Final Battles
of Patton's Vanguard

ALSO BY DON M. FOX

Patton's Vanguard: The United States Army Fourth Armored Division (McFarland 2003; paperback 2007)

Final Battles of Patton's Vanguard

The United States Army Fourth Armored Division, 1945–1946

Don M. Fox

McFarland & Company, Inc., Publishers
Jefferson, North Carolina

ISBN (print) 978-1-4766-8009-5
ISBN (ebook) 978-1-4766-3899-7

LIBRARY OF CONGRESS AND BRITISH LIBRARY
CATALOGUING DATA ARE AVAILABLE

Library of Congress Control Number 2020006163

© 2020 Don M. Fox. All rights reserved

No part of this book may be reproduced or transmitted in any form or by any means, electronic or mechanical, including photocopying or recording, or by any information storage and retrieval system, without permission in writing from the publisher.

On the cover: A Fourth Armored Division column in Germany (United States Army)

Printed in the United States of America

*McFarland & Company, Inc., Publishers
Box 611, Jefferson, North Carolina 28640
www.mcfarlandpub.com*

Table of Contents

Acknowledgments	vii
Author's Notes	ix
Preface	1
1. The Western Front	5
2. Goodbye Bastogne	9
3. Rest and Recuperation	20
4. To Hell and Back	32
5. The Armored Infantry—Again	49
6. Attack into Germany	57
7. The Drive to Bitburg and the Kyll River	66
8. The Drive to the Rhine	93
9. Between the Rhine and Moselle	110
10. From the Moselle to the Rhine	127
11. Jumping the Rhine	159
12. Task Force Baum	178
13. The Road to Hammelburg	187
14. The Only Mistake	204
15. Breakout from the Main River Bridgehead	215
16. Ohrdruf	233
17. Beyond the Restraining Line	249
18. Czechoslovakia	266
19. The Occupation	284
Bibliography	295
Military Unit Index	299
General Index	303

Sure, we want to go home. We want this war over with. The quickest way to get it over with is to go get the bastards who started it. The quicker they are whipped, the quicker we can go home. The shortest way home is through Berlin and Tokyo. And when we get to Berlin, I am personally going to shoot that paper-hanging son-of-a-bitch Hitler. Just like I'd shoot a snake!
—Lieutenant General George S. Patton, Jr.,
addressing his troops before Operation
Overlord, June 5, 1944

Acknowledgments

The precursor to this work is *Patton's Vanguard: The United States Army Fourth Armored Division*, by the present author. Published in 2003, the book tells the division history from its activation on April 15, 1941, through the Battle of the Bulge. The present volume completes the story, starting with the closing days of the Bulge and ending with the deactivation of the division in 1946.

When I commenced work on the first book, the youngest veterans of the division were in their mid-seventies. Fast forward to 2019, and the youngest of those remaining are in their nineties. As I reached out to rekindle relationships or develop new ones, the unanswered phone calls and emails served as a frequent reminder of the inevitable dwindling of their generation.

Fortunately, I remained in contact with several veterans after the publication of the first book. In ways both large and small, the following men added value to this book:

Nicholas Alexander	T/Sergeant, Company A, 53rd Armored Infantry Battalion
Jack Ammon	Chaplain, Fourth Armored Division
Edward Bautz	S-3, 37th Tank Battalion
Robert Calvert, Jr.	Company C, 51st Armored Infantry Battalion
Harry Feinberg	Sergeant, 37th Tank Battalion HQ Company
John Harris	Battery First Sergeant, 22nd Armored Field Artillery Battalion
Albin F. Irzyk	Lieutenant Colonel, 8th Tank Battalion
Leonard H. Kieley	Captain, Company A, 8th Tank Battalion
Milton B. Koshiol	Company A, 10th Armored Infantry Battalion
Jimmie Leach	Captain, Company B, 37th Tank Battalion
Joe Morris	C Battery, 22nd Armored Field Artillery Battalion
King Pound	35th Tank Battalion
Paul H. Stephenson	Captain, Company C, 8th Tank Battalion
John Whitehill	Captain, Company A, 37th Tank Battalion

Others who provided valuable feedback, insights, or material include:

David Baum	Son of Major Abe Baum, 10th Armored Infantry Battalion
Bruce Cooperman	Son of Captain Barnet Cooperman, 10th Armored Infantry Battalion
Tracy Donahue	Daughter of Captain Richard Donahue, Company D, 37th Tank Battalion
Rochelle Dwight	Daughter of Captain William Dwight, 37th Tank Battalion
Reinier Groeneveld	Researcher on the 46th Armored Medical Battalion
Martin Heinlein	Expert on Task Force Baum
Gregory Himebauch	Son of Sergeant Gordon Himebauch, Company A, 8th Tank Battalion
Mark Homa	Son of Sergeant Joseph Homa, Service Battery, 22nd AFAB

Acknowledgments

Al Irzyk, Jr.	Son of Lieutenant Colonel Albin F. Irzyk, 8th Tank Battalion
James Kelly	Son of 1st Lieutenant Earl J. Kelly, 10th Armored Infantry Battalion
Jamie Leach	Son of Captain Jimmie Leach, 37th Tank Battalion
Michael Malone	Friend of Major Harry Rockafeller
Marcia McFarland-Gray	Daughter of Corporal Edward McFarland, 8th Tank Battalion
Darren Neely	Author, *Forgotten Archives, Volumes 1 and 2*
Ivan Steenkiste	Belgian citizen dedicated to the Fourth Armored's legacy
George P. Waters	Son of Lt. Colonel John K. Waters
Jim White	Son of Sergeant Joseph White, C Troop, 25th Cavalry Reconnaissance Squadron
Joe Whitehill	Son of Captain John Whitehill, 37th Tank Battalion

Special thanks go to Belgian citizen Erwin Verholen, who invested a day with me touring the battlefields where the 704th Tank Destroyer Battalion supported the 94th Infantry Division. Also to Germany's Peter Domes, who provided invaluable mentorship regarding Task Force Baum.

My gratitude to cartographer Jason Petho. The maps he created for this work are an invaluable complement to the narrative.

I have been honored by the citation of *Patton's Vanguard* in the works of other authors and historians. They are a unique breed, and I am fortunate and thankful when I receive a tacit nod of approval from those more skilled in their craft than I. Additionally, I appreciate the use of *Patton's Vanguard* as reference material during the production of two television documentary series, *Patton 360* and *Greatest Tank Battles*.

There is one individual above all others who I must single out for recognition and gratitude, and that is Brigadier General Albin F. Irzyk, to whom I dedicate this book. Irzyk exemplified Major General John S. Wood's credo of being known by one's deeds alone. On September 10, 2018, he passed away at the age of 101. Just three weeks before his death I shared with him that I had commenced work on the balance of the division history. I looked forward to visiting with him to discuss that period of the war. Arrangements were made, but unfortunately, his health did not prevail. There is not a day that goes by that I fail to think of him. I thank you, the reader, for taking time to learn more about him and his brothers-in-arms.

Author's Notes

While writing this history, I was mindful of maintaining continuity with *Patton's Vanguard*. However, when comparing the two works, the reader may notice some differences in respect to the literary protocols. For instance, in this book military time is used instead of the 12-hour clock convention (i.e., A.M. and P.M.). By doing so, the narrative aligns best with most of the source material (official military records, in particular).

When referring to military units, I have retained military conventions that typically use numerals. An exception is reserved for the Fourth Armored. From time to time, *Olympic* is used as an alternate designation for the Fourth (*Olympic* being the division's code name).

The first book contained a list of abbreviations for the benefit of the reader. I did not repeat the list in the second book but have presented the basis for most abbreviations upon their first appearance in the narrative.

The use of *italics* applies most commonly to words of Germanic origin. Also, all German military units are presented in *italics* to readily distinguish them from their American counterparts. *Italics* are also used on some occasions for emphasis. Such instances should be obvious to the reader. For cities, towns, and geographic features, I have endeavored to apply the spelling and character usage of their native origin.

As was the case in the first book, an extensive bibliography is provided, listing all the source material drawn upon for the work. Responsibility for any errors of fact or omission rests solely upon the author.

Preface

To best understand the history about to unfold, the reader is well served if they have a basic understanding of the preceding events. While it might seem safe to assume the reader has digested *Patton's Vanguard*, it would be unwise to leave it to chance.

The first book opened with a description of the training that forged the division and its reorganization into the "light" armored division table of organization and equipment. The transport of the division to England and its continued training was explored. The first chapter also detailed the arrival and impact of the Fourth's new and (eventually) beloved commander, Major General John Shirley Wood. Universally, Wood was considered the embodiment of the Fourth Armored. He forsook a nickname for the division and, as a result, forever wedded the Fourth to the motto, "They shall be known by their deeds alone."

The narrative continued with the boarding of ships on July 9, 1944, for delivery of the division on Utah Beach. The battles and daring drives that followed became legendary as Wood's division served as the vanguard for Lieutenant General George S. Patton's United States Third Army.

The Fourth Armored (code name *Olympic*) led the breakout from Normandy during *Operation Cobra*. The division drove across the base of the Brittany peninsula, severing it from the interior of France. Turning east, Wood's men charged toward the Seine River. Colonel Bruce Clarke's Combat Command A overran the city of Orleans en route to the dramatic, classic armored assault on Troyes. *Olympic* sprinted from the banks of the Seine toward the German border, the drive stalling at the line of the Moselle River only for want of gasoline.

During the delay imposed by General Eisenhower upon a frustrated Patton, the *Wehrmacht* scraped together enough men and matériel to form a thin defensive line. What had been a void between the Fourth Armored and the Rhine River now contained a patchwork of units threatening to slow the advance of Patton's vanguard.

With fuel tanks replenished, Wood's division surged across the Moselle River both north and south of the city of Nancy, forming a noose around its German occupiers.

Then came the greatest tank-versus-tank battle on the Western Front. When Hitler deployed an arsenal of fresh *Panzer* brigades to thwart the advance of Lieutenant General Omar Bradley's 12th Army Group, *Olympic* responded by inflicting grievous, disproportionate losses upon the *Wehrmacht*. Major General Wood's men cemented the reputation of the Fourth as America's premier armored division. A legend was born.

During much of the month of October, the division rested and regained its strength. By early November, Patton's Third Army was prepared for a new offensive.

The Third United States Army (TUSA) called upon the Fourth Armored to play a key role in its drive to the German border. Miserable weather conditions, coupled with a reinforced and resilient opponent, resulted in a grueling advance to the northeast. On November 24, *Olympic* collided with the flank of a counterattack launched by the respected *Panzer Lehr Division*. The timely arrival of Wood's tanks disrupted the German attempt to squelch the progress of the U.S. Seventh Army. After sending the *Panzer Lehr* into retreat, the Fourth Armored continued its drive toward the *Westwall*.

With the division less than 10 miles from the German border, a festering conflict between Major General Wood and the commander of XII Corps (Major General Manton Eddy) came to a head. The differences between the two men were apparently unresolvable, and Lieutenant General Patton relieved Wood of his command. The men of the Fourth Armored were shocked and dismayed. In a matter of days, the beloved Wood returned to the United States for eventual assignment as head of the Armored Replacement Center at Fort Knox. His replacement, Major General Hugh Gaffey—hand-picked by Patton from his Third Army staff—took the reins just before the Fourth Armored left the front line for rest and refitting.

Then came Hitler's surprise counteroffensive. On December 16, the Germans burst through the thinly held American lines in the Ardennes. As portions of Lieutenant General

XII Corps commander Major General Manton Eddy (left) and Major General John S. Wood (right) (U.S. Army photograph).

Hodges' First Army reeled under the weight of the attack, General Eisenhower called upon Patton to wheel elements of his Third Army 180 degrees from their positions south of the "Bulge" to strike the underbelly of Hitler's offensive.

Lieutenant (Lt.) General Patton in turn chose the Fourth Armored to lead the attack. In an impressive feat of logistics and rapid movement, *Olympic* traveled more than 160 miles and moved into positions opposite the *5th Fallschirmjäger Division*. The 8th Tank Battalion, under the command of Major Albin F. Irzyk, led the charge for Brigadier General Dager's Combat Command B. Dager's men moved quickly and efficiently, even sending Task Force Ezell into Bastogne on December 20.

By the time the Fourth Armored assembled en masse for their attack, the Germans had surrounded the defenders of Bastogne. Thus, the primary focus of Patton's offensive became the relief of the encircled American forces.

The ensuing effort to reach Bastogne lasted five grueling days. From December 22 through December 26, the Fourth Armored fought some of its toughest battles and suffered its heaviest losses. The towns of Chaumont, Bigonville, Warnach, and Assenois were etched in the minds of the veterans who fought there. The feats accomplished in those towns by men named Irzyk, Leach, Whitehill, Abrams, Dwight, Hendrix, Boggess, Trover…—the list really knows no end—would be recorded indelibly in the historical accounts that followed over the decades to come.

The Fourth Armored Division's role in the Battle of the Bulge was far from over when the M4A3E2 Sherman tank dubbed *Cobra King* rolled within sight of the front lines of the 101st Airborne Division. The balance of the division slogged its way north over the next several days against German defenders who refused to give way without a fight.

On December 30, the *1st SS Panzer Division* spearheaded an attack to cut the relief corridor leading into Bastogne. The 35th Tank Battalion and other elements of the Fourth blunted the attack and inflicted crippling losses upon the infamous German division.

On January 1, 1945, the Fourth Armored Division, though battered and bruised after the arduous task of relieving Bastogne, stood ready to continue the fight. This is their story.

1

The Western Front

Eisenhower

General Dwight David "Ike" Eisenhower served as the Supreme Commander of the Allied forces facing the Germans in Western Europe. His command, the Supreme Headquarters Allied Expeditionary Force (SHAEF), was comprised of armies from several nations having both common and competing interests and personalities. Ike possessed not only the formidable challenge of balancing the interests within his team, but also the responsibility for managing the military relationship with Marshal Joseph Stalin (the leader of the Soviet Union and Eisenhower's military counterpart).

Despite the complexities of the Western Alliance, Eisenhower did without an overall ground commander. After the establishment of three army groups on August 1, 1944, Ike maintained direct reporting relationships with the commanding generals of each of those forces (British Field Marshal Bernard Montgomery leading the 21st Army Group, U.S. Lieutenant General Omar Bradley the 12th Army Group, and Lieutenant General Jacob Devers the 6th Army Group). The arrangement made possible a more hands-on approach compared to what might have resulted had an overall commander of ground forces been appointed (a position Field Marshal Montgomery lobbied for relentlessly, to the point of annoyance). But the command structure also made Eisenhower a lightning rod for criticism as he managed the distinct wants and needs of the three army group commanders.

The Plan

As expressed in the original directive from the Combined Chiefs of Staff, the strategic plan for the invasion of France and subsequent advance into Germany had one objective prioritized above all others: the destruction of the German army. Yet at the same time, it was recognized that the German military machine could be brought to its knees by capturing two important geographic regions: the Ruhr in the northern part of central Germany and the Saar Basin to the south. Combined, they accounted for a critical portion of Germany's production of war matériel.

The pre-invasion plan called for two major thrusts into Germany. The primary drive would be delivered north of the Ardennes with the objective of seizing the Ruhr. The secondary thrust would come south of the Ardennes to provide flank protection for the primary drive and remove the Saar industrial region from German hands.

The original plan for *Operation Overlord* did not anticipate a substantive penetration into Germany within the first year following the invasion. Indeed, it was not envisioned that

Allied forces would advance as far east as the Rhine River within the first 12 months (the Rhine being the most formidable natural obstacle standing between SHAEF and ultimate victory).

For members of the Western Alliance, the Rhine River and the 22 road and 25 railroad bridges spanning it represented both a barrier and an opportunity. But the Allies were getting ahead of themselves if they overlooked the fact that west of the Rhine, tracing much of the German border, resided the most formidable *man-made* obstacle: the *Westwall*. Eisenhower envisioned from the start that before his armies punched across the Rhine, all German forces west of the river would be cleared out, thus allowing a concentration of divisions on the main points of thrust into the German interior. Sweeping the *Westwall* and all the land between it and the Rhine was a component of the plan destined to impact the course of events.

The Execution

As is so often the case in war, the plan did not survive the commencement of battle. Following the invasion of Normandy, progress was less than expected and Eisenhower fell behind the original timetable for expanding the lodgment area. However, in the wake of *Operation Cobra* and the collapse of the German defenses in Normandy, much time was gained.

The rapid advance across France was unexpected and, in many respects, unplanned. There were opportunities gained and opportunities missed. In large part, the misses resulted from a failure to prioritize the campaign's number one objective: *the destruction of the German ground forces.* In any event, by almost any measure, the breakout from Normandy and subsequent pursuit across France and the Low Countries was one for the ages. Logistics strongly influenced much of what happened during the autumn months, and as winter approached, Eisenhower focused on gathering his strength and returning to many of the tenets of the pre-invasion plan.

By mid–December 1944, many believed the end of the war in Europe to be a foregone conclusion. Allied forces pressed inward on the German frontier from both west and east. Most of the territory seized by Hitler during the expansion of the *Third Reich* had been taken back by either the Soviets or the Western Allies. During those short, daylight-starved days of December, the vaunted *Wehrmacht* compared little to the stature achieved at the height of Hitler's power. The prospect of Allied victory was so certain, the United States curtailed production of armaments, scaled back the formation of new divisions, and reduced the rate of draftees called upon for use as replacement troops.

Then came Hitler's surprise counterattack in the Ardennes. Bursting across the German border into Belgium and Luxembourg, the *Führer's* bold move cast sudden doubt on the course of the war. To some, the outcome … so certain just days before … was at risk. But to those familiar with the art of war, the German offensive threatened the timetable for victory and little else. Save for the development of an atomic bomb by German scientists, defeat of the Nazis remained a foregone conclusion.

While the outcome may have indeed been inevitable, there was one complicating factor that affected the lives of every member of the United States Army Fourth Armored Division: war is not fought on paper. For as long as Hitler maintained his iron-fist rule over the *Wehrmacht*, fighting, death, and destruction would continue.

1. The Western Front

On January 1, 1945, the Western Front stretched 450 airline miles, tracing an uneven but generally north to south line from the North Sea to the border of Switzerland. The Allies held positions within 25 miles of the Ruhr industrial region, wherein lay the cities of Essen, Düsseldorf, and Wuppertal. The most uneven section of the line was located where the remains of the Bulge extended 40 miles west of the German frontier. Another prominent bulge existed in the Alsace region, west of the Rhine River. Dubbed the "Colmar Pocket," the Germans were determined to hold on to this appendage for as long as possible.

All of this came at great cost. By January 3, more than 3.7 million Allied soldiers had come ashore to wage war against the Nazis. Of those, 516,244 became casualties (though many of those returned to duty). The Americans alone suffered 335,090 casualties, with 55,184 killed in action.

Eisenhower's command stood at 49 infantry divisions, 20 armored divisions, and three airborne divisions (not to mention a plethora of supporting units). He held a strong superiority over the Germans in virtually every category: at least two-and-a-half to one in artillery, 10 to one in tanks, three to one in aircraft, and two-and-a-half to one in troops. His armies were both larger and faster than their German counterparts. For the most part, his ground forces were motorized while the Germans still relied heavily on horse-drawn transport.

The Germans possessed a seemingly impressive 80 divisions. However, these formations were typically a shell of their normal complement. The German forces facing the Western Allies were led by *Generalfeldmarschall* Gerd von Rundstedt. His command looked mighty on paper, but he was aware of its limitations.

While the situation looked bleak in many respects, there were some positives for Rundstedt to consider. The Allied strategic air campaign, launched with the intention of bringing German manufacturing to its knees, did not work as intended. Germany's production of war matériel *peaked* in the fall of 1944. Tank and assault gun production from November 1944 to February 1945 ran at about 1600 vehicles per month.

What *did* work for the Allies was the portion of the air campaign aimed at reducing Germany's production and distribution of petroleum-related products. The *Wehrmacht*, whether on land, sea, or air, was subsequently limited in its fighting ability due to crippling fuel shortages.

The state of German manufacturing was one concern. The availability of human resources was another. While replacement soldiers were hard to come by, the proverbial well had yet to run dry ... but it was getting close. It was not until January 1945 when Hitler required both older and younger men to serve. At that time, the upper age limit was moved to 45, while at the opposite end of the spectrum, 17-year-olds were pressed into service.

While disadvantaged in several ways, *Generalfeldmarschall* Rundstedt possessed one strategic advantage: the benefit of fighting and managing logistics within interior lines. While both the Western Allies and Soviets struggled with supply routes that grew longer over time, the German armies, by the contraction of their front lines toward Germany, drew closer to their resources.

Under these circumstances, the United States First and Third Armies tightened the vise on the Bulge. Beyond the prospect of trapping German forces west of the point where the two American armies would eventually link up, Lt. General Patton was further motivated (in his own words, "delighted") when he received a directive from SHAEF indicating that, once the two armies were joined, the First Army would pass back to the control of Lt. General Bradley's 12th Army Group (thus wresting control of the First Army from Field Marshal Montgomery).

A battle consists of two sides, and Hitler, while conceding that his original objectives were out of reach, had no appetite for yielding ground in the Ardennes. He engaged his troops in yet another attempt to seize Bastogne, attacking from the north and northeast (having given up on cutting the relief corridor carved out by the Fourth Armored Division). A dozen days would pass before the two American armies came together.

After the Bulge

As the vestiges of the Bulge were erased, Eisenhower turned his attention toward the resumption of the Allied offensive. He remained true to the original plan of clearing the enemy from their positions west of the Rhine and maintaining a focus on their destruction. Field Marshal Sir Alan Brooke argued for a concentration of force solely to the north. He also remained insistent regarding the appointment of a single ground commander. Ike stood firm on both counts: the supporting attack in the south would not be cancelled, nor would a ground commander be placed between he and the generals in command of the army groups.

Eisenhower, bitten once by Hitler's unexpected accumulation of force for the conduct of the Ardennes offensive, commissioned the creation of a reserve maintained under the direct control of SHAEF. Much to Patton's dismay, this created an ongoing internal battle over where the divisions for the reserve would be drawn from. SHAEF had to pull the units from *somewhere*. All too often, Patton's Third Army was the source, and from Patton's perspective, this jeopardized the success of his campaign. Questioning the wisdom of Eisenhower's strategy, he asked,

> *Reserve against what? This seemed like locking the barn door after the horse was stolen. Certainly at this period of the war no reserve was needed—simply violent attacks everywhere with everything ... the Germans do not have the resources to stop it.*

As the Western Allies closed in on Germany from the west and the Soviets from the east, Eisenhower was aware of the need for communication and coordination between the two forces. In mid–January, Air Chief Marshal Sir Arthur Tedder, accompanied by Major General Harold R. Bull (the SHAEF G-3) and Brigadier General T.J. Betts (deputy assistant chief of staff for intelligence at SHAEF) arrived in Moscow to coordinate battle plans with the Soviets. Prior to this, the Combined Chiefs of Staff advised Eisenhower of the Soviet's plans and intentions. But now, with the two great forces closing in on Germany from both sides, closer coordination was required in anticipation of a linkup somewhere inside Germany.

Dispatched by Eisenhower, the trio met with Stalin and his staff. In the wake of the meeting, the Combined Chiefs of Staff authorized Eisenhower's direct communication with Stalin on topics concerning the conduct of military operations.

So as the calendar turned to 1945, the Allied command structure, lines of communication, and protocols were in place for the final drive to destroy Hitler's forces and to bring Germany to its knees in surrender. The resources of manpower and matériel were heavily in favor of the Allies. As has been the case for centuries, all that remained was the conduct of the battle itself. Victory now depended upon a soldier's willingness to leap from his foxhole, M1 Garand in hand. And on that count, the American soldier was ready.

2

Goodbye Bastogne

Defending the Corridor

At the stroke of midnight, American artillery in the Ardennes signaled the start of 1945 with a massive 30-minute artillery barrage. The Germans aspired to celebrate in similar fashion but lacked the ammunition and guns to match the American salute.

For King Pound, parked in a new replacement tank positioned near the Arlon-Bastogne highway, the threat of enemy artillery provided ample reason for he and his crew to be buttoned up inside their steel home. Pound, who belonged to the 35th Tank Battalion of the United States Army Fourth Armored Division, was the tank's driver. In their old tank—destroyed during the drive to open a relief corridor to the encircled 101st Airborne Division—King and his fellow tankers maintained a stash of wine. It would have come in nicely on this occasion. But the wine, along with the tank, was long gone. Their only indulgence this night was a box of Powerhouse candy bars. Pound ate 10 of them. He never touched a Powerhouse bar again.

The Fourth Armored Division, having beaten back a powerful attack by the *1st SS Panzer Division* just two days prior, had as its primary mission the defense of Highway N4. Also called the Arlon-Bastogne highway, it was a quality paved roadway stretching for 22 miles between the two Belgian municipalities. Although the attack by the *1st SS Panzer* was masterfully repulsed by the Fourth, the threat of enemy action remained. Combat Command A (CCA), commanded by Brigadier General Herbert Earnest, had the largest share of responsibility for defending the highway.

Earnest was a relatively new face to the Fourth Armored, having been sent by Third Army HQ less than a month prior as a replacement for the struggling Colonel William P. Withers. He disclosed to Lt. Colonel Hal Pattison (executive officer of CCA throughout the division's campaign in Europe) the hope that he would earn command of the Fourth Armored. According to Pattison, Earnest had been told (presumably by Patton), "if he did well with CCA he would get a division of his own." When he accepted command of CCA, he did not expect Hugh Gaffey to hold on to the division for so long, and he gambled that Major General Wood would not return to the helm.

During the predawn hours of January 1, Brigadier General Earnest issued an alert for a possible enemy counterattack emanating from the direction of Lutrebois. The small town lay east of his defensive line, which ran parallel with N4. The 51st Armored Infantry Battalion (AIB), commanded by Major Dan C. Alanis, held a key section of the line that extended through the woods separating the highway from Lutrebois. The enemy was close at hand. Opposite A Company and C Company (i.e., A/51 and C/51) a pocket of enemy troops held a position in the woods a hundred yards wide.

M4A3E8 tank in position south of Bastogne (U.S. Army photograph).

The anticipated German attack never materialized. However, with the arrival of great flying weather, fighter-bombers from the XIX Tactical Air Command came out in force. The pilots rose to the occasion, literally and figuratively.

The following day, a patrol from C/51 reported that the enemy pocket facing the battalion contained 30 to 40 Germans equipped with about 10 machine guns. At noon, a well-coordinated attack was launched by A/51 to reduce the enemy position. Mortars, rocket launchers, tanks, and flame throwers were added to the small arms firepower of the armored infantrymen. They advanced through the woods and arrived at the far edge without encountering resistance.

The attack to the east provided extra buffer between the 51st AIB's front and the vital highway they were charged with defending. A/51 and C/51 assumed defensive positions along the edge of the woods, and in most cases, took over the improved positions abandoned by their opponents. B/51, having remained in place on the battalion's right flank during the advance, sent two platoons forward to close the gap that developed with the other companies.

Such was the cleanup work performed along the relief corridor on January 1 and 2; a corridor through which so many members of the Fourth Armored Division spilled their blood during the final 10 days of December 1944.

Cold and Quiet Days

While CCA stood guard against possible German threats, much of the division was blessed with the opportunity to rest and refit. However, being off the front line didn't remove them from harm's way. On the first day of the year, a German aircraft dropped fragmentation bombs near the 37th Tank Battalion's positions close to Chaumont, injuring 11 and killing an enlisted man from D/37.

On January 2, the Fourth Armored was released from Major General John Millikin's III Corps and assigned to Major General Troy H. Middleton's VIII Corps. Elements of Combat Command B (CCB) and Combat Command Reserve (CCR) held positions near small towns south and southwest of Bastogne. Major Albin F. Irzyk's 8th Tank Battalion and Major Harold Cohen's 10th Armored Infantry Battalion maintained their command posts at Assenois. The 22nd Armored Field Artillery Battalion (AFAB), commanded by Lieutenant Colonel Arthur C. Peterson, held a position near Grandru and remained active firing time-on-target (TOT) and harassment and interdiction (H&I) missions in support of the 35th Infantry Division (the 35th ID held positions along the corridor immediately south of CCA).

Replacements filtered into the division, coming in the form of green troops and men reassigned from other units. Soldiers wounded in action, now healed, returned to their old units.

Some of the existing officers were given new assignments, which usually had a ripple effect on others. For example, when Captain Diamantes (the commanding officer of A/10) was transferred to the role of battalion intelligence officer (S-2), Lieutenant Kelly was placed in command of A Company. Given the much higher casualty rate among company commanders in the infantry and tank companies, the opportunity to serve on the battalion staff was not an unwelcome development for an officer so appointed.

January 3 was marked by a heavy, wet snowfall that accumulated to a depth of five inches in some areas. Visibility was very poor. The Germans didn't threaten the east side of the corridor that day within CCA's zone, which was probably a good thing for them … considering the moves about to be made by the Fourth Armored Division's commander, Major General Hugh Joseph Gaffey.

Born in 1895, Hugh Gaffey became a career soldier and served in field artillery during the First World War. He arrived on the Western Front during August of 1918, just three months before the armistice. During the peacetime years before the Second World War, he remained primarily in the artillery arm. On August 5, 1942, he received the star of a brigadier general and was eventually assigned to lead Combat Command B of the 2nd Armored Division while in Morocco. After his promotion to the rank of major general, he was given command of the 2nd Armored prior to its participation in the invasion of Sicily. A successful campaign on the Mediterranean island was followed by the division's departure for England, where they prepared for the invasion of France. Prior to D-Day, he was reassigned and became the chief of staff for Lt. General Patton's Third Army (the two having served together with I Armored Corps prior to the North Africa and Sicily campaigns). In the wake of the controversial relief of Major General Wood, Gaffey was the man hand-picked by Patton to fill the role of division commander. January 3 marked one month since commencing his turn at the helm of the Fourth Armored Division.

After Major General Wood's departure from the Fourth Armored, hope remained among the ranks that he would return to command the division. However, as the days and weeks passed, the odds became increasingly remote that "P" would ever again wear the shoulder patch of the Fourth Armored Division in combat. Lt. Colonel Pattison later offered this assessment of the prospect of Wood's return:

> Rumor current in the Division at the time was that General Wood would return, that a new Corps Headquarters was to be activated soon and that General Gaffey was being purified in a combat division for corps command and that General Wood would return when Gaffey moved to the new Corps. If this has had been the plan fate intervened in the form of the battle of the bulge.

The realignment of Gaffey's units on January 3 demonstrated the great flexibility inherent in the combat command organizational model. In this case, CCA, still in the role of defending the Arlon-Bastogne highway, was reinforced with the 10th AIB and the 8th Tank Battalion. The 51st AIB and the 35th Tank Battalion continued their assignment with CCA, making this combat command a very formidable fighting force. Additional units assigned to CCA were the 94th and 66th Armored Field Artillery Battalions, Company A of the 24th Armored Engineer Battalion, Company A of the 704th Tank Destroyer (TD) Battalion, Battery B of the 489th Anti-Aircraft Artillery (AAA) Battalion, Company A of the 46th Medical Battalion, and Company A of the 126th Ordnance Battalion.

Other shifts took place within the division. The 37th Tank Battalion, 53rd Armored Infantry Battalion, and 22nd Armored Field Artillery Battalion were assigned to CCB. Meanwhile, two companies from the 704th TD Battalion were detached from the Fourth Armored and sent to support the 101st Airborne Division. C/704 (-one platoon) went into position near Longchamps (north of Bastogne) and B/704 (-one platoon) worked with the 101st east of Bastogne.

January 4 brought poor weather punctuated by more snowfall. CCA's front remained relatively quiet as the men fought the elements and little else. Major General Middleton placed CCB on a one-hour alert in anticipation of an attack against VIII Corps. Intelligence reports predicting hostile enemy activity once again turned out to be false alarms. This was not the case near Longchamps, where C/704 assisted the 101st in turning away a German assault. But for the Fourth Armored, the front remained quiet.

Brigadier General Earnest formed three task forces to handle CCA's position on the line. Defending the northern sector was Task Force Withers (Colonel Withers now being cast in the unorthodox role of assistant to the commander of CCA), which consisted of the 8th Tank Battalion, 10th Armored Infantry Battalion (-B Company), and a platoon of tank destroyers from A/704. The south sector was held by Task Force Alanis, which consisted of the 51st AIB, A/35 and a platoon of A/704. Task Force Oden (Lt. Colonel Delk Oden, commanding officer of the 35th Tank Battalion) served as a mobile reserve positioned west of the line. Oden's force included the 35th Tank Battalion (-A Company), B/10, and A/704 (-two platoons). The Fourth Armored Division's artillery continued to support the 35th Infantry Division, which remained directly south of CCA.

The German forces opposite CCA remained passive on January 5. The 51st Armored Infantry Battalion combat diary noted that it was the quietest day they had experienced during the entire Ardennes campaign to date. The battalion received 71 replacements and the news of Captain Harry Rockafeller's promotion to the rank of major (Rockafeller continued as the battalion's executive officer). Major Alanis took advantage of the relative tranquility to pull one platoon out of the line for a 12-hour visit to the chateau being used as the battalion's command post. The infantrymen had the luxury of warming up, drying out their clothes, and grabbing some much-needed rest. Plans were made for all companies to repeat this process during the next couple of days, with a new platoon being rotated off the line every 12 hours.

Though the front-line action was light, there was no shortage of work to do. Away from the battlefield, the 126th Armored Ordnance Battalion invented a method to help tanks from slipping on the icy roads: two-inch calks were cut out from steel grousers and welded to every fifth block of the steel tracks. Welders from the 126th traveled 50 miles to Étain, France, where they fitted the calks on the tracks of replacement tanks destined for *Olympic*.

An American crew at work on maintenance. Note the extenders on the outer part of the track; the crew is likely in the process of installing them, given their absence on the other track (U.S. Army photograph).

On January 6, another warning was issued about the possibility of enemy attacks. This time, the threat was more specific: a German prisoner revealed that a strike would be made at 0400 the following day. The Fourth Armored divisional artillery placed interdicting fire into the area thought to be where the Germans were assembling. With friendly aircraft grounded due to the weather, the result of the fire could not be observed.

Later that day, Lt. Quigley and four enlisted men from the 10th Armored Infantry Battalion departed for the rear. They were fortunate recipients of a 30-day furlough to the United States. One enlisted man was selected from each of the three armored infantry companies and the fourth came from the Medical Detachment.

The privilege wasn't limited to the 10th AIB. In total, three officers and 36 enlisted men from the division departed for the United States on January 6 and 7. While the rotation system impacted a modest number of men, having even the slightest chance of being chosen for a return trip to the U.S. was a great morale booster.

On January 7, the division remained on alert for the German counterattack disclosed the day before by the prisoner. The appointed time came and went without incident. Later that day, another prisoner stated that the prior day's artillery barrage aimed at the German's assembly area caused heavy casualties and disrupted their plan (reports received later from friendly units verified this).

The 6th Armored Division, positioned north of the Fourth, was not as fortunate. Seven hundred German infantrymen, supported by 10 to 12 *Panzers*, struck the positions held by CCA/6. The Fourth Armored Division's own CCA was placed on alert to offer support. The order to move never came, however, as the 6th Armored managed to contain the attack.

Lt. Colonel Abrams spent part of the day trying out a new .50 caliber machine gun mounted in the co-axil position on the M4A3E8 Sherman tanks. An additional .30 caliber machine gun, mounted atop the turret, received his personal trial as well. When he returned to the command post of the 37th Tank Battalion, he expressed high praise for the new configuration.

Preparing to Attack

From the start of Lieutenant General Patton's attack against the south flank of the Bulge, units had been thrown into the line as they became available. Rather than conducting an attack in depth, the Third Army's divisions were aligned side by side. Patton's offensive was conducted along much of the length of the north-facing line. This was not his preference. From the beginning, he relished the opportunity to sever the Bulge at its base to trap as many Germans as possible west of his intended penetration. However, higher command denied him the opportunity. The appetite for such a bold move did not exist among his superiors.

Now, 24 days after the Germans initiated their overambitious drive toward Antwerp, Patton possessed a formidable array of divisions with which to continue his attack against the enemy's southern flank. His objective: shaking hands with Hodges' First Army.

Patton wished to employ nine divisions in an attack commencing January 9. However, he met resistance from one of his generals when Major General Middleton, commander of VIII Corps, called him and asked for a delay. Middleton expressed his concern about the fighting condition of the 87th Infantry Division, 17th Airborne Division, and Fourth Armored. He lobbied for a delay until January 10.

Patton denied Middleton's request. However, for another reason altogether, the commitment of the Fourth was delayed one day after all: the division's artillery battalions were still lending support to the 35th Infantry Division and their guns could not be relieved in time.

The plan was recast for January 10. Under the original scheme, CCB was attached to the 101st Airborne Division. But now, *Olympic* would have its own zone to the east of the 101st and would attack through the line held by the 6th Armored Division. Within their zone, CCB and CCA would operate side-by-side, each attacking on its own axis of advance.

While the Fourth prepared to go back on offense, there was an undercurrent of something else being afoot. It was rumored that the enemy might launch an attack farther south against the east-facing flank of the Third Army. At 0930 on January 9, elements of the 24th Armored Engineer Battalion and the 704th Tank Destroyer Battalion were dispatched on a mission to reconnoiter a route toward the area of concern in Luxembourg.

The M18 tank destroyer was particularly well suited for this type of mission. The combination of its light weight (only 20 tons) and high horsepower radial engine (350 or 400 hp, depending upon the engine variant) resulted in a top road speed of 55 to 60 miles per hour. Nicknamed the "Hellcat," its speed was nearly double that of a Sherman tank and equaled the nimble, six wheeled M8 armored car. The Hellcat's armament of a 76mm high-velocity gun and .50 caliber ring-mounted machine gun, coupled with its high speed and maneuverability, made it a unique and effective armored fighting vehicle.

The Revised Plan of Attack

On January 9, having been relieved of its short-lived attachment to the 101st Airborne Division, Brigadier General Dager's CCB received orders to move to an area northeast of Bastogne. The 53rd Armored Infantry Battalion arrived in their assembly area at 1700, and at 2100, the company commanders met to review the plan. Their orders were to attack at 0900 the following day in conjunction with the 37th Tank Battalion. The tanks and infantry would strike on an axis extending to the northeast while using the railroad tracks leading out of Bastogne as the boundary line between them and the 101st Airborne.

The units of Brigadier General Earnest's CCA prepared to move into position as well. At 1030, the company commanders of the 10th Armored Infantry Battalion met with Earnest at the battalion's forward command post. They received orders to move to an assembly area between the small villages of Mont and Neffe, about one mile east of Bastogne. Following the meeting, Major Cohen was evacuated due to illness and was temporarily replaced by Captain Hugh F. Young (Captain Abraham Baum moved into Young's slot as executive officer).

At 1500, Young and Baum traveled to Bastogne for a meeting with the 6th Armored Division. The two captains then went to the front line to take a personal look. At 1705, the companies left for their assigned positions from whence they would initiate the following day's attack. The officers of the 10th met again at 2100 and received their attack orders.

The third combat command (Colonel Wendell Blanchard's CCR) went into position near Chaumont. The 51st AIB moved on foot to a temporary assembly area and set up an all-around defense to prevent infiltration during the night. The 8th Tank Battalion was positioned nearby.

By the end of the day, all units of the Fourth Armored were assembled and prepared to attack on the morning of January 10.

Back on the Offensive

Now under the command of VIII Corps, the division's primary objective on January 10 was the town of Bourcy, five miles northeast of Bastogne. CCB would attack on the left and CCA on the right. Troop D of the 25th Cavalry Reconnaissance Squadron filled the gap between the two combat commands, while Troop C maintained contact with the 101st Airborne Division to the left of CCB. Each cavalry troop normally consisted of a dozen M8 armored cars, each mounting a 37mm main gun plus two machine guns: a co-axil .30 caliber and a ring mounted .50 caliber. The road speed for an M8 was a spry 55 mph, making it perfect for reconnaissance and patrol work of this sort.

The two combat commands moved out of their assembly areas at 0600. After a preparatory barrage delivered by the artillery of the 6th Armored Division, CCA and CCB crossed their respective lines of departure at 0900.

In the CCA sector, Brigadier General Earnest organized his command into two task forces: Task Force (TF) Young (commanded by Captain Hugh Young, still filling in as CO of the 10th Armored Infantry Battalion) and Task Force Oden. TF Young would lead the attack while TF Oden remained in reserve. The initial objective was to clear the woods on the high ground northeast of Neffe.

Task Force Young advanced on the heels of an additional preparatory barrage delivered by the M7 105mm howitzers of the 66th Armored Field Artillery Battalion. Two platoons of A/10 climbed aboard some of the tanks of B/35. Laden with infantrymen, the Shermans churned their way across the snow-covered ground toward their objective. The lead elements were followed by the remainder of A/10 and B/35, then C/10, the mortar and machine gun platoons of the 10th AIB Headquarters Company, one section of the 704th Tank Destroyer Battalion, and one squad from the 24th Armored Engineer Battalion.

The attacking force made its way to the line of the woods and proceeded to move among the timbers. The only opposition up to that point came from enemy small arms fire. The advance went well, with the infantry clearing about half the woods by 1400. Ten minutes later, the attack continued into the remainder of the woods. The situation changed abruptly when a withering barrage of hostile artillery and direct tank fire erupted. The shelling continued unabated for the next hour. Despite the volume of fire, the armored infantrymen pressed through the woods and moved beyond onto open ground.

Casualties and equipment losses mounted. A/10 suffered 41 casualties in less than 60 minutes. B/35 began the attack with 11 tanks and saw their Shermans whittled down to only two (four being lost to enemy fire and five running into maintenance problems when their tracks ran afoul on severe ice). Forced to withdraw in the face of murderous fire, the Americans moved back over the crest of a hill and secured defilade positions in the woods. They dug in to protect their gains.

During the intense battle, there were numerous examples of courageous action. Sergeant Curtis D. Jackson crawled under fire to reach one of his unit's machine guns that had fallen idle. As the enemy continued to rake his area with a stream of bullets from automatic weapons, Jackson single-handedly brought the machine gun to life and engaged the enemy positions. S/Sgt. Lawrence L. Curtis teamed up with Pfc Charles C. Davenport to wage a two-man war against a German machine gun and mortar position. Davenport provided covering fire with his M1 Garand rifle and pinned down the Germans manning the weapons. S/Sgt. Curtis then used a bazooka to take out the enemy nest.

M8 Armored Car in action (U.S. Army photograph).

Some of the bravest acts were performed by soldiers trying to help their fallen comrades. S/Sgt. Joseph L. Noel exposed himself to the intense barrage to pull back one of the wounded men 20 yards to the protection of his own foxhole. Medical aid man Private Curtis L. McDonald took his peep (commonly referred to after the war as a "jeep") back and forth into the woods to evacuate the wounded. Several times during the battle, his vehicle was struck by shrapnel from the relentless enemy artillery fire. Corporal Russell V. Black took a page out of Private McDonald's book. Even after the last of the able-bodied infantrymen withdrew, Black made return trips with his peep to evacuate the wounded they had left behind. Technician 5th Grade Salvatore E. Rodriquez of A/10 jumped into his halftrack as shells continued to fall. He drove into the open battlefield where lay the wounded and dismounted to render aid. He helped several of the fallen into his halftrack, and with shells still descending around him, drove the men to safety. Sergeant Morriston L. Westberry also drove his halftrack into the face of the withering artillery barrage to help evacuate the wounded.

The men who risked their lives to rescue their brothers-in-arms were remarkably like those who fought in the manure-strewn village of Chaumont just 18 days prior. It was yet another example of the resilience and courage of the 10th Armored Infantry Battalion.

CCB's advance faced heavy resistance as well. The attack kicked off at 0925, and after 25 minutes, moved no more than 600 yards. The armored infantry continued a methodical advance in the face of heavy small arms, mortar, and artillery fire as the Sherman tanks crept behind them. After a robust firefight, the 53rd Armored Infantry Battalion reached the first phase line at 1140. Fifteen prisoners captured in the area were from the *7th Company, 696th Regiment* of the *340th Volksgrenadier Division*.

The advance continued, and then things really heated up at 1235 when the Germans, firing from the north, hit the attacking elements of CCB with mortar fire and heavier direct weapons. Enemy infantry took aim at the Shermans with *Panzerfausts*.

As some of the American infantrymen fell wounded, Private Sam Capri moved forward to tend to them. While the medic administered aid, a bullet pierced his steel helmet, momentarily stunning him. When he recovered, he continued his work, maintaining his composure despite the swirl of combat all around him. His luck ran out when he received a severe leg wound … but that didn't stop him from dragging himself from one wounded man to another (he was awarded the Distinguished Service Cross).

The Germans brought their own armor to the party. The 37th Tank Battalion's A Company, commanded by 2nd Lt. John Whitehill, destroyed two self-propelled guns and damaged another, while also destroying a towed anti-tank gun. Lt. Pendergast, the forward observer for the 22nd Armored Field Artillery Battalion, directed the fire of B Battery against two enemy tanks.

Another Fire Call

At 1350, an abrupt and dramatic change took place when CCB received orders to disengage and reassemble near Bastogne.

It is no small task to halt an attack and conduct a withdrawal while in direct contact with the enemy. As the 22nd Armored Field Artillery Battalion fired TOT and H&I missions, the 37th Tank Battalion pulled back a few vehicles at a time, moving them initially to an area near the Bois D'Hazy. By 2040, the 53rd Armored Infantry Battalion and 37th Tank Battalion were back in their assembly area near Assenois.

At 1700, CCA received a similar order: break off the attack and remain in position until relieved by elements of the 6th Armored Division. The 10th Armored Infantry Battalion began moving before dark into a bivouac area near Mont and were settled in by 2030. The night was calm and free of enemy interference, interrupted only by the steady cadence of friendly artillery fired by nearby units.

What happened? Why was the attack broken off so abruptly?

Earlier that day, Patton received an order to dispatch an armored division into a reserve position in Luxembourg (the idea must have been percolating earlier, given the reconnaissance mission conducted the day prior by the task force from the 704th Tank Destroyer Battalion and the 24th Armored Engineers). There was sudden fear—though not on Patton's part—that the Germans might attack toward Luxembourg City, with a strike coming either from the base of the Bulge or a point farther to the southeast where Patton had thinned his lines to accommodate the build-up of divisions for his attack against the south flank of the Bulge. As Charles McDonald (author of the official U.S. Army history *The Last Offensive*) put it so masterfully, "…intelligence staffs at SHAEF and the 12th Army Group these days were seeing burglars under every bed."

The Fourth Armored Division received the assignment. According to Patton, Gaffey's division was chosen because only one of their combat commands was engaged at the time, thus making a withdrawal easier (though in fact, two of their combat commands were attacking). So, the attack of the Fourth Armored was abruptly halted. The division was pulled from the line, detached from VIII Corps, and placed in TUSA reserve. By the end of the day on January 10, the division's battalions were made aware of their next stop: they would leave in the morning and head south toward Luxembourg City.

As the Fourth Armored prepared to depart, the members of the division did something never asked of them before: they removed the unit patches from their uniforms and painted over or otherwise concealed the unit identification markings on their vehicles. Not having enough paint, some of the men had to rely on mud, grease, or motor oil to cover the unit designations. Removing the patch from their uniform was sacrilegious (such a source of pride was their unit identity). But the move required secrecy, so the order was executed.

At 0500 on January 11, *Olympic's* headquarters received their orders for the road march. The division would use the familiar Arlon-Bastogne highway and move south to positions below Luxembourg City. Some units would travel a little farther south and head for billets in France (including the division headquarters, which relocated from Bastogne to Rodemack). Radio silence was to be maintained until further notice.

The temperature was well below freezing and the roads were covered with ice. A heavy snowfall blanketed the area overnight. It would be an uncomfortable trip, especially for the units on the tail end of the column moving at night. But it was certainly better than another bone-rattling night in the frozen hell of a foxhole.

The 51st Armored Infantry Battalion moved out at 0920 and reached their assembly area at 1600. The companies dispersed to their billets in several small French towns located less than four miles south of the border with Luxembourg. A/51 went to Roussy le Bourg, B/51 to Evange, C/51 to Roussy le Village, and the 10th AIB Headquarters Company to Breistroff-la-Grande.

The 10th Armored Infantry Battalion, slated for departure at 1100, didn't get underway until 1215 (their departure delayed due to the pace of movement of CCA's forward elements). Seventy miles and nearly 11 hours later, the battalion arrived at their billets in the French towns of Fixem, Gandren, and Beyren.

The 53rd was the last of the armored infantry battalions to depart. After almost eight hours on the road, they arrived at Hassel, Luxembourg 15 minutes before midnight.

The 8th Tank Battalion billeted at Boust and Soetrich, France, while the 25th Cavalry Reconnaissance Squadron found their new homes at Contern, Luxembourg. The 37th Tank Battalion (one of the last units to depart the Bastogne area) didn't arrive at the Luxembourg village of Itzig until 0300 on January 12.

The speed and skill with which the Fourth Armored executed the move warranted praise from Lt. General Patton: "The remarkable ability which Gaffey has of doing what he is told fast was well exemplified here." It was indeed an impressive feat given the weather and road conditions, coupled with the order to maintain radio silence.

Bastogne was in the Fourth Armored Division's rear-view mirror. But Lt. General Patton still had work to do. With the loss of the Fourth Armored from VIII Corps, TUSA didn't resume the offensive near Bastogne until January 12.

The 11th Armored Division assumed the Fourth's role in the attack. On January 16, they contacted the First Army's 2nd Armored Division near the town of Houffalize, an act which triggered the agreement to bring the First Army back under control of Lt. General Bradley's 12th Army Group. From Patton's perspective, "This will be very advantageous, as Bradley is less timid than Montgomery."

3

Rest and Recuperation

Third Army Reserve

When Patton placed the Fourth Armored into reserve, he chose a position where the division could use the road net to respond to threats against either XII Corps or XX Corps. When asked at a January 12 press conference about the new role of the division, Patton replied, "Just waiting to bite this fellow in the ass when he comes through."

The men of *Olympic* wasted little time once established in their assigned area. Major General Gaffey's staff conducted contingency planning, and at the combat command level, Brigadier General Earnest reconnoitered routes he might use to counter a German attack in XII Corps' zone. While their commanders conducted planning sessions, the soldiers were ordered to apply winter camouflage to their vehicles.

Unlike Patton, SHAEF still had a case of the jitters from their Bulge hangover. Fearing a repeat of the German airborne assault conducted during the opening phase of that battle, units of the Fourth Armored were placed on alert against possible enemy paratroopers. As a precautionary measure, the 53rd Armored Infantry Battalion established a security patrol running along the two-and-a-half-mile road between their location at Hassel and the 25th Cavalry Reconnaissance Squadron's position at Contern, Luxembourg.

On January 13, wary of a German attack from yet another direction, the division was ordered to move to an area west of the Thionville-Luxembourg highway. By 1400, all units had identified suitable locations for billets. CCR moved first, followed by CCA and CCB. The division headquarters relocated seven miles due west to Dudelange.

While not officially in a rest period, the net result from being in reserve was essentially the same. The veteran Fourth Armored, knowing the value of time, used every possible moment to service their equipment and absorb replacements. The time away from the front line was much needed and well deserved.

Not all the men received the same opportunity to rest and refit. At various times during the next several weeks, the division's artillery supported other units. Immediately after moving into Luxembourg, the 66th Armored Field Artillery Battalion fired missions in support of the 4th Infantry Division, while the 94th Armored Field Artillery Battalion reinforced the 255th Field Artillery Battalion in support of the 2nd Cavalry Group. The 22nd AFAB had its turn when they relieved the 94th AFAB. During this period, the armored field artillery battalions drew satisfaction from firing at enemy targets inside the German border.

Ideally, a rest period would be used to replenish the division. But the Third Army faced a shortage of supplies (not to mention the dearth of infantry replacements that still plagued the combat units). Hospitals were critically shy of blankets and litters. Winter clothing remained in short supply (though local manufacturing of camouflage snowsuits had just

3. Rest and Recuperation

Civilians at Hayange, France, manufacturing winter camouflage suits for American troops (U.S. Army photograph).

commenced with up to 10,000 suits per week being produced). One-inch steel cable—critical for recovering tanks and other heavy vehicles—was scarce (local manufacturing sources were used for this as well). There was a critical shortage of artillery replacement parts. The daily coal ration was reduced to half the normal allowance of four pounds per man. Even K rations were in short supply, so much so that Patton issued a directive that combat troops should be the only recipients.

An Army Marches on Its Stomach

As the saying goes, an army marches on its stomach. Of all the armies to fight during the Second World War, the Americans were certainly the best fed. Advances in food processing created new options that made it more likely that the calories required to keep a soldier moving and fighting would be delivered.

The G.I. had five options for sustenance (excluding what might be scrounged from the land they occupied):

The A ration was fresh food prepared by a unit's mess crew. Mobile kitchens could bring hot meals relatively close to the front line, but they were typically enjoyed when a unit was farther off the line in reserve.

The B ration (also known as the 10-in-1) consisted of canned and packaged goods, including items such as meat, vegetables, biscuits, soluble coffee, sugar, salt, candy, and gum. Accessory items included a can opener, toilet paper, and water-purification tablets (Halazone). The package was designed to supply 10 men with one meal each. Unable to store the 10-in-1 crates inside their vehicles, the tankers usually stacked them on the exterior engine deck of the tank. As Captain Len Kieley recalled, incoming artillery spoiled many a meal. "I can't tell you how many times there were beans and franks all over the tank."

The C ration was a canned ready-to-eat "wet" food. Among the varieties to choose from were meat and beans, meat and potato hash, and meat and vegetable stew.

The D ration was a nutrient-infused chocolate bar yielding approximately 600 calories. While it might look appealing, it was hard and unappetizing. The bar was formulated to resist melting and intentionally designed to taste bitter (it couldn't taste *too* good, lest the soldier over-consume it as a treat).

The K ration closely resembled the components of the 10-in-1. However, the K ration was an individual meal that provided between 3000 and 3500 calories, with the items bundled together in a single carton. It was produced in three varieties: breakfast, dinner, and supper. It included some confections and a small version of the D ration.

John Harris, First Sergeant of C Battery, 22nd Armored Field Artillery Battalion, shared his personal view about what was good … and what was not:

> The ten-in-one ration was the best of all. Next would be the C-Ration. We relied heavily on issued rations. The French gave us some hot food once in a while. In Germany we would look up in fireplaces, and if we were lucky we would find hams hanging there being smoked. Very good for hungry GI's. The Ten-in-one ration came in a heavy cardboard box and fed ten men. The Ten-in-one's always had fresh baked bread. Ten-in-one is my first choice and C rations is second, K rations are third. Of course, K rations are best for assault troops (invasion). Depending on the combat situation, we would have our kitchen trucks come forward to our position and cook us a hot meal. This was great! I like the C Ration's canned potatoes. We usually ate mostly C rations. The hard chocolate bar in the K ration was always good for trading, wine, food, etc. They lacked somewhat in taste. Not too many ate the chocolate bars. They were solid as a rock. Used a lot for trading. The Europeans seemed to like chocolate.

The Pressure Mounts on Hitler

On January 12, the Soviets launched a large-scale offensive, hurling nearly three million soldiers against 750,000 German defenders along a 400-mile front. As the Russians pressed forward, German troops and everyday citizens retreated to the west. The civilians had much to fear, as the Russians had earned a reputation for brutality, including widespread rape and murder. Rather than fall subservient to the invaders, almost five million Germans left their homes in pursuit of safe havens.

Also headed west were thousands of American prisoners of war. Often on foot, they were evacuated from camps soon to be overrun by the Russian horde. Marching under terrible winter conditions and sapped of their strength by weeks, months, or even years of captivity, many did not survive the journey. In some instances, Russian forces caught up to the columns and liberated the prisoners. In very rare cases, Americans took up arms alongside the Russians and opted to fight their way west. Their German guards, if not fortunate enough to take refuge and flee, were often executed.

The situation on the Western Front was in a state of flux. The American First and Third Armies had yet to join hands in the Ardennes. Until that transpired, Montgomery controlled Lt. General Hodges' First Army, leaving Patton's TUSA as the lone Army under Bradley's 12th Army Group. Beyond the task of pushing the Germans back inside their December 16 start line, the American commanders were uncertain about the road ahead.

On January 12, Bradley and Patton discussed the prospective long-range plans which they might propose to General Eisenhower. Lt. General Bradley favored a thrust by Hodges' First Army toward Cologne (in which case Patton's Third Army would protect the southern flank of Hodges' attack). Lt. General Patton, on the other hand, lobbied for an attack by his own XX Corps. In his opinion, an attack "straight east through Saarlautern would bring better results and would certainly be more crippling to Germany, as it would get the whole Saar valley."

A Time to Recover

The days to come provided the Fourth Armored Division with time for sorely needed rest and recuperation. The small towns and villages they occupied were more alike than not. Many houses were marked by piles of manure along the main street. While unsightly, its use as fertilizer come springtime made it a necessity. The opportunity to sleep under a roof, out of the winter elements, was a tremendously welcome change. The comfort of being indoors rendered a town's cosmetics immaterial.

Sergeant Robert Calvert, leader of the 1st Rifle Squad of the 1st Platoon of C/51, was assigned to the family home of the Fischbachs, who ran a small store out of their residence. Calvert recalled that the Fischbachs were "a couple in their 40s with three children. We lived in their front room for eight days and became good friends." (Calvert stayed in touch for the next 60 years, exchanging Christmas cards and seeing the family on at least two occasions after the war.)

Calvert's unit, just like the other armored infantry companies in the division, needed reinforcements, renewed training, and reorganization. As Calvert explained:

> The company had to be restructured and almost every leadership post had a new incumbent. Chris became platoon sergeant and was promoted to T/Sgt. Clovis Alphonse took the 2nd rifle squad and Mutschmann the machine gun squad. As they had been in the company for some time, they were made staff sergeants. Larry (mortar squad) Shorty Chaffee (3rd rifle) and I (1st rifle) were made sergeants. We discovered they made a lot of us Pfc's in late December, nice of them since it paid a few more dollars a month. In January, I was awarded the Combat Infantry Badge which, along with the honor, increased your pay $10 a month.

Calvert's platoon was led by Lt. Laughlin. He described the lieutenant as "a popular and fair leader." However,

> His weakness was that he drank too much and when we were not in combat, his driver generally had to cover for him. Each morning, when we were in a combat situation, there would be a squad leader's meeting where the plans for the day would be announced. Tasks were assigned to each squad, and some were obviously more dangerous than others. Laughlin would rotate the risks; the squad which had suffered the least recently was given the most difficult task. I almost always agreed with the logic behind his assignments.

Two sure signs of a unit being in a rest area were the screening of movies and the appearance of a Red Cross Clubmobile. The Clubmobiles were a particularly welcome sight. The donuts and hot coffee were enjoyable, but it was the treat of visiting the American women who staffed the unit that made the G.I.'s trip worthwhile.

January 22, 1945. A member of the Red Cross dances with men of the 919th Field Artillery Battalion during a break in firing near Tunting, France (U.S. Army photograph).

T/Sgt. Nick Alexander joined A/53 in July as a replacement. Initially, he served as a front-line medic. During February, he became a combat squad leader and eventually rose to platoon sergeant. He shared distinct memories of his time away from the front line in January:

> It was a restful and peaceful time. We stayed with a nice family, man and wife two young children, boy about 8 yrs and daughter about 6yrs. We had leave in Luxembourg City and even attended an American movie (Sgt York starring Gary Cooper) in the local cinema. I had seen the movie before in Boise, Idaho prior to entering the service. Some movies were shown in a local barn by our special services. The Luxembourg people were very gracious even though our entire squad of 8–9 occupied most of the house. We spent about 4–5 days there before shipping out. The sister of the father and her young daughter (8–9 yrs) visited also for three days. I spent some of my time entertaining the kids and also accompanying the matron of the house on her chores in the village delivering milk and crops to the villagers, to the dismay of the platoon leader. We were also reinforced with new replacements at this time. We gave our hosts tobacco and chocolate bars … and food from the kitchen if available. It was a very pleasant resting period before moving back to the attack.

For some, the rest period generated more work than usual. The 126th Armored Ordnance Battalion was particularly busy. On January 14, the battalion reported that all company shops were crowded with vehicles for repairs. This was the peak day for the month-to-date, with 53 inoperative vehicles in the battalion shops.

For Major Albin F. Irzyk, the down time allowed him to take on the solemn task of writing letters to the next of kin of those killed in action. Each family had presumably

3. Rest and Recuperation

Major Albin F. Irzyk, who assumed command of the 8th Tank Battalion on December 2, 1944 (author's collection).

received the standard notification from the War Department. But it was Al's responsibility as the battalion commander to provide a level of personalization and detail that would hopefully answer the questions many families asked in the wake of the formal notice from the War Department. Irzyk went to great lengths to understand the events that led to each soldier's death. The process of crafting the letters took an emotional toll on him, but he remained committed to doing his best to honor the courage and sacrifice of his men by providing as much information and comfort as possible to the families.

On January 15, *Olympic* was reassigned from Third Army reserve to Major General Eddy's XII Corps. The move came in conjunction with orders for XII Corps to commence an attack on January 18. Eddy's instructions were to establish a bridgehead across the Sûre River near Diekirch and then drive north to cut into the base of what remained of the Bulge. XII Corps was stacked for the occasion, consisting of (in addition to the Fourth Armored) the 87th, 80th, 4th, and 5th Infantry Divisions.

There were no immediate plans to utilize the Fourth in conjunction with the attack, so rest and recuperation continued. Around this time, the division began issuing passes to Luxembourg City and Paris. On January 15, the 53rd AIB granted several passes to lucky members of the battalion. A few days later, an order was given allowing units to issue passes to as much as five percent of their troop strength at any given time.

January 15 was a typical day during the rest period. The 10th Armored Infantry Battalion scheduled two showings of the movie *San Diego, I Love You* at a theater made from a large barn in Frisange; unfortunately, the shows were cancelled because of generator issues. The theater was back up and running the following day, with performances held at 1930 and 2130. It was described as "a diverting comedy" that was "well attended and enthusiastically received." The men of the 10th Armored Infantry Battalion had the opportunity for hot showers, but they had to be shuttled by truck to a shower point at Mann, Luxembourg to take advantage. Six trucks kept a continuous stream of soldiers moving to and from the facility.

Entertainment continued over the next several days. On January 17, the men were treated to two showings of *A Guy Named Joe* starring Spencer Tracy and Irene Dunn. The division band toured around the division while the Red Cross Clubmobiles made appearances that brightened up the day. The division clergy held a Protestant service in the area near C/10 which drew a large group of attendees from many units. Catholic and Jewish services were conducted as well.

Like the other tankers in the division, the men of Major Irzyk's 8th Tank Battalion settled into their billets in Luxembourg. The local citizens embraced their American guests with open arms. The weather had been miserable, making the temporary homes in the towns of Mondercange and Monnerich valued havens from the elements. The battalion's kitchen trucks were able to operate on a regular basis and served three hot meals every day. There was more than enough food, and some of the citizens were treated to leftovers. The children came out bundled up for protection against the severe winter weather and seemed to particularly savor the meals.

Around this time, Lt. Colonel Hal Pattison traveled to Thionville to meet with the G-4 of XX Corps, who was an old friend and fellow battalion commander from his days with the 37th Armored Regiment. At lunch, he met with one of Major General Walton Walker's aides who had served as a platoon leader in Pattison's old battalion. Speaking privately, the aide asked how the division had reacted to Wood's relief and whether they expected him to return to command the Fourth. When Pattison told him that they had resigned themselves to Wood not coming back, the aide indicated that he shared Patton's opinion. He went on to divulge that Walker had urged Patton to relieve Wood "sometime earlier than the actual event."

M7 self-propelled howitzer of B Battery, 22nd Armored Field Artillery Battalion (U.S. Army photograph).

The Big Guns Keep Firing

The division's artillery battalions remained hard at work. The 66th Armored Artillery Battalion fired preparatory barrages in support of an attack by the 4th, 5th, and 80th Infantry Divisions. Reinforcing fires continued until January 30, at which time they were relieved by the 94th Armored Field Artillery Battalion. The men of the 66th moved into billets until February 5. Commencing on January 19, the 22nd Armored Field Artillery Battalion provided reinforcing fire for the 255th Field Artillery Battalion. Their most notable fire mission occurred the following morning when they participated in a "Serenade" (code for the simultaneous firing of multiple artillery units). The target was a *Nebelwerfer* (rocket) unit under observation by an American observation plane.

While life within one of the armored field artillery battalions had its own share of hardships, the chance of becoming a casualty was significantly less than that of their brothers in the armored infantry and tank battalions. Since entering combat in July through the end of January, 171 members of the 66th Armored Field Artillery had been wounded in action and 23 men killed. Forty-nine had been injured in action and 13 had non-battle injuries. There were 14 cases of combat exhaustion and 44 men transferred due to disease. By contrast, the armored infantry divisions suffered a similar number of casualties in a fraction of the time. For example, in the month of November *alone*, the 53rd Armored Infantry Battalion suffered 402 casualties, of which 34 men were killed in action, 135 wounded, and 233 sick or listed with battle fatigue.

Realignment

On January 17, a new troop list was issued for the combat commands:

CCA: 10th AIB, 35th TB, A/25, A/24, A/704, B/489, A/46, A/126
CCB: 53rd AIB, 37th TB, C/25, B/24, B/704, A/489, B/46, B/126
CCR: 51st AIB, 8th TB, D/25, C/704, D/489, C/24

There were also changes in store for the division's leadership. On January 22, Brigadier General Earnest was released from duty as the commander of CCA (he assumed command of the 90th Infantry Division). Earnest's replacement was Colonel Hayden A. Sears, who transferred from the 17th Armored Group.

Colonel Sears wasn't a stranger. Prior to the reorganization of the division to the "light" format, he commanded the 35th Armored Regiment while part of the Fourth. He was a familiar and welcome face to Al Irzyk (promoted this very day to the rank of lieutenant colonel).

Another change was the reassignment of Colonel Withers, who was relieved of his assignment as assistant commander of CCA and appointed division assistant chief of staff. Withers' role as assistant commander was highly unusual to begin with, since the official Table of Organization and Equipment (TO&E) did not call for such a position. Also unusual prior to this was the simultaneous presence of two brigadier generals within the division (Dager and Earnest).

On January 24, in a sign that the rest period might soon end, both the 51st and 53rd Armored Infantry Battalions conducted reconnaissance of the positions currently held by units of the 4th Infantry Division. A move to the front line was imminent.

Accolades

The relief of Bastogne, now a memory generated almost a month ago, was destined to be an accomplishment never to be forgotten. On January 20, the mold for cementing the legacy of the Fourth Armored was partially cast when the division received a letter from Lt. General Patton:

The outstanding celerity of your movement and the unremitting, vicious and skillful manner in which you pushed the attack, terminating at the end of four days and nights of incessant battle in the relief of Bastogne, constitute one of the finest chapters in the glorious history of the U.S. Army.

The American press arrived to capture more details of the Fourth's role in the Battle of the Bulge. On the day of Patton's letter, Will Lang from *Time-Life* magazine and Ernest Hauser of the *Saturday Evening Post* sought information about the battle from the Fourth Armored Division's G-2. Hauser also interviewed Al Irzyk and several men from B/8.

On January 21, the division received a letter from SHAEF which read in part:

The 4th Armored Division is both feared and hated by the German front-line troops because of its high combat efficiency. Some American PW's who could speak and understand German were told by enemy soldiers and officers that the 4th Armored Division has gained a reputation amongst the Wehrmacht of being a crack armored unit dangerous to oppose.

The Ebb and Flow on the Western Front

By late January, as evidenced by the withdrawal of troops from the area, Hitler had tacitly conceded defeat in the Ardennes. On January 22, he ordered the *6th SS Panzer Army* to leave the Ardennes to help protect the oil fields in Hungary from the advancing Soviet forces. At 1530, pilots reported a significant amount of German armor on the move north of Diekirch (they described it as "the biggest concentration they had seen since the Falaise Gap"). XIX TAC's fighter groups conducted 627 sorties against German positions facing TUSA near Prüm and along the Our River. Air strikes destroyed the bridge at Dasburg, restricting German movement toward the east and creating a target-rich environment on the west side of the river.

On the American side of the line, the generals wrangled over the best course of action to take following the reduction of the Bulge. On January 23, Bradley called Patton into a meeting and proposed a plan to attack with a single corps through the Eifel. The following day, Bradley, Patton, Hodges, and their staff met to coordinate plans for future attacks by the First and Third Armies.

Just as their plans were finalized, General John Whiteley (deputy to the assistant chief of staff operations for SHAEF) contacted Bradley, wishing him to transfer a corps headquarters to the 6th Army Group. Bradley lost his temper (according to Patton, it was the first and only time he witnessed Bradley flare up). In his diary, Patton recounted Bradley's response to Whiteley's request:

If he (Whiteley) wanted to destroy the whole operation, he could do so and be damned, or words to that effect, and to take all the corps and divisions.... Bradley was very firm, and even angry.

Patton later added:

Bradley, Hodges and myself are determined to carry on our attack no matter how much they deplete us. Personally, I am convinced that the Germans are pulling out, probably as far as the Rhine, and if we go

3. Rest and Recuperation

ahead, we will get to the Rhine, and very soon. To do otherwise at this moment would, in my opinion be criminal.

Meanwhile, the Soviets ... unencumbered by such vacillation ... were driving hard. By January 27, Russian tanks and infantry were situated only 100 miles from Berlin. The Oder River was the last major physical obstacle separating Marshal Georgy Zhukov's forces from the German capital. On that day, the Germans did what they could to wipe out all trace of their criminal actions at the concentration camp near Auschwitz, but they were unable to mask the horrors perpetrated there. The Russians soon liberated the camp but failed to announce the discovery to the Western Allies.

Had the Soviets revealed their find, it would not have been the first the world had heard of the atrocities committed by the Germans. The first reports by American newspapers appeared during June of 1944. On November 25, the War Refugee Board made public a report describing the murder of more than one-and-a-half million people at Birkenau and Auschwitz during the two years between April 1942 and April 1944. Three eyewitnesses testified as part of the report: two of them were young Slovak Jews who escaped from the Birkenau camp on April 7, 1944. The third was a non–Jewish Polish major, previously held prisoner at Lublin and later transferred to Birkenau.

The Jewish youths provided details about the gas chambers and crematoria. They described the herding of prisoners into a hall where the unwitting victims were told to undress under the pretense they were going to bathe. They relayed how the poor souls were crowded into the gas chamber, unaware of its purpose, and packed into as tight an area as possible before the heavy doors were sealed behind them. The men of the *Schutzstaffel (SS)* climbed to the roof, and from there poured powder out of tin cans labeled *Cyklon*. In a direct quote from the report:

It is presumed that this is a cyanide mixture of some sort which turns into gas at a certain temperature. After three minutes everyone in the chamber is dead.

The Polish major offered a separate but similar account.

Writer John H. Crider's story was published by the *New York Times* on November 26, 1944. Even though the article appeared on the bottom fold of the front page, his report failed to make a notable dent on the American psyche. The G.I.s pushed eastward into Germany unaware of the horrors awaiting discovery.

By January 28, the Allied line was restored much to its pre–Bulge appearance. However, the disposition of Allied divisions was far different than it was prior to Hitler's attack. As January drew to a close, the First Army began its drive into the Eifel with the Third Army attacking in support of Hodges' right flank. Patton noted in his diary:

We are starting a new attack today and it is snowing like Hell. However, I think that the Germans are in a bad way and that we will be able to get through. Unfortunately we have to storm the Siegfried line as a starter.

At the same time, Soviet forces crossed the Oder River at Kienitz, placing them less than 50 miles from Berlin. If there was a race for the German capital, the Soviets were winning.

Patton's attention was squarely focused on the resumption of his offensive. On January 31, he reflected on his interaction with the perennially cautious Major General Eddy of XII Corps. When Patton directed Eddy to attack on February 4, Eddy asked for a delay until February 6.

He (Eddy) said I never gave him time to get ready and did not appreciate time and space factors. I told him that had I ever given a corps commander the time he asked for, we would still be on the Seine (river in France).

Little did Patton know that he would be the one to put the brakes on Eddy's attack.

Sharpening the Blade

While rest, recreation, and recuperation continued to be important elements in the division's life, it was also a time to ready *Olympic* for a return to the battlefield. During the latter part of January, training and the adoption of new weapons became routine. Firing ranges were constructed so that small arms and tanks could be put to work. Additional training was especially important for the new replacements joining the division.

Throughout the ETO, most of the replacements were not prepared to enter combat. A regimental commander from the 5th Infantry Division (Colonel Charles W. Yuill) noted that,

> About 75% of our rifle company replacements are not qualified for rifle combat when we receive them. One group included 150 men who had been trained as AA (anti-aircraft) men and had no infantry training except the six or seven weeks' basic training given to all soldiers. Infantry replacements should have at least four months of infantry training before being sent to combat units.

Sergeant Nick Alexander offered his thoughts about the replacements he received for his armored infantry battalion:

> Most of the replacements were young newly inducted 18–19-year-old kids with just 3–4 months of basic training experience. A small number of older men were transferred in from other non-combat units (cooks, clerks, air corps, etc.), some of whom were married and even had children at home. Most assignments were to the rifle squads with an M-1 rifle, while others went to the mortar and machine gun squads carrying a carbine and receiving quick lessons on the use of those weapons. A bazooka man practiced once or twice, if possible, shooting at distant targets (shot-up and abandoned vehicles like tanks and trucks). We had a 2–3 fold turnover and very few of the original well trained "fourthers" were "still around when the war ended."

A new piece of equipment introduced to the division was the E4–5 flamethrower, designed

The M24 light tank, a late-war replacement for the M5A1 (U.S. Army photograph).

for use with a Sherman tank. Fueled by two 25-gallon tanks, it fired through the machine gun aperture at a range of 50 to 70 yards and could last 50 seconds. If exhausted, it could be swapped out for the normal machine gun in as little as 30 seconds. The weapon was installed on one of the medium tanks from B/37 and put through extensive demonstrations and training.

Ultimately, it was decided not to install any beyond the single example in B Company. The Army's original intent was to outfit nine Shermans per tank battalion with the E4–5, but after trials and initial use in the field, it quickly fell out of favor with tankers.

The tank battalions continued to receive the new M4A3E8 Sherman tanks. The 37th Tank Battalion was informed that their light tanks would soon be replaced by a new model, the M24 "Chaffee" light tank. Driver training on the M24 was undertaken in advance of their delivery. On February 5, the cavalry reconnaissance units took possession of their first Chaffees.

The HQ units of the armored infantry battalions received upgrades to their assault guns. The M8 howitzer carriages (75mm guns mounted on a light tank chassis) were replaced by Sherman tanks armed with 105mm howitzers (the same model used by the tank battalions). The assault gun crew members underwent training on the new tanks. In the case of the 10th AIB, the training was supervised by officers of the 35th Tank Battalion, who possessed ample experience with the gun.

The 126th Armored Ordnance Battalion made more improvements to the division's armored vehicles. Crews were sent out to weld chicken wire to the exterior of the light and medium tanks, which allowed natural camouflage to be inserted once the foliage of spring returned (a practice that the 8th Tank Battalion was famous for). With the gradually improving weather and road conditions, the steel-cleated blocks were removed from the tank treads.

The white-washing of vehicles came to a halt and the crews' attention turned toward returning the vehicles to their normal appearance. During the days ahead, unit identification markings were restored.

On February 1, TUSA began the process of up-armoring Shermans by applying two-and-a-half inches of extra plating on the forward hull (the steel was salvaged from destroyed tanks). The job of welding the supplemental armor in place was contracted out to local civilian factories. The upgrade saved untold lives, especially as the dreaded *Panzerfausts* became a prevalent threat. The M4A3E2 Sherman tanks had proven popular among their crews, and the up-armoring process was an attempt to provide similar attributes to more tanks. Colonel Toben, the XII Corps ordnance officer, said of the "Jumbo" tank,

> *Crews who have used the medium tank M4A3E2 with increased armor on turret and front like it. The increased weight has not seriously reduced mobility. Hits on the front and turret that would have knocked out other tanks have bounced off the M4A3E2.*

The Fourth Armored Division was back in full fighting form. Their equipment was better than ever. The coordination of air and artillery support had been fine-tuned over the course of months of battle. Even though the number of original members of the division had been thinned after months of heavy fighting, a strong contingent of experienced officers and enlisted men remained. They would provide the ongoing training and motivation needed to turn new recruits into effective soldiers. *Olympic* was primed and ready to take the battle to German soil.

4

To Hell and Back

The 704th Tank Destroyer Battalion

On January 11, the three tank destroyer companies of the 704th were reunited with the Fourth Armored. A/704 and B/704 were attached to CCA and CCB, respectively, while the balance of the battalion was attached to CCR.

At 1230, the 704th (-A-B) left the Bastogne area for billets at the French town of Volmerange, 43 miles to the south. After their arrival, they commenced training exercises for replacement personnel and conducted vehicle maintenance. The battalion staff also reserved time for the enlisted men to enjoy a dose of much needed rest and recreation.

The 704th's command post was more than a dozen miles west of the German border. This might have been considered a haven from threats other than the *Luftwaffe*, but any feeling of immunity was shattered when a massive 340mm railway gun fired on their position, dropping two rounds within 50 feet of the command post. Three men from the reconnaissance unit were sleeping in a house across the street from the CP when another shell brought the building down around them. Miraculously, not one of the soldiers received a scratch. Another shell hit across the street from the battalion headquarters. The explosion and concussion blew out the window of the operations room, tore down the stove, and punched holes in the opposite wall. A huge steel fragment collapsed into the building. Incredibly, T/Sgt. Baloga slept through the entire shelling.

That excitement aside, the battalion settled in and enjoyed life off the front line. Little did they know that just one week later their lives would be intertwined with those of the 94th Infantry Division.

The 94th Infantry Division

The 94th Infantry Division, led by Major General Harry Malony, arrived in France on September 8, 1944. Rather than being sent toward the German border, the *"Pilgrim Division"* headed west into the Brittany Peninsula. Their mission: assume responsibility for containing the German troops holed up in the port cities of Lorient and St. Nazaire. While this was light work compared to the fighting near the German frontier, it offered an opportunity to engage the enemy. During their nearly four-month assignment in Brittany, the 94th inflicted 2700 casualties and captured 566 Germans.

On January 1, the 66th Infantry Division took over the 94th ID's role in Brittany. Even though the *Pilgrim Division* had been in action for nearly four months, it was still viewed

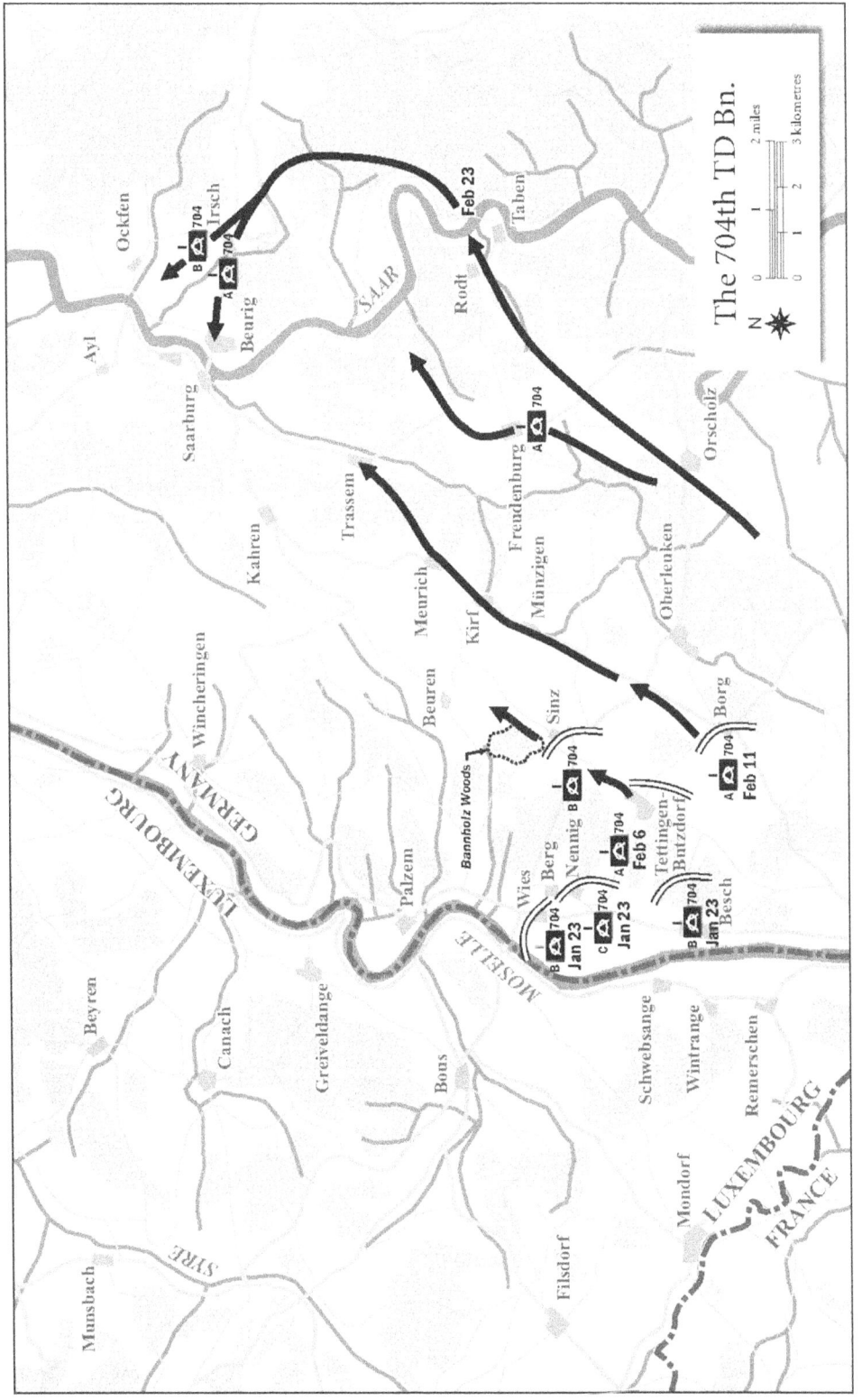

The 704th TD Bn. (© Petho Cartography, 2020).

as a green unit in need of further development. Assigned to Major General Walton Walker's XX Corps, Malony's division headed east. At the time, Walker's units held positions on the far right of TUSA. While Patton's other corps engaged in fighting at the Bulge, Walker's primary role was to stand his ground in front of the *Westwall* and guard against anything Hitler might have up his sleeve.

On January 7, the 94th began the process of taking over the front held by the 90th Infantry Division. Due to the repositioning of XX Corps in response to the battle in the Ardennes, the 94th ID's line extended a tenuous 13 miles.

Malony had his infantrymen improve their positions. They dug into the frozen, snow-blanketed earth and planted mines and demolitions in the event the Germans launched an attack in their zone.

On January 14, the 94th began limited offensive operations (intended in part to help their maturation). Malony's general mission was to reduce the *Westwall* defenses along their front and tie down German forces that might otherwise be deployed at the Bulge. Their initial opponent in the coming battle was the under-strength *714th Regiment* of the *416th Infantry Division*.

The 94th's first objective was the small town of Tettingen, located a short distance inside the German border. Advancing without the aid of tanks (the division did not yet have the benefit of an attached tank battalion), one of their infantry battalions headed north along the axis of the main road leading to the town.

The southern edge of Tettingen was marked by the town church, its masonry steeple clearly visible to the infantrymen as they made their approach. When they got closer, they saw the belt of *Westwall* fortifications extending from the town toward the east. The con-

January 19, 1945. Soldiers of the 94th Infantry Division move toward cover across dragon's teeth of Siegfried Line near Tettingen, Germany (U.S. Army photograph).

January 19, 1945. This 94th Infantry Division outpost between Besch and Nennig has repulsed enemy patrols and is now awaiting a probable attack. The machine gunners are Tec5 Eruink Topmiller (left) and Pfc Charles H. Scott. This position directly faces two German pill boxes (U.S. Army photograph).

crete triangular spikes known as "dragon's teeth" were arranged in tidy rows across an open field and then disappeared from sight as they flowed into the nearby woods.

Tettingen was secured with relative ease. Malony doubled down on the gain and captured the neighboring village of Butzdorf. The 94th Infantry Division's advance resulted in a mile-deep salient beyond the American front line.

The following day, another infantry battalion from the 94th moved north toward Nennig, one mile and three-quarters northwest of Tettingen. Nennig fell much as Tettingen had. However, when the Americans pressed farther north toward Wies, they found a more determined foe. After suffering many casualties, the town was finally cleared on January 16.

The separate attacks at Tettingen and Nennig resulted in two finger-like appendages protruding into German territory. Over the course of January 16 and 17, the 94th closed the gap between the salients.

The Commitment of the 704th

The 704th Tank Destroyer Battalion was detached from the Fourth Armored on January 18 and assigned to XX Corps. The following morning, elements of the battalion departed for a cluster of towns in France 15 miles south of the border with Luxembourg. The 704th Headquarters Company traveled 28 miles and established their command post at

Bouzonville. Company A billeted at Brettnach, B Company at Vaudreching, and C Company at Anzeling.

Two of the tank destroyer companies didn't remain in their billets very long. On the afternoon of January 19, B/704 moved 30 miles south to Saint-Avold to support the 5th Ranger Battalion. On January 20, A/704 moved north for seven miles to the vicinity of Halstroff, where they supported the 301st Infantry Regiment of the 94th Infantry Division. The 1st Platoon reported to Waldwisse, the 2nd Platoon to Obernaumen, and the 3rd to Büschdorf. C/704 and the other elements of the 704th remained in reserve.

On January 23, the entire 704th was attached to the 94th Infantry Division. The battalion headquarters moved 14 miles to the northwest and entered billets at Oberperl, a German town tucked in the area where the borders of Germany, France, and Luxembourg converge. B Company, relieved of its work with the 5th Ranger Battalion, established billets at the German town of Besch, two miles north of the 704th's command post. They dispatched one platoon of Hellcats to the vicinity of Nennig and another platoon to Weis. C/704 billeted along with the battalion headquarters at Oberperl while sending its 2nd Platoon to the vicinity of Tettingen and another platoon to Wochern.

A Sea of Mines

One of the primary threats facing the 704th was the sea of deadly mines planted by the Germans. On January 26, after knocking out a pillbox and machine gun position, Sergeant John Jesky's Hellcat struck a mine which severely wounded T/5 Canio Costanzo, forcing his evacuation. Jesky, his gunner Corporal Lyndon Stephenson, Private First Class (Pfc) Frank Heger, and Private Salvatore Tripodi were all badly shaken up by the same blast. That same day, Lieutenant Leonard (the reconnaissance officer attached to C/704) stepped on a land mine and was evacuated due to serious leg wounds.

The following day, T/Sergeant Willard Fox took a maintenance crew to retrieve Sergeant Jesky's Hellcat. After struggling for two hours without success, they abandoned the effort. On January 30, while attempting to retrieve another disabled tank near Butzdorf, Fox's wrecker struck a mine, causing the recovery vehicle to throw a track. Fortunately, none of the crew were injured, but it took until 0400 the next morning to repair and return the vehicle.

The proliferation of mines was unlike anything the battalion had yet seen. Every type of mine was present. *Teller-mines* were used against tanks and other heavy vehicles. *Topf-mines* were primarily designed for use against tanks, and because of the absence of metal components, they were not revealed by American land-mine detectors. *Schu-mines* were an anti-personal mine housed in a wooden box, making it difficult to detect. *S-mines* (nicknamed the "bouncing Betty") drew the most fear from American infantrymen. When triggered, the explosive charge launched into the air and detonated at a height of about three feet, sending shrapnel flying at the most vulnerable areas of the body.

The 11th Panzer Division Strikes

The 94th's penetration through the *Westwall* did not go unnoticed by the enemy's higher headquarters. The veteran *11th Panzer Division*, already en route to the area, was directed to first blunt the American attack and then counterattack and push their enemy back outside the line of the *Westwall*.

By German standards at this stage of the war, the *11th Panzer* was well equipped. Handicapped by the late arrival of their complement of 50 *Panther* tanks, they chose to attack

February 3, 1945. An American engineer works on mines as an M18 Hellcat of the 704th Tank Destroyer Battalion stands by. Near Nennig, Germany (U.S. Army photograph).

without them and deployed two regiments of *Panzer Grenadiers,* 30 *Mark IV* tanks, and 16 assault guns. Though short the formidable *Panthers*, it was nevertheless a powerful offensive force.

The *11th Panzer's* first action was to send a *Kampfgruppe* to reinforce the defensive positions held by the weaker German infantry. At 2100 on January 21, the *11th Panzer* fought their way to the center of Nennig. The Americans abandoned the north section of the town, including a prominent castle located on the high ground that dominated the approaches. Here, the German advance reached its zenith, but it didn't spell the end of bitter fighting between the *11th Panzer* and the 94th Infantry Division.

On January 22, American reinforcements from the 8th Armored Division entered Nennig. Sherman tanks from CCA/8 reinforced the infantry, but the tankers from the inexperienced 8th Armored were driven out by the veteran *11th Panzer*. A brief clearing in the very poor weather that dominated the day allowed American B-24 bombers to hit German artillery and mortar positions. Clearer skies on January 23 invited the use of P-47s to strike targets in Sinz and the Bannholz Woods, where *Panzers* and other German vehicles sought refuge from the American fighter-bombers.

February 2, 1945. At a demolished chateau in Nennig, Germany, an M-18 of the 704th Tank Destroyer Battalion, left, guards a road next to a German *Mark IV*, destroyed during the attack on Nennig (U.S. Army photograph).

On January 26, blizzard conditions set upon the battlefield. The 94th Infantry Division launched an attack toward Sinz but made little progress. In the face of counterattacks by German infantry and newly arrived *Panthers*, the Americans pulled back.

The weary 94th attacked again the following day. This time, assisted by tanks and armored infantry from CCA/8, the Americans succeeded in taking a portion of Sinz. As daylight ended, CCA/8 withdrew on orders to join its parent division elsewhere, leaving the infantry of the 94th to their own devices. Under renewed pressure from the relentless German opposition, elements of the 376th Infantry Regiment were forced to withdraw on January 28, which left Sinz open once again for occupation by the *11th Panzer Division*.

The 94th Infantry Division's perceived lack of results garnered the personal attention of Lt. General Patton. On January 31, he told the division commander that his unit had the worst performance in the Third Army when it came to the ratio of non-battle casualties to battle casualties. As historian Martin Blumenson recounted, "If conditions did not improve, he said, Maloney (sic) himself would become a non-battle casualty." Patton described the interaction, saying, "I was intentionally rough." Patton later recounted the admonishment he gave to Malony and several of his officers:

(I) told them very frankly that the 94th has lost more men as prisoners of war than all the other troops I had committed during my entire military service and that they must wipe out this disgrace. I then patted General Maloney (sic) on the back, and believe that this technique will have the desired effect.

February 1, 1945. Lt. General George S. Patton (front left) is greeted on arrival by Major General Harry J. Malony (right), commanding general of the 94th Infantry Division (U.S. Army photograph).

The 704th Comes into Play

After the setback at Sinz and the withdrawal of the 8th Armored Division's combat command, Major General Malony regrouped before commencing further offensive action. In the absence of supporting tanks, elements of the 704th were deployed as if they were Shermans. Things were about to get a lot tougher for the Hellcat crews.

On January 27, C/704's 3rd Platoon moved out for Besch and Nennig. A section of Hellcats protected a crossroad near the *Westwall* south of the latter town. The tank destroy-

February 2, 1945. Bodies of dead Germans lay in front of the chateau they tried to hold in Nennig, Germany (U.S. Army photograph).

ers remained there for only a day before rejoining the rest of the platoon at Besch. The 1st Platoon held a position in the rear area at Oberperl.

On January 29, C/704 received heavy indirect shelling. The Germans maintained excellent observation outposts and called in constant artillery and mortar fire. To evade the enemy shells, the 3rd Platoon moved a section of tank destroyers into the woods near Nennig. They found the dense forest "littered with dead Germans" along with many American casualties. Neither side had risked sending men into harm's way for the retrieval of their dead. Instead, the bodies were left to freeze in the harsh winter conditions.

The 704th saw their own ranks thin out as well. Before the end of January, the battalion experienced several losses among the ranks of its officers. Captain David Lamb transferred out of the battalion, while Captain Leonard Wilson, commanding B Company, was wounded and evacuated after a mortar shell burst near his peep. Lt. Leonard, a recon officer attached to C Company, stepped on a mine while trying to find an alternate route for one of the tank destroyer platoons (he suffered a severe injury to his foot and was evacuated). In addition to the loss of three officers, eight enlisted men were wounded during the month. To help offset these and other losses, 56 enlisted men arrived as replacements. The officer ranks were replenished when Captain Buchanan returned to service and two new replacement officers arrived (Lt. Douglas McKeown and Lt. Robert Matheson).

In stark contrast to the slashing assaults carried out by the Fourth Armored, where the mobility and firepower of the Hellcats were utilized to the fullest, the coming days and weeks placed the M18s largely in the role of conventional tanks. Perhaps the most frequent way the tank destroyers were used was to assist the 94th Infantry's attack on pillboxes. The Hellcat's 76mm shells weren't powerful enough to break through the reinforced concrete, but a carefully placed shot into the aperture of the pillbox could jam the steel shutters and stun the defenders. The infantry could then close within range to assault the pillbox.

A Reprieve for C/704

On February 6, rumors circulated that C/704 would be reattached to the Fourth Armored Division. Lt. Edwin Leiper (C Company's executive officer) sought confirmation and returned with the news that the company would leave the following day.

The three platoons of C/704 were relieved by A/704. On the morning of February 7, they departed on a 40-mile road trip that took them across the border into Luxembourg, where they eventually settled at the town of Bettembourg. The men were billeted at homes there, a setting which the company diarist described as, "...the best setup we have yet had." The company was more than ready to embrace some rest. By 1900 they were enjoying movies and a band. Their brothers in A and B Companies were still in the thick of it and would remain so for four more agonizing and brutal weeks.

On February 8, the 704th experienced more personnel changes. Major Charles L. Kimsey, the battalion's executive officer, was relieved from command and transferred to the Fourth Armored. This wasn't unusual, since the 704th had long been a breeding ground for leadership positions in the Fourth. This resulted in a frequent shuffling of other command positions. In this case, Captain Crosby P. Miller moved from S-3 to executive officer, which led to Captain William Horn moving from S-2 to S-3. Captain Evans moved from command of HQ Company to replace Horn as S-2, and 1st Lt. William F. King assumed command of HQ Company.

Bloody Bannholz

Just before daylight on February 7, the 1st Platoon of B/704 and one section of the 2nd Platoon moved out in direct support of the 2nd Battalion, 301st Infantry Regiment as they prepared for a limited attack against two objectives: the town of Sinz and Bannholz Woods. The woods were located on the high ground overlooking Sinz from the north, making its capture an important part of any attempt to hold the town. The 94th was no stranger to Sinz, having already made two attempts at capturing it. This time, E Company would give it a try.

After dodging incoming artillery and the ever-present mines, American infantry moved into the houses on the edge of town. With a foothold established, they proceeded to clear most of Sinz over the course of the day. The Germans hung on tenaciously, and by nightfall, were left holding a lone house on the edge of town. They abandoned the position sometime before sunrise. The third time was apparently the charm.

February 7, 1945. Infantrymen of the 301st Infantry Regiment, 94th Infantry Division, take cover in a muddy ditch beside the road to escape an enemy barrage near Sinz, Germany (U.S. Army photograph).

Meanwhile, at 0700 the same day, F Company advanced up the open slope between Sinz and Bannholz Woods. The doughboys attacked without armor support and ran into heavy resistance once they entered the tree line. Experienced *Panzer Grenadiers* and well-positioned *Panthers* from the *11th Panzer Division* kept the American infantry at bay. German mortar and artillery fire rained down on F Company and inflicted serious casualties. The enemy fire was too much to handle, and F Company retreated to the initial start line. Most of the men returned, but one of the platoons failed to receive the order and remained in position at the edge of the woods.

Heavy fighting continued near Sinz on February 8. The American position inside the town was tenuous due to the enemy's hold on the dominant high ground to the north. Plans were thus made for a second attack on Bannholz Woods. Elements from Companies E and G were combined with men from the 94th Intelligence and Reconnaissance Platoon (I&R) to create a combat team 100 strong. They would attack the following morning.

The assault team advanced under cover of darkness during the early morning hours of February 9. The American infantry moved deep into the woods and dug in. Before sunrise, German infantry began to close in on the American foxholes while their artillery poured shells through the treetops. The men of the 94th were in a tough spot.

At dawn, five Hellcats from B/704 moved toward the woods to support the hard-pressed infantry. The lead tank destroyer (dubbed "*Blondie*" and driven by Harry Traynor) approached an enemy pillbox pinning down some of the doughs. *Blondie's* gunner slammed two high-explosive rounds into the fortification, silencing the Germans within.

As the Hellcats advanced, Traynor saw a German *Panzerfaust* team in front of them. His gunner placed the Germans in his sight, and Traynor saw the result: "They disappeared in a cloud of smoke." *Blondie's* crew then spotted two *Panzers* (almost certainly *Panthers* from *Panzer Regiment 15*) on the edge of the woods. A sergeant from the 94th came up to the side of Traynor's Hellcat and told the tankers not to worry about them. The sergeant proclaimed that the *Panthers* had been knocked out earlier in the engagement.

Lieutenant Marion Taake (the commander of B/704) proceeded into the woods on foot. *Blondie* followed close behind. Suddenly, the crew saw Lt. Taake with his pistol drawn, firing at a *Panther*. The Hellcat's gunner drew a bead and hit the *Panther's* turret with an armor-piercing round. The explosion was so close to Taake that Traynor feared for the lieutenant's life. Taake was apparently unscathed and waved the tank destroyers deeper into the woods.

High-explosive rounds rattled the trees around the tank destroyers (an environment feared by the crews in the open-turret Hellcats). Indirect fire wasn't their only concern: they sensed the enemy infantry closing in. Suddenly, artillery and *Panzer Grenadiers* became the least of their worries when another *Panther* appeared. In the time it took the *Panther* to get off one shot, two rounds flew from the Hellcat, knocking out the enemy tank (this marked the 17th tank destroyed by *Blondie* during the campaign).

Traynor nudged *Blondie* down the trail toward the north side of the woods. He parked the destroyer between two trees and turned off the engine. His position was at the edge of the tree line and afforded a view of the barren slope gradually descending from the woods. At that moment, looking out over the open field below him, he saw a *Panzer* moving in his direction, followed by a slew of enemy infantry. The gunner on Traynor's M18 fired, but the shells deflected off the thicker, angled frontal armor of the heavier German tank. The tank destroyer commander, Johnny Prusaczyk, yelled "Harry! Back out of here! The whole damn German Army's coming up the hill!"

Traynor hit the starter but the engine didn't crank. The commander ordered the two other crewmembers to bail out, which they did without hesitation. Then suddenly, a high velocity shell hit the rear of the tank destroyer. Presumably, the enemy tanks reportedly knocked out at the entrance to the woods were manned and operative, and at least one of them had made its way down the trail behind *Blondie*. The round from the *Panther* sliced through the tank destroyer, causing catastrophic damage. Traynor was severely wounded but managed to get out of his driver compartment. Before he fled the destroyer, he summoned the strength to pull his commander from the turret and got him far enough away from *Blondie* before it exploded.

Prusaczyk drew his last breath in Traynor's arms. Harry, his leg severely injured and his head ringing, passed out. The advancing German soldiers captured him and moved him to the rear for treatment. When Traynor regained consciousness, he was in a German hospital in Augsburg.

The battle was far from over. The *Panthers* hit one of the other Hellcats from the rear, and mortar fire damaged another M18 and wounded one of the crewmen. The Hellcat was still mobile, so the driver used the TD to bring the wounded tanker to Sinz while the other two able-bodied crewmen stayed with the platoon. As the German infantry swept through the woods, they overran and destroyed the other two Hellcats. During the melee, five men from B/704 were killed and another five taken prisoner. The rest of the tankers, along with Lieutenant Taake, managed to escape from the woods on foot.

The Germans proceeded to shoot up the remaining infantry. The *Panthers* roamed the woods, firing into the American foxholes at point-blank range. The lightly-armed doughs could do little to fight back.

On February 10, the 94th Infantry took another run at the woods with a fresh infantry battalion. The 2nd Platoon of B/704 supported the attack, but they were restricted in their movement due to very soft ground conditions made worse by an afternoon rain.

The battle raged the entire day with a level of intensity even greater than the two efforts preceding it. After the American infantry regained the woods, the Germans brought their tanks into the open to engage them. The Hellcats jockeyed for position as best they could over the difficult ground. After skillfully maneuvering into an advantageous spot, Lt. Buell Mankin's gunner knocked out a *Panther* using a high-velocity armor-piercing (HVAP) round. Before the fight was done, gunners from the 704th knocked out another three *Panthers*.

B/704's success against the *Panthers* wasn't enough to turn the tide. The infantry remained under intense pressure, and by nightfall, the remnants of the battalion filtered back from the woods, unable to hold their positions. The 1st Platoon of A/704 and one section of B/704's 3rd Platoon moved into Sinz, only to end up on the receiving end of heavy mortar and tank fire emanating from the high ground north of town. It was simply too easy for the *Panzers* to roll to the crest and let loose.

Having been denied their objective after three separate attacks, Malony altered his plan. For the time being, he reformed his line to exclude the Bannholz Woods. The following day, B/704 was placed in reserve while A/704 maintained its support of the 94th Infantry. A/704 moved to Borg, and on February 14, two of their three platoons returned to Tettingen. On February 15, A/704 supported the infantry while attacking two pillboxes east of town (knocking out one of them).

The Grind Continues

American attempts to push deeper into German territory were bitterly contested. The Germans benefited from fighting on familiar territory with perfect observation from their network of pillboxes. They launched tank and infantry counterattacks whenever the Americans moved into position to attack the *Westwall* fortifications.

The ground conditions added to the level of difficulty for the 704th. Whenever a tank destroyer moved off-road, it risked bogging down, making it a proverbial sitting duck. Indirect fire was a continuous threat. The woods offered concealment for the Hellcats, but the risk from tree bursts remained ever-present. The proliferation of mines continued to take a toll on the battalion. The blanket of snow made the task of identifying and clearing the mines a more difficult one for the engineers.

B/704 returned to the fight and spent two days dodging shellfire while jockeying for a position to nail a *Panzer* harassing the infantry near Besch. The enemy tank had perfect cover near a castle. With the Hellcats unable to hit the tank, a 155mm self-propelled artillery gun was brought to bear. A blast from the gun collapsed part of the castle wall on top of the tank, setting it on fire.

North of Borg, the M18s led by Lt. Fred Rodgers helped the 94th clear Campholz Woods and the pillboxes found a short distance to the north. Once again, the enemy counterattacked and beat back the doughboys. The enemy mortar fire was so accurate that Americans moving through Borg were chased by shell bursts landing between the buildings with surgical precision.

The Tide Turns

On February 19, Major General Malony gained the freedom to deploy his entire division on offense. Supported by A and B Companies of the 704th, the infantry moved out across the mine-studded hills to the east.

The German defense buckled under the weight of the heavier attack. Making the task easier for both the 94th and the 704th was the fact that the *11th Panzer Division* had gradually withdrawn from the battlefield. The veteran division's replacement was the far less imposing *256th Volksgrenadier Division*.

The Hellcats remained in support of the 376th Infantry Regiment. Once again, a key objective was Bannholz Woods. Following an artillery preparation, the 1st Battalion made the 94th ID's fourth assault up the slope between Sinz and the woods. Resistance was notably less than it had been during the prior attempts. The heaviest return fire came from 20mm guns located in the nearby Geisbüsch Woods. Once the German position was identified, Hellcats from the 704th placed direct fire on the guns and silenced them. By 0815, the 1st Battalion declared Bannholz Woods clear of the enemy.

As the infantry continued their attack toward the northeast, six Hellcats from A/704 took up positions on the northeast edge of the woods. The tank destroyers provided covering fire, shooting over the heads of the infantry as they advanced.

Another important objective was Der Langen Woods, due east of Bannholz Woods. After the infantry secured the woods, the Hellcats moved to join them. As the tank destroyers moved across the open ground between the two woods, 88mm fire erupted from the edge of Moscholz Woods, located to the north. Three tank destroyers were hit, and the remaining Hellcats scrambled for cover. As the lead destroyer approached the relative safety of woods, another 88mm shell found its mark, knocking it out of action. The infantry later hunted down the German gun position and destroyed it. But it was a tough day for A/704.

Once Bannholz Woods was declared secure, Captain Harry Burkett (the battalion maintenance officer) returned with his adjutant (Captain John Tytus) to recover one of the M18s from B Company. Though abandoned, the TD was reportedly still drivable. They also hoped to find some trace of the men reported missing from B Company.

Upon reaching the tank destroyer, Burkett fired up the engine and discovered that he could maneuver it. With Captain Tytus riding on the rear deck, he started down the road toward the 704th Battalion HQ. As Burkett churned his way south, he saw the body of an American soldier on the roadway. To avoid running over the corpse, he drove the tank destroyer onto the shoulder of the road. What Burkett didn't know was that the Germans had buried several 105mm howitzer shells along the roadside and topped them off with a *Teller-mine*. The blast "blew the whole side of the tank off and turned it over, upside down." Burkett was killed instantly. Captain Tytus was thrown clear and survived. Burkett was a popular officer, and the battalion took his loss very hard. In the wake of his death, Lieutenant Leiper became the battalion maintenance officer.

As the attack pressed on toward the Saar River, the towns of Münzingen, Trassem, Kastel, Orcholz, and Tavern were key way-points. Münzingen was initially bypassed, setting the stage for the trailing infantry and tank destroyers to clear the town. The TDs were positioned on a reverse slope, ready to fire into the town in support of the assaulting infantry. As an enemy tank fled the village, one of the destroyers engaged it in a duel. A round from the *Panzer* narrowly missed the turret of the Hellcat, striking a bedroll strapped to the back. As the bedding erupted in flames, another destroyer joined the fray and knocked out the enemy tank. The infantry mopped up Münzingen by 1620.

The attack moved forward at a pace the 94th Infantry Division was unaccustomed to. During the advance, B Company lost one tank destroyer to anti-tank fire and another to a mine which blew a hole in the bottom of the M18. But in return, B Company knocked out a *Panther* tank and two anti-tanks guns while delivering solid blows to the enemy infantry.

At Freudenberg, Lieutenant Rodgers of A/704 was fired on by an enemy sniper. An unusual twist was the sniper's use of wooden bullets. Rodgers was furious about being targeted with the relatively harmless projectile. When he located the sniper's position in a church steeple, he blasted the gunman's perch with his 76mm main gun. When later confronted with two anti-tank guns, Lt. Rodgers marched several prisoners over the crest of a hill between his tank destroyers and the enemy emplacements. Rather than shoot through their fellow soldiers, the German gun crews surrendered. In the 704th's unit history, it was surmised that, "The Krauts didn't fancy the idea of being caught in the line of fire of the battle royal that would have resulted."

The success of the attack on February 19 led to the commitment of the 10th Armored Division. With the 10th advancing on the left of the 94th Infantry, the divisions moved steadily toward the Saar River, an objective roughly seven miles from where the 94th initiated their offensive.

Malony's division reached the Saar near Serrig and Taben-Rodt. Heavily contested crossings were made at both locations on the morning of February 22. Once the engineers installed a bridge, the 704th moved up to support the attack. A/704 and one platoon from B/704 crossed the river on February 23 using the bridge at Taben-Rodt. The remainder of B Company crossed on February 25.

The Hellcat crews assisted in the expansion of the bridgehead. In one instance, German defenders holding a position in a house were delaying the infantry's advance. A Hellcat came to assist and fired a high-explosive round into a window. The blast collapsed the wall, revealing a well-disguised pillbox. The gunner switched to an APC round and fired a direct shot into the pillbox aperture, which rendered the defenders silent. Another pillbox was blasted into submission by a Hellcat working in tandem with an M16 halftrack mounting quad .50 caliber machine guns. Twenty Germans emerged from the battered enclosure and surrendered.

A platoon of A/704, commanded by Lt. Mankin, participated in an attack on Beurig (just north of Saarburg on the east side of the river). Mankin's tank destroyers knocked out several more pillboxes, paving the way for the infantry. Later in the engagement, a platoon from B/704 supported the 5th Ranger Battalion, which had embarked upon a special mission to cut off a critical road behind enemy lines. The Rangers fought on their own until a relief force from the 94th made contact after driving from the south. The M18s joined and

The town of Serrig, Germany (U.S. Army photograph).

February 2, 1945. A Hellcat tank destroyer (right) from the 704th Tank Destroyer Battalion guards a road next to a destroyed German *Mark IV* tank. Nennig, Germany (U.S. Army photograph).

assisted the Rangers in an attack on the high ground east of Serrig, where they drove off members of the *2nd Mountain Division*. After the attack, the Hellcats "took a terrific pounding by giant rockets and mortar fire."

On March 4, the order came down for the 704th to rejoin the Fourth Armored. The deadliest chapter in the tank destroyer battalion's story was finis.

5

The Armored Infantry—Again

XII Corps Attacks

On January 16, the U.S. First and Third Armies linked-up at the battered and cratered town of Houffalize. A photographer recorded the moment when G.I.s from the two armies shook hands. The image represented closure of the gaping wound inflicted on the American front. It also captured the event that triggered the reassignment of Lt. General Hodges' First Army to Bradley's 12th Army Group. Montgomery was out of the picture. It was now Bradley's battle, with Hodges and Patton united again as his army commanders.

After a month of bitter fighting, the enemy penetration extended 16 miles beyond the German border. Much to Patton's chagrin, the plan for the final reduction of the Bulge lacked boldness. Rather than a surgical strike aimed at severing the appendage at its base, pressure was to be applied broadly around the perimeter of the German line with the goal of pushing the enemy back to their starting point. In sharp contrast, Patton wished to snare and destroy the enemy divisions before they retreated to the protection of the *Westwall*.

By mid–January, Manton Eddy's XII Corps, holding the line at the southeast base of the Bulge, had fought its way back to the banks of the Sûre River. Most of his divisions faced north on a line running west to east. The XII Corps' positions extended to the juncture of the Sûre and Our Rivers (a place punctuated by the German town of Wallendorf). There, the American line turned southeast and followed the course of the Our River (the river defining the border between Germany and Luxembourg).

On January 18, while the Fourth Armored Division sat out and regained its strength, the rest of XII Corps launched an attack against the south flank of the Bulge. The operation began at 0330 with an assault across the Sûre River. Searchlights reflected off the low-hanging clouds improved visibility for the infantry. To maintain an element of surprise, the American artillery remained silent. The 5th Infantry Division, already veterans of many river crossings, employed the 10th Infantry Regiment as the primary assault unit.

The crossing was executed with relative ease. During the dark early morning hours that followed, the American infantry slipped behind the enemy positions. The initial objectives were secured by 0600, with much credit given to the many days of aggressive patrolling conducted prior to the main assault. By the break of dawn, they were well established in the German rear, and by the end of the day, the 2nd and 10th Infantry Regiments held a bridgehead 2000 yards deep. Engineers quickly bridged the Sûre, enabling tanks and tank destroyers to reinforce the infantry.

The 4th Infantry Division joined the fray, attacking on the right of the 5th Infantry

January 16, 1945. Men from the U.S. First and Third Armies achieve contact near Houffalize, Belgium (U.S. Army photograph).

Division. For the next several days, the two divisions pushed north under very tough conditions. On the night of January 24, the 5th Infantry Division captured the town of Hoscheid, a little more than seven miles from where the division crossed the Sûre River. The pace of one mile per day served as a grim indicator of the degree of difficulty imposed by the terrain, the weather, and the enemy.

By January 28, the 5th Infantry Division's objectives were in hand. Along with other elements of XII Corps, their focus shifted to the east. In their sights were the pillboxes and bunkers of the *Westwall,* embedded upon German soil on the opposite side of the swollen Our River.

Task Force Oboe

On January 29, in a move reminiscent of *Olympic's* first engagement in Normandy, all three of the division's armored infantry battalions were assigned to CCB. The Fourth's divisional artillery (excluding the 22nd Armored Field Artillery Battalion, which continued to reinforce the 255th Field Artillery Battalion supporting the 2nd Cavalry Group) and other indirect fire elements (among them the six 105mm assault guns from the 8th Tank Battalion) joined the armored infantry under the banner of *Task Force Oboe*.

Task Force Oboe would play a supporting role in XII Corps' upcoming offensive aimed at crossing the Our River and forging a penetration into Germany. Initially they were sent to relieve the 319th Infantry Regiment of the 80th Infantry Division, which held positions facing the Our River north of its juncture with the Sûre River. Major Dan Alanis's 51st Armored Infantry Battalion would hold the north half of CCB's line and Major Hal Cohen's 10th Armored Infantry Battalion the south. The 53rd Armored Infantry Battalion (commanded by Lt. Colonel George Jaques) was held in reserve.

The 51st AIB arrived at Gilsdorf at 1700 on January 29. They donned white camouflage gear before starting on foot toward the positions of the 3rd Battalion. A/51 took over the positions held by I Company in the area east of Fouhren, where they faced the German fortified positions on the opposite side of the Our River (this marked the far left of the 51st AIB's line). To avoid drawing fire from the enemy pillboxes, the transfer took place after dark.

B/51 occupied the center of the battalion line near Longsdorf, a little over a mile south of A/51.

C/51 moved through Bettendorf and continued to the northeast before reaching the positions held by K Company on the forward slope of the densely forested Niederberg Ridge, which commanded the west bank of the Our River. By 2200, all three armored infantry companies were in position.

The 10th Armored Infantry Battalion took over the positions held by the 319th Infantry Regiment's 1st Battalion. Before the transfer, Major Cohen and Captain Baum, along with the recon platoon and one officer from each of the armored infantry companies, traveled 20 miles from their command post to Moestroff, where they coordinated with the 1st Battalion. The 10th AIB moved out of Frisange at 1530 and arrived at Moestroff at 1930.

A/10 and C/10, supported by the battalion's mortar and assault gun platoons, occupied a line a little over a mile to the east of the town, close to the Our River and just south of the right flank of the 51st Armored Infantry Battalion (the Germans greeted A/10 by sending a few rounds of mortar fire, inflicting two casualties). B/10 was held in reserve at Reisdorf, a village nestled on the south bank of the Sûre River. All three of Major Cohen's armored infantry companies were in position before midnight.

The 53rd Armored Infantry Battalion received their orders at 1300. The infantrymen left their billets at Rollingen at 1400 and arrived two hours later at Bettendorf, where they relieved the 2nd Battalion of the 319th Infantry Regiment. Of the three armored infantry battalions, they had the easiest go of it because of their reserve status.

Once in position, the armored infantrymen began sizing up their environs. At 1800 on January 30, C/10 sent a patrol to reconnoiter the village of Hoesdorf, located on the west bank of the Our River near the base of the commanding Niederberg Ridge. The houses in Hoesdorf were packed tightly together like a jigsaw puzzle, the two- and three-story homes hugging the narrow, jagged streets on their sharp descent toward the river. The patrol drew enemy fire from the village and suffered one casualty before returning.

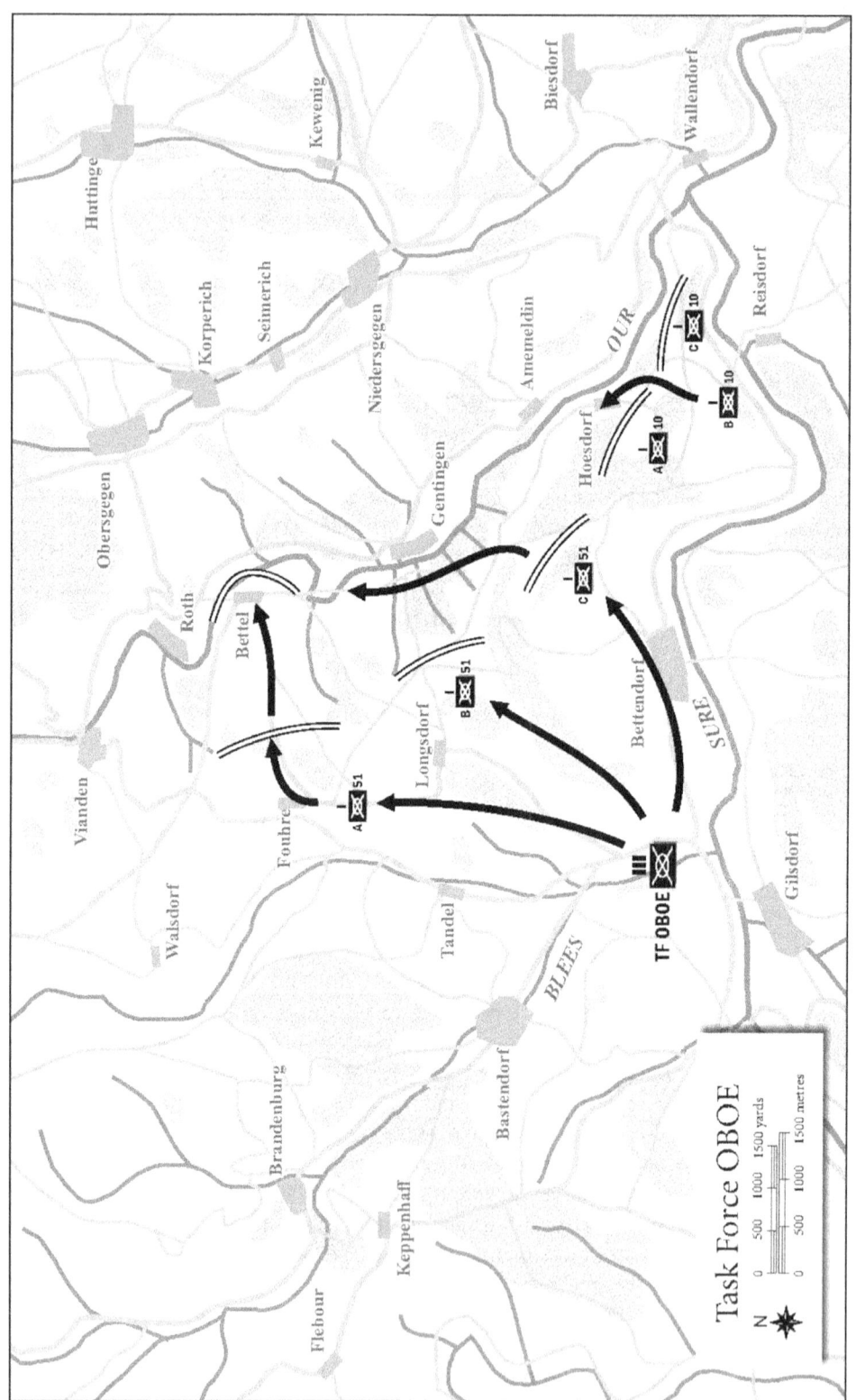

Task Force OBOE (© Petho Cartography, 2020).

The remainder of the night passed quietly for the 10th AIB. The armored infantry, looking east across the Our River, redoubled their vigilance in anticipation of any moves made by the Germans. The enemy-held pillboxes and other positions were in clear sight.

January 31 saw an increase in activity as both sides tested their opponent's lines. At 0630, B/51 fired on an enemy patrol that appeared in front of the platoon holding the company's right flank. At 0800, the 10th AIB captured a German identified as a member of the *2nd Company, 915th Regiment, 352nd Volksgrenadier Division*. At 1330, two more prisoners were brought in that belonged to the *7th Company* of the same regiment. Off and on throughout the day, the right flank of A/10 received small arms fire from the vicinity of Hoesdorf. At 1500, four rounds of heavy mortar fire struck farther to the rear near Reisdorf.

After dark, B/51 sent a 17-man patrol to conduct reconnaissance in front of their position. Their mission was to locate enemy pillboxes, outposts, and bridges. They were also instructed to check the depth and current of the river, and if possible, cross and conduct reconnaissance on the other side. The patrol succeeded in locating two pillboxes, but their attempts to get to the river were thwarted by German outposts.

Pushing the Envelope

On February 1, General Eisenhower ordered Bradley to break off his attack. The 12th Army Group was forced to shift units back to the U.S. Ninth Army for its part in the northern thrust being led by Field Marshal Montgomery. Patton received permission to continue his offensive, but in very limited fashion. The direct quote from Eisenhower's order: "Continue the probing attacks now in progress."

Patton's subsequent scheme went well beyond that of a probing action. His plan called for Major General Middleton's VIII Corps (the 87th, 4th, and 90th Infantry Divisions, plus the 11th Armored Division) to penetrate the *Westwall* and capture Prüm, 18 miles to the northeast. As Middleton's attack progressed, Eddy's XII Corps (the 5th, 80th, and 76th Infantry Divisions, 2nd Cavalry Group and the Fourth Armored) would drive northeast from the vicinity of Echternach to capture the city of Bitburg ... a "probe" of a dozen miles. Major General Millikin's III Corps (the 6th Cavalry Group, 17th Airborne Division and 6th Armored Division), positioned in between the other two corps, was confined to conducting patrols to remain connected with their neighbors. Lastly, Major General Walker's XX Corps (the 26th and 94th Infantry Divisions plus the 3rd Cavalry Group, positioned to the right of XII Corps) would conduct limited attacks in their zone. At a meeting with his corps commanders on February 3, Patton unveiled the plan and issued orders for the offensive. The night of February 6 was chosen for the kickoff.

Patton believed he was putting one over on Eisenhower. The reality was that Ike and Bradley had consulted previously on the topic of just how far the envelope should be pushed. Eisenhower blessed a more aggressive posture for the 12th Army Group (and Patton in particular) than his "probing" directive suggested. Bradley kept this to himself as a means of tempering the depth of Patton's attack, lest he go so far as to disrupt SHAEF's overall plan (which still favored the northern thrust by Montgomery).

Holding the Line

While Patton plotted to turn his authorized probes into an outright drive toward some of the largest cities in his zone, the Fourth Armored Division's armored infantry battalions remained relegated to a defensive posture.

The mission for the 53rd Armored Infantry Battalion changed abruptly when they were dispatched to an area east of Beaufort, five miles southeast of their reserve position at Bettendorf. Lt. Colonel Jaques' battalion was attached to the 318th Infantry Regiment and ordered to relieve the regiment's 3rd Battalion, which held the far-right flank of the 80th Infantry Division's line. From their new position, they were to provide fire support when the 318th crossed the Sûre River south of Dillingen.

Over the course of the first five days of February, the 51st Armored Infantry Battalion held its position facing the Our River, limiting their activity to patrol work near the river. Reconnaissance and listening parties were pushed to within 25 yards of the river's edge. Each night, the Germans shot off flares that illuminated the front. However, the enemy apparently abandoned aggressive patrolling in the 51st Armored Infantry Battalion's area. Instead, they settled on harassing the Americans with occasional artillery and mortar fire.

On February 5, several German soldiers deserted and swam across the frigid Our River. After surrendering to the 51st's forward elements, the prisoners were taken back for interrogation. They were forthcoming and revealed the locations of their company and battalion command posts. They also revealed that the bridge between Bettel and Roth was out.

As February unfolded, the 10th Armored Infantry Battalion's main point of focus became the Germans holding out on the west bank of the Our River. During the dark, early morning hours of February 1, A/10 dispatched a patrol to blow up a pillbox located southeast of Hoesdorf. Faced with a vertical cliff fronting the pillbox, the G.I.s were unable to attack. At about the same

An example of the terrible conditions faced during the sudden thaw during late January and early February (U.S. Army photograph).

time the Americans were stalking the pillbox, an enemy patrol was discovered near the positions of A/10. The G.I.s chose not to engage, and the Germans passed by without firing a shot.

Later that morning, Major Cohen visited A/10. Thirty minutes after his arrival, six rounds of heavy mortar fire fell near the company. Other than that, the day was quiet enough to allow for two hot meals to be brought up to the men on the line. The relative inaction also allowed the battalion to send groups of 50 men on leave to Luxembourg City. Smaller groups were granted 72-hour passes to Paris. Some additional comfort was had due to the weather warming up. The consequence, however, was a thaw that transformed the ground and roads into rivers of mud. The melting snow increased the power of the Sûre River, washing out the footbridge connecting Kleinreisdorf and Reisdorf.

The day had been quiet, but things heated up that evening. At 2015, an outpost of A/10 observed an enemy patrol tying to infiltrate their line. A firefight erupted. When a German tried to throw hand grenades into their ranks, G.I.s brandishing their M1 rifles drove him off. A heavier amount of rifle and machine gun fire erupted on the company's right flank but was apparently of no consequence.

The Battle for Hoesdorf

On February 2, Major Cohen's staff spent most of the day perfecting a plan for a night attack against Hoesdorf. The effort would be led by B/10, with A/10 and C/10 firing in support. Though the waning gibbous moon rose later in the night, the battalion noted that visibility was limited to a matter of inches in the pitch-black darkness. Among the officers leading B Company's attack on Hoesdorf was Lt. Leech. Wanting to be with his men for the upcoming action, he tucked away a coveted pass to Paris.

Under cover of darkness, Leech and the other members of B/10 crossed the line of departure for the attack. The route of advance took the armored infantry up a steep, muddy slope. After reaching the summit, they moved beyond the positions of C/10 and entered a forested area separating C Company from Hoesdorf.

The Americans found the woods littered with *Schu* mines. By the time daylight arrived, the anti-personnel devices claimed every officer of B/10 as a casualty. Three officers were wounded, and tragically, the devoted Lt. Leech killed (the pass for Paris later found in his possession). When one of the platoon leaders fell wounded and his men were left "panicked and confused," T/Sgt. Dennis Hassell seized the initiative and assumed command. He reorganized the platoon and led them to safety.

The situation in the woods was indeed confused. T/Sgt. Clifford C. Turner spent several hours in total darkness trying to clear a path through the minefield, even as artillery and mortar fire fell in the area. Sergeant William T. Rowe of Headquarters Company worked diligently to clear the minefield as well. His effort ended when he was mortally wounded by one of the mines.

The disruption created by the minefield brought B/10's attack to a halt. Major Cohen took personal control of the situation and got the company reorganized. At midnight, Captain Newton and 2nd Lieutenants Adrien J. Tessier and Barnet M. Cooperman were hurriedly brought forward from other assignments to replace the fallen officers of B Company.

Major Cohen revised the plan of attack. B Company would continue as the assault force, but they would abandon the line of attack through the woods in favor of a road running between the positions of A/10 and C/10.

The attack resumed at 0030 with the armored infantry advancing down the steep road toward Hoesdorf. The rushing sound of the Our River provided a backdrop and probably helped conceal the sound of the rubber-soled combat boots descending toward the village. A G.I. inadvertently leaned on the horn of his peep, causing Lt. Cooperman a moment of apprehension … but it didn't stir a response from the enemy.

As B Company advanced into Hoesdorf under the cover of darkness, they apparently caught the German defenders by surprise. Resistance was light, and some of the Germans stumbled out in a state of undress. By 0500, the armored infantry cleared the village. During the attack, B/10 suffered 14 casualties of their own while capturing 19 Germans. Afterward, Captain Newton retained command of B/10.

Marking Time

On February 2, the thaw continued to play havoc with the movement of troops and vehicles. Rivers throughout the region burst at the seams. The Sûre River, normally about 30 feet wide, expanded to more than 100 feet in some sections. The height of the Moselle River rose over a dozen feet, dislodging the temporary pontoon bridges. This was just the start of several days of miserable weather. Days of cold, hard rain added to the effects of the thaw, making living conditions completely miserable.

On February 4, the 51st Armored Infantry Battalion joined the 53rd in being attached to 80th Infantry Division. Their role was to support the 80th in their upcoming crossing of the Our River.

The 10th Armored Infantry Battalion went a much different direction that day. The 3rd Battalion, 319th Infantry Regiment began to relieve the 10th from their positions facing the Our River. By 2200, the armored infantrymen were off the line and headed south for bivouac areas at Evrange and Frisange. Transferred from CCB to CCA, the men were soon enjoying hot meals and showers. The next several days were enhanced with movies and parties (one of which was thrown by Delk Oden's 35th Tank Battalion and attended by Major Cohen and Captains Newton and Seaver).

On February 5, the 66th Armored Field Artillery Battalion moved out of their rest area and took up positions north of Consdorf, Luxembourg. They were given the general mission of supporting the 5th Infantry Division's 10th Infantry Regiment.

That same day, Lt. General Patton's plan suffered a blow that not even the Germans could deliver. SHAEF ordered the 12th Army Group to cease its attack in the Eifel so that Hodges' First Army could shift farther to the north, closer to the area of the Roer River and the vital dams that controlled its flow.

The Third Army commander was called to Bastogne for a photo opportunity with Eisenhower. Patton later noted that Ike "never mentioned the Bastogne offensive, although this was the first time I had seen him since the nineteenth of December, when he seemed much pleased to have me at the critical point." In a letter to his wife that day, he lamented the possible change in posture for the Third Army: "You may hear that I am on the defensive but it was not the enemy who put me there."

6

Attack into Germany

The 5th Infantry Division Crosses the Sûre

Despite the change in plans for the disposition of the U.S. First Army, Patton moved forward with his offensive. The XII Corps' plan of attack called for the 5th and 80th Infantry Divisions to establish separate bridgeheads across the Sûre River at points south of the convergence of the Our and Sûre Rivers.

The 5th Infantry Division would make the main assault within a four mile stretch of the river between the towns of Bollendorf (on the German side of the river) and Echternach (on the Luxembourg side). The 417th Infantry Regiment (part of the 76th Infantry Division and now attached to the 5th) would conduct its own crossing farther south to protect the right flank of the 5th ID's attack.

Farther north, the 80th Infantry Division would cross the Sûre along a winding section of the river between Wallendorf (the confluence of the Our and Sûre Rivers) and Bollendorf. Once the bridgehead was established, the *Blue Ridge* men would advance toward Mettendorf, a town just over five miles northeast of Wallendorf. By doing so, they would protect the left flank of the 5th Infantry Division's advance toward Bitburg.

The assault forces of the 5th Infantry Division moved to the line of the river on the night of February 6. The crossing was scheduled to commence at 0100 on February 7.

Weather conditions were not for the faint of heart. As noted by the campaign historian Charles McDonald, a "fitful rain turned to light snow." Due to the thaw that began four days prior, the river, swollen beyond its normal dimensions to a width of 60 yards, flowed at a brisk 12 miles per hour.

The forces of nature inflicted damage before the Germans ever did. As the men of the 5th Infantry Division paddled to the opposite shore, some of the rubber boats capsized. Others were tossed about and sent uncontrollably off course. Approximately 60 soldiers drowned.

The enemy was prepared. Some of the Americans made it as far as the middle of the river before the Germans added their own weight to the forces of nature. As flares illuminated the boats laden with vulnerable infantrymen, the Germans opened fire with automatic weapons that decimated the first wave. From among the two regiments leading the assault, only two boatloads of eight men each made it to the east bank of the river and German soil. The withering fire denied them reinforcement.

The Fourth Armored Division's 66th and 22nd Armored Field Artillery Battalions fired in support of the assault. The M7s delivered smoke to help conceal the river crossing. They employed counter-battery fire to help silence German artillery positions, along with harassing and interdiction fire on road junctions. Time-On-Target (TOT) missions were fired on towns (this type of barrage coordinates the fire of all guns to hit the target at the same time). Fire missions against enemy troops were called in by observers (Lt. Doran was the ground observer from the 66th). Between the hours of 0100 and 0530, the 22nd fired more than 1500 rounds in support of the assault. But all this was not enough to turn things immediately in favor of the 5th Infantry Division.

The Armored Infantry Supports the 80th Infantry Division

On February 6, the 51st AIB received orders to seize Bettel, one of the towns still in German hands on the west bank of the Sûre River. Additionally, in the area south of Bettel, they were to clear the terrain between their positions and the river (all of this being done to protect the left flank of the 319th Infantry Regiment during their crossing of the river farther south). The attack would take place the following day.

At 0120 on February 7, the artillery provided 40 minutes of preparatory fire. A/51 moved forward through the dark as C/51 and B/51 provided fire support with small arms. The assault guns and mortars fired a final concentration on Bettel at 0220. The enemy returned fire with artillery and used white flares to illuminate the battlefield.

A/51 encountered no resistance as they entered the town. However, anti-personnel mines once again took their toll, inflicting 11 casualties. The armored infantry cleared the buildings and consolidated their position by 0430. The battalion also contacted the 6th Cavalry Group on their left (that unit covering the far right of III Corps' zone).

After daylight, the men of A/51 were under the observation of enemy troops hunkered down in pillboxes on the opposite side of the river. To avoid drawing fire, they remained in the cellars of the town. Any movement out in the open during the daytime was tantamount to poking the proverbial bear.

Meanwhile, C/51, charged with clearing the west bank of the Sûre, embarked upon a confused attack through the woods as they searched for the riverbank. Captain Hope's men reached their objective on the river without contacting the enemy, but they spent hours in the dark dealing with men getting lost and wandering aimlessly in search of their units. Once dug in along the riverbank, they drew small arms fire, artillery, and mortar from across the river. The battalion's total casualties were 15 from mines and three from enemy artillery.

Robert Calvert, Jr., who joined C/51 during the previous November, adopted a perspective on the fate of those struck by enemy fire:

> *I developed the theory that men were wounded by the weapon they feared the most. Somehow, I assumed the chance of my being hit by an artillery shell was pretty minimal and I wasn't too worried about rifle fire. I assumed that if I were hit, it would be by a machine gun. German machine guns were really rapid fire, and one soon learned to distinguish them from ours. Anyway, I subsequently proved my own theory correct.*

At 0200 on February 7, the 53rd Armored Infantry Battalion commenced fire across the river into the area between Bollendorf and Dillingen. This was done to draw the German's attention away from the 80th Infantry Division's 318th Regiment as they made their way toward the line of the Sûre River. The diversionary fire drew a considerable reaction from German artillery.

While the 51st and 53rd Armored Infantry Battalions provided support, the 318th Infantry Regiment attacked across the swollen Sûre River. Word of the ill-fated attacks conducted by the 5th Infantry Division had already reached the leadership of the 80th Infantry. Fearing that the level of resistance might be similar at their crossing sites, the 80th employed a ruse to divert German attention. Chemical mortars were used to create smoke screens in areas *other* than the intended crossing sites. This helped enable the leading assault companies to slip across in other locations with far fewer losses than incurred by the 5th Infantry Division.

The situation at the 318th Infantry Division's crossing sites became more tenuous at daybreak. German observers directed a heavy volume of fire in the form of small arms, self-propelled guns, artillery, *Nebelwerfers* (rockets), and other heavy weapons. The swift current continued to toss about the assault boats, capsizing some and pitching both the able-bodied and wounded into the frigid, rushing water. By nightfall, the 80th Infantry Division held the high ground northeast of Wallendorf, and one company of infantry slipped into the town. By 2300, the final elements of the 318th Regiment's 2nd Battalion were across the river.

The rain ceased during the early morning hours of February 8. The 3rd Battalion of the 318th Infantry Regiment, still on the west bank of the Sûre, carried out an assault across the river near the town of Dillingen (midway between Bollendorf and Wallendorf). Throughout the day, the 318th fought to expand its hold on the east bank. It was a difficult task as they came up against hard-core defensive positions within the *Westwall*. Over the course of 10 hours, an attack by the 318th's 2nd Battalion gained only 1200 yards.

The 51st and 53rd Armored Infantry Battalions continued to lend support to the 80th Infantry Division. C Company of the 305th Engineer Battalion, assigned to support the 51st, worked diligently at clearing Teller mines from the supply road leading into the newly captured town of Bettel. As the engineers removed the mines, they stacked them in piles next to a building. The tight cluster of explosives had grown to about 40 mines when the Germans started shelling Bettel from across the river. One of the enemy rounds hit the mines, creating a massive set of secondary explosions that killed one man and injured five. It was a hard lesson learned by the engineers. After that event, it became accepted practice to destroy mines as quickly as possible after their removal. If this was impracticable, they would stack the mines in small piles several yards apart.

On the evening of February 8, much farther behind the Sûre River, Major General Gaffey outlined for his staff the new plan for their division. They would sit tight until the two infantry divisions seized crossings over the rivers Sûre, Prüm, and Nims. The Fourth Armored would then attack through the infantry and drive to the city of Bitburg.

Expanding the Bridgeheads

On February 8, the 5th Infantry Division continued their attack across the Sûre River. The Fourth Armored was called upon to offer support. The 66th Armored Field Artillery Battalion provided a smoke screen to help the 10th and 11th Infantry Regiments make their crossing. The 1st and 3rd platoons of C Company, 24th Armored Engineer Battalion ferried men of the 10th Regiment across the river throughout the day and night.

The Fourth's armored engineers found themselves in the thick of the action. Sergeant Woodrow R. Anderson took one of the assault boats across the river and single-handedly placed smoke pots to help cover the crossing. But the smoke cover provided by the engineers and artillery was not enough to immunize the crossing site from enemy fire. The

Germans lobbed mortar shells toward the assault boats carrying the *Red Diamond* infantrymen. One shell scored a direct hit, wounding and throwing five infantrymen into the swift current. They clung to the remains of a damaged bridge until the 24th's Corporal Willard Beaulieu made his way onto the span and pulled them out of the freezing water.

Slowly but surely, the 80th and 5th Infantry Divisions expanded their control of German soil. The 5th Infantry finally managed to get a footbridge in place. Later that night, the engineers started constructing a vehicle bridge.

The role of the 51st and 53rd remained strictly on the west bank of the Sûre River where they guarded the left flank of the 80th Infantry Division. The support they provided primarily took the form of indirect fire with their assault guns and mortars, aimed at targets called out by the 80th Infantry Division and its 319th Regiment.

On February 10, higher command once again stepped in and limited Patton's advance. Bradley called his subordinate and asked how soon he could go on the defensive. Patton told him that, if he had to go on the defensive, he would ask to be relieved.

Bit by bit, the units of the Fourth Armored Division returned to Gaffey's control. On February 11, the 53rd Armored Infantry Battalion reverted to the Fourth and moved to Rollingen. Upon the release of the 53rd, the commanding officer of the 318th Infantry Regiment heaped praise on Lt. Colonel Jaques' battalion for its role in drawing the enemy's attention from his regiment's bridgehead. The following day, after being assigned to CCB, the 53rd moved to Leudelange, where Jaques' battalion remained in reserve until February 19. During that time, the men engaged in an active schedule of maintenance, range firing, and the training of replacement troops.

The 51st Armored Infantry Battalion remained under the control of the 80th Infantry Division for several more days. During the battalion's time on the line, A/51 had the toughest time of it. After capturing the town of Bettel on February 7, the company's movement was severely restricted. Their positions in the town were under close observation from enemy pillboxes across the river. Any movement on the part of the infantrymen presented a risk of drawing deadly fire. The threat was so pervasive that supplies could not be delivered. As a result, the men were forced to subsist on K rations for 10 days. On February 17, Major Alanis's men were relieved under cover of darkness by units of the 80th Cavalry Reconnaissance Troop.

After moving to the vicinity of Berdorf (just a mile and a half west of the Sûre River), the 66th Armored Field Artillery Battalion continued to support the 5th Infantry Division. The 22nd Armored Field Artillery Battalion and the 35th Tank Battalion worked together to provide indirect fire support as well. On the night of February 20–21 and throughout the day of February 21, the combined battalions fired approximately 6000 rounds in support of XII Corps. (On February 23, the 22nd AFAB and 35th Tank Battalion would rejoin the Fourth Armored Division in their normal roles.)

By the end of February 11, bridges were finally in place over the Sûre. However, the 5th Infantry Division's penetration beyond the river was only one mile deep and three miles wide. Also, there remained a gap of several hundred yards between them and the 80th Infantry Division to the north. Additionally, the two regiments of the 80th that had crossed the river had not yet managed to tie their *own* bridgeheads together. Faced with defending their native soil, the enemy resisted with great tenacity. And the Germans were not leaving well enough alone. American air reconnaissance spotted columns of enemy vehicles moving south and southeast from Bitburg.

It was also on February 11 that Bradley removed Major General Millikin's III Corps from Patton's control and shifted it to General Hodges' First Army. While not stopping his advance completely, higher command had seen to it that Patton would have to make due with less resources.

On the heels of the reorganization of TUSA, Patton visited Major General Eddy on February 12 and offered him the opportunity to halt his attack for a day. Patton was confident that the crossing sites were secure and that the troops might benefit from a brief respite. Somewhat uncharacteristically, Eddy insisted on pressing the attack. Spurred by their corps commander, the two regiments of the 80th Infantry Division connected their bridgeheads. Later that day, they also connected their right flank to the 5th Infantry Division's left flank.

The Respite Continues

The 10th Armored Infantry Battalion, having enjoyed the relative luxury of being in a rest area for several days, had the special opportunity on February 12 to send three men back to the United States on furlough for 30 days. The opportunity was extended to other battalions as well. That same day, Captain Jimmie Leach, commanding officer of B/37 and future recipient of the Distinguished Service Cross for his actions during the Bastogne campaign, was another member of the division chosen to make the long trip back to America. Lt. Bernard Liese was assigned command of B/37.

Passes were doled out in greater numbers for trips to Luxembourg City and in smaller numbers for Paris. Closer to the front, the bowling alley in Frisange was converted into a makeshift movie theater (likely a better spot than the barn used during their last stay). The men enjoyed feature films virtually every day (*You Can't Ration Love* received great attendance at back-to-back screenings). Catholic and Jewish services were held. The main church in Frisange was used for the conduct of confession and mass. The popular Red Cross Clubmobiles made their way to the battalions.

Parties became a somewhat common event. The 53rd Armored Infantry Battalion, only two days removed from the front line and now in billets at Leudelange, hosted an officers' party. A couple of days later, Major Cohen threw a party. Among the attendees were Major General Gaffey and CCB's commanding officer, Brigadier General Dager. The party was described as "an extremely successful affair" and an "excellent time ... enjoyed by all."

The time off the line wasn't consumed exclusively by rest and relaxation. In anticipation of the type of fighting expected in the future, the companies honed their skills by rehearsing assaults on fortified positions. The training regimen over the following days included field stripping the .30 and .50 caliber machineguns, conducting a fast road march, calisthenics, and an orientation on the composition of an armored division.

Up and down the chain of command, time was taken to recharge. While he did not carry out his threat of asking to be relieved when his offensive was neutered, Lt. General Patton *did* decide to go on leave. He departed for Paris on February 15.

While most of the division rested, there were still men of the Fourth Armored closer to harm's way. On the morning of February 14, Lt. Colonel Wallace (commanding officer of the 66th Armored Field Artillery Battalion) and his peep driver (Private Hubert J. Plecinski) became the first members of the 66th to enter Germany when they rolled across the Sûre River via the treadway bridge erected between Echternach and Bollendorf. (A treadway bridge was a form of pontoon bridge. Parallel steel tracks were laid across the pontoons, over which wheeled and tracked vehicles would cross.) Wallace and Plecinski were followed

A pontoon bridge on the Rhine River near Boppard (U.S. Army photograph).

by Lt. Sanders, the recon officer for Battery B who was conducting reconnaissance for the establishment of a ground observation post.

On February 17, the 51st Armored Infantry Battalion returned to the Fourth Armored Division's control. It was finally their turn to head for the rear. The battalion retuned to the same billets they had enjoyed prior to entering the line. The next several days were spent servicing their vehicles and going through general rehabilitation. For C/51, that meant returning to the town of Pontpierre. Sergeant Calvert had the pleasure of staying once again at the home of the Fischbachs, where he and his squad cleaned up and rested.

The respite for Sergeant Calvert and his fellow G.I.s of the 51st lasted only four days. On February 21, the battalion was assigned to CCB and placed on alert. When the soldiers departed Pontpierre for the second time, the residents assembled at the town square to say a tearful goodbye. They had become good friends with their American guests.

Breaking the Logjam

Expansion of the American bridgehead was laborious. A combination of enemy will, terrain that favored the defense, and oppressive weather conditions tempered the pace of the American advance. Eleven days after the first assault boats crossed the Sûre River, there were few signs that German resistance was softening.

On February 18, the 66th Armored Field Artillery Battalion, still firing in support of the 5th Infantry Division, moved out of Berdorf and crossed the Sûre River. The batteries of M7s moved into firing positions near the town of Ferschweiler, two miles beyond the German border. In doing so, the 66th became the first complete battalion of the Fourth Armored to enter Germany.

The 35th Tank Battalion deployed to provide indirect fire support. Four officers and four computers (people, not machines) from the 22nd Armored Field Artillery Battalion were sent to the 35th to assist with fire control. Performing in the role of an improvised artillery battalion was not something the Fourth's tankers were accustomed to.

On that same day, the 80th Infantry Division attacked out of their bridgehead. The strike by the 80th was XII Corps' right-hook counterpart to a left-hook being delivered from the northwest by Major General Troy Middleton's VIII Corps. In effect, this was a pincer movement aimed at the destruction of German forces holding out in what was known as the Vianden Bulge. The plan called for the two attacking forces to close the encirclement at the village of Mauel, 10 miles northwest of Bitburg and roughly 15 miles north of the 80th Infantry Division's bridgehead.

The Vianden Bulge was 22 miles wide and 11 miles deep. Its defenders occupied inhospitable terrain favorable to the defense. The western border of the Vianden Bulge was primarily the line of the Our River, which presented a major obstacle on its own. Before the penetration by XII Corps across the Sûre River, the Germans within the Vianden Bulge had relied on the Our and Sûre Rivers, coupled with the *Westwall* fortifications, as the primary guardians of their left (southern) flank. The defenders were eager to withdraw to better positions on the east bank of the Prüm River, but Hitler would not allow it.

Two regiments of the 80th Infantry Division led the attack, striking from the area of Wallendorf. Their immediate objective was Mettendorf (five miles to the north-northwest) and Hill 408, the most commanding height in the area. The 319th Infantry Regiment drew the assignment of isolating the German pillboxes facing the Our River. Their attack to the north and northeast would cut the pillboxes off from behind, isolating the defenders. The Germans would have the Our River in front of them and the Americans behind them.

The 80th Infantry Division required assistance on their left flank. The 53rd Armored Infantry Battalion drew the assignment and was attached once again to the 80th. On February 19, the battalion traveled 40 miles to take up positions at Ammeldingen, a small German village on the east shore of the Sûre River. The 53rd's mission: mop up the defenders remaining in the pillboxes after the 319th Infantry Regiment cut them off from behind.

The 53rd Armored Infantry Battalion attacked on the morning of February 21, striking along a line that followed the course of the Our River. A/53 and B/53 moved abreast as friendly artillery and mortars laid down a barrage on the pillboxes confronting them. A/53 captured Gentingen at 1130 and B/53 seized Roth at 1415. C/53 was later committed out of reserve to strike farther east of the river. At 1320, they took Obersgegen, nearly three miles from the battalion's starting line.

By nightfall, the 53rd AIB's mission was complete. Three hundred and thirty seven Germans emerged from their pillboxes and surrendered to Lt. Colonel Jaques' men.

The battalion was relieved by elements of the 80th Infantry Division and returned to the control of the Fourth Armored. The 53rd's immediate task upon their return was to guard the five bridges in place near the junction of the Sûre and Our Rivers.

On February 21, the 66th Armored Field Artillery Battalion displaced to positions just north of Shankweiler. The howitzers were placed behind infantry that were dug-in along the river. The battalion remained in these positions and provided fire support until February 25.

On February 19, Patton expressed in writing to Bradley that the Third Army was the only American force attacking while all others "were doing nothing at all." Given that he was the only commander on offense, he believed his Third Army to be deserving of more divisions (anywhere from one to three he felt his due). If given the resources, he would deliver results. He knew how to make a compelling argument. Later that day, in Bradley's absence, Patton convinced Major General Harold Bull (SHAEF G-3) to give him the 10th Armored Division, which he then assigned to Major General Walker's XX Corps.

Putting Together the Final Pieces

February 21 began with an air of peace. The men of C/704 even enjoyed playing football and basketball that morning. This all changed at noon when the Hellcat crews learned they were attached to Combat Command B and placed on alert for a move at any time. The platoons of C/704 were parceled out among the armored infantry battalions, with the 1st Platoon assigned to the 10th Armored Infantry Battalion, the 2nd Platoon to the 51st, and the 3rd Platoon to the 53rd.

For the 10th Armored Infantry Battalion, what had become a familiar daily routine during the rest period came to an abrupt halt at 1100. All passes to Luxembourg were cancelled and the battalion was shifted from CCA to CCB. At 1230, Major Cohen left for CCB's headquarters while the battalion prepared for movement. The balance of the day was spent preparing for a move, but the order never came. The companies remained in place overnight.

Signs of heightened activity also appeared in the skies. The XIX TAC flew 504 sorties on February 21. Pilots claimed as damaged or destroyed 318 vehicles, 28 tanks and armored vehicles, 575 railroad cars, and 14 guns. It was also an ugly day for the German *Seventh Army* when American planes targeted their headquarters. *General* Hans-Gustav Felber had just taken command of the *Seventh Army* the day prior. It was a rude welcome, courtesy of the XIX TAC's P-47 Thunderbolts.

The same day, Bradley visited the Third Army headquarters to brief Patton and his staff on the status of future operations. It was not good news for the offensive-minded Patton. His army was to remain static as the Allied armies to the north worked their way toward the Rhine River. Hodges' First Army would attack for the sole purpose of providing flank protection for the 21st Army Group and the U.S. Ninth Army. The Third Army would hold in place until the city of Cologne was invested. Only then would Patton be allowed to strike from the direction of Prüm toward Koblenz. During the next phase, while the First Army remained on the west bank of the Rhine, the Third Army had the green light to attack from the area of Saarlautern and advance along what was known as the Frankfurt corridor. Patton asked specifically if he could advance sooner toward Koblenz if the opportunity presented itself (i.e., prior to the investment of Cologne). He received the go-ahead to do so.

Having just returned from his own trip to Paris, Patton thought it best for the commander of XII Corps to take some time away from the front. He provided Major General Eddy the use of his C-47, which Eddy elected to take to London. Major General Gaffey was placed in command of XII Corps until Eddy's return on February 28.

7

The Drive to Bitburg and the Kyll River

Time to Roll

After several weeks in the comfort of billets tending to maintenance and engaging in the rigors of training for replacements and veterans alike, the men of the 8th Tank Battalion were ordered to move out. The tankers savored a hot breakfast during the predawn hours of February 22 before the rally cry of "Mount up and turn 'em over" echoed through the streets of Mondercange. As the first evidence of daylight cast itself upon the gray, cold sky, the men and women of the town, who had been such gracious hosts and hostesses, lined the streets to say goodbye. The *Rolling Eight Ball* formed into a familiar column and snaked its way out of the town, the lead tank heading north toward the 80th Infantry Division's bridgehead on the Sûre River.

The 8th Tank Battalion was just one element of CCB rolling toward the Sûre River. In addition to the 8th, the combat command now included the 10th Armored Infantry Battalion, 51st Armored Infantry Battalion, 53rd Armored Infantry Battalion, C/704, C/24, a platoon of the 995th Engineer Treadway Bridge Company, and the 94th Armored Field Artillery Battalion. A formidable force, the most unusual aspect was the attachment of the combat command to the 80th Infantry Division.

The role that Brigadier General Dager's men were about to play was not what they were accustomed to. Rather than using their armor and mobility for exploitation, CCB would attack in a fashion that focused on its infantry-heavy composition. Another peculiarity was the employment of the 8th Tank Battalion. Rather than remaining together as a unified command, each medium tank company was doled out to one of the infantry battalions. A/8 (commanded by Captain Len Kieley) worked with the 10th, B/8 (Captain Ben Fischler) with the 53rd, and C/8 (Captain Eugene Bush, who returned to the battalion on January 22 after a lengthy hospital stay) with the 51st.

Other elements of CCB were already across the river. The 53rd Armored Infantry Battalion, having fought on February 22 east of the Sûre River near Obersgegen, relieved the 2nd Battalion of the 319th Infantry Regiment near Geichlingen (a mile-and-a-half northeast of Obersgegen). The 51st Armored Infantry Battalion assembled near Obersgegen and the 10th Armored Infantry Battalion, still in Luxembourg, moved 45 miles to join the 53rd near Geichlingen.

The territory occupied by the armored infantry showed stark signs of the battles that preceded their arrival. The 51st Armored Infantry Battalion recorded:

> *The area shows all indications of having taken a terrific beating from our artillery and the countryside is strewn with debris and dead animals. Evidence of horse drawn artillery is found along all roads with*

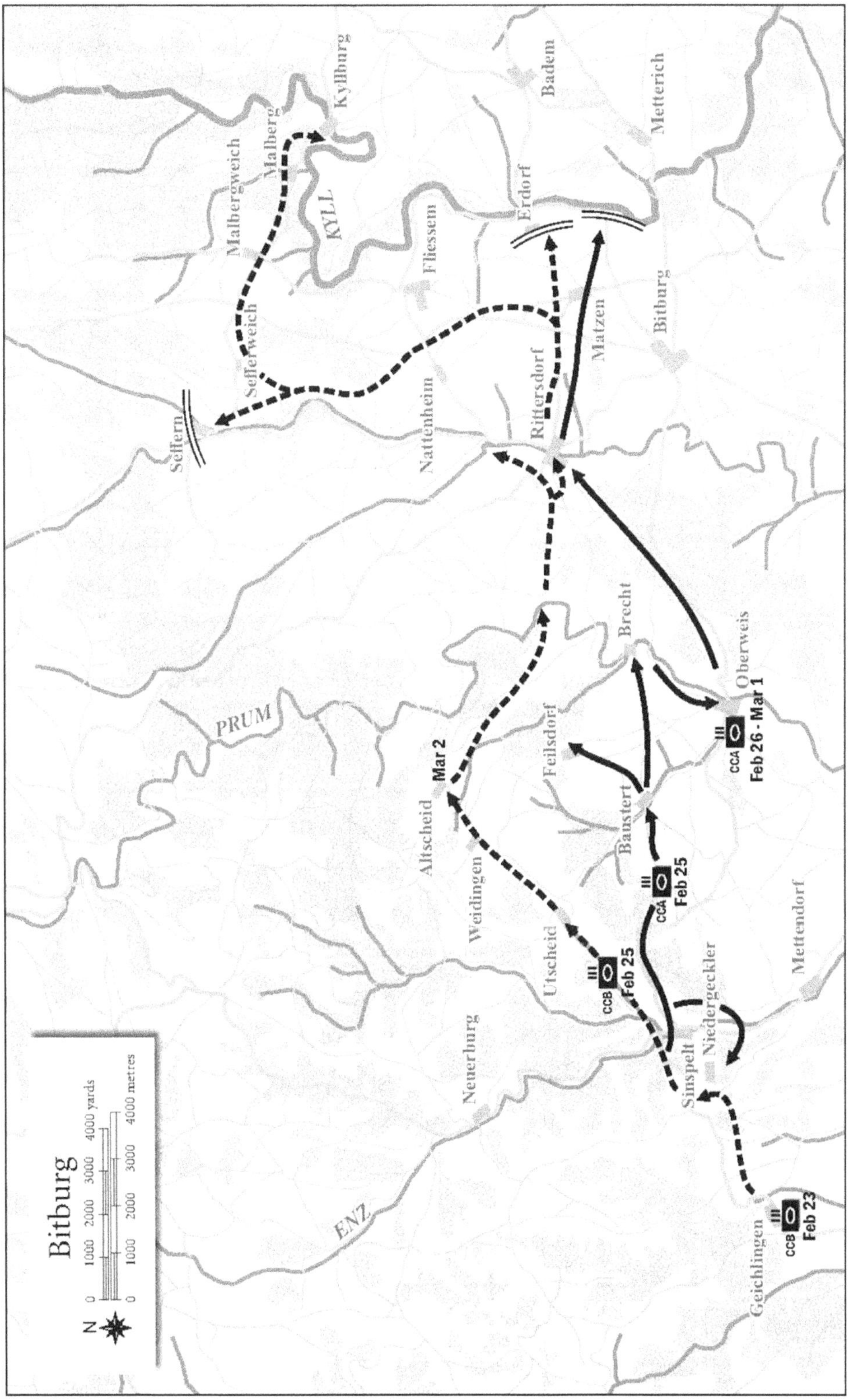

7. The Drive to Bitburg and the Kyll River 67

Bitburg (© Petho Cartography, 2020).

horses being killed in harness. The atmosphere is anything but pleasant, civilians are segregated and confined to particular sections of towns and forced to stay inside.

After CCB assembled east of the Sûre, the plan was to launch an attack that same day to capture Sinspelt, approximately one mile beyond the 80th Infantry Division's forward positions. They also hoped to seize a bridge over the Enz River, which ran through the town itself.

The 94th Armored Field Artillery Battalion would support the attack. The liaison officers assigned to the battalions were Captain Cook with the 53rd, Captain Temple with the 10th, and Lt. Roger Boas with the 51st. Each of the officers were assigned two observers. Additionally, one observer was attached to each of the tank companies from the 8th Tank Battalion. Lt. English was assigned as the liaison with CCB.

The attack, already scheduled to take place after dark, was postponed until the 1st and 2nd Battalions of the 319th Infantry Regiment made contact in front of the 51st Armored Infantry Battalion. This took place at 2330, and the three armored infantry battalions were ordered to begin their advance immediately thereafter. The 10th and 53rd AIBs formed the assault force while the 51st remained behind to the southwest.

The Medal of Honor

At 1000 on February 22, 1st Lt. James H. Fields of the 10th Armored Infantry Battalion reported to the Fourth Armored Division HQ and met with the Division G-1, Colonel John Himelick. Fields knew exactly why he was invited: he was about to become the Fourth Armored Division's first recipient of the Medal of Honor. None other than Lt. General Patton would be in attendance to bestow the honor.

Lt. James H. Fields receives the Medal of Honor from Lt. General George S. Patton (U.S. Army photograph).

Patton arrived at 1145 and joined the throng of participants and observers. The formal ceremony commenced, and a company of cavalry and a color guard paraded before the assembled troops and dignitaries. After Colonel Himelick read the citation, Lt. Fields and the colors came front and center. Patton placed the medal upon the honoree and expressed his pleasure in the lieutenant being the first Medal of Honor recipient for the entire Third Army. The magnitude of the event was reflected by the many photographers in attendance. Patton topped off the occasion by inviting Lt. Fields to dinner that evening. They were joined by Major General Gaffey, whom Patton told to refrain from sending Fields back to the front.

It has been my unfortunate observation that whenever a man gets the Medal of Honor or even the Distinguished Service Cross, he usually attempts to outdo himself and gets killed, whereas in order to produce a virile race, such men should be kept alive.

The Battle at Niedergeckler

The 53rd Armored Infantry Battalion kicked off the attack at midnight. C/53 led the advance along with B Company of the 8th Tank Battalion. For the first 90 minutes, Lt. Colonel Jaques' men advanced through the darkness unopposed. When they arrived at a sparsely populated and elevated crossroads 400 yards west of Niedergeckler, they received heavy small arms fire and encountered enemy tanks. For the next three hours, C/53 clawed its way through the darkness only to gain 200 yards. But that was enough to do the job, and the enemy was cleared from the crossroads by 0440. A/53 then moved through C/53's position and prepared to carry the attack the final distance toward Niedergeckler. However, they would wait until daylight before striking.

Before the 53rd AIB attacked Niedergeckler, the 10th AIB was tasked with securing the higher terrain east of the town. B/10 and C/10 commenced their attack at 0800. As they advanced (presumably circling north of the town), they encountered two enemy machine guns positioned to interdict the road leading into Niedergeckler.

T/Sgt. James W. Hoy left his cover to take out the machine gun nests. After reaching a vantage point from which to engage the German positions, a 20mm anti-aircraft gun opened fire in his direction. Ignoring the torrent of deadly lead, he maintained his position and fired until both machine guns fell silent.

Another enemy machine gun threatened one of the infantry platoons. While under intense fire, Staff Sergeant Gomer D. Smail adjusted the fire of a pair of 60mm mortars, enabling them to knock out the machine gun nest.

Machine guns were perhaps the least of the 10th Armored Infantry Battalion's worries. On the road outside of Niedergeckler, the Shermans of Captain Len Kieley's A/8 entered a sharp engagement with several *Panther* tanks belonging to the *2nd Panzer Division*. The terrain around the crossroads is gently rolling farmland, making it an ideal place for a tank duel.

Kieley's citation for the Bronze Oak-leaf Cluster to the Silver Star Medal tells the story:

> Besides directing the operation himself, Captain Kieley employed his vehicle as a fighting tank and knocked out one enemy Mark V tank which was obstructing his axis of advance. Captain Kieley's force reached the high ground on the other side of town, accounting for 10 enemy tanks, 1 vehicle, 62 killed and approximately 200 prisoners of war, without loss to any of his force.

The German *Leutnant* commanding the disemboweled *Panzer* unit reported his losses to the commander of the *2nd Panzer Grenadier Regiment*, *Oberstleutnant* Karl-Richard von Puttkamer. The *Leutnant* warned Puttkamer that American tanks were headed in their direction. As told in the Fourth Armored Division's history authored by Ken Koyen, the *Oberstleutnant* instructed the *Leutnant*, "You are now in command of an infantry company. Organize a defense of Sinspelt with stragglers and personnel from regimental headquarters." The officers departed to set up a machine gun position on the east bank of the Enz River, where they hoped to keep the Americans from crossing the bridge.

By 0900, B and C Companies of the 10th Armored Infantry controlled the high ground east of Niedergeckler. The Germans didn't ignore them, however, and hit the hilltop with heavy artillery and mortar fire, which inflicted several casualties. Lt. Barnet Cooperman (C/10) later recounted how the barrage planted dark scars across the snow-covered ground … each succeeding round becoming another deadly blemish on the landscape.

With the back door of the town sealed, A/53 attacked at 1000. After 40 minutes of tough fighting, B/53 was sent in to assist. Doubling the size of the attacking force made the difference, and the last hold-outs gave up within a matter of minutes. Seventy-one Germans were taken prisoner and four enemy tanks destroyed.

During the battle, the 51st Armored Infantry Battalion was released from its assembly area. They had two assignments: seize the high ground south of Niedergeckler (Hill 405) and relieve the elements of the 10th AIB on the high ground east of town. The latter task was easy enough. Elements of the 51st Armored Infantry Battalion took over the 10th AIB's position at 1100. The former assignment was another matter altogether.

The Battle for Hill 405

At 1330, the 51st Armored Infantry Battalion moved toward Hill 405. C/51 drew the assignment to attack the hill, and Sergeant Calvert's squad was chosen to lead the way.

While Calvert attended a squad leader's meeting to review the plan of attack, his men rested in an open area at the base of Hill 405. When enemy fire erupted around them, they retreated to the shelter of some nearby trees. Two of the squad members (Yelton and Ferguson) were hit by enemy fire. Fellow soldiers drug Ferguson back to the cover of the woods and he was taken to an aid station. Yelton was not as fortunate. Having fallen 50 yards beyond the wood line, he was too far away for the medics to make what would surely be a suicide dash to reach him. Even if they managed to make it to his side, dragging him back half the length of a football field at a fraction of the pace would certainly do them in. He lay where he fell.

Others from the platoon were also hit. One soldier was struck in the back but was lucky enough to have his entrenching shovel stop the projectile. A soldier not nearly as fortunate lost his leg.

The attack to seize Hill 405 stalled before it ever really started. The Americans didn't know where the Germans were firing from, so they pulled back to the safety of a nearby house.

At 2030, a platoon leader returned to the battalion command post and reported that Hill 405 was held in such strength that the company could not advance to the crest. He was ordered to return to his platoon along with instructions to take the hill. The subsequent night attack was successful, with the hill secured by 2300. Several Germans were killed during the assault and three prisoners were taken. At 0300 the next day, C/51 was relieved by Company G of the 319th Infantry Regiment. They returned to the battalion assembly area near Niedergeckler.

While the stalemate at Hill 405 was in progress, A/51 (commanded by 1st Lt. Robert L. French) was ordered to clear a roadblock consisting of felled trees. It was reported that the barrier was defended by infantry and three tanks. When the roadblock was attacked, just one enemy tank was encountered, and it withdrew after firing several rounds. In the process, A/51 took 16 prisoners and killed several Germans while suffering no casualties themselves.

The 51st AIB's situation was further complicated at 1700 when enemy infantry appeared on a ridge 500 yards south of B/51's position. American artillery and assault guns pounded the Germans, leaving several of them wounded. Twelve prisoners were taken.

Stubborn Resistance at Sinspelt

The 10th Armored Infantry drew the assignment of continuing the attack toward Sinspelt, a town nestled deep within the valley carved out by the Enz River. B/10 and C/10, which had taken the high ground east of Niedergeckler, would be the companies to carry the load. In addition to securing Sinspelt, their orders were to capture the bridge crossing the Enz and then seize the high ground to the east, which dominated the exit from the bridge area.

The attack by B/10 and C/10 began at 1620. Problems arose at the outset when B/10 was pinned down at Niedergeckler by enemy artillery, leaving the doughs of C/10 to advance alone toward Sinspelt. One of the forward observers for the 94th Armored Field Artillery Battalion, Lt. William Steele, was wounded and evacuated (he was replaced by Sergeant Nicholas Yocca from B Battery).

The enemy artillery took its toll. Medic James E. Wyland left the safety of his cover and raced ahead through the falling artillery rounds to render aid to the wounded. Even after receiving shrapnel wounds to both legs, he continued to deliver first aid to those in need. After working valiantly to save many of the fallen, he succumbed to his wounds and drew his last breath on the battlefield.

Rescuing the wounded was a common theme during the attack on Sinspelt. Pfc Bryon Stewart and Pfc Clifford Van Auken, medics attached to B/10, made repeated trips to aid the stricken. Though wounded themselves, they kept working until all casualties were cared for. Pfc Lester H. Heinold went to the assistance of a wounded soldier, and while rendering aid, received a leg wound. Though hobbled, he still managed to load the soldier into a peep and drive him to safety.

B/10 remained pinned down by artillery fire, but C/10 kept advancing. As they drew closer to Sinspelt, small arms fire erupted from the woods located northwest of the town. American artillery responded with high-explosive shells that ripped into the treetops. The enemy position had to be neutralized, so A/10 (which had previously entered Niedergeckler and was subsequently relieved by C/51 and a platoon from C/704) was dispatched to attack the woods.

A/10 attacked over open ground toward the tree line. Enemy machine gun fire emanating from the woods pinned down the armored infantrymen. Pfc Donald D. Snyder was undeterred and continued to advance. Firing a .30 caliber machine gun from his hip, Snyder single-handedly wiped out the enemy machine gun nest. When other infantrymen rallied behind Snyder and pressed their attack toward the woods, the Germans emerged and surrendered.

With the threat on their flank neutralized, the American tanks and infantry descended into the town, moving with urgency for fear the bridge would be destroyed before they had a chance to grab it. No matter how desperately they wanted to get there, 1st Lt. William N. Martasin's armored infantry platoon was pinned down by direct tank and small arms fire. Seeing his men hit, Martasin stood up and charged alone toward the enemy. This inspired his men to increase their fire and resume their advance toward the bridge.

The American infantry and tanks pushed through the narrow streets, working their way toward the bridge. As they closed in, interdicting fire from the 94th Armored Field Artillery Battalion was called for to prevent the Germans from destroying the bridge.

The M7 firing on the bridge site was the 6th section of C Battery. They fired so fast and furiously that the loader, Pvt. Edward J. Makowski, was overcome by smoke and fumes generated by the howitzer. As the crew worked feverishly to pour high-explosive shells onto the bridge site, an ejected brass cartridge slashed the face of T/5 Elmer A. Wachal. While they couldn't see the results of their fire for themselves, it was working.

The Sherman tanks of Len Kieley's A8, fresh off their destruction of two platoons of *Panthers,* charged the narrow bridge. The Germans apparently had nothing available to stop them, and the American tanks surged across. The tankers turned their guns against *Oberstleutnant* von Puttkamer and his men defending the bridge site, killing him and the crew of the gun emplacement.

C/10 closed in on the bridge and joined Kieley's tanks on the far bank. At 2015, two companies of the 53rd came across the bridge as well. The Shermans were joined by several Hellcat tank destroyers and took up defensive positions near the houses on the east side of the river.

The east end of the bridge at Sinspelt. Note the dominating high ground beyond the town (photograph by author).

7. The Drive to Bitburg and the Kyll River

With the bridge secure, A/10 and B/10 came forward and attacked the dominating high ground east of Sinspelt. During the assault on the hill, the advancing American infantry were pinned down by small arms and automatic fire. Pfc Richard Lucas, armed with a Browning Automatic Rifle (BAR), advanced in the face of enemy fire and silenced a machine gun, taking two prisoners in the process. As he walked the prisoners back, a pistol rang out, seriously wounding him. Despite being shot, he eliminated the gunman who fired at him and managed to bring the prisoners back to his lines.

T/Sgt. William J. Mackin also played a critical role in A/10's attack. When his platoon was held up by light machine gun fire, Mackin took a small group of his men and worked around the flank to knock out the enemy position. Later, his unit was pinned down by 88mm fire. Mackin took the lead and called for his men to follow. Inspired by his actions, his platoon overran the enemy positions. Carried forward by such acts of courage, the 10th Armored Infantry Battalion secured the high ground east of Sinspelt by 2130. B/10 moved to a road junction north of Sinspelt and was subsequently relieved by A/51 at 0320 on February 24.

There was an unanticipated benefit derived from CCA's attack at Sinspelt. The combat command's actions disrupted the fledgling counterattack plans of the *2nd Panzer Division*, which was in the process of moving from Prüm with hopes of attacking through the lines of the *352nd Volksgrenadier Division*.

Battle Fatigue

The intensity of combat at Sinspelt was a stark reminder that the war was far from over. Those who believed that the campaign in Europe was anticlimactic after the Battle of the Bulge were not among the men who continued to face the danger that came with being on the front line. Even the most seasoned veteran could succumb to the pressure. Such was the case for Captain Stanley Lyons, commanding officer of the 10th Armored Infantry Battalion's Headquarters Company.

At the start of the division's campaign in Normandy, Lyons served as the commanding officer of the battalion's reconnaissance platoon (a component of the HQ Company). After nearly seven months of combat, he had earned his stripes as a hardened veteran. Little remained of war that was beyond his experience. Yet he was as susceptible as anyone to the effects of war.

Lyons was inspecting the firing positions of the battalion's assault gun platoon. When he arrived, T/Sgt. Charles O. Graham was in the process of surveying the guns within the aiming circle. One of his crew (the "recorder") was nearby posting the data. When Graham finished his task, he told Lyons that he was going to check on his basic load at the ammunition trailer. The recorder headed back to the guns while Lyons walked in another direction to inspect a concrete bunker. About 30 yards separated Lyons from the G.I. when a German artillery shell passed so close over his head that, in his words, "it sucked my steel helmet off." That same shell killed the recorder.

Lyons, terribly shaken, went back to his peep where his driver awaited him. Lyons' hands were shaking "almost uncontrollably." Having never been rattled like that before, he asked his driver to take him to the battalion aid station.

Captain Lyons saw the battalion surgeon, Captain John Mabee, and asked for something to help him with the "shakes." Lyons was told to sit on a bed of straw in the makeshift hospital (it was a converted barn). He was soon visited by an aid man who gave him a "can of soup made out of mixed rations and water." Lyons fell into a deep sleep. He woke up a few hours later free of the shakes and feeling relieved. Lyons felt there was something extra in the "soup" that aided his recovery (though Captain Mabee insisted that it was nothing more).

The psychological impact of combat was something the American Army had planned for. Clinically, a soldier who fell victim was labeled as a "neuropsychiatric casualty." The objective given the medical units was simple: keep as many men fit for duty on the front line as possible. As stated in the Third Army Medical after-action report,

> Emphasis was therefore placed on <u>preventative</u> neuropsychiatry. Since virtually all preventative measures were command functions, the division neuropsychiatrists, by virtue of their assignments, were in a position to disseminate pertinent information to officers of the line. Especial importance was placed on the necessity for differentiation between cases of physical fatigue and neuropsychiatric casualties. Provision was made to handle these in unit rest areas at the regiment or battalion level to prevent their being placed in medical evacuation channels. The Army policy included the statement "no such case will be evacuated unless he has unmistakable symptoms which are neither mild nor transient. The decision (to evacuate) is essentially one of command unless the symptoms are clear and pronounced." The avoidance of indiscriminate evacuation and the proper selection for treatment on the spot were considered to be imperative. Formal neuropsychiatric diagnosis leaves in the mind of the soldier the firm conviction that he will never again perform combat service. It was directed, therefore, that no diagnosis other than "exhaustion" would be placed on the Emergency Medical Tag except in the case of the obviously psychotic.

The Army acknowledged that this field was "relatively new and untried in military experience." In retrospect, the resources devoted to it were modest: each division was assigned a neuropsychiatrist, as was each evacuation hospital. Their support team consisted of two nurses and six enlisted men trained in narcotherapy.

In all likelihood, there *was* a little something else in the soup.

A member of C Troop, 25th Cavalry Reconnaissance Squadron, grabbing sleep where he can (courtesy Jim White).

Driving Beyond Sinspelt

At 0820 on February 24, the Germans struck before the 10th Armored Infantry renewed its own attack. Three *Panzers* appeared and engaged the American infantry. The Sherman tanks of A/8 moved up and engaged, forcing the Germans to break off their attack. The threat repulsed, A/10 and two platoons of Shermans moved forward and cleared the enemy from the high ground.

At 1030, the 10th Armored Infantry Battalion's command post moved from Niedergeckler to Sinspelt. An hour later, the battalion staff held a meeting with the company commanders and issued orders for the next phase of the attack. The plan called for the 10th AIB to seize Brimingen and the high ground to the south while the 51st AIB covered their left flank by capturing Utscheid to the northeast.

The 10th Armored Infantry attacked at 1400. A/10 and B/10 advanced with the Shermans of A/8 in support, moving over high ground and through a section of woods toward the small village of Newhaus. Meanwhile, C/10 moved in retrograde toward the wooded high ground south of Niedergeckler to guard the rear of CCB.

As C/10 entered the woods, their commander, 1st Lt. Earl Kelly, was shot in the thigh

Passing a knocked out German vehicle at Sinspelt are Fourth Armored infantrymen Pvt. Mike DiMartino, Cpl. Joseph Savage, Pvt. Frank Volpe, and PFC Keith Floyd (U.S. Army photograph, courtesy Darren Neely).

and evacuated. During the ensuing attack, platoon leader 1st Lt. Barnet M. Cooperman directed the assault and seized the objective without suffering any casualties within his unit. After securing the high ground, his luck ran out when enemy machine guns opened fire on the flank, wounding several of his men. Cooperman brought up two mortar squads from other platoons, put them in a battery with his own mortar squad, and directed the return fire that knocked out the enemy positions. Cooperman contacted the medics and supervised the removal of all the wounded.

When A/10 and B/10 approached Newhaus, they found the town heavily defended. The Germans responded with small arms and mortar fire that inflicted heavy casualties on B/10. When A/10 received sniper fire emanating from a house near the road, a bazooka team came forward and destroyed the building. Newhaus fell, but only after a period of intense fighting.

Lt. Earl Kelly, before departing for Europe in 1944 (courtesy James Kelly).

B/10 and the tanks of A/8 and C/8 pressed on toward Brimingen. The Germans responded with heavy artillery fire against the combined arms team. Direct fire knocked out two Sherman tanks, but the team carried the attack forward despite the losses. It was clear, however, that a direct assault on the town would not be a wise approach.

The Sherman tanks left the infantry behind and circled the town to the north. While moving along that route, the tankers came upon the German artillery hampering their advance and proceeded to overrun the enemy position on Hill 236. The Shermans then occupied defilade positions on the high ground northeast of Brimingen and hit the town with a heavy dose of shells from their main guns. After the tanks lifted their fire, B/10 moved into the town and engaged in house-to-house fighting. Brimingen was cleared out by 1900 and outposted for the night by the armored infantry and tanks.

While B/10 tackled Brimingen, A/10 fought to secure the high ground west of the town. After the infantry occupied Hill 426, they received heavy artillery fire but continued to hold the terrain.

B/10 paid a high price during their attack on Brimingen, and it took many acts of courage to get the wounded to safety. Corporal Dave Fisher (a medic) went into the teeth of an artillery barrage to administer aid and arrange for the evacuation of the wounded. After four medics were wounded while assisting the fallen, S/Sgt. Charles Lipsitz voluntarily rendered aid, making several trips until all were evacuated. Similarly, when several members of B/10 were struck by enemy mortar and machine gun fire, Pfc John Macik went forward to treat and evacuate the wounded. Even though later wounded himself, Macik refused to be evacuated until the casualties were cared for. Private William W. Murschell made many attempts under fire to evacuate casualties. And not to be overlooked or forgotten was Private Ralph E. Coutcher, who left his cover to provide help until he was mortally wounded.

Perhaps the most heroic act by the members of the 10th Armored Infantry Battalion occurred after Brimingen was secured. T/Sgt. Samuel K. English and two other soldiers were preparing a defensive position. Sergeant English suddenly realized that a grenade attached to his cartridge belt had become armed. He immediately sensed the danger to the two men standing near him and sprinted away as far as he could before the detonation occurred, saving their lives while losing his own.

The 51st Armored Infantry Battalion continued the attack. After being relieved by F Company of the 319th Infantry, the plan called for the 51st (continuing to work in tandem with Company B from the 8th Tank Battalion) to drive on the left of the 10th Armored Infantry Battalion with the mission of seizing Utscheid (two miles northeast of Sinspelt) and two separate points of high ground north and east of the town. B/8 and B/51 would take the lead and occupy the high ground to the east. Lt. French's A/51 would follow and take the high ground to the north. C/51 would then seize and outpost the town.

An enemy artillery barrage forced a delay in the attack until 1245. Once underway, B/8 and B/51 (aka the "B Team") advanced only 600 yards before encountering a crater in the road. The road ran through a long, narrow strand of woods, thick enough to limit off-road movement of the tanks and other vehicles.

The lead tank came to a halt while another tank took to the shoulder of the road to maneuver around the crater. The attempt was foiled when the tank's tread hit a well-placed

German civilians gather outside of Utscheid (U.S. Army photograph, courtesy Darren Neely).

mine. With the column stymied, some of the infantry dismounted from the tanks and conducted a reconnaissance to find an alternate route for the column. As this went on, the tank crews of Captain Fischler's B/8 located and destroyed two *Panzers*.

The infantrymen discovered an alternate route and the advance resumed. After B/8 and B/51 gained the high ground, they observed three enemy self-propelled guns and a *Panzer* retreating toward the northeast from Utscheid. The Shermans opened fire, destroying the tank and one of the self-propelled guns. Utscheid was cleared and the other objectives secured, but not before taking 106 prisoners. The armored infantry consolidated their positions near Utscheid and dug in.

At 1730, the 37th Tank Battalion joined the 51st Armored Infantry Battalion. This relieved B/8, which moved to the rear to rejoin the 8th Tank Battalion (the 37th crossed the Sûre River earlier that morning and assembled in an area a quarter of a mile south of Obersgegen before receiving the order to support the 51st). Meanwhile, the 53rd Armored Infantry Battalion moved their command post to Sinspelt and deployed their companies on the high ground northeast of town. Of the three armored infantry battalions, they were the only unit to experience a relatively calm day (though heavy artillery fire hit Sinspelt at 2000).

The Germans continued to offer stiff resistance, sending a statement that they were not yet a beaten army. The prisoners taken during the day came from the *2nd Panzer Division*, the *9th Volksgrenadier Division*, the *276th Volksgrenadier Division* and the *352nd Volksgrenadier Division*.

Patton Presses the Attack

As the Fourth Armored Division pushed generally eastward on February 24, the XII and VII Corps completed a pincer movement just north of Obergeckler. Over 3000 prisoners were taken within the enveloped area. It was a loss the Germans could ill afford.

On the heels of his tactical victory, Patton hosted a lunch the following day for his three corps commanders: Major Generals Middleton, Walker, and Gaffey (the latter still filling in for Major General Eddy, who was on leave). Major General Otto Weyland, commander of XIX TAC, was also invited to the affair. Aware of the gathering, General Bradley called and asked if he and his Chief of Staff (Major General Leven Allen) could attend. Patton welcomed them enthusiastically. But before Bradley arrived, the Third Army commander coached up his generals on how they might gain Bradley's permission to carry their attack onward to Trier.

Over lunch, Patton and his subordinates persuaded Bradley to allow the offensive to continue until the end of daylight on February 27. There was horse trading involved, as the approval came with the condition that the 90th Infantry Division would be designated as part of the SHAEF reserve. (It came to pass that Patton failed to secure Trier on the timeline granted by Bradley. But as the battle progressed, Bradley removed the shackles and allowed Patton to keep up the attack. On March 1, the 10th Armored Division entered Trier.)

In his diary, Patton expressed his sentiment regarding the weeks that had passed since the Bulge. "I wonder if ever before in the history of war, a winning general had to plead to be allowed to keep on winning."

The Fourth Armored Division's zone was more than 20 miles north of Trier, but their role in Patton's drive into Germany was of no less consequence. Gaffey, acting as temporary commander of XII Corps, released CCB from the 80th Infantry Division, thus bringing the full weight of the Fourth Armored back under division command. On February 25, he directed the entire Fourth Armored to attack to the northeast. CCB and CCA would strike in tandem along parallel paths. CCB was aligned on the left (north) and CCA on the right (south). The plan: cross the Prüm and Nims Rivers and then cut the major roads leading north from Bitburg. The Fourth would then draw up to the line of the Kyll River, which extends north to south approximately two miles east of Bitburg. The 5th Infantry Division would advance approximately six miles from its current position and have responsibility for the urban fighting likely necessary for the capture of Bitburg.

Crossing the Prüm River

While Brigadier General Dager served as the temporary commander of the division, Lt. Colonel Abrams took the helm of CCB. In Abrams' absence, Major William Hunter assumed command of the 37th Tank Battalion.

On February 25, the 10th Armored Infantry Battalion rose at 0600 and got ready to move. After being relieved by the 53rd Armored Infantry Battalion, C/8 and A/10 were ordered to attack and take Hill 399 northeast of Brimingen. The B Team (B/8 and B/10) was instructed to advance by road to Baustert (a little over a mile northeast of Brimingen) while A/8 and C/10 advanced on their right.

The 10th AIB advance commenced at 0830. Before reaching Baustert, the Americans received direct fire from woods northeast of Brimingen. The 94th Armored Field Artillery Battalion was called upon to deliver a TOT in response. The 105mm howitzers silenced the enemy guns and the advance continued.

Resistance at Baustert was limited to rear-guard elements, and the town was occupied by noon with little effort. The 10th Armored Infantry's command post closed the growing gap with its forward companies by moving from Sinspelt to Brimingen. Prisoners taken during the morning battles came from a hodge-podge of enemy units including artillery, anti-aircraft, and the *Luftwaffe*. The captives revealed that their orders were to fight a delaying action. The low state of their morale was evident (perhaps a reflection of units of their type being asked to carry out a mission normally reserved for others better trained for the task).

At noon on February 25, a realignment of the combat commands took place. Colonel Hayden Sears' CCA now consisted primarily of the 10th Armored Infantry Battalion, 8th Tank Battalion, and 94th Armored Field Artillery Battalion. The 276th Armored Field Artillery Battalion and 974th Field Artillery (155mm howitzers) were attached for additional artillery support. For Al Irzyk, the alignment came as a bit of a surprise, as it was the first time his 8th Tank Battalion served under the command of CCA.

At 1400, CCA launched an attack to capture Brecht, two miles due east of Baustert. The infantry of B/10 advanced on foot among the tanks of B/8 as they made their way east along the road connecting the two towns. C/8 and A/10 moved in similar fashion along the high ground to the left of the road, sweeping up the village of Feilsdorf in the process. C/10 advanced across the open fields to the right of the route taken by the B Team.

Ample artillery and mortar fire met the advancing troops. Lt. Colonel Cohen went to the high ground overlooking the attack. In full view of the Germans, and with constant shelling near his position, he directed the fire of the 8th Tank Battalion. When friendly artillery struck too close to his own men, he personally ordered the fire to be lifted (Cohen received the Distinguished Service Cross for his actions that day ... though not until 1996).

The bridge over the Prüm River at the town of Brecht in 2019 (photograph by author).

With their left flank protected by the capture of Feilsdorf, CCA continued its attack toward Brecht and the Prüm River. The river runs from northwest to southeast directly through Brecht, splitting the town almost evenly. A lone bridge crossed the river at a spot near the center of town, and it was everyone's hope that it could be captured intact.

At 1645, the leading combat elements came within sight of the bridge. The German propensity for denying their infrastructure to the invading Allied forces was displayed once again. Before the tanks and infantry ever had a chance, the Germans destroyed the bridge. Unable to cross, the armored infantry turned their attention to the houses and cellars on the west side of the river. Cohen's men cleared out the last of the defenders by 1800.

Robbed of the opportunity to cross the Prüm at Brecht, A/25 dispatched their scouts to the south, tracing the line of the river in search of a spot where the engineers might place a temporary bridge. About a mile and three-tenths downstream, near the town of Oberweis, the armored cavalrymen encountered a German patrol, which they dispersed after a stiff engagement. They soon located an area in the river valley where the terrain was level enough from the edge of the road down to the river bank. No bridging equipment was immediately available, so A/25 and elements of the 10th Armored Infantry Battalion improvised by summoning forward some Sherman tanks, which turned their guns against a series of telephone poles, bringing them to the ground. Some of the soldiers rolled the telephone poles down to the bank while others waded into the river to arrange them into a footbridge. The armored infantry moved across the river and established a bridgehead deep enough to allow the engineers from A Company of the 150th Engineer Battalion to work overnight on the installation of a Baily bridge. They completed the 90-foot span at 1315 the following day.

Colonel Sears' CCA secured the objectives assigned to him for February 25. During the day's action, 136 prisoners were taken (including six officers) from the *2nd Panzer Division* and *9th Volksgrenadier Division*. The 10th Armored Infantry Battalion suffered the loss of two men KIA, 25 WIA, and 10 non-battle casualties.

On the morning of February 26, as the engineers worked feverishly on the Baily bridge, the 10th Armored Infantry Battalion and elements of the 25th Cavalry Recon Squadron expanded the bridgehead. A/10 pushed beyond the river and by 0830 captured the high ground and woods overlooking the crossing site, taking several prisoners in the process. The 25th Cavalry protected the terrain to the right of A/10. After the area was secure, C/10 came forward and joined A/10 in a march up the road toward Rittersdorf, three miles to the northeast. At 1030, B/10 crossed the river and proceeded in column along the same route.

At noon, the lead elements of A/10 contacted tanks from the 37th Tank Battalion at a point about two miles southwest of Rittersdorf. The infantry continued their march all the way to the town, where they subsequently set up their command post while positioning two of the armored infantry companies on the high ground to the northeast. Farther back, the vehicles of the 25th Cavalry and the 8th Tank Battalion made their way across the completed bridge and closed in on the positions held by the infantry.

By 1930, all units and the command post were in place. The 10th Armored Infantry's casualties for the day were light, with two men KIA and five WIA. The following day (February 27) the 10th AIB was transferred to CCR (having been replaced in CCA by the 53rd AIB).

CCB's Blitz

CCB's axis of advance was only a little more than a mile north of the route followed by CCA. As we are about to see, their drive to the east outpaced that of Colonel Sear's command. In effect, CCB pinched CCA out of the line (which explains the aforementioned contact between the 10th AIB of CCA and the 37th Tank Battalion of CCB near Rittersdorf).

Action on the morning of February 25 began at 0715 when B/37 and B/51 attacked Weidingen. An artillery preparation paved the way into the town, while an artillery strike and mortar smoke were delivered on the high ground to the northeast. During the day, the 22nd Armored Field Artillery Battalion fired a battalion-record 2628 rounds.

At 0855, C/37 and C/51 attacked and seized Altscheid, less than one mile to the northeast of Weidingen. Sixty-seven prisoners were taken and nine enemy killed. Four trucks, two halftracks, and a 75mm anti-tank gun were destroyed.

A/37 and A/51 advanced southeast toward the town of Koosbüsch by way of a winding road running through a valley flanked on both sides by woods. As they moved through the area southeast of Altscheid, German anti-tank fire destroyed one of the Sherman tanks. After reaching Hill 472, the Americans attacked from the heights above Koosbüsch, seizing it and pushing on to the high ground to the east. There, they had a perch overlooking the town of Hermesdorf and the Prüm River.

Following an artillery barrage, B/37 and B/51 led the attack against Hermesdorf, which lay entirely west of the river. The main road led through the town to the lone bridge crossing the Prüm, which hugged the east edge of Hermesdorf. Unlike the bad luck CCA had at Brecht, CCB drove through the heart of Hermesdorf and found the span intact. The armored infantry secured the bridge and quickly pushed across. The only glitch was that

Crewmembers working an M7 self-propelled howitzer (U.S. Army photograph).

the bridge was not adequate for supporting the weight of the Shermans, so Lt. Liese's tanks from B/37 forded the river on their own (at this point in its course, the Prüm was more akin to a creek than a river).

The armored infantry pushed beyond the Prüm and gained control of the high ground to the east. C/37 and C/51 received orders to advance another mile-and-a-half east and secure Hill 366, overlooking the town of Rittersdorf from the west. The prize located near the center of Rittersdorf was a bridge spanning the Nims River (another narrow but nevertheless vehicle-stopping obstacle). Once the C Team secured the high ground and was positioned to provide fire support, the A Team would attack and seize the town and the bridge.

C/37 and C/51 used unsurfaced trails for their advance over the open, hilly terrain toward Hill 366. The dominating terrain was secured by 1530.

Before the A Team began its attack on Rittersdorf, P-47 Thunderbolts descended from the sky and hit the town with bombs and machine gun fire. After the P-47s departed, C/37's tanks shelled the town, paving the way for A/37 and A/51 to advance toward the village streets.

The attacking forces captured the bridge and moved across the river, after which they consolidated and held their positions. A/51 occupied the high ground east of Rittersdorf and along the river. B/51 held a position farther north and east of the river, while C/51 controlled Hill 366 and the road leading from Rittersdorf north-northwest to Ließem. The Sherman tanks of B/37 and C/37 took up positions west of the river on the high ground overlooking the approaches to Rittersdorf from north and south, as well as the town itself. The light tanks of D/37 took up positions to the west of C/37 to protect the combat command's north flank.

In the process of clearing Rittersdorf, CCB took 1000 prisoners—a spectacular bag for Abrams' men (a task force led by 1st Lt. French from the 51st Armored Infantry Battalion was credited with capturing 80 percent of the total). The combat command decimated a battalion of infantry from the *2nd Panzer Division* (the Germans lost 200 men killed in action at the hands of CCB). The 37th Tank Battalion accounted for a dozen artillery pieces and six 88mm anti-tank guns. American tanks and tank destroyers also inflicted losses on the *2nd Panzer Division's* dwindling complement of tanks. The gunners in the Shermans of the 37th and the Hellcats from C/704 accounted for nine enemy tanks and five self-propelled guns. One of the *Panzers* was taken out by Sergeant Stasi's Hellcat from C/704. His gunner, Corporal Dominik Sorrentino, received credit for the kill.

Unfortunately, C/704 did not emerge unscathed. Sgt. Frank Orleno, one of C/704's original members, was mortally wounded by mortar fire at Rittersdorf, as was his gunner, Corporal Michael Bodinsky, when he went to Sgt. Orleno's aid. The battalion's diary reinforced that "they were both among the very best of our men," further describing it as a "tragic loss."

At 1655, artillery support for CCB was bolstered when the 66th Armored Field Artillery Battalion arrived at Brimingen. Thereafter, their M7s reinforced the fire of the 22nd Armored Field Artillery Battalion.

By the end of the day, Abrams' tanks were only one-and-a-half miles northwest of Bitburg. At 2300, the company commanders and battalion staff from the 37th Tank Battalion, 51st Armored Infantry Battalion, and C/704 met to review the plan for the following day. At its core, the mission was to cross the Kyll River and capture the town of Badem, 1.75 miles east of the river.

CCB Meets Resistance at the Kyll

On February 26, the Fourth Armored Division smashed over the Nims River. The weather turned for the worse that morning with rain and only fair visibility. During the dark early morning hours, German 88s and mortars hit the firing positions of the 22nd Armored Field Artillery Battalion. The harassment extended over a period of nearly five hours, not abating until 0700 (one of the M7s from C Battery was put out of action when an enemy round punctured the recoil tube).

The enemy fire failed to disrupt the American attack. At 0600, the remaining companies of the 51st AIB and 37th Tank Battalion west of the Nims River crossed over to the east side and joined the A Team.

At 0800, the combat command launched their strike toward the Kyll River. D/37 had the mission of protecting the north flank of the advance while the nimble tank destroyers of C/704 protected the south. B/37 and B/51 spearheaded the drive to the east.

Shortly after initiating movement, anti-tank fire erupted from the woods less than a half-mile to the south, midway between Rittersdorf and Matzen. Three Sherman tanks from B Company were knocked out. The Shermans destroyed one enemy tank during the engagement, and fire from the M7s knocked out an anti-tank gun.

The B Team continued its advance toward Matzen and seized the high ground west of town. Direct anti-tank fire hit B/37 again, taking out another Sherman. As the armored infantry drew closer to the Kyll River, they were driven back by direct fire from the opposite shore and heavy small arms fire from their right. The 105mm howitzers of the 22nd Armored Field Artillery Battalion poured indirect fire into the nearby woods where German anti-tank guns were positioned.

With the B Team protecting their right flank, the A Team's orders were to advance to the river, after which they would attempt an assault on the town of Erdorf, located on the east bank. The wooded terrain on the west bank sits well above the river and town, affording an excellent view of the objective.

The A Team's advance to the high ground was uneventful. When the team drew up to the woods flanking the Kyll, the infantry dismounted from the tanks and moved into position for the assault on Erdorf. The degree of the slope and the woods precluded the tanks from participating in the attack, so it was up to the infantry alone to capture the town on the far shore.

The G.I.s weaved their way through the barren trees, balancing themselves as they descended the slope and guarding against slipping on the thick carpet of leaves turned brown and dead by winter. Despite being inside the woods, the absence of underbrush coupled with the naked branches left them visible to their opponents.

A hail of small arms fire, machine guns, 88mm, and 20mm fire pinned them to the slope. After a grueling seven hours of failed attempts to close with the enemy, the company was ordered to withdraw. Given their position on the forward slope, this was no easy task. At 1625, the 179th Field Artillery Battalion fired a smoke mission to help the infantry retreat without further loss. The 22nd Armored Field Artillery Battalion added to the smoke cover at 1725. The last men of A/51 came back under the cover of darkness at 2230.

The 22nd Armored Field Artillery Battalion fired well over 2000 rounds during the day. First Sgt. Harris summed up the effort of the howitzer crews:

> Being on the receiving end of 2632 rounds of 105mm high explosive would not be my idea of a fun day. It must have been a day of hell for the Germans. My battery received enemy artillery fire several times today. Luckily only two men were injured. We received only a fraction of enemy fire compared with what we fired at them.

As the B Team drove toward the Kyll River, the C Team advanced on their left. Enemy artillery put one of the Shermans out of action and knocked the blade off the battalion's bulldozer tank. The C Team's return fire destroyed one 88mm gun and a half-track prime mover.

The tankers and armored infantry reached their objective near the Kyll at 0910. After drawing direct fire from across the river that cost them another Sherman, they withdrew to a covered position and regrouped.

At 1630, C/51 and C/37 assaulted a strip of woods. The armored infantry took the lead and the Shermans followed, firing over the heads of the infantrymen. Within 30 minutes, the doughs did the tough work of clearing the woods. Whatever enemy troops remained fled the woods and retreated south toward Bitburg. The C Team then moved into a defensive position extending east of Hill 418, where they tied in

S/Sgt. John Harris, 22nd Armored Field Artillery Battalion (courtesy John Harris).

with the A Team's position on their left. To the left of the A Team, D/37 and C/704 held the ground leading down to the river.

The night of February 26 ended with Combat Command B coming up somewhat short of their goals. The 51st Armored Infantry Battalion history described the action as "the tightest spot they have been in during this phase of combat. This has been a rough day, particularly for Co B and the men are tired."

The following day, the decision was made by TUSA to delay the crossing of the Kyll. Instead, CCB turned its attention to securing their flank to the north.

After an artillery preparation, the A Team attacked Nattenheim. Resistance was light, and the town yielded 85 prisoners. Simultaneously, the C Team moved into position to occupy the high ground overlooking Fleißem in preparation for an attack. With the A and C Teams in place, the B Team moved through Nattenheim and advanced toward Hill 431. Their attack was delayed by enemy fire coming from woods located to the north and west. In the process of neutralizing the threat, they took approximately 20 prisoners.

Having cleared the woods, the B Team turned their attention back to Hill 431, which they occupied without difficulty. The C Team then descended on Fleißem on the heels of an artillery preparation. By midday, all objectives were secured, and the combat command sat tight. But at 1245, a dozen enemy tanks were spotted in the woods near the 51st Armored Infantry Battalion. A fire mission was called in for the 22nd Armored Field Artillery Battalion, and the weight of their barrage scattered the *Panzers*.

One more opportunity presented itself that afternoon. Word circulated that a footbridge over the Kyll might be intact. At 1305, a patrol consisting of a platoon from A/51 and a platoon of tanks from A/37 headed toward the river to check it out. The patrol returned empty-handed, reporting that no such bridge existed.

CCB Attacks Sefferweich and Malbergweich

By 1500 on February 27, the teams consolidated their positions and the right flank of CCB was tied in with CCA's 53rd Armored Infantry Battalion. The following day, the 37th Tank Battalion and 51st Armored Infantry Battalion held in place and were instructed to spend their time on maintenance and cleaning their weapons.

This changed at 1030 when word came down that CCB was to capture the towns of Sefferweich and Malbergweich, two and-a-half to three miles north of their current positions. The towns were modest in size, with Malbergweich being the slightly more dominant of the two and located one-and-a-half miles due east of Sefferweich.

A prominent feature in the area was a large stretch of woods atop higher ground south of Sefferweich. The woods extended along a mile-long axis running south to north. At its widest point, the woods were half a mile wide. A road ran down the spine of the woods and continued north over the open terrain separating the towns. The woods were also laced with several trails entering and exiting from many directions. An elaborate plan was developed for the attack, and the A and B Teams drew the assignment for executing it.

B/37 kicked off the advance at 1330. Working with B/51, their first objective was to clean out the woods and high ground overlooking the towns. As the tanks reached the area where the main road and one of the trails entered the woods, they were held up by an anti-tank gun well-positioned to control the approaches. After a delay, a decision was made for B/37 and B/51 to bypass the woods to the west. The tanks and infantry circled around on the open ground and eventually landed on the heights overlooking Sefferweich from the southeast. The woods were now at their back.

As B/37 and B/51 maneuvered, the A Team attempted to move into the woods using the secondary trails. Enemy artillery and small arms fire made it impossible for Lt. Whitehill's tanks to gain access. Unable to progress, the A Team attempted to mirror the B Team's maneuver by circling the woods over the open ground to the east. Unlike the west perimeter, the Germans had the east side covered. The A Team's advance ground to a halt.

With no other avenues to consider, a second attempt was made to drive up the main south-north road. This time, the tanks penetrated the woods. Soon after entering, however, they discovered that the road was heavily mined. Three of Whitehill's tanks detonated explosives and were disabled. The immobilized armor blocked the road and held up the column. When engineers came forward to clear the minefield, they received heavy artillery and mortar fire, which hampered their work.

CCB was far behind schedule and made even more so when the commanding officer of A/51, 1st Lt. Robert L. French, was killed during the attack. French was the prior recipient of two Silver Stars, a Bronze Star, and two Purple Hearts. His loss was a blow to the battalion. (Lt. French was posthumously awarded the Distinguished Service Cross for his actions between February 22 and 28). In the wake of French's death, a pause was taken to reorganize. Complicating things further was the temporary loss of contact between the A and B Teams.

The attack resumed at 1700. The A Team encountered lighter resistance this time and reached the north edge of the woods, where they joined the B Team at 1910. The armored infantry dug in for the night on the high ground southeast of Sefferweich.

At 0625 on March 1, before CCB began its attack, heavy enemy artillery and mortar fire hit the positions of the A and B Teams. Fifteen minutes after the commencement of the barrage, 12 enemy tanks and approximately 100 infantrymen counterattacked from the direction of Sefferweich. The Germans headed directly for the positions held by the armored infantrymen of A/51 and B/51.

The *Panzers* sought defilade cover and opened fire on A/37. Both B/37 and A/37 returned fire. Though the Americans lost two Sherman tanks, they destroyed three German assault guns and a *Panther* tank. Despite the accuracy of the American gunners, the German infantry and remaining armor pressed their attack.

The heaviest thrust came against the positions of A/37 and A/51. The 22nd Armored Field Artillery Battalion and machine guns of the 51st Armored Infantry combined forces to hit the softer targets, forcing the enemy infantry into retreat (the 22nd AFAB, firing under the direction of forward observer Lt. Dufoe, also claimed kills on two enemy tanks and an assault gun). The Americans suffered numerous casualties, including the commanding officer of A/51 (just one day after taking command in the wake of Lt. French's death). Lt. Smith, a forward observer for the 22nd AFAB, was also killed. Despite the weight of the German attack, the Americans held their positions. In addition to the loss of the irreplaceable armored vehicles, the enemy suffered 55 killed and 35 taken prisoner. The remainder of the enemy force withdrew.

That morning, Lt. Colonel Abrams resumed command of his battalion (Brigadier General Dager having returned to his command of CCB after filling in as the commander of the Fourth Armored). At 1830, Abrams sent a message to the 22nd Armored Field Artillery Battalion stating that, "Today's artillery was superb. The best I have ever seen."

Praise from Lt. Colonel Abrams was high praise indeed. He was as tough as they came. He knew that for his men to have the best chance of winning the war—and coming out of it alive—they must attack. Relentlessly. As the war progressed, he pressed for night attacks for the simple reason that it was one more way to keep the enemy off balance. The quicker work they made of the Germans, the sooner they were headed home. While he maintained a tough outer shell, he was always concerned about the welfare of his men. What he dished out in terms of rigorous workload and high expectations was as much for the preservation of his men as it was for the achievement of the mission. The two goals were never mutually exclusive.

The effective strength of the 51st Armored Infantry Battalion was very low. They needed a break and were ordered to hold their positions until elements of the 25th Cavalry Recon Squadron arrived to relieve them. By noon, the armored infantrymen were off the line. The companies moved on foot to an assembly area near Nattenheim, where they reorganized.

At 1000, the 10th Armored Infantry Battalion was assigned to replace the 51st in CCB. The battalion left Rittersdorf at 1300 and arrived at Bickendorf at 1430. All three companies of armored infantry proceeded on a one-mile foot march toward CCB's line south of Sefferweich. Contact was made with the 25th Cavalry and the 37th Tank Battalion.

Cohen and Abrams, who had become great friends and exceptionally proficient teammates, prepared to resume the offensive. The objectives for the attack: securing the town of Sefferweich (from whence the Germans had commenced their attack that morning) and seizing the two hills on the far north side of Sefferweich and Malbergweich.

Before the attack commenced, the Germans greeted them with another round of heavy artillery and mortar fire. A mortar shell struck one of the 10th Armored Infantry Battalion's ammunition halftracks, setting it afire. Sensing the danger, Tech 4 Joseph C. Metz valiantly went about extinguishing the blaze, even though he was knocked off his feet several times by exploding ammunition.

In preparation for CCB's attack, the 22nd and 66th Armored Field Artillery Battalions fired a preparatory barrage on Sefferweich. American aircraft added their weight to the preparation, softening up the Germans by bombing and strafing their positions in and near the town.

At 1545, all companies jumped off simultaneously. The Germans met the attack with small arms fire that was described as "troublesome" but casualties among the attacking forces were light. During the attack, Lt. George J. Perkins, while advancing to his observation post to direct the fire of the mortar platoon of the 10th Armored Infantry Battalion's HQ Company, was wounded by sniper fire. He refused to be evacuated until he finished the job. A/37 and C/10 drove into the town but found no opposition as they worked their way through the streets.

The tanks and infantry of C/37 and A/10 advanced and seized the high ground between Sefferweich and Malbergweich. B/37 and B/10 then came forward and relieved those units, after which B/37 advanced to a higher point on the ridge. There, approximately 200 Germans held prepared positions. The Shermans routed the enemy infantry, which allowed C/37 and A/10 to attack and secure Malbergweich.

Cleaning Up Farther to the North

The 37th Tank Battalion and 10th Armored Infantry Battalion shifted to defensive positions. The Germans had responded in strength, but CCB had the upper hand for the day. The tally was 400 German prisoners, four enemy armored vehicles destroyed, several guns knocked out, and 65 enemy troops killed.

The town of Malberg in 2019 (photograph by author).

The day's work was incomplete, however, as it was necessary to gain additional protection on the division's northern front. At 2200, C/10 sent a platoon of armored infantry a mile west of Sefferweich to the town of Seffern. Meeting no resistance, they captured an intact bridge spanning the Nims River and secured the town.

Exploring to the east, A/10 sent a patrol into Malberg (a little over a mile east-southeast of Malbergweich). The venture almost ended in disaster when 1st Lt. Alfred F. Albert's men were ambushed by a deadly crossfire of concealed weapons. Realizing they had to withdraw if they were to survive, Lt. Albert contacted each man personally. The patrol retreated behind a curtain of falling snow.

The following day, A/10 departed at 1000 and moved one-and-a-half miles to the high ground southwest of Tittendorf where the vehicle park had been established. They were joined by B/10 and C/10 later that afternoon. The vehicles were used to form a perimeter and the troops dug in and erected pup tents. At 1900, the battalion kitchens were brought up to serve hot food. Before the day ended, Lt. Colonel Cohen was pleased to learn that his battalion received a commendation from the commanding general of the 80th Infantry Division for their attack on Hoesdorf on February 2, along with a congratulatory statement from his own division commander, Major General Gaffey.

CCA Attacks Matzen

The battlefield on the morning of February 27 was obscured by rain and fog. At 0745, B/53 and a platoon of tanks from A/8 moved out through the muck to attack Matzen.

The Sherman tank commanded by the 94th Armored Field Artillery Battalion's forward observer, Lt. Griffith, moved with the attacking elements. As he approached Matzen, his tank was hit four times by enemy rounds. One of the shells skirted high on the turret, striking the hatch cover. Sgt. Anthony Mazza was hit by a flying piece of the hatch and Lt. Griffith was struck in the eye by a steel splinter. After the crew bailed out of the tank, Griffith realized that Sgt. Mazza was not among them. The lieutenant led a party back to the tank with the hope of rescuing their comrade. Advancing through enemy fire, he reached the Sherman only to discover that the sergeant had been killed. He and his team were able to retrieve the tank, but it was no consolation for Mazza's death.

The forward elements entered Matzen at 0830. Small arms greeted the American infantry as they moved among the houses. After a two-hour engagement, Matzen was cleared of all resistance. By 1310, the high ground south of the town was taken and defensive positions established. A machine gun platoon was attached to B/53 for additional firepower. During the action in and around Matzen, two enemy tanks were destroyed. Additionally, 26 Germans were killed and 45 were taken prisoner.

Following the attack, the 53rd Armored Infantry Battalion remained in a defensive posture south of the town. Lt. Colonel Jaques' command post relocated from Rittersdorf to Matzen. Not long after his arrival, the Germans sent him a warm greeting by shelling the

February 27, 1945. German POWs pass a burning building in Irsch, Germany, as they are brought in for interrogation (U.S. Army photograph).

command post with heavy artillery. The battalion remained in its rest area until March 6. During that time, they rehabilitated their personnel and took care of vehicle maintenance. In their battalion journal, they took stock of their personnel losses for the month of February: 78 wounded in action, nine missing in action, and 19 killed in action. Having lost only a single halftrack during the month, their matériel losses paled by comparison.

Tightening the Noose on Bitburg

The Fourth Armored had firm control of all roads leading north from Bitburg, and reports from air reconnaissance indicated that German forces were fleeing the city.

While flying over Bitburg, Lt. Billy Wood's observation plane was hit by enemy machine gun fire. The gas tank was punctured, and Wood suffered an injury to his leg. He managed to land the damaged plane near friendly tanks. After patching both his leg and the fuel tank (according to the battalion history, using "chewing gum and string" as his instruments of repair), he flew his plane back to the 94th Armored Field Artillery Battalion.

Elements of the 80th Infantry Division followed behind *Olympic* and were kept busy collecting the prisoners left behind by the advancing armor. Meanwhile, a battalion from the 5th Infantry Division's 2nd Infantry Regiment arrived at the Nims River at a spot one mile west of Bitburg.

The 11th Infantry Regiment cut off the city from the southeast. Lt. Colonel Irzyk dispatched a patrol from Lt. Erdmann's D/8 to contact the 11th Infantry. The patrol returned with 20 prisoners mounted on his tanks.

With the encirclement of Bitburg complete, other elements of the 5th Infantry Division advanced into the city. By midday on February 28, the task of securing the city was complete.

Cleanup West of the Kyll Continues

On March 1, Major General Gaffey returned from temporary duty as the commander of XII Corps. Brigadier General Dager, who commanded the division in Gaffey's absence, returned to the command of CCB. Lt. Colonel Abrams in turn resumed command of the 37th Tank Battalion. On that day, Patton and Major General Eddy visited the 76th, 5th, 80th, and Fourth Armored Divisions.

The early days of March were punctuated by poor weather. Rain and damp fog kept the XIX TAC fighter-bombers out of the skies above the Fourth Armored Division's zone. After the failed German counterattack near Sefferweich, enemy resistance consisted primarily of ineffective shelling.

When CCB shifted its axis of attack to the north, it required the units of CCA to extend their left flank to the north as well. The 8th Tank Battalion and 53rd Armored Infantry Battalion, facing east toward the Kyll River, remained in defensive positions extending south along a two-and-a-half-mile line running from Fließem to the area southeast of Matzen. After receiving two direct hits from German artillery at their command post in Matzen, the 53rd Armored Infantry moved their CP farther west to Bitburg, which by then had been cleared by the 5th Infantry Division.

After darkness settled in on the evening of March 2, Lt. Colonel Irzyk moved the 8th

Tank Battalion's B, C, and D Companies, the assault guns, and the mortar platoon up to the west bank of the Kyll River. The purpose was to create a diversion for the upcoming river crossing to be conducted by the 5th Infantry Division. Under pouring rain, the armored units occupied the river line running from the vicinity of Matzen north to Fließem. The Germans took note and poked at the area around Fließem with sporadic mortar and artillery fire during the night.

The 53rd Armored Infantry Battalion and 8th Tank Battalion remained in those positions through March 3. Patrols were sent out by the 53rd, but no enemy contact was made west of the river. There was much activity observed east of the river, where it appeared the Germans were preparing defensive positions. On March 3, the 53rd Armored Infantry Battalion pulled back to Bitburg to prepare for the resumption of offensive operations.

The Hellcats of C/704 outposted and guarded the flanks of CCB (the balance of their parent battalion remained far to the south in support of the 94th Infantry Division). They maintained that role until March 3, when the company moved to the Bitburg area in preparation for the next stage of the advance. The 1st Platoon was assigned to escort the trains supplying the 37th Tank Battalion, while the 3rd Platoon was attached to C Troop of the 25th Cavalry. The 2nd Platoon was assigned to accompany CCB's headquarters. At the command post of C/704, they noted that the Germans seemed to be giving up with little resistance. They also observed that the prisoners of late were increasingly young boys and old men.

The new arrangement of the .30 and .50 caliber machine guns. This added considerable firepower to the standard Sherman (U.S. Army photograph, courtesy Darren Neely).

While the division coiled up behind the Kyll River, the mechanics of the 126th Armored Ordnance Battalion equipped many of the 76mm Sherman tanks with a powerful modification: the standard .30 caliber machine gun mounted next to the tank's main gun (aka the coaxial machine gun) was removed and replaced with the Air Corps' high-speed .50 caliber machine gun. The welders were also busy up-armoring the Shermans.

On March 2, CCB continued to expand its lines. A platoon of Sherman tanks entered Seffern to reinforce the platoon from C/10 that had occupied the town the evening before. Nearly four miles to the east-southeast, a patrol from C/37 took a second stab at entering Malberg. This time, they encountered only scattered fire from small arms. The town was occupied with little difficulty.

Less than three-quarters of a mile to the southeast of Malberg, the town of Kyllburg nestles deep within the valley containing the Kyll River. The river makes a magnificent loop that embraces the town on three sides. High, forested ground overlooks the west side of the town, which begins midway down the valley wall. The streets descend steeply toward the river, with tightly-packed houses stair-stepping their way in unison with the pavement. In peacetime, it would be an idyllic setting.

Based upon intelligence provided by a local citizen, the Americans about to investigate the town did not expect to find any German resistance at Kyllburg. Their new-found ally promised that the Germans had abandoned the town.

During the midafternoon of March 2, a patrol consisting of a platoon each of armored infantry and medium tanks set out for Kyllburg. The infantry from A/10 were led by Lt. Albert, while the tanks were supplied by Lt. Whitehill's A/37. Near the front of the patrol was their civilian guide. Their hope upon entering Kyllburg was to find a bridge intact over the Kyll River.

The patrol snaked its way down the steep, curving mountainside road leading to Kyllburg. They entered the town at 1500 and were shocked when they were greeted with small arms, automatic weapons, and mortar fire which killed one soldier and wounded several others. The patrol was forced out of the town. The civilian—who turned out to be an ardent Nazi—was killed. The method of his death, and at whose hands, is left to conjecture.

8

The Drive to the Rhine

Patton's Plan

The next phase of Patton's offensive was a drive to the Rhine River. The plan called for the 5th Infantry Division, veterans of multiple river crossings, to forge a bridgehead across the Kyll through which the Fourth Armored would launch two combat commands. CCA and CCB would move north on parallel roads for eight miles, cutting behind the enemy positions along the river. Still working side by side, the commands would then swing to the northeast and advance to the Rhine near the town of Andernach. With luck, there might be an intact bridge ready for the taking. The 5th and 80th Infantry Divisions would follow in *Olympic's* wake. The 76th Infantry Division, growing in experience by the day, would advance on the right and protect XII Corps' flank.

Patton's attack posed a serious threat to the entire German front. If TUSA's drive to the Rhine met the left hook landed by Hodges' First Army, two corps of the German *15th Army* would be trapped. The German *7th Army* was the primary opponent standing in Patton's way. And the biggest threat to the *7th Army*, as viewed by its commander, *General* Hans-Gustav Felber, was the veteran U.S. Fourth Armored Division.

Like so much of the *Wehrmacht* at this stage of the war, the *7th Army* was a shell of what it might have been during the glory years of Nazi Germany. Felber had three corps aligned from north to south: *LIII Corps*, *XIII Corps* (positioned near Bitburg opposite the Fourth Armored Division) and *LXXX Corps*. On paper, the three corps summed up to 10 divisions. But these were divisions in name only, with most being reduced to effective strengths a small fraction of their normal complement. The two strongest divisions were the *2nd Panzer Division* (an increasingly familiar foe of the Fourth Armored) and the *246th Volksgrenadier Division*. These divisions were placed deliberately opposite the Fourth Armored in anticipation of their attack.

General Felber possessed little in the way of reserves. The only noteworthy unit was an understrength battalion of *Tiger* tanks (battalion in name only, as it currently consisted of only 10 to 15 pieces of armor). But for want of gasoline, the *Tigers* were not able to move into the zone of *XIII Corps*.

Crossing the Kyll River

The first step in securing a bridgehead over the Kyll took place in the dead of night. At 2300 on March 1, the 11th Infantry Regiment dispatched the I&R platoon leader (2nd Lt. Leonard J. Duston, Jr.) and two engineers to the river to conduct a reconnaissance. Lt.

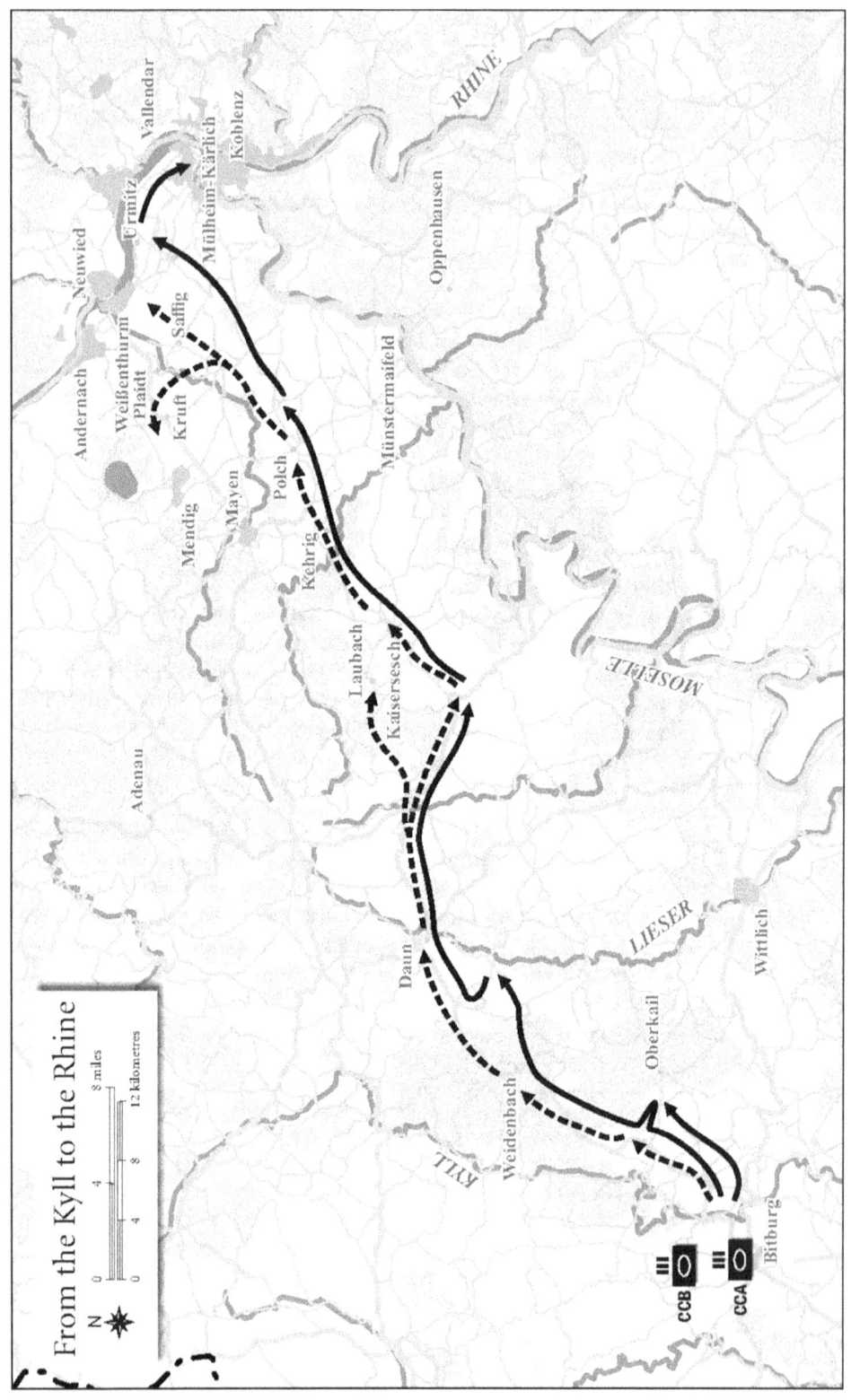

From the Kyll to the Rhine (© Petho Cartography, 2020).

8. The Drive to the Rhine

Duston waded across the Kyll and advanced another 100 yards into German territory. He returned without incident ... a good sign of things to come.

To help the 5th Infantry Division achieve surprise, there would be no preparatory fire by artillery when the crossing began on March 2. The 2nd Battalion of the 11th Infantry would cross on the left. Once established, they would capture the town of Erdorf, tucked in close to the east bank. The 3rd Battalion of the 11th Infantry would establish a bridgehead on the right, and subsequently drive east to capture Badem, 1.75 miles beyond the river.

The operation began after sunset, with A and C Companies of the 7th Engineer Battalion constructing footbridges over the 25-foot-wide river. For a diversion, the Sherman tanks of C/37 fired at enemy positions on the east side of the river.

February 26, 1945. German POWs carry rations for American front-line troops across a pontoon footbridge over the Saar River at Taben, Germany. The bridge was built by U.S. Army combat engineers (U.S. Army photograph).

Shortly after midnight, members of the 2nd Battalion crossed the river unopposed. It took only 12 minutes for the first company to reach the opposite shore. The bridgehead expanded steadily until a German counterattack at 0245 stalled the advance. By daylight on March 3, the 2nd Battalion had expanded the bridgehead to a depth of 600 yards.

The crossing did not go as well in the 3rd Battalion sector. Problems with the bridging dictated a shift in the plan, and another crossing site was used west of Metterich. It was much later in the day before troops of the 3rd Battalion were moving east. Construction soon began on a vehicle bridge near Erdorf. The work was completed before daylight on March 4.

On March 5, Third Army Headquarters received Letter of Instruction 16 from the 12th Army Group. Relative to the Third Army, the directive said,

> *The Twelfth Army Group was to clear the enemy of the area west of the Rhine and north of the Moselle Rivers to ensure security of the main lines of communication to the north, with the front of the southern zone (Third Army) to remain on the defensive.*

Conspicuously absent was any mention of conducting a crossing of the Rhine River, by capture of a bridge or any other means.

CCB's Breakout from the Kyll Bridgehead

At 0730 on March 5, the Fourth Armored began its drive across the Kyll River. Brigadier General Dager's CCB led the attack and pushed through the 5th Infantry Division bridgehead between Erdorf and Huttingen.

The primary elements of CCB were the 37th Tank Battalion, 10th Armored Infantry Battalion, C/704, B/24, B/46, B/126, C Troop of the 25th Cavalry Reconnaissance Squadron, and the 66th and 22nd Armored Field Artillery Battalions. Artillery forward observers for the 66th were Lt. Doran (riding with the 25th Cavalry Reconnaissance Squadron) and Lt. Osborne (supporting the 37th Tank Battalion), while the 22nd Armored Field Artillery Battalion forward observers were Lieutenants Fife, Duty, and Markowski. The Sherman tanks of A/37 and armored infantry of C/10 formed the spearhead of the column. Due to fog and rain, there was no air support.

Despite artillery and rocket fire directed against the American column, the lead tanks advanced quickly toward Badem, the first village beyond the 5th Infantry Division's bridgehead. The defenders surrendered quickly, and the Sherman tanks continued to roll. After exiting Badem, the column made a hard turn to the north and headed for Orsfeld, just under two miles up the road. By 0845 the village fell into American hands.

The route of advance continued to the northeast across heavily wooded and hilly terrain. The destination was Meisburg, seven miles distant. Throughout the advance to Meisburg, the 37th reported frequent opposition from tanks, anti-tank guns, infantry, and artillery. A/37 and C/10 continued to serve as the vanguard for CCB and overran German supply lines and rear-echelon troops as they sliced deeper into German territory. As it had done so many times before, the Fourth was cutting into the bowels of its enemy.

Upon reaching Meisburg, the Fourth found a stiffer opponent. The German artillery was heavy and accurate … a sign that they probably had a forward observer in play. Private Francis Crevier of the 10th Armored Infantry Battalion went on a one-man mission to hunt the observer down. Crevier advanced into Meisburg, located the enemy OP, and forced the surrender of the observers. He then found the communication equipment used to call in the artillery fire and cut the lines. Shortly thereafter, the opposing artillery fell silent ... but not before inflicting heavy casualties upon the Americans. After the dust settled, the 10th Armored Infantry Battalion established their command post inside Meisburg. The 66th Armored Field Artillery Battalion set up their firing positions nearby.

After the main column jogged to the northeast, protection was needed for their left flank. The 25th Cavalry was called upon to advance along a parallel route to the west of CCB's main axis. Along this route, they captured the towns of Kyllburgweiler, Seinsfeld, and Steinborn. The M8 armored cars continued farther north, protecting CCB's left as they advanced. When they came to the area west of Meisburg, they seized a large ammunition depot (which may have been one of the reasons the Germans offered such a staunch defense of the town). The cavalrymen then moved north to the town of Salm, where they received heavy artillery fire at a road block.

The next objective for the main column was Weidenbach, a mile-and-a-half to the northeast. The Germans mounted a spirited defense, throwing a *Nebelwerfer* brigade into the breach. It was the toughest fighting CCB experienced all day. When one of the tanks in the column received a hit by a high-explosive shell, infantrymen riding on the tank were thrown violently to the ground. S/Sgt. Robert L. Brown, riding on the next tank in the column, leapt down and pulled from harm's way one of the infantrymen about to be crushed by the oncoming Sherman. S/Sgt. William McGinnis, riding on the tank that was hit, also had the presence of mind to pull a fallen armored infantryman out of the path of the oncoming machine's treads.

After the fall of Weidenbach, A/10 pushed beyond the town to seize the wooded high ground to the east. During the assault on the hill, the Germans inflicted severe casualties. Medical aid vehicles were unable to negotiate the rough terrain, leading 1st Lt. Alan I. Moses to expose himself to direct fire as he aided the wounded and saw to their evacuation.

Two more towns were on the American agenda before the advance halted for the night: Salm (which the 25th Cavalry had stopped short of) and Wallenborn. Both towns were less than two miles from Weidenbach (Salm being to the north-northwest and Wallenborn to the north-northeast).

C/37 and A/10 carried out the assault on Salm. Stiff resistance led to several casualties among the armored infantry. Some of the wounded were unable to move. With no medics available, Pfc Theodore Janetos and Pfc William Lee braved continuous shelling to treat and evacuate those in need. By the time the battle was over, the Americans destroyed three 105mm guns and several 75mm weapons.

Lt. Donahue's D/37 carried out the attack on Wallenborn. His light tanks assaulted the town without infantry support and destroyed a large column of wagons and guns during the process of securing the objective.

Spearheaded by the 37th Tank Battalion, CCB had advanced 13 miles to the northeast from the point where it crossed the Kyll River. The men of the 10th Armored Infantry complained about the bad roads hindering their advance as much or more than they did the constitution of the enemy (the tankers of the 37th characterized the opposition as being a bit stiffer). The German troops they encountered were cobbled together from a stew of different units and disciplines: artillery, *Panzer*, *Panzerfaust*-equipped infantry, personnel clerks, and quartermasters. According to the 10th Armored Infantry Battalion, the enemy lacked equipment and suffered from low morale. The Americans captured half of a brigade of the *53rd Artillery* and destroyed the other half. The total prisoner count for the day was approximately 1500. Many tanks and artillery pieces were destroyed, including three *Tiger* tanks and five *Panthers*. Some of the units they opposed were elements of the *79th, 340th, and 246th Volksgrenadier Divisions,* plus the seemingly ever-present *2nd Panzer Division*.

CCA Faces a Challenge

CCA crossed the Kyll using the same bridge as CCB. As a result, Brigadier General Dager's command was well on its way to the northeast before CCA started across the river. To draw alongside CCB, Colonel Sears would have to push aggressively to close the gap.

After crossing the river, the leading tanks of C/8 turned south toward Metterich. Following in column behind C/8 came C/53, a platoon of Hellcats, C/24, C battery of the 94th, and A/25. As the Sherman tanks moved beyond Metterich, they found the unpaved road on their assigned route to be in extremely poor condition. The fields on each side were even worse, and any vehicle moving off-road was likely to become mired. Nevertheless, the tankers pushed onward.

Resistance cropped up almost immediately after the column left Metterich, but the element of surprise was CCA's friend. Colonel Sears' men rounded up a sizeable number of prisoners and moved on.

The Sherman tanks progressed a little over a mile before coming to the narrow Katzengraben River. The column drew to a stop upon discovering that the bridge had been destroyed. A quick survey of the area revealed no alternate routes. The only way across was to ford the river.

Channeling the spirit of the Moselle crossing nearly four months earlier, Lt. Colonel Irzyk ordered C/8 to send their tanks across. As they had done near Bayon when under the command of Lt. William Marshall, the tankers of C Company successfully pushed their armor to the other side. As each tank crossed, it broke down the bank of the river, making it easier for the next Sherman in line. But the tanks stood alone in making the crossing, as the nature of the river prevented the halftracks and wheeled vehicles from making a similar attempt.

What choice did Lt. Colonel Irzyk have? He could slow down the pace of the attack by drawing up the tanks on the far side of the river to form an outpost while the engineers came forward to install a bridge, or he could push the tanks without infantry support toward the next objective: Gindorf.

Tanks operating without infantry are more vulnerable in an environment such as a town or a wooded area, where enemy infantry can draw close enough to use personal anti-tank weapons. But knowing that time was of the essence for CCA to draw abreast of CCB, Irzyk ordered C/8 to drive onward without infantry support (a platoon of Hellcat tank destroyers, also able to ford the river, accompanied the Shermans). C Battery of the 94th Armored Field Artillery Battalion managed to move forward into firing positions near Badem, less than a mile west of Irzyk's crossing site.

As the Shermans of C/8 and the Hellcats drew close to Gindorf, enemy tank fire erupted from a wooded area to the northeast. The Shermans returned fire and knocked out four tanks ... but not before losing two of their own (one to an enemy tank and the other to a mine). The tankers carried the battle into the town, driving their Shermans through the narrow streets sans infantry support. Enemy small arms fire rang out, punctuated by the sound and fury of *Panzerfausts*. Another tank fell prey to the lethal anti-tank weapon.

More German tanks appeared on the outskirts of Gindorf. The American tank gunners destroyed two of them, but at the cost of another Sherman. The M7 howitzers from C Battery fired in support of Irzyk's tanks, and in return they were subjected to harassing fire from German artillery and mortar units. Friendly tanks from the other companies of the 8th Tank Battalion arrived and provided the extra weight needed to clean out the town.

The day was waning, and CCA had advanced a little less than four miles from the Kyll River, well short of the advance made by CCB's spearhead. The column had barely turned north, so with every passing hour, the gap between the vanguards of the two combat commands grew wider.

Lt. Colonel Irzyk made a bold decision. He ordered his advance units to return to an assembly area near Metterich. Fervently believing that his assigned route was impassible due to the road conditions, he radioed Colonel Sears and recommended a change in CCA's route of advance. If he remained on the original path, he was confident that he would not close the growing gap between the two combat commands. The alternative, from his perspective, was to backtrack and fall in line behind CCB. Using the better road in CCB's zone, CCA could keep pace with their advance. Colonel Sears agreed.

With permission granted, Irzyk reconfigured the column. The armored infantry and other supporting units reversed course and picked up CCB's route. Rather than send the medium tanks all the way back from Gindorf, Irzyk ordered them to advance due north along a poor secondary road (being fully tracked, they were able to negotiate it). The shortcut placed them back at the head of CCA's column and behind the rear elements of CCB.

CCA completed its movement for the day near the town of Oberkail, a little over two miles northeast of Gindorf and just slightly more than a mile east of CCB's primary road. CCA's original route was turned over to the 5th Infantry Division, now drawing up on the division's right.

The Germans were at risk of having a substantial number of troops snared in Patton's trap. The commander of *LIII Corps*, *General* Kau von Rothkirch, ordered the *340th Volksgrenadier Division* to escape. They planned on setting up a blocking force at Oberstadtfeld to cover the division's retreat. Unbeknownst to Rothkirch, Oberstadtfeld had already fallen into American hands. The only recourse was to abandon their vehicles and heavy equipment and escape on foot. To do so, they had to make a treacherous pass through CCB's column.

The tally of losses suffered at the hands of the Fourth Armored on this day alone provided ample evidence of the strength of the trap. Three hundred Germans were killed, 200 wounded, and 1,375 captured. Five *Tiger* and two *Panther* tanks were destroyed. Thirteen guns ranging in caliber from 75mm to 150mm were eliminated. Two hundred miscellaneous vehicles and a hundred horse-drawn vehicles were wiped out.

CCB's Blitz to the Rhine Continues

A hard snow fell on the morning of March 6. The poor weather kept American fighter-bombers on the ground and restricted the tanks to the roads for fear of bogging down. Even though the terrain and conditions favored the defense, the Germans often seemed more interested in surrendering than putting up a fight. But there were exceptions.

CCB renewed their drive at 0715 with B/37 and B/10 spearheading the attack. In a familiar scene, the armored infantry mounted the tanks (even those near the front of the column). The infantrymen that couldn't find a place on a tank rode in the halftracks that followed. Leaving their assembly areas near the towns of Weidenbach, Salm, and Wallenborn, the column formed up and proceeded through Oberstadtfeld, which had been outposted by the 25th Cavalry Recon Squadron the night prior. From there, the column proceeded to Pützborn.

Near Pützborn, a German staff car carrying *General* Rothkirch approached what he thought to be an assembly of his troops. Instead, it was a cluster of German prisoners of war being secured by tankers of the 37th Tank Battalion. Unaware of the nature of the situation, Rothkirch's car drove directly in front of the Sherman tanks of B/37. On the scene was 1st Lt. Bernard Liese, commanding officer of the medium tank company. He said to the general, "Where do you think you're going?" It didn't take long for Rothkirch to size up the situation. He replied, "It looks like I'm going to the American rear."

Rothkirch was escorted away from the front and placed under guard at the Brasseur Hotel in Luxembourg. Lt. General Patton personally interviewed the German corps commander. He asked Rothkirch why the German army continued to fight in the face of such overwhelming firepower and matériel superiority. Rothkirch replied as one would expect a professional soldier to respond. As paraphrased by Patton, "They were under orders and would have to carry on as soldiers in spite of personal opinions and beliefs." Certainly, had the roles been reversed, Patton would have responded in kind.

CCB continued to surge ahead. The tankers and their accompanying infantry pushed through the German villages undaunted. As they approached each town, the lead elements often had to deal with roadblocks constructed of timbers … though with increasing frequency, the barriers were not well defended. Rather than focus on the roadblocks, the Germans seemed to put more effort into hitting the American column with artillery, rockets, and mortars while the vehicles were in between towns. Direct fire was also employed against more vulnerable units trailing farther behind the spearhead.

One such instance involved the 66th Armored Field Artillery Battalion. Having left their positions near Meisberg at 0800, their vehicles were well back in the column (as would be the norm for the mobile artillery). As the M7s churned down the road, three enemy tanks appeared on one of the flanks. In response, Captain Edwards (commanding Battery C) placed an M7 from Battery A into position and adjusted its fire on one of the enemy tanks. A smoke screen was laid down, which allowed the column to continue without being directly targeted.

The M7 crews of the 22nd Armored Field Artillery Battalion found themselves in a similar situation. At 1030, Battery A went into position to fire on four enemy tanks located on top of a hill overlooking the column. The fire, directed by the battalion S-3, chased the *Panzers* from their perch. At 1115, C Battery applied direct fire against two *Panthers* and managed to destroy them. The Germans had a modicum of success when they knocked out Captain Wilhelm's halftrack … but that was hardly worth the price of two valuable *Panthers*.

At 1230, three enemy tanks placed the column under fire close to Oberstadtfeld. M7s from B/22 went into position and placed direct and observed fire on the tanks, knocking out one of them. Unfortunately, C/22 lost two M7s to direct fire from the *Panzers*. At the same time, A/22 joined the fray. Captain Vogel adjusted their aim, and a smoke screen laid down by the M7s allowed the column to pass (the two remaining enemy tanks withdrew). Those weren't the only gun losses for the 22nd AFAB. Before the day was out, the 22nd lost two more M7s due to mechanical difficulties (one suffering from a burned-out motor, the other a bad transmission).

After Pützborn, the next town to fall to CCB was Neunkirchen, followed quickly by the much larger town of Daun. The Germans tried to stunt the American advance by applying rocket fire and armor. But the 3rd Platoon of C/704 brought the threat under control when they knocked out two *Panther* tanks and a self-propelled gun.

By end of day, CCB squeezed in the capture of three more towns. First came Darscheid and Shönbach, the latter being five miles east of Daun. Then at 1330, after pushing another mile to the east, they approached the village of Ulmen. Heavy small arms fire was encountered, but the town was taken with few American casualties. An unexpected boon was the capture of a large stockpile of German supplies (Ulmen was the headquarters for a German quartermaster unit).

It was near Ulmen that T/Sgt. Clifford C. Turner (10th Armored Infantry Battalion) took a peep patrol ahead of his column to reconnoiter the area. Several men in olive drab uniforms opened fire on the patrol, seriously wounding Turner. When he saw one of the enemy soldiers aiming his burp gun at the soldier riding alongside him in the peep, he threw himself across his comrade, saving his life but giving up his own. He was posthumously awarded the Distinguished Service Cross for his selfless act.

The head of the column pushed beyond Ulmen and cleared the terrain to the northwest. It was here that Brigadier General Dager stopped for want of daylight and roads in sound enough condition to withstand the weight of his armor. Sporadic artillery fire was received throughout the night.

CCA Closes the Gap

While CCB made its impressive drive, CCA attempted to break away to the east on its own route. The effort was short-lived when the destruction of the bridges at Oberkail stopped them in their tracks. After remaining at the town on the night of March 5–6, they fell in line once again behind CCB. They used a parallel route whenever possible, but the opportunities were limited. Throughout March 6, they attempted to close a 17-mile gap between the combat commands. As measured by the 53rd Armored Infantry Battalion, they covered approximately 16 miles, having started at Gindorf and finishing at Üdersdorf at 1950.

Though little resistance was met along the way, a bigger challenge arose for CCA when a truck belonging to the supporting engineer company collapsed the bridge at Niederstadtfeld. CCA's column was split in two.

Battery C of the 94th Armored Field Artillery Battalion had already crossed the bridge. Separated from the rest of the battalion, the lone battery of howitzers continued to move forward and joined the 53rd AIB near Üdersdorf. Shortly after they placed their guns in position, a volley of *Nebelwerfers* hit their area but caused no damage or casualties. Meanwhile, the rest of the 22nd set up their M7s near the damaged bridge.

Because CCA trailed CCB, Colonel Sears' men spent plenty of time sweeping up the Germans bypassed by Brigadier General Dager's column. The prisoners came from more than 70 rear echelon outfits, including the *40th Wood-Chopping Command* and the *226th Snow-Shovel Company*. For the first time, the Fourth encountered replacement training battalions. The speed of the American advance caught the green troops before they were ever assigned to a unit.

At times, the Germans were compelled to surrender through the power of persuasion. Psychological warfare agent Alexis Ureyvitch Sommaripa, using a loudspeaker mounted on

The specially equipped M5A1 tank of Alexis Sommaripa (the "Mad Russian"). He was tremendously effective at gaining the surrender of German troops (U.S. Army photograph).

an M5A1 Stuart light tank, developed a sterling reputation for bringing the enemy out with their hands held high. A typical negotiation went like this:

> *Achtung! Achtung! German soldiers, come on out. Civilians, stay in your homes and put white cloth from your windows to show there are no soldiers. The Fourth Armored Division surrounds your town and is prepared to destroy it if you do not surrender. Do not expect to fire your last shell and then surrender! Surrender now—or else!*

An Unsung Hero

Alexis Sommaripa's story is unique. Born in Russia in 1900, he immigrated to the United States in 1918. Already possessing a law degree, he enrolled at Harvard and earned a master's degree. Alexis then became a successful manager at DuPont, where he engaged in work that included research in the use of synthetic fabrics.

In the wake of Pearl Harbor, Sommaripa attempted to enlist in the U.S. Army. Though 41 years of age, he was accepted. After going through training, the Quartermaster Board put Alexis' knowledge of fabrics to work, assigning him the job of testing new materials being considered for the Army. He was later sent to England as a member of the Office of Strategic Services (OSS) as a civilian technician.

Sommaripa eventually worked his way into the Special Operations Branch of the OSS, where he could put his language skills to better use. On June 9, 1944—three days after D-Day—he landed at Omaha Beach and was assigned the task of gathering intelligence. Finding this work not as exciting as he would like, he successfully lobbied for the role of talking the enemy into surrender (something he had observed at the village of Carentan). Assigned to the 2nd Mobile Radio Broadcasting Company (MRBC), he soon perfected his methods for convincing the enemy to lay down their arms. Initially assigned to support the 82nd Airborne Division during their time in Normandy, he was later assigned to the 37th Tank Battalion.

In late August, Sommaripa's role was changed to that of a recruiter for the OSS Morale Section. Unhappy with his work there and yearning to be back near the front, he returned to his prior role and subsequently reconnected with the Fourth Armored Division as it completed its drive across France. Lt. Colonel Abrams bestowed upon Sommaripa the nickname the "Mad Russian." Abrams later said of him, "The progress of the Division was greatly enhanced by Alex's batting average of surrenders."

CCB's Final Dash to the Rhine

From CCB's starting position on March 7, the mighty Rhine River was just two dozen miles to the northeast. The combat command's primary objective for the day was the high

March 9, 1945. A "peep" (a.k.a. jeep) of the Fourth Armored Division, only five kilometers from Koblenz, Germany (U.S. Army photograph).

ground between Andernach and Koblenz, northeast of Ochtendung. The elevated terrain offered a commanding view of the river and could serve as an ideal staging area from which to conduct future operations. If luck was on the side of the Fourth Armored Division, they might find one of the bridges spanning the fabled river intact.

Poor weather continued to be a factor in operations. Another round of snow limited visibility, while the cold and damp made conditions miserable for all. Secondary roads were often impassible due to the mud. The motorized columns were often limited to the higher quality paved roads and highways. Fortunately, due to Hitler's commitment to building a superior infrastructure, the highways (*Autobahnen*) inside of Germany were considered by many to be the best in the world. The *Autobahnen* now served a purpose Hitler may have never imagined: carrying a foreign invader deep into the heart of the *Reich*.

CCB moved out of Ulmen at 0730. After an initial advance of four to five miles, they had to reverse course at Laubach when a road indicated on the map turned out not to exist. Under relentless fog and rain, they returned to Ulmen and took a detour to the southeast and the town of Büchel.

The column advanced through Büchel without opposition. The lead tanks of the 37th Tank Battalion turned to the northeast and moved toward Kaisersesch. On the outskirts of the town, the column halted and brought forward the "Mad Russian," who used his amplifier and speaker

Sherman tanks from the 37th Tank Battalion—an M4A3E2 "Jumbo" on the left, and an M4A3E8 "Easy eight" on the right (U.S. Army photograph, courtesy Darren Neely).

system to broadcast the demand for surrender. The defenders complied, and the Americans entered Kaisersesch unopposed. In addition to capturing 200 Germans, approximately 300 allied prisoners of war and slave laborers of many different nationalities were rescued.

CCB's advance continued another five miles toward Kehrig. During the approach, the light tanks of D/37 overran a 20mm flak gun regiment located in a valley to the south of town. The Stuart tanks then climbed to the high ground overlooking the approaches to Kehrig. As the lead tanks advanced, *Panzerfausts* and anti-tank guns erupted, destroying two of Lt. Donahue's tanks. Alexis Sommaripa's specially equipped M5A1 Stuart tank was brought to the front once again. This time, the demand for surrender met a different response: gunfire.

An artillery concentration helped accomplish what the ultimatum could not. Following a punishing barrage, A/37 and C/10 attacked and secured Kehrig without further American loss.

CCB forged onward. At 1430, five *ME-109s* were sighted overhead. One of the enemy planes made a pass at the head of the column, but a quick response from the .50 caliber machine guns drove it away. As the advance continued between Kehrig and the larger town of Polch (four miles to the northeast), the Americans received direct fire from 20mm anti-aircraft guns. Return fire from American tanks and artillery silenced the opposition. At 1448, the column entered Polch unopposed.

Ochtendung, a little more than five miles to the northeast, was the next town along the route. It was here that two enemy trains and a column of troops were caught trying to flee. 1st Lt. Edgar C. Smith, flying for the 66th Armored Field Artillery Battalion, provided overhead reconnaissance from his Piper Cub. After spotting the retreating German column on the road toward Koblenz, he made radio contact with Lt. Liese of B/37, who didn't have a line of sight to the Germans due to the intervening hills. Lt. Smith spurred on Liese's tanks.

A Piper Cub observation aircraft, grounded during poor weather. The Piper Cub pilots played a critical role conducting reconnaissance and spotting artillery fire (U.S. Army photograph).

"They're only 1,500 yards from you now, go faster." As the Shermans closed the gap, Smith radioed, "They're around the next curve, go get 'em!" The Shermans finally closed on the enemy column and attacked it from the rear.

The 75mm and 76mm main guns and machine guns ripped into the fleeing Germans as the tank drivers spurred their killing machines down the road. Once the Shermans reached the head of the column, the tankers reversed course and worked the column over again from front to back. The Americans unloaded on the target-rich environment. Hundreds of prisoners were taken. The town was cleared by 1730.

The majority of the combat command remained close to Ochtendung for the night. The total advance for CCB that day was a stunning 26 miles.

Ochtendung provided a vivid memory for Captain Lyons of the 10th Armored Infantry Battalion. It was a memory not of combat, but something that took his mind off the grind of warfare. At the center of town was a masonry church, within which remained a functioning organ. One of the men in his battalion played piano and wanted to give the organ a shot. The instrument only operated by way of a bellows, which required someone to operate the foot pedals that brought the instrument to life. Lyons did the pumping, while Howard (Lyons did not mention his last name) filled the church with music that poured into the streets of the town.

CCA Approaches the Rhine

By the arrival of dawn on March 7, the damaged bridge at Niederstadtfeld was repaired and the balance of CCA moved toward Üdersdorf. Battery C of the 94th Armored Field

The church in Ochtendung in 2019 (photograph by author).

Artillery Battalion had spent the night there separated from the rest of the battalion. Except for the lone salvo of fire from the *Nebelwerfers,* the night had been uneventful. But as the balance of the 94th came within sight of Üdersdorf, the *Nebelwerfers* struck again, hitting the road leading out of the town. Unlike the day prior, the rockets came at the steady pace of "sixty rounds at a clip every minute or two." Lt. Donald Guild, the battery executive for A/94, adjusted the fire of C/94 in an effort to hit the *Nebelwerfers.* Reinforcements came in the form of a Piper Cub observation plane piloted by Lt. Herbert L. Bothwell, who took the spotter reins from Lt. Guild.

A pitched duel took place between the M7s and the *Nebelwerfers.* The German rockets found their mark, damaging the battalion commander's peep and those of the battery commanders. Lt. Boas was among a group of officers and enlisted men standing together when a half-dozen shells fell close by and inflicted several casualties. Among the injured was Captain John Merriam, who received a serious leg wound and was evacuated. Also wounded were four men from C/94: Corporal Walter J. Zelinski, Pfc Elden F. Rorem, and Privates George Wood and Paul Emmett. After moving other vehicles to safety, Sgt. Francis O'Conner was wounded as he tried to help the fallen.

Battery C hammered away with their 105mm howitzers. Pfc James Powers took over the M7 of Corporal Zelinski and kept it firing with the rest of the battery. As the M7s maintained a fierce rebuttal, the pace of fire from the enemy rockets slowed and eventually stopped.

During the artillery engagement, the CCA column still trailing to the west ceased movement. When the duel ended, the advance resumed. The lead elements of the combat command subsequently departed Üdersdorf at 0900, and it wasn't long before the tail end of CCA closed the gap with the rest of the command.

Upon breaking out into the Rhine Plain, CCA and CCB finally separated, with CCA peeling off to the east in the direction of Bassenheim. Late in the day, the bulk of CCA drew into an assembly area between Polch and Ochtendung. The 53rd Armored Infantry Battalion and 94th Armored Field Artillery Battalion stopped for the night near Kerben (two miles northeast of Polch). The 8th Tank Battalion occupied the towns of Minkelfeld and Waldorferhof (the latter being three-quarters of a mile south of Ochtendung). CCA was finally in position directly on the right flank of CCB.

It was near Ochtendung that CCA saw its first substantive action of the day. Three Germans were captured outside of the town. Upon questioning, they revealed themselves as an advance billeting party for the rear echelon of the *7th Army.* Subsequently, the lead truck in an eight-vehicle column came face to face with the Sherman tank commanded by 1st Lt. Irvin J. Ferguson of A/8. Machine guns fired by the tank platoon commanded by Lt. Truman Basham, working from the flank, sent the column up in flames.

It was everyone's aspiration to grab an intact bridge over the Rhine. Little hope remained for achieving that when American aerial reconnaissance covering the front of the Third Army reported that no bridges remained. Presumably, the Germans had destroyed them all, even though thousands of their own troops remained west of the Rhine. Armed with that intelligence, the forward elements of the Fourth held in place behind the heights facing the river, safely out of sight and range of any German guns poised near the Rhine.

CCR finally joined the rest of the division east of the Kyll River. At 0715 on the morning of March 7, the combat command (which included the 51st Armored Infantry Battalion and 35th Tank Battalion) moved along the route taken by CCB. The column came to a temporary halt near Seinsfeld and resumed movement at 1400 with Ulmen as their destination.

Poor road conditions and heavy traffic caused the advance to move at a slow pace. Unable to make it as far as Ulmen, Colonel Blanchard (commander of CCR) ordered the column to move off-road and assume defensive positions near Darscheid. No enemy contact occurred during the night, which was certainly not a surprise given that CCB and CCA had previously moved through the area in force.

Fifty-eight hours. That's all the Fourth Armored Division required to advance from Bitburg to the Rhine. The spearheads covered 65 miles and rounded up somewhere between five to six thousand prisoners along the way. They inflicted 700 casualties and destroyed or

A captured German 88mm multi-purpose gun, being put to use by American forces (U.S. Army photograph).

captured 34 enemy tanks and 29 assault guns. The tally in all other categories included 444 motor vehicles, 417 heavy duty vehicles, 36 105mm guns, 125 20mm guns, 16 *Nebelwerfers,* seven 75mm guns, 17 *Volkswagens,* 42 halftracks, 39 88mm guns, 21 motorcycles, two armored cars, and two ammunition depots with 80,000 rounds of 88mm and 4,000 rounds of 20mm. Patton noted in his diary that the Fourth Armored "reached the Rhine north of Koblenz, making 65 miles in about 36 hours—a very remarkable performance."

The cost for the Fourth Armored, while not as severe as the battles of past months, was not inconsequential. Twenty-nine men were killed, 80 wounded, and two reported missing.

The German forces west of the Rhine were in complete disarray. Three German Corps (*LIII, LXVI,* and *LXVII*) were now at serious risk of being trapped on the wrong side of the river. A major contributor to their plight was Hitler, who remained intolerant of yielding ground.

What none of the advance elements of either CCA or CCB knew was that 15 miles to the northwest, the U.S. 9th Armored Division had seized a bridge, allowing American forces to breach the Rhine River. As they paused for the night of March 7/8, the officers and enlisted men of the Fourth Armored Division were also unaware that German columns were desperately trying to cross the Rhine River via the Kronprinz-Wilhelm railroad bridge at Urmitz.

9

Between the Rhine and Moselle

The Other Rhine Bridge

By the end of the day on March 7, the 9th Armored Division, spearheaded by Brigadier General William Hoge's Combat Command A, seized the Ludendorff Bridge at Remagen and established a slim bridgehead on the far side of the river. The crossing of the Rhine was a dramatic, unexpected development. The impact was felt across the entire Western Front.

The capture of the bridge brought about an immediate change in plan for General Bradley (it also led Hitler to relieve *Generalfeldmarschall* Gerd von Rundstedt of his command of German forces in the west). Upon conferring with Lt. General Hodges, the decision was made to push three infantry divisions across the Rhine as soon as possible to reinforce the gains of the 9th Armored. Eisenhower, once brought into the fold, agreed to further increase the reinforcement of the bridgehead above and beyond the initial four divisions.

While Eisenhower remained willing to allocate additional resources for the defense of the bridgehead, he would not endorse or allow an effort to exploit the capture of the bridge by breaking out deeper into Germany. His concern was singular: he would not detract from Montgomery's pending offensive to the north.

CCB's Attack on Kettig

On March 8, yet another change took place in the command structure of *Olympic* when Brigadier General Dager left to take over the 11th Armored Division. With his departure, Lt. Colonel Abrams was named the new commander of CCB. In the wake of Abrams' new assignment, Major Hunter was awarded command of the 37th Tank Battalion. Captain William Dwight became Hunter's executive officer and Captain John McMahon assumed the role of his S-3.

Abrams' first assignment was to attack the towns of Plaidt, Saffig, and Kettig (the latter being one mile shy of the Rhine). Both Plaidt and Saffig fell into American hands after meeting little opposition. A/37 and C/10 accounted for Plaidt, while B/37 and B/10 swept into Saffig. A/37 and C/10 then moved from Plaidt and outposted Saffig, allowing the B Team to continue the offensive toward Kettig. A/10 was dispatched to cut the road leading from Saffig to Ochtendung.

At 1300, B/37 and B/10 advanced toward Kettig. Leading the way were two platoons of armored infantry mounted on Sherman tanks. To reach Kettig, the tanks left the highway

9. Between the Rhine and Moselle

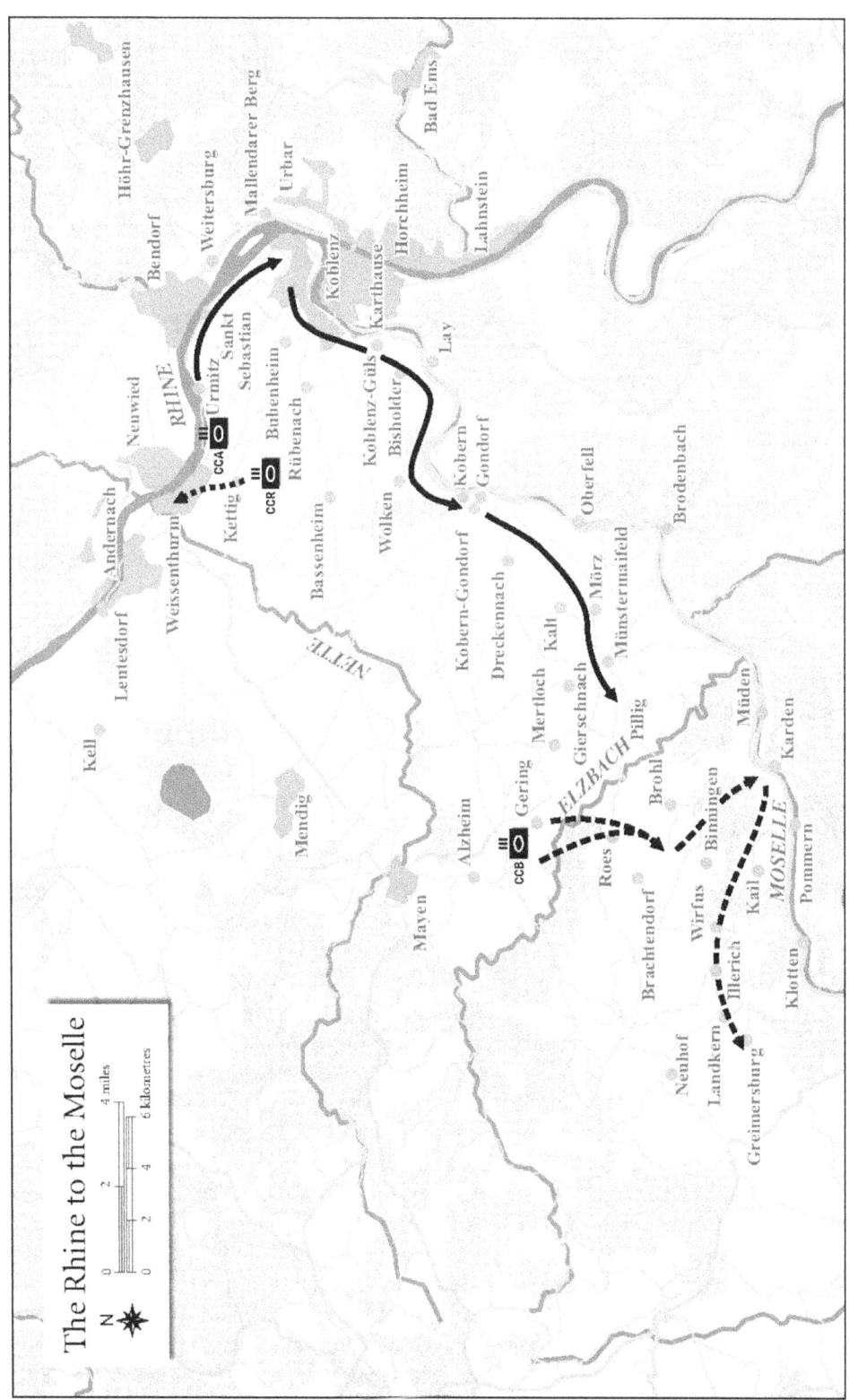

The Rhine to the Moselle (© Petho Cartography, 2020).

and traveled over open ground for more than a mile. One platoon of B/10, unable to follow off road, remained behind in their halftracks. As the B Team navigated across the field, the Germans hit them with small arms and artillery fire emanating from the woods on their left (200 prisoners were later extracted from the woods).

The attack on Kettig began in earnest at 1545. Direct fire from German anti-aircraft guns originated from both sides of the Rhine River. S/Sgt. Lumpkin H. Glenn and his squad, while conducting reconnaissance in front of the main attack, found the Germans on the verge of commencing a counterattack against B/10. He and his men held the enemy in check until their own ammunition ran low. S/Sgt. Glenn then personally covered their withdrawal.

The 66th Armored Field Artillery Battalion was called upon to support the B Team's attack. They delivered a very effective barrage, and the Americans cleaned out Kettig by 1700. Prisoners were taken from the *80th Battalion, 34th Regiment* of the *172nd Volksgrenadier Division*.

After the capture of Kettig, the Sherman tanks of B/37 advanced to the high ground between the town and the Rhine River. The top of the ridge overlooked the main highway that ran parallel with the river between Andernach (to the west) and Koblenz (to the east). The route was jammed with enemy vehicles, both motorized and horse-drawn, all moving toward Koblenz. Ferries were also in use, frantic in their effort to move men and equipment across the river.

It was a target-rich environment. The guns of CCB, including those of the 66th Armored Field Artillery, fired at the congested highway and ferry crossings throughout the evening and then again from 0300 to 0700 on March 9. The damage inflicted on the fleeing Germans was considerable, but the American tanks and armored infantry advanced no further. Their commanders were apparently content to hammer away at the enemy from a distance.

While CCB approached the Rhine, several German tanks, trapped on the wrong side of the Rhine, cut the combat command's column farther to the rear. The *Panzers* were in position to wreak havoc on the supply train's lighter vehicles. Lt. Andrew C. Pluff, commanding the 10th Armored Infantry Battalion's assault gun platoon, received a radio message regarding the threat and raced his guns to the scene. He launched a savage attack against the enemy tanks, forcing one of the crews to abandon their vehicle while the others tank commanders chose to retreat.

Not all action in CCB's zone happened in the direction of the Rhine River. On March 8, C Troop of the 25th Cavalry Reconnaissance Squadron remained on the move toward the west. With the support of the 3rd Platoon of C/704, they captured the town of Kruft and one other village, which secured the left flank of the combat command. In the process, another 300 German prisoners were taken along with some vehicles. The 1st Platoon of C/704 kept busy as well, taking 25 prisoners and destroying three vehicles.

After the Americans took hold of Kruft, two German vehicles loaded with weapons, ammunition, and other supplies—and apparently unaware of the American presence—came charging into the town. Corporal Albert Cardenas, 3rd Platoon C/704, fired his M3 "grease gun" to bring the vehicles to a halt. With the help of Private Donald Crise and Corporal Morris Rupprecht, they captured the entire lot of enemy soldiers, trucks, and cargo. Caught in the net along with the prisoners and equipment were 15 five-gallon jugs of 5 Star Cognac. By the end of the day, C/704 had assembled at Kruft and outposted the town. They were also assigned guard duty over a large group of prisoners.

CCA and the Bridge at Urmitz

CCA, operating to the east of CCB, moved out at 0800 on March 8. The first task was the capture of Bassenheim and Wolken. Both towns fell without opposition.

At 1400, D/8 and B/53 attacked Rübenach, a little less than three miles to the northeast of Bassenheim and the last major town along the primary highway leading to the Rhine River. The companies came under heavy shelling from depressed anti-aircraft guns firing from the vicinity of Metternich, a town off to their right. The German gunners enjoyed an open field of fire from there to Rübenach and the highway. Despite the heavy incoming fire, D/8 and B/53 captured Rübenach. The Germans did not give up easily, and the armored infantry and light tanks were still mopping up as late as 1800.

The action at Rübenach provided flank protection for the main body of CCA as it drove toward the twin towns of Mülheim-Kärlich. When the 53rd Armored Infantry Battalion (-B) and 8th Tank Battalion (-D) entered Mülheim-Kärlich, there was no opposition in Kärlich. At Mülheim, direct fire hit the column, taking out three tanks (one of which was recoverable) and inflicting some casualties among Irzyk's men. The Germans also struck back with artillery and mortars while snipers picked away at the Americans inside the town.

While CCA went about the business of clearing Mülheim, Lt. Colonel Irzyk took his M4A3E8 Sherman command tank to the high ground just south of the town. Upon reaching a promontory, he gazed upon the prize sought after by the Fourth Armored since the breakout from Normandy: the Rhine River. The coveted "shortest way home" was tantalizingly close.

From his perch two miles south of the river, Irzyk described the Rhine as "majestic and regal." He added that it was "not the brilliant blue that I had expected but more of a gray green." Between his vantage point and the river, much of the terrain was "flat, level, and

An M5A1 light tank, likely belonging to the 8th Tank Battalion. Unlike the 35th and 37th Tank Battalions, the 8th routinely used foliage for camouflage (U.S. Army photograph).

The railroad bridge at Urmitz as it appeared in 2019, viewed from the south bank of the Rhine River (photograph by author).

open as a tabletop." But much more alluring than the river and its natural environs was the man-made structure rising above it: an intact bridge.

The bridge itself was a railroad span carrying two tracks across the river. By its nature, it made vehicle crossings slow and labored. Irzyk surmised that planks had been laid across the tracks so that vehicles could navigate it more easily.

The web of roads leading to the bridge teemed with traffic as German soldiers worked their way toward the crossing. The bridge was crammed with men and equipment from one side to the other. Irzyk described the merging forces as "fighting desperately, even violently to squeeze in." A menagerie of motor vehicles, both armored and thin-skinned, crept slowly forward along with horse-drawn wagons and carts. Irzyk described the jostling for position "as though rams had locked horns and fought each other all the way to the bridge."

Lt. Colonel Irzyk salivated over the military situation:

> Never before in the war had there been anywhere near such a vast array of lucrative, tempting, mouthwatering targets. It put Coney Island to shame. Here was an intact bridge over the Rhine River with hundreds of men with hundreds of vehicles and wagons, helplessly bogged down, defenseless and out there for the taking.

Though daylight was fading, Irzyk seized the opportunity to strike. He alerted two of his tank companies to prepare for a charge over the open terrain with the objective of seizing the bridge. The veteran tankers quickly moved into position. Irzyk sent the tanks on their way with a simple command. "Go!"

The Shermans had barely started across the field when a tremendous volume of 88mm anti-tank fire came flying in their direction. The lethal high-velocity weapons were well positioned to defend the approach to the bridge. The veteran tank battalion commander described the German response as "the most concentrated 88mm fire that we had yet experienced." Coming from Irzyk, the statement speaks volumes about the intensity of the German reaction to his assault.

Irzyk immediately realized the foolhardiness of sending his tanks churning across two miles of open terrain in the face of such withering fire. He halted the charge and pulled the Shermans back to safety.

Irzyk settled for calling in his supporting artillery. A torrent of high-explosive shells rained down upon the massed enemy. Explosions and flames rocked the vicinity of the bridge and town throughout the night, producing a deadly man-made source of illumination.

In the meantime, Mülheim-Kärlich and Rübenach were outposted for the night with the tank and armored infantry companies tied in together. At 2000, Irzyk met with Colonel Sears, at which time the directive was given "to prepare to drive at first light to the Rhine River and to seize the bridge over it." At 2145, a meeting was conducted at the command post of the 53rd Armored Infantry Battalion to cast plans for establishing a bridgehead across the Rhine.

The Mission Changes

Back at higher headquarters, Eisenhower had second thoughts on how the Ludendorff Bridge might be utilized. Unwilling to strip Montgomery of the resources necessary for a successful northern thrust, he limited his investment in the Remagen bridgehead to no more than five divisions. Hodges protested to Bradley, but to no avail. No exploitation would be made until Ike granted permission.

A plan was submitted to Eisenhower that called for Patton to make a crossing of the Rhine farther south. The Third Army would then turn north to drive behind the Germans fronting the river. In combination with the divisions of the First Army poised to break out of the Remagen bridgehead, they would attack with a mighty right hook, ultimately connecting with Montgomery's forces. A bold plan, it never earned the favor of Eisenhower (he formally turned it down on March 13). In addition to rejecting the plan, Ike reinforced that Hodges' First Army was not to advance more than 10 miles beyond the Rhine. Neither Patton nor Hodges hid their disgust with the decision.

Events at Remagen influenced the balance of the 12th Army Group. Given Eisenhower's vacillation about the exploitation of the First Army's success, another crossing of the Rhine was out of the question. And so, it was on March 9 that the mission for the Fourth Armored changed in a significant way. Indeed, the mission of the entire Third Army was modified, as General Bradley approved a turn to the south for Patton's forces. The new plan was one that Patton himself had previously proposed, as he was eager to devour the German forces still holding valued ground in the Saar-Palatinate region.

At 0930, the unit commanders held a meeting at the Fourth Armored Division's headquarters. There they discovered that the division's mission had changed rather dramatically. The Fourth Armored would continue to search for a bridge, but it would not be one crossing the Rhine. The Moselle River was the new target.

More specifically, orders called for CCA to clear the remaining enemy from the west bank of the Rhine River. CCR would relieve CCB, and then Lt. Colonel Abrams' new command would spin south some 20 miles toward the twin towns of Treis-Karden (Treis laying astride the south bank of the Moselle, and Karden, the smaller of the two towns, nestled on the north shore of the river). CCB's mission was to seize a bridge across the Moselle River. Should Abrams' combat command not find a bridge intact at Treis-Karden, they would reconnoiter along the Moselle for other crossing sites.

The move for the combat units of CCB was not quite that distant. That morning, the 10th Armored Infantry and 37th Tank Battalion were released from CCB and assigned to CCR. CCB was in turn assigned the 35th Tank Battalion and 51st Armored Infantry Battalion. What sounded like a complex movement of units was more of an administrative realignment, with the combat command headquarters making the farthest move.

The 11th Infantry Regiment, having been attached to the Fourth Armored the day prior, was ordered to guard the areas farther to the south and west of the Fourth's current positions. This move protected the right flank of the supply routes serving *Olympic*.

CCA's Assault on the Urmitz Bridge

At 0500 on March 9, Lt. Colonel Irzyk issued an order to stand fast and not advance on the bridge. However, no mention was yet made to him of the plan to advance toward the Moselle. The fact that CCA held in place did not preclude them from inflicting damage upon the enemy.

Between 0600 and 0830, the Americans used their artillery to pound the approaches to

The church from which Lt. Colonel Irzyk observed the Rhine River bridge at Urmitz on the morning of March 9, 1945 (photograph by author, 2019).

the bridge and the suspected locations of the 88s that had thwarted the 8th Tank Battalion's drive to the bridge the evening prior. Irzyk ascended to the steeple of a prominent church ... the centerpiece of the town ... that afforded a view of the bridge and its approaches. Despite the barrage by the American howitzers, the roads and the bridge itself remained as jammed as they had been the day before.

Apparently, confusion existed within the higher levels of American command. Word of the new mission for TUSA had not yet flowed to all elements of the Fourth Armored Division, as evidenced by Colonel Sears' subsequent order for Irzyk to mount another drive for the bridge.

Irzyk returned to his command tank to join his battalion in the assault. With infantry now mounted on the tanks and artillery shells continuing to descend on the German caravans, Irzyk's task force descended toward the bridge. He fully expected the shrill, screeching sound of the 88s to come at any moment. The tanks picked up speed, steadfastly churning down the slope. Much to their surprise, the dreaded 88s were silent. Perhaps the American artillery had been effective.

When the tanks reached the halfway point to the bridge, Irzyk's hopes were dashed. A series of violent explosions rang out. Before his eyes, the bridge's superstructure was torn to pieces. An arch of debris ascended above the river. The lighter bridge fragments and dust rose higher as the heavier elements succumbed to gravity and plunged into the river. To the horror of the tankers and infantrymen watching the scene unfold, the debris wasn't confined to the structure of the bridge. Lifted into the sky in torn, bloody, and mangled pieces were German soldiers, vehicles, horses, tanks ... every bit of material that was crammed onto a bridge measuring over five football fields in length. When the debris and smoke settled, some strands of metal were left hanging on as grotesquely contorted appendages to the still intact piers and abutments.

No matter the cost, the Germans made sure that a second Remagen would not occur.

After the demolition, German troops and matériel were trapped on the south bank of the Rhine. The highway tracing the river became a target-rich environment and the artillery battalions showered the highway with a rain of explosives. Irzyk's tanks, which halted at the sound and sight of the bridge's destruction, advanced the rest of the way toward the vestiges of the bridge and began firing on the stranded vehicles. The Germans had no escape route.

Bruce Donald Fenchel, a tank driver in the 8th Tank Battalion, described the scene:

> Fleeing German soldiers tried to cross the Rhine ... only to be picked off with machine guns and rifles. Their makeshift rafts were blown out of the water by tank guns. Broken planks and riddled rowboats with dead men at the oars drifted downstream.

When little else remained to be accomplished at the river's edge, Irzyk pulled his battalion back to Mülheim. Come morning, he learned that crossing the Rhine was no longer the goal. Instead, he would be revisiting a familiar water obstacle: the Moselle.

CCA Sweeps the Moselle

Who among the members of the Fourth Armored Division would have imagined yet another encounter with the Moselle River? Six months had passed since the waterway factored so prominently in the division's history. Now, they chomped at the bit once more to secure a crossing. To their surprise, they would not attack east along a route that would seem to be the shortest way home. Instead, they would strike south, deep into the rear of the German *7th Army.*

At 0630 on March 10, Colonel Sears arrived at the command post of the 8th Tank Battalion and issued new orders to Lt. Colonel Irzyk. CCA would work its way south to where the Rhine and Moselle Rivers meet, and then advance southwest down the line of the Moselle in search of a bridge. Unlike so many recent days, March 10 was sunbaked and beautiful. It was a welcome change.

The armored infantry and tanks were quick to get on the road. Lt. Colonel Irzyk took his place with the C Team (C/8 and C/53, plus his assault gun platoon). Starting from a point along the Rhine just east of Urmitz, patrols from C/8 and C/53 moved expeditiously through the towns of Kaltenengers, Sankt Sebastian, Kesselheim, and Lützel (where the Moselle meets the Rhine). Due to the main road being littered with the debris of war, the column was often forced to leave the pavement (the ground conditions were now good enough to allow it without appreciably slowing down the tanks and halftracks). Occasional bursts of 20mm fire came from across the river, but it was of no consequence. German soldiers stranded on the American side of the Rhine surrendered throughout the sweep of the area.

The C Team turned southwest and followed the line of the Moselle. The hope was that among the three known bridges leading over the river into Koblenz, at least one might be found intact. But the patrols soon confirmed that all the bridges had been destroyed.

The task force returned to Mülheim at 1200. They didn't remain there long, for at 1400, orders were received to conduct a sweep farther down the line of the Moselle. Irzyk turned once again to the C Team, which conducted a reconnaissance extending several miles along the river. They captured the towns of Güls and Winningen in the process, having met only light opposition at both towns. The A Team also went to work, leapfrogging ahead of the C Team to clear the towns of Kobern and Gondorf.

CCA also redeployed the 53rd Armored Infantry Battalion, ordering it to move closer to the Rhine near Rübenach. During the day, a German prisoner reported that a bridge was intact near the town of Neuendorf, which rests just above the confluence of the Rhine and Moselle Rivers. The 53rd AIB dispatched a patrol which returned with the news that no such bridge existed. The 53rd AIB remained in the area through March 13, primarily snagging German stragglers trying to make their way east.

On the left flank of CCA, the 704th Tank Destroyer Battalion (-B) patrolled a two-and-a-half-mile section of the Rhine River between Kettig, Kärlich, and Mülheim, while maintaining contact with CCR to its left. Working farther out on the opposite (right) flank of CCA, the 25th Cavalry Reconnaissance Squadron cleared the towns of Lehmen, Moselsuersch, Münstermaifeld, and Wierschem, which filled in the gap between CCA and CCB.

No Unit is Immune

On March 10, the 53rd Armored Infantry Battalion welcomed back (in a manner of speaking) 28-year-old Private Silvio F. Podesta. When he returned, it was not of his own volition. Originally a member of the 22nd Armored Field Artillery Battalion, he was reassigned as an infantryman prior to the Battle of the Bulge (not an uncommon fate at a time when units were dealing with a severe shortage of infantry replacements). Not happy with his new role, he went absent without leave (AWOL) before reporting to the 53rd AIB. Evidence presented at his court-martial told the story:

> He was at the Service Battery of the Field Artillery and he liked it and (said) he would not soldier in the infantry and (he said) that he went AWOL. He never reported to the company. He came up with the trains vehicle and stopped there at the Service Company. He got off the vehicle and was shown where to report and when the vehicle left he departed. He went to Nancy, France.

Podesta was picked up by the military police in Nancy and instructed to report to the 53rd's Service Company. Once he arrived by vehicle back at the front, he repeated the entire act. This time, he managed to remain in Nancy until February 18. At that point, opting for a more glamorous location, he made his way to Paris. There he was later apprehended and returned to the 53rd Armored Infantry Battalion on March 10.

Podesta's court-martial took place on April 21 in Meerane, Germany. Found guilty, his sentence was a dishonorable discharge, total forfeitures, and confinement at hard labor for life. His confinement was scheduled for the United States Penitentiary at Lewisburg, Pennsylvania.

Compared to other American divisions in the ETO, a thorough inspection of the records for the Board of Review of the Branch Office of the Judge Advocate General revealed only two other cases of desertion within the Fourth Armored Division that came before the Board for review (and the judgment in one of those cases, involving two members of B Company, 8th Tank Battalion, was vacated upon review). The total number of Fourth Armored Division cases reviewed by the JAG was remarkably low: only nine individuals in total, inclusive of the two vacated judgments. Many other divisions, by contrast, had dozens of convictions reviewed.

Approximately 2000 cases were considered by the members of the ETO Board of Review, whose role was to take a second look at the most serious convictions in the theater. For perspective, there were over 1.7 million courts-martial conducted across all theaters during the war.

A reading of the cases heard by the Board of Review reveals the challenge of maintaining law and order among the hundreds of thousands of soldiers in the ETO. Whether on the front line or in rear echelon units, the cases range from hideous and senseless murders to devastating rapes, theft of government and civilian property both large and small in magnitude, black market activity, drunkenness on duty, assault on or disrespecting an officer, being absent without leave, and desertion. Many of the cases are as gritty and raw as any found in the toughest areas of civilian life. The fact that the number of incidents involving men of the Fourth Armored is so low on a comparative basis is noteworthy.

Grasping at Straws

As the Allies pushed deeper into Germany and the *Wehrmacht* was rendered less capable of stopping the advance, the Hitler Youth operating near the Moselle were called upon to engage in sabotage. The underlying hope was that a strong effort behind the American lines would force the Third Army to divert resources from their spearheads. The officers in charge of the training were advised to "plant in the young minds a heroic romantic psychosis." The captured documents describing the techniques to be employed included the admonishment:

THE ENEMY WANTS TO DESTROY YOU AND YOUR FAMILY, THEREFORE HARM HIM WHEREVER YOU CAN.

Among the tactics: Placing sugar in gas tanks, erecting steel street obstacles during darkness to cause accidents and flatten tires, stretching wires across roads (especially dangerous for motorcyclists and peep drivers), putting nails on boards in the road, jamming railroad switches with stones in hopes of causing train derailments, using needles to perforate the diaphragm on telephones, cutting telephone wires, and stealing enemy equipment.

Their training prepared them for little more than juvenile vandalism. While annoying, it was hardly sabotage on a scale that would materially change the course of events. But the captured document (issued on March 1) further illustrates how desperate the Germans had become.

The Hard Road to Karden

The new units of CCB, having been in reserve, were starting from assembly areas nearly 17 miles west-southwest of the other Fourth Armored Division elements nestled against the line of the Rhine River. As was the norm for the operation of a combat command, the two maneuver battalions were cross-reinforced (a typical scheme being a company of tanks reinforcing the armored infantry battalion, and conversely, a company of armored infantry reinforcing the tank battalion).

On the morning of March 9, the 51st Armored Infantry Battalion departed from Kehrig, some eight miles north-northwest of Treis, while the 35th Tank Battalion departed from an assembly area east of Kehrig, near the town of Einig. As the battalions advanced south along their routes, they meshed the teams.

The primary artillery support for the 35th Tank Battalion and 51st Armored Infantry was provided by the 66th Armored Field Artillery Battalion, which took up firing positions near the town of Binningen, 2.5 miles north of the Moselle River. Lt. Mitchell was the forward observer (FO) working with C/35, Lt. Livingston the FO with A/51, Lt. Sanders with C/51, and Lt. Doran with C Troop of the 25th Cavalry Recon Squadron. Captain Wendell served as the liaison officer between the 66th Armored Field Artillery Battalion and the 35th Tank Battalion. Additional firepower was available from the 276th Field Artillery Battalion, which reinforced the 66th (the 66th would remain in position near Binningen until March 11, from whence they supported CCB as they cleared the area on the north bank of the Moselle).

Once the 35th Tank Battalion and 51st Armored Infantry Battalion came together, the team of C/35 and C/51 combined to lead the drive south. The armored infantry rode on the decks of the Sherman tanks rather than in their halftracks. Lt. Bryan's platoon of armored infantry rode on the lead tank platoon, and on the lead tank itself was the squad of Sergeant Calvert (as he later pointed out, "not a great position").

All proceeded smoothly as the C Team headed south down the road connecting the towns of Brohl and Karden. The first sign of trouble occurred where the winding road began its descent into the valley of the Moselle. The column was initially flanked on the left by a steep wooded slope, but this changed after a short distance as the road carved its way into the side of the valley wall on their right. From that point all the way to the town, the steep, rock-strewn forested side of the valley hemmed in the right side of the road, while the ground dropped precipitously into the woods on their left.

It was at the initial point in the descent that the lead tank ran over a mine and erupted in flames. Smoke and dust blinded the infantrymen as the tank lurched to the side and ran

The start of the descent toward Karden, where C/51 and C/35 first made contact with the Germans defending the approach to the town (photograph in 2019 by the author).

into a ditch. Small arms fire raked the column. Lt. Bryan and four other men were wounded, and Mickey Barbieri was killed by a sniper. The rest of the infantrymen in the column dismounted and assumed defensive positions along the narrow sides of the road. The enemy positions had not yet been spotted, and the American casualties continued to mount as German small arms and artillery fire pounded the column.

The company commander of C/51, Lt. Mulregan, came forward to Sgt. Calvert's position and asked, "Who's the squad leader here?" After Calvert identified himself as the commander, the lieutenant said, "Sergeant, crawl up to that gully and drop some hand grenades into it." Calvert moved some 50 yards toward the bend in the road without drawing fire. He reached the point where the ground dropped to the left and tossed the grenades into the abyss below the road, then crawled back to his lines.

More men fell, wounded or killed. Muschmann, the machine gun squad leader, had his foot run over by a tank and was out of the fight. Also wounded was Sgt. Alphonese, leader of the 2nd Squad. John Pruett was killed while trying to set up a machine gun position.

Calvert's squad was reduced to six men. When Browning Automatic Rifle (BAR) gunner Gordon Miner went down wounded, Calvert traded his M1 rifle for the more potent weapon. Two Germans suddenly jumped up from a hiding place in some nearby bushes and started running down the road. Calvert took aim, but the BAR jammed, allowing them to get away.

The column was at a dead stop. As the clock ticked past 1600, Calvert went to the rear to see if there were any orders. He saw that the artillery observer had been killed and learned that the commander of his own C Company was seriously wounded and taken back for aid. Lt. Laughlin, his old company commander, was coming up from A Company to take over command of the stalled and stricken C Company. At the same time, engineers got to work clearing out the mines that had brought the column to a halt.

Now under orders to get the attack moving, the platoon sergeant ordered Calvert to take what was left of the 1st and 2nd Squads and move down the road. Calvert approached the commander of the tank now at the head of the column and told him that he would have his infantrymen follow the tanks. The tank commander made it clear that his tanks weren't going anywhere unless the infantry led the way. With German artillery still falling around them, Calvert got his men started down the road, leading his under-strength squad on the left side of the road while Charles Slaninka volunteered to take the 2nd Squad down the right.

The infantry had not advanced far when Calvert saw a line of machine gun bullets hitting the road in front of him, carving a path straight in his direction. There was nothing he could do in that split second other than harbor the thought of being struck square in the chest. A bullet struck the back of his leg, spinning him about. Another round cut through his boot. He rolled over to the side of the road, thankful and overjoyed to be alive. As he lay on the roadside watching the infantry and tanks advance, Lt. Laughlin, whom he held such great respect for, knelt beside him and asked if he was okay. Calvert later said, "I could not have been more honored if General Eisenhower had asked how I was doing."

The American infantry kept moving and began methodically cleaning out the enemy foxholes along the road. At the same time, the tanks, which were confined to the road the entire way to the town, used their machine guns to support the infantry as best they could.

The road to Karden as it carves into the valley wall leading to the Moselle River (photograph in 2019 by the author).

The terrain made it nearly impossible for the infantry to maneuver and outflank the enemy dug in among the trees and rocks, but they pushed on with determination. Within 20 minutes, the remaining enemy were killed or captured.

Meanwhile, Sergeant Calvert lay back along the road, his wound treated with sulfa powder by a passing platoon sergeant. Once the attacking forces moved on, he was alone, save for the lifeless bodies strewn near the road.

Some unaccompanied German prisoners walked by, headed to the American rear. Calvert eyed them with suspicion as they passed. One of his squad members, slightly wounded, came walking back as well. Eight of the 11 men of his squad were casualties in the battle.

Calvert crawled a short distance and armed himself with an abandoned carbine, lest any uncooperative Germans appear. After some time had passed and no medics came within sight, he grabbed a stick and used it for support as he hobbled toward the rear. He was finally transported to an aid station, where he found himself amidst many from his company.

The lead tanks reached the outskirts of Karden. A German 50mm anti-tank gun covered a roadblock, imposing a brief delay. Though this initial obstacle was mopped up quickly, the job of pushing through the town to the river turned out to be a more difficult affair.

The task of clearing out the houses within Karden was difficult in part due to the very narrow streets. The Germans took full advantage of the urban landscape by employing snipers and *Panzerfausts*. The nature of the German opposition was described by the 66th Armored Field Artillery Battalion as "the first organized resistance which we had met since crossing the Kyll River. Resistance consisted of arty and mortar fire, mines, machine guns, and small arms fire, and a few tanks."

The A Team (A/35 and A/51) was committed to the battle and advanced through the C Team. Tanks and infantrymen worked their way through Karden, hoping to seize the bridge before it was blown. Just as the lead tank reached the near end of the bridge, the Germans set off explosives. Denied a crossing, the A and C Teams concentrated their effort on clearing out the town.

Unable to advance on Treis, the 51st Armored Infantry moved back to the high ground from whence the initial attack was launched. By 2030, they settled into position there. During the night, the battalion sent patrols back into Karden to see if the Germans had returned.

The day's fighting took a heavy toll on the 51st AIB: two of the armored infantry companies suffered a combined 70 casualties.

The 66th Armored Field Artillery Battalion, firing their 105m howitzers from positions just shy of three miles to the rear, spent the night hitting targets across the river. The 35th Tank Battalion joined the 66th near Binningen.

The following morning (March 10), rather than search for another crossing site, the 51st Armored Infantry and 35th Tank Battalion advanced west and secured the towns of Wirfus, Illerich, Landkern, and Greimersburg. The four towns were stretched out in a line from east to west, all within less than three miles of the Moselle. The goal was to clear out any remaining enemy pockets that might threaten the Fourth Armored Division from the south. It turned out to be a relatively easy task, as none of the towns were occupied by German troops.

It was a different story back at Karden. Elements of the 51st Armored Infantry conducted a reconnaissance to investigate a warehouse where a large store of supplies were kept by the Germans. As the Americans attempted to make off with a stash of wine, preserves, and other edibles, German mortar fire, originating from across the river, tried to interfere with their mission. It did not deter them from escaping with a substantial quantity of goods. It was a booty that served as a nice supplement to their own rations.

A Brief Rest

When the 11th Infantry Regiment relieved CCB from their positions along the line of the Moselle, it allowed Lt. Colonel Abrams to move his units into an assembly area near Gamlen. The 53rd Armored Infantry Battalion assumed billets at Roes while the 35th Tank Battalion settled in at Kaifenheim.

Still assigned to CCB, the tank destroyers of C/704 moved to billets at Brachtendorf. Like the other units of CCB, they were about to enjoy a brief respite from the battlefield. The mess kitchen was set up, which the men took to be an indicator that they might be staying put for some time. As noted in the company journal, "Most of us celebrated our first night in over two weeks away from rugged combat by sampling a bit of that Beaucoup Cognac from the supply so generously contributed by the Jerries we captured at Kruft." The company took advantage of the lull to send all but three of the tank destroyers to ordnance. They subsequently learned they would receive new M18s, the most distinguishable feature of which was the addition of a muzzle break on the main 76mm gun.

C/704 didn't remain in place for long. After the company had breakfast in Brachtendorf, the M18s departed town. The skies cleared and the temperature was much more comfortable for the tank destroyer crews in their open-top turrets as they cruised to their final stop at Gillenbeuren. After their arrival, the tankers "disposed the Kraut families" and moved into the comfort of their homes. The mess truck arrived and served up a hot supper for the evening. The following day, the company sent the tank destroyer drivers and assistant drivers to Metz, well over a hundred winding miles to the rear, where their new tank destroyers were waiting for them (they arrived back at the company command post on March 15).

CCR Covers the Left Flank

When the men of the 10th Armored Infantry Battalion awoke at 0615 on March 9, they were still assigned to CCB. The day began with a hot breakfast served to all companies. Still working with the 37th Tank Battalion, C/37 and A/10 were located at Kettig and the team of A/37 and C/10 at Plaidt.

At 1020, the two battalions were officially assigned to CCR. Due to CCB's movement toward the Moselle River, CCR was now positioned on the division's left flank.

The 10th AIB had little to report for most of the day, with the only enemy activity noted being a harmless fly-over of four *Messerschmitt Bf 109* fighters. The inactivity came to an end at 1800 when B/10, supported by tanks from the 37th, attacked Weißenthurm, a town on the south bank of the Rhine three miles west of Urmitz. It turned out to be an easy affair against Germans armed only with light small arms.

On March 10, CCR worked the area along the Rhine River west of Urmitz. C Company of the 37th Tank Battalion, teamed with the 10th Armored Infantry Battalion, severed the Andernach-Koblenz highway.

An M4A3E2 "Jumbo" Sherman advances through the streets of Koblenz (U.S. Army photograph, courtesy Darren Neely).

A tougher task awaited them at Weißenthurm. Apparently, a substantial enemy force moved back into the town during the night, and the task force was sent back to clean out the town for the second time. On the second go-round, CCR rang up a hefty tally of German losses: 15 anti-aircraft guns, 16 anti-tank guns, 16 artillery pieces, five rocket guns, six heavy mortars, eight halftracks, one tractor, 70 trucks, nine motorcycles, eight peeps, 11 cars, 296 wagons, 42 kitchen wagons, two *Panzerfausts*, four 88's, 875 rifles, 80 machine guns, and 55 machine pistols. The American tankers killed 15 Germans and took 475 prisoners.

Even with the Rhine River at their back and little hope for survival, not every German was willing to surrender. Such was the case when enemy armor threatened the 10th Armored Infantry Battalion's main supply route. 1st Lt. Brooks McElwrath, the 10th AIB's transportation officer, noticed that some of the tanks of the 37th were having difficulty observing the enemy tanks and self-propelled guns. He worked his way to a superior vantage point where he could see the enemy. He then directed the fire of the Shermans, which in turn knocked out some of the German tanks and forced the others to withdraw. McElwrath carried out his mission while under direct enemy fire, and he lost his life in the process.

On March 11, the 10th Armored Infantry Battalion's Assault Gun Platoon was on point of an American column moving out of Kaisersesch. Stubborn German stragglers continued to filter through the area, and when a *Tiger* opened fire on the column from the flank, Sgt.

Carl H. McGee led his section off road and returned fire with his 105mm gun. Sergeant Dominic F. Larrocco took another section of the assault guns off road as well and took aim on the *Tiger* with high-explosive rounds. When too many trees in the line of fire prevented him from hitting the *Tiger* directly, he had his gunner, T/4 Alfonso D. Casanova, switch to white phosphorous shells to screen the flank of the column. The volume and accuracy of his fire enabled the column to continue.

Late in the day on March 12, it was determined that *Olympic* would move to an area farther to the west near Duan. At 1730, an overlay for a new division assembly area was distributed. There were reports that Germans might still be in the proximity, so a task force commanded by Captain McMahon (the 37th Tank Battalion's S-3) was assigned the job of mopping up the area before the division moved in. His command consisted of B/37, C/10, the 37th Tank Battalion's assault gun platoon, two platoons of tank destroyers, and a squad of engineers.

As March 12 came to an end, the areas west of the Rhine and north of the Moselle had been sufficiently cleared of the enemy. The next phase of the operation would lead to one of the most dazzling drives in the history of the Fourth Armored Division.

10

From the Moselle to the Rhine

The Plan to Destroy the German Seventh Army

On March 13, the HQ of 12th Army Group issued Letter of Instruction 17:

> *The Third Army was to defend the line of the Rhine River in zone and attack in conjunction with the Seventh Army in order to protect the Seventh Army's flank and rear.*

The directive was of greater consequence than its brevity might lead one to believe. The zone of attack and advance for the Third Army would cut deep into the rear of the German *7th Army*, which predominately faced west in opposition to the U.S. Seventh Army. Patton's attack, spearheaded by the Fourth Armored, had the potential of closing a catastrophic trap that could snare tens of thousands of Germans.

Bradley had previously discussed the plan with Eisenhower. On March 13, he flew to Luxembourg to disclose it to Patton in person. When Bradley arrived at Patton's headquarters, he found the Third Army commander in the middle of having his hair trimmed. Patton called for another barber so that Bradley could join him. As the barbers worked, the two generals discussed the plan that Bradley had sold to Ike. While turning away from the Rhine was a disappointment to him, Patton embraced the opportunity to execute a swift and violent maneuver across the Moselle that could lead to the destruction of a large German force. Employing his trademark salty language, Patton summed up his sentiment for Bradley's benefit: "At any rate, it'll save us from sitting on our asses, while SHAEF makes up its mind as to whether we're going to cross the Rhine."

Manton Eddy's XII Corps, stacked with five (and soon to be six) divisions inclusive of the Fourth Armored, would play the most critical role in Patton's offensive. By this time, most of the commanders shared deep experience as a team, and their effectiveness would soon be on full display.

Olympic moved to a new assembly area. The units of CCB relocated from positions south of Polch to an area west of Cochem. The 51st Armored Infantry Battalion moved near Wollmerath, while the 35th Tank Battalion moved to Alflen. The combat command's 66th Armored Field Artillery Battalion moved from Binningen to Schmitt.

Farther north, the 87th Infantry Division took over the positions held by CCA's 8th Tank Battalion and 53rd Armored Infantry Battalion. Both battalions moved into new areas where they caught up on vehicle and equipment maintenance in preparation for the offensive action soon to follow.

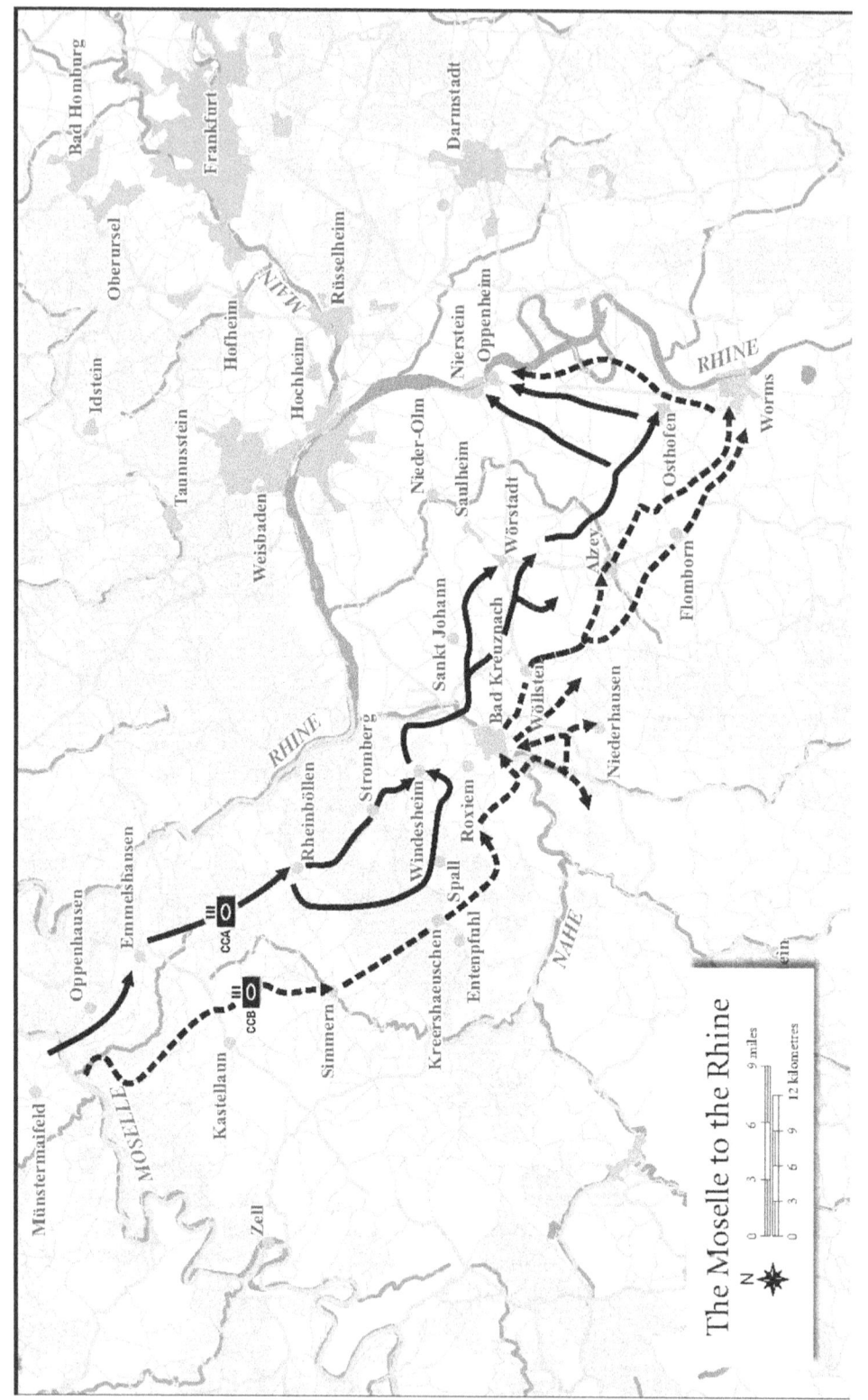

The Moselle to the Rhine (© Petho Cartography, 2020).

An up-armored M4A3E8 Sherman (U.S. Army photograph, courtesy E. Verholen).

Forging the Moselle Bridgehead

Before dawn on March 14, troops from the 90th and 5th Infantry Divisions crossed the Moselle River. Opposition at the 5th ID's crossing site was light, and by 1830 the doughs captured the town of Lutz, almost two miles beyond the river. Elements of the 2nd Infantry Regiment moved south and attacked Treis. There, they faced heavy resistance from elements of the *159th Volksgrenadier Division*. As the 5th ID expanded its hold on the south bank of the Moselle, the engineers began construction of a pontoon bridge near Müden.

The 90th Infantry Division crossed the Moselle near the town of Brodenbach, a little over five miles from the 2nd Infantry's site at Müden. The *159th Volksgrenadier Division* had responsibility for this area as well, along with elements of the skilled *6th SS Mountain Division Nord* just slightly to the east. The crossing met little resistance, and the American infantry moved with relative ease outside of the villages, sweeping across the terrain and occupying high ground outside of the populated areas. The engineers quickly went to work installing a bridge at Hatzenport while the leading elements of the 90th ID expanded their bridgehead to a depth of six miles.

There was little the Germans could do to stop the Americans as they pushed beyond the Moselle. In fact, the 5th Infantry Division commander, Major General Stafford LeRoy Irwin, was eager to motorize one of his regiments so that he could push forward on his own toward the XII Corps' objective of the Nahe River. The plan called for the Fourth Armored Division to play that role, but Irwin believed he could get the job done sooner if given the chance. Eddy, however, stayed with the original plan of relying on the Fourth Armored to stage the breakout.

While the infantry divisions carved out the bridgeheads, the Fourth Armored Division's day began just like the handful that had preceded it. At C/704's company command post at Gillenbeuren, it was described as a second consecutive pleasant day. The tankers read coverage of the Fourth Armored Division's prior exploits in *Stars and Stripes* and enjoyed the luxury of another day of hot meals served by the kitchen crew. The promise of a real shower awaited them. But upon arriving back at their billets, they received word that they would soon be on the move. At 1600, the company of tank destroyers traveled a dozen miles and bivouacked for the night, not knowing that more fabled stories about the division were yet to be written.

The combat commands were reconfigured for the new offensive. The 51st Armored Infantry Battalion and 35th Tank Battalion moved to CCR. The 10th Armored Infantry Battalion and 37th Tank Battalion were both reassigned from CCR to CCB. The 24th Armored Engineer Battalion's A Company, the 22nd and 66th Armored Field Artillery Battalions, and B Company of the 46th Medical Battalion also joined CCB. The 53rd Armored Infantry Battalion, 8th Tank Battalion, and 94th Armored Field Artillery Battalion remained assigned to CCA.

The assignment of the 37th Tank Battalion was welcome news for CCB's new commander. Lt. Colonel Abrams was certainly delighted to have his old unit back underneath his command umbrella. Among the three armored infantry battalions, there was none he respected more than Lt. Colonel Cohen's 10th Armored Infantry. He and Cohen had developed a deep mutual respect both as warriors and friends; it was a friendship that would last well beyond the war. Even though Abrams was one level of command more distant from the front line, no one would know it. He didn't embrace the trappings of the typical leader of a combat command and preferred to spend his time forward among his front-line commanders. Working side-by-side with Cohen was exactly where he wanted to be.

Across the Moselle.... Again

Starting at 1300 hours on March 15, *Olympic* passed through the Moselle River bridgeheads of the 5th and 90th Infantry Divisions near Müden and Hatzenport, respectively. CCA crossed the river at Hatzenport and formed the division's east column, while CCB crossed at Müden, forming the west column.

CCA was led by two platoons of light tanks from D/8 and the Shermans of B/8. After contending with heavy traffic in the bridgehead, the armored vehicles started their ascent from the valley of the Moselle. For almost two miles, they followed the twists and turns of the road carved into the valley wall. Upon emerging from the depths of the valley, they were treated to a wide-open vista of rolling hills. Compared to the preceding miles, it was like landing on another planet. Freed of the handcuffs of the steep grade, the combat command picked up speed and advanced through the towns of Morshausen and Beulich unopposed. The first Germans they encountered were at Gondershausen, where resistance was light and easily brushed aside.

The M7s of the 94th Armored Field Artillery Battalion deployed neat Gondershausen

10. From the Moselle to the Rhine

The Moselle River at Hatzenport in 2019 (photograph by author).

to provide fire support if called upon. Cub pilots Lt. Billy Wood and Lt. Bothwell flew until daylight was nearly exhausted, calling out missions against retreating enemy columns and 88mm guns. Some of those 88s may have been the ones encountered near CCA's next objective: Liesenfeld.

It was at Liesenfeld that the Germans made their first strong stand of the day in front of CCA. Three 88s were spotted in some woods outside of the town, and Irzyk's tanks dispensed with them before they could do any harm. The Germans also positioned four anti-tank guns closer to the town and complemented their fire with a heavy dose of small arms. Two of the anti-tank guns were destroyed near a railroad crossing and the others captured. The German infantry were routed after a determined fight spearheaded by the armor.

Before halting at 1830, Emmelshausen (a much larger town butting up against Liesenfeld) and Schwall were cleared. The command post of CCA moved to Gondershausen for the night. Colonel Sears' combat command had advanced approximately 10 miles beyond the Moselle.

After crossing the Moselle, CCB's mission was to advance parallel to CCA. After an initial drive to the south, they would turn east and draw up alongside Colonel Sears' combat command and protect his right flank. As with CCA, the long-term objective was the seizure of Bad Kreuznach, 33 miles to the southeast astride the Nahe River.

CCB's advance across the Moselle did not get off to a good start. Considerable traffic congestion between the vehicles of the 5th Infantry Division and those of the Fourth Armored slowed the pace of movement. C/704 (equipped with six brand-new M18s) and C Troop of the 25th Cavalry Recon Squadron crossed the Moselle first. They moved through the zone of the 90th Infantry Division at Burgen and proceeded three miles to Macken, where they met tough resistance in the form of 88mm anti-tank guns. After clearing Macken, they pushed on for 10 miles over a road littered with wrecked enemy equipment, dead soldiers, and mutilated horses beyond counting. Many felt the greatest sorrow for the horses.

At the town of Laubach, they captured an executive commandant's command post. Among the booty they collected from a well-stocked supply room were several dozen brand new wrist and pocket watches. They finished the day there, with the tank destroyers manning the outposts.

Behind the nimble Hellcats and armored cars came the bulk of CCB. A/37 and C/10 led the column, the final elements of which crossed the Moselle by 1300. The lead tanks picked up speed as they moved through Macken, Eveshausen, and Dommershausen (approximately four miles over winding roads). The only resistance along the route came in the form of roadblocks erected at the entrance of each town, some of which were accompanied by a small number of defenders armed with light weapons. The obstacles were often dealt with by direct fire from the main guns of the leading tanks, which splintered the timbers typically used to form the barrier. If the roadblocks were defended, the combination of fire from the tanks and an assault by the accompanying infantry were more than enough to clear the way. In more extreme circumstances, indirect fire would be brought in to soften up the opposition.

A Fourth Armored column passes a destroyed horse-drawn transport and gun (U.S. Army photograph, courtesy Darren Neely).

The village of Dorweiler, just one mile east of Dommershausen, presented a more formidable obstacle. A strong roadblock of fallen trees was protected by mortars and 20mm fire, resulting in a delay of 45 minutes. Some of the lead elements bypassed the roadblock to keep the column moving, leaving other units to deal with the enemy. The roadblock was cleared using direct fire from the tanks, and the balance of the column resumed movement by 1500.

CCB's advance continued for almost three miles before anti-tank fire was received from the town of Beltheim. Rather than conduct an assault over the open terrain leading into the town, the combat command's 105mm howitzers were called upon to silence the enemy guns.

The advance continued with spotty interference. At 1530, the column received fire from several 20mm guns, but the tanks neutralized them without much trouble. The rear of the column received sniper fire at 1600, but no casualties were suffered. The column moved through Gödenroth and Laubach in quick succession, bringing the main body of CCB 12 miles beyond the Moselle.

At 1715, the leading elements of Abrams' command reached Simmern, five miles south of Laubach. The town was seized at 1800, with 500 Germans taken prisoner. But most importantly, the bridges over the Simmern River were captured intact. Many of the town's buildings were in flames when Abrams' men departed. The mayor was an ardent Nazi, which may have influenced matters.

The prisoners were predominately from the *326th Regiment* of the *198th Infantry Division*. The strength of the regiment was reportedly 1200 men before they encountered the Fourth Armored. Other prisoners taken that same day belonged to the *3rd Company*, *13th Battery* of the *9th Flak Division*. The *3rd Company* had orders to go from Hamburg to Bad Kreuznach, and while in transit, suffered the misfortune of running into tanks of the 37th Tank Battalion and P-47s of the XIX TAC. The flak unit suffered heavy casualties and most of their guns were destroyed.

CCB had traveled almost 17 miles. With Simmern secured, the infantry companies proceeded to dig-in outside the town while the supporting tanks were positioned nearby.

As for CCR, by late that evening, the command had moved to an assembly area near Düngenheim. The plan was for Colonel Blanchard's force to follow in the wake of CCB the next day. To help exploit and reinforce the heady advance made by the Fourth Armored, Major General Eddy attached to CCB an infantry regiment from the 5th Infantry Division. A regiment from the 90th Infantry Division was attached to CCA.

CCB's Advance to the Nahe River

Sensing the Germans' weakness, Patton issued verbal orders on March 16 for *Olympic* to attack toward the city of Mainz on the Rhine River, 33 miles east of the division's forward elements. To the south of the Fourth Armored, the 11th Armored Division would strike toward the Rhine River and the city of Worms. The 10th Armored Division, on the far right of the Third Army, would attack in a southerly direction toward Kaiserslautern, cutting deeper into the rear of the German *7th Army*.

After a brief overnight respite, the leading elements of CCB left Simmern at 0630 on March 16. The column headed south-southeast toward the town of Tiefenbach. Little resistance was encountered, and the town was cleared without incident.

Major General Hugh Gaffey (far left, back to camera) and Major General Manton Eddy (facing Gaffey at far left) observe elements of the Fourth Armored on March 16, 1945 (U.S. Army photograph, courtesy Darren Neely).

At this point, the geography begs description. Tiefenbach stood at an entrance to the Soon Forest ... a prominent, elongated, mountainous ridge five to six miles wide and extending some 60 miles from southwest to northeast. The ridge's southernmost point begins between the towns of Rhaunen and Simmertal and terminates at its northernmost extent above Bad Homberg. At a point approximately one third of the way to the northeast, the Main River carves out a valley through the ridge. Had they the resources, the Germans could have made a stand on this imposing piece of terrain. They had to settle for less, but it turned out to be a worrisome factor for the Americans nevertheless.

After securing Tiefenbach, the lead elements of CCB made their way into the Soon. The vanguard of the column moved rapidly through the forest, and before 1100, emerged near Winterbach. Once beyond the town, the 10th Armored Infantry Battalion encountered German workers and captured about 100 of them.

The Americans were lulled into a false sense of security as they entered the Soon Forest. German snipers allowed the forward elements to pass, opting to ambush the softer rear elements of the combat command as they followed the route blazed by the leading tanks and armored infantry.

The 22nd Armored Field Artillery Battalion, farther back in the column, was hit the hardest. Three of their trucks were ambushed, resulting in one being destroyed and another damaged. Six enlisted men were wounded and an officer (1st Lt. Carvel C. Hood) reported missing in action after the ambush.

After leaving the forest behind them, the column advanced over friendlier terrain. The increasingly familiar roadblocks were found at most of the towns that followed, but they were all undefended, making it easy for the tanks leading the column to either destroy or bypass them. Winterburg, Bockenau, Sponheim, Mandel, Weinsheim, Rüdesheim, and Hüffelsheim all fell into American hands within the hour. Hüffelsheim became a particularly attractive gift when CCB overran the headquarters of what was left of the *560th Volksgrenadier Division*. At that point, the lead elements had advanced approximately 10 miles east of the forest.

At 1200, CCB reached the Nahe River at the town of Norheim, approximately two miles southwest of Bad Kreuznach. No bridge was found, so C/37 and A/10 (the latter being under the command of Captain Lange since March 12) took the lead and headed east along the winding, twisting course of the Nahe in pursuit of a bridge at the larger town of Bad Münster.

The Germans had destroyed the road bridge at Bad Münster. Fortunately, a railroad bridge, 960 feet in length, was discovered intact. Two platoons of Shermans from C/37 made a quick crossing while under fire from 20mm guns and enemy aircraft. Over the next 45 minutes, American P-47s and the assault guns from the 37th Tank Battalion combined to silence the enemy guns. By this time in the war, the harmony and synchronization between XIX TAC and the Fourth Armored was superb.

While C/37 and A/10 secured the rail crossing, A/37 located another bridge at the town of Oberhausen, three miles west of Norheim. Abrams opted to have the rest of CCB cross the Nahe at this location, leaving D/37 to outpost the bridge after the column had crossed. Out of this bridgehead, A/37 and C/10 advanced four miles southeast to Hochstätten, which they attacked and cleared.

Meanwhile, C/37 and A/10 advanced out of their bridgehead at Bad Münster and drove

A German *ME-262* jet fighter aircraft (U.S. Army photograph).

south toward Altenbamberg, securing it by 1315. The companies then continued to Hochstätten, where they joined A/37 and C/10.

CCB dispatched a task force to the west to clear the village of Feilbingert, which had been surrounded by the trajectories of A/37 and C/37. Abrams' final move of the day was a mile-and-a-half drive to the southwest to secure Hallgarten and Dreiweiherhof on the combat command's right flank.

The deep penetration made by CCB caught the enemy by surprise. During the night of March 16 and through the following morning, numerous vehicles and troops stumbled into CCB's positions near Altenbamberg. The Germans realized the danger represented by the bridgeheads gained by the Americans over the Nahe River, so they summoned what strength they could from the *Luftwaffe* to bomb and strafe the bridges. The attacking force included *ME-262s* ... the new jet fighter aircraft. In total, 39 German planes attempted without success to destroy the bridges. The 489th Anti-Aircraft Battalion reportedly downed 12 enemy aircraft and damaged eight. The *Luftwaffe* also attempted to strike the supporting artillery farther to the rear. The 452nd Anti-Aircraft Battalion was credited with four certain kills, and likely downed another four.

For some of the German ground forces facing the Fourth Armored, the writing was on the wall. The *2nd Panzer Division* attempted to break out of the trap being set by the Third Army. They tried desperately to reach Bingen on the Rhine River. The men of the *2nd Panzer* were not alone. *General* Felber, commander of the German *7th Army*, also tried to escape. Driven into the woods to avoid the strafing aircraft of the XIX TAC, he and his staff were under concealment when a column from the Fourth Armored skirted by them. An hour later, he and his chief of staff, *General* von Gersdorff, where able to make their way out of the trap via a back road.

CCA's Drive to the Nahe

CCA, driving east on the left of CCB, had a tougher go of it. The combat command departed from the area of Liesenfeld at 0630 with the light tanks of D/8 in the lead, followed closely by the A Team. Other than an encounter with a single anti-tank gun, they had smooth sailing at the outset, at times cruising at speeds as fast as 20 miles per hour (rapid for an armored column). The advance went seamlessly until 1000, when they approached Rheinböllen. The town is located at the western base of the Soon Forest, about seven miles northeast of where CCB entered the forested ridge. One of the higher quality roads in the area led to the east, and it would have been the most expeditious way to transit the dense Soon Forest ... had the Germans not made other plans.

Approximately 150 men from the *6th SS Mountain Division's* reconnaissance battalion were ready and waiting, poised on the north edge of the Soon Forest and within the town itself. Roadblocks were in place and the *SS* troops were prepared to defend them. As the light tanks of D/8 approached, two were hit by *Panzerfausts*. The commanding officer of D Company (Lt. Roy Erdmann) was wounded, as was Staff Sergeant Ellsworth Ranson, whom Lt. Colonel Irzyk called "that great warrior ... whose tank uncovered the large nest of anti-tank guns at Marthille in Lorraine many months before."

More firepower was required. Irzyk brought forward the Shermans of A/8 and infantry of A/53. Lt. Colonel Irzyk also called in artillery support from the 94th Armored Field Artillery Battalion, which fired their guns expeditiously. It took the A Team two hours to destroy the roadblocks and clean out the village. In the process of clearing Rheinböllen, A/8 lost two more Sherman tanks to *Panzerfaust*-wielding SS troopers.

Rather than hold up the entire advance while Rheinböllen was dealt with, Irzyk had the balance of the combat command circle back to the southwest nearly two miles to the smaller town of Ellern. From there, they took a modest, winding secondary road that ran to the southeast through the forest. The forest hugged the roadway from both sides, which restricted the column to the roadway.

Not long after entering the woods, the column halted in front of a roadblock constructed from felled trees. Tankers and infantrymen combined forces to cut up the timbers and remove the debris, with tanks hauling off the larger logs. The column moved on with C/8 and C/53 in the lead, their pace now akin to what CCB had experienced. It was almost five miles through the forest before they reached the first village. It is hard to say that Gräfenbacherhütte was even a village, as it consisted of not more than a dozen buildings. From that point, only one more mile separated the column from the east edge of the forest.

Once outside the confines of the forest, CCA sprinted six miles through the towns of Argenschwang, Spabrücken, Dalberg, Wallhausen, and Gutenberg. The towns fell like dominos, with little opposition other than unmanned roadblocks.

After clearing Gutenberg, CCA turned to the north and sliced two miles to the town of Windesheim, where they would pick up the main road. The Germans made a stand there, employing direct fire weapons and *Panzerfausts*. The attack cost the 8th Tank Battalion one of its valued officers (Lt. Gill) when a *Panzerfaust* round hit his tank, killing one of his crew and wounding him seriously enough that he had to be evacuated.

What of A/8 and B/53, left far back at Rheinböllen? After clearing the town, they moved through the villages of Rheinboellerhuette, Neuhuette, Stromberg, and Schweppenhausen (a trek of about eight miles). They joined the rest of CCA at Windesheim.

With his command consolidated, Colonel Sears spurred CCA to the east and the Nahe River. Waldlaubersheim was the first town along their route, and a *Panzerfaust* claimed one of the Shermans there. The column moved on to Langenlonsheim, nestled on the west bank of the Nahe north of Bad Kreuznach (about seven miles north of where CCB had reached the Nahe at Bad Münster). Directly across the river was the town of Gensingen, where a single bridge provided the only direct link to Langenlonsheim. The Germans were ready, and as the Americans approached the bridge, they destroyed the span. With darkness fast approaching, CCA stopped for the night, drawn up to the west bank of the Nahe River.

For CCR, it was an uneventful day as they trailed behind CCA and CCB. Colonel Blanchard's units set out at 0800. Nearly 10 hours later, they closed in on their assembly area near Simmern, now well to the rear of the primary combat commands. The 51st Armored Infantry Battalion secured the main roads and bridges in the area. At 2115, the 51st received an order attaching it to CCB, but at 2350, the order was rescinded, and the battalion remained with CCR.

Over the course of March 15 and 16, the Fourth Armored Division advanced 33 airline miles, crossing the Hunsruck Mountains and taking 1200 prisoners along the way. They inflicted serious losses upon the *Wehrmacht*. On the last day alone, they tallied 84 enemy killed and 115 wounded. They also destroyed 18 75mm guns, one *Panther* tank, and over 200 assorted vehicles. By contrast, the losses suffered by the Fourth Armored were remarkably light: six men killed and 24 wounded.

There was little to stop the division from reaching the Rhine. CCA was only five miles south of the mighty river. The city of Mainz, which had been their primary objective, lay just 16 miles to the east.

Before the end of the day, there was a change in leadership at the high end of the division ladder. Colonel William L. Roberts joined the Fourth Armored as the Assistant Division Commander. Some members of the division—Captain Abe Baum and Lt. Bert Ezell, in particular—were already familiar with Roberts from his time commanding CCB of the 10th Armored Division (they had met during the foray into Bastogne with Task Force Ezell).

Patton Unleashed... Almost

At 1100 on March 16, General Bradley called Patton and informed him that Eisenhower's plane was unable to land near 12th Army Group's headquarters for a planned meeting. Rather than return, the plane was rerouted to Luxembourg for an unscheduled visit to Patton's headquarters.

Patton called a staff conference, which Eisenhower attended as a guest (the primary topic at the meeting was the supply situation faced by Third Army). Patton and Ike then drove to Trier to visit the front. That evening, they dined together in the company of four Red Cross girls. The two generals stayed up talking until the early morning hours of March 17.

After a short sleep, Ike attended the Third Army morning briefing. Patton noted afterwards that,

> Eisenhower spoke and paid me the first compliment he has ever vouchsafed. He stated that we of the Third Army were such veterans that we did not appreciate our own greatness and should be more cocky and boastful... (Ike was) extremely complimentary and stated that not only was I a good general but also a lucky general and that Napoleon preferred luck to greatness.

Eisenhower and Patton then departed by plane for the town of Luneville, located in the Lorraine region of France. The impressive gains made by TUSA compelled Eisenhower to hold a meeting with Patton, General Jacob Devers (commander of 6th Army Group, fighting to the south of Patton), and Lt. General Alexander Patch (commander of the U.S. Seventh Army and a subordinate of Devers).

The purpose of the meeting was to establish how best to capitalize on Patton's gains. One option was for Patton's Third Army to advance across part of the zone designated for Patch's Seventh Army. Lt. General Patch showed no hesitation in accepting the proposition, emphasizing that, "We are all in the same army." Given that the Seventh Army still faced stiff opposition holding out in the *Westwall* fortifications, an advance by Patton farther into the rear of the German *7th Army* would make Patch's own mission easier in the end. The authority granted to the Third Army created an even more fervent desire on Patton's part to press the advantage. This in turn resulted in Patton applying greater pressure on his direct reports to hasten their advance.

After returning to Luxembourg, Patton held a press conference. One of the reporters asked, "What is more important, a bridge across the Rhine or the fighting down there?" (i.e., near the Moselle River). Patton replied, "A bridge across the Rhine."

Patton would eventually turn his attention to the Rhine. But in the meantime, another mission stood between TUSA and the famed river. And the Fourth Armored Division would lead the way.

Snaring Bad Kreuznach

It was March 17, and before Lt. Colonel Abrams continued CCB's drive to the east, there was cleanup work to be done. The three-mile stretch of road leading north from Hochstätten to Bad Münster had to be cleared of the enemy. The road was heavily wooded on both flanks (especially to the east), making it ripe for sniping and interdiction by the enemy. B/10 drew the assignment of clearing the route as well as Bad Münster itself.

At 0830, the armored infantry and some supporting tanks headed north from Hochstätten. No resistance was met along the route, and at 0930, with the doughs riding on the tanks, they crossed the bridge over the Nahe and got to work clearing the enemy from Bad Münster. During the attack, an *ME 109* flew over and was shot down. Four more planes appeared at 1030, but neither side drew blood. By 1130, Bad Münster was in American hands.

Back at the southern end of the road, it was around noon when a machine gun and burp gun located on a hilltop south of Hochstätten opened fire on the 10th Armored Infantry Battalion's command post. The HQ personnel silenced the enemy with a torrent of fire from their .50 caliber machine guns.

After securing Bad Münster, B/10 and the supporting tanks moved south to ensure the road leading back to Hochstätten was clear. By 1430, the mission was accomplished.

Having rested during the morning and early afternoon, the B and C teams of the 10th and 37th were ordered to attack Fürfeld and Frei-Laubersheim. The towns are located about three miles east of Altenbamberg (Fürfeld being to the south of Frei-Laubersheim). The 66th Armored Field Artillery Battalion fired preparations and harassing and interdiction fire in support of the attack. By 1630, both towns were in American hands. The Germans offered only minor small arms fire in opposition. Later that evening, the 66th moved their howitzers into the vicinity of Fürfeld, where they remained until March 20.

Now came the more substantive task of surrounding and consuming Bad Kreuznach (most of which sits on the east side of the Nahe River). CCB was in position to attack the city from the rear, with the most direct approach being from the southeast. Orders were issued at 1630 for B/37 and B/10 to lead the attack, followed by A/37 and A/10. The mortar and machine gun platoons from HQ Company were attached for additional support.

The leading elements met considerable resistance as they approached the city. Germans fired *Panzerfausts* and small arms from the cellars and dug-in positions. The *Panzerfausts* were particularly effective, accounting for one tank and several men.

As darkness approached, only a small section of Bad Kreuznach had been cleared. Given the inherent challenges of urban night fighting, the attack ceased, and a perimeter defense was established. Enemy snipers remained at work during the night, but they failed to find any targets.

While CCB encircled Bad Kreuznach from the south, CCA continued its search for a crossing site over the Nahe River somewhere north of the city. A bridgehead was needed to execute their part of the pincer movement.

Starting at 0600, the main force of Colonel Sears' combat command reconnoitered along the Nahe River in the area near Langenlonsheim, approximately three-and-a-half miles north of the center of Bad Kreuznach. A/8 and A/53 moved south and entered the town of Bretzenheim, where to their delight, they found a bridge intact. An old wooden structure some 50 yards in length, it appeared that it had been tampered with for demolition.

Captain Kieley (commanding officer of A/8) looked at the bridge with suspicion. Normally, the armored infantry or engineers would inspect the bridge before armored vehicles attempted to cross. But Colonel Sears (whom Kieley later said "was dying to get a star") insisted that the Shermans move across immediately, barking his orders over an open radio channel. Kieley recognized the risk and pushed back, telling Sears "The bridge is in, but it's not in." An argument ensued, with Kieley saying to Colonel Sears, "If I go down, I'm after your ass."

According to Irzyk's account, with the assistance of covering fire provided by the tanks, the armored infantry crossed in the face of small arms fire and carved out a modest bridgehead. According to Kieley, his tank was the first to hit the bridge. When his Sherman reached the midpoint, the span buckled, splintered, and collapsed, sending Kieley and his crew into the river with a "hard, dull thud." Fortunately, the depth of the river was not enough to submerge the tank. While delivering an incredible jolt to the crew, the engine kept running and the treads were able to gain traction on the riverbed.

Kieley's tank made it up and over the riverbank, but it wasn't a suitable place for other vehicles to ford the river. A better spot was found not too distant, and the other tanks pushed across while the engineers went about the task of repairing the damaged bridge so that the wheeled vehicles could join them. (Captain Kieley was later disarmed, placed under guard, and threatened with court martial by Colonel Sears. It was likely that Lt. Colonel Irzyk intervened and saved the day.)

Rather than wait for the engineers to complete their work, Lt. Colonel Irzyk ordered his tankers to continue the offensive on their own (a bold move, especially when fighting through towns, but this wasn't the first time he had taken such a risk). The Shermans pushed three miles to the east, capturing Ippesheim, Biebelsheim, and Zotzenheim without opposition.

As the day progressed and the bridge repair continued, a threat began to develop much farther to the rear. Enemy infantry trying to escape the developing envelopment presented a danger to CCA's supply lines, so B/8 was ordered to patrol the route leading back to Simmern, more than 20 miles behind the lead elements of the combat command.

The threat was real … or at least had the potential to be. In desperation, *General* Felber planned a two-division counterattack against the Fourth Armored. One of his divisions failed to assemble for the attack. The other was the *2nd Panzer Division*, which managed to cobble together a force of four tanks, three assault guns, about 200 *Panzer Grenadiers,* and some artillery support. The attempt was for naught, as they were delayed by the very roadblocks and anti-tank barriers they had erected to delay the Americans.

A German attack *did* come to fruition when a force of several hundred enemy infantry attempted to ambush CCB's main supply route at a point some 10 miles west of Bad Kreuznach. During recent days, most Germans surrendered once caught behind American lines. But there were exceptions … and this was one of them. There would soon be others.

A Threat Emerges to the West

Colonel Blanchard's CCR began March 17 near the town of Simmern, some 20 miles to the rear. At 1230, his command moved east to close on the rest of the division but was held up when a column from the 11th Infantry Regiment cut in front of them. After the road congestion cleared, the column resumed movement and reached Tiefenbach. During the road march, sporadic mortar fire fell along the route (fortunately, there were no casualties).

When the head of the column arrived at Winterbach, CCR was informed that a large force of enemy infantry was attacking from the south toward Winterburg, about a mile-and-a-half southeast of Winterbach. The Fourth Armored Division's main supply route ran through this town, making the enemy movement an immediate threat.

Colonel Blanchard formed a task force composed of the light tanks of D/35 and the armored infantry of C/51. Major Charles L. Kimsey was placed in command. His mission: repel the attack and ensure the supply line was open and secure.

Kimsey ordered the M5A1 tanks to lead the assault. Since the enemy had no anti-tank weapons, the tanks were able to "cruise freely through the entire area, killing many of the enemy infantry." Many of the Germans surrendered to the dismounted infantry that followed. A medium tank company, a section of tank destroyers, and the assault gun platoon of the 35th were then added to the task force. They moved around the left flank of D/35, destroying three 40mm anti-aircraft guns placed on a ridge east of Eckweiler. The Germans responded with heavy artillery fire, which forced the light tanks to withdraw. The Shermans and armored infantry moved to the commanding high ground overlooking the towns of Eckweiler, Daubach, and Ippenscheid.

The following morning, the task force sent patrols into Daubach and Eckweiler to see if they contained enemy troops, and if so, in what strength. The patrol sent into Daubach found the town already occupied by friendly forces of the 5th Infantry Division.

The patrol that had been dispatched to Eckweiler, just a little over a mile to the west, found the opposite: the town was strongly held by German infantry. Enemy machine gun nests overlooked the entrances to the town. There were no tanks or anti-tank guns observed, but it was clear that a stronger force was required for an attack.

The medium tanks from the 35th and the assault guns from the 51st hit Eckweiler with a heavy opening barrage. Many of the buildings were set on fire by the high-explosive rounds sent screaming into the midst of the enemy stronghold. A platoon each of tanks and armored infantry moved into the blazing town. The German machine gun positions had been knocked out by the advance fire from the tanks.

The surviving Germans offered little opposition. Sixty-one prisoners were scooped up and seven enemy killed. The only casualty among the Americans was a single armored infantryman slightly wounded by mortar fragments. After clearing the town, the tanks and infantry withdrew back to the high ground overlooking the devastation. Later that day, the task force was relieved by the 1st Battalion of the 11th Infantry Regiment.

By 1700, CCR assembled near Weinsheim with orders to move out at 0630 the following morning. Their mission was to reinforce CCB. However, the situation faced by Abrams' combat command called for immediate support, so B/35 and A/51 were placed in a task force led by Major Harry Rockafeller, which departed immediately to reinforce the American positions at Fürfeld.

CCB's Attack on Volxheim

Over the course of March 18 and 19, German resolve stiffened. The combination of the encirclement of Bad Kreuznach and having the Rhine River at their back created an air of desperation among the Germans. As a result, General Gaffey's attempt to digest the city and draw up to the line of the Rhine River bore a close resemblance to the fighting experienced back in November. However, there was at least one clear difference when comparing the two periods, and that was the magnificent weather that allowed the fighter-bombers of XIX TAC to play a prominent role in the current battle.

CCB's first task was the clearing of Bad Kreuznach. But before the attack commenced, the Germans launched their own strike at Hochstätten, scraping together tanks and assault guns for the effort. American fighter-bombers arrived to lend a hand in repulsing the attack (the 22nd Armored Field Artillery Battalion reported that three enemy tanks were destroyed by P-47s).

At Bad Kreuznach, the armored infantry of B/10 and Sherman tanks of B/37 carried the load. The Americans pushed deep into the city and block by block, they flushed the enemy from the many buildings and cellars. The strong German resistance exhibited the day prior was multiplied when citizens took up arms alongside the soldiers of the *Wehrmacht*. A civilian brandishing a *Panzerfaust* managed to knock out an American tank.

At times during the attack, the armored infantry rode upon the tanks. One of the men mounted on a Sherman of B/37 was Pfc John W. Jennings. When a *Panzerfaust* round barely missed the Sherman upon which he was riding, the concussion of the blast threw him to the ground. Incensed, he rose to his feet and rushed through enemy fire, single-handedly assaulting the German position. He killed three of the enemy and captured 35.

After considerable effort, Bad Kreuznach was deemed clear by noon. During the process of sweeping the city, CCB liberated a hospital where they discovered 50 American soldiers. A medic from the 10th Armored Infantry saw to it that the repatriated G.I.s were evacuated to the rear for treatment. Among the losses suffered by the Americans—and it was a tough one—was the commanding officer of B/37, Lt. Bernard Liese.

While Bad Kreuznach was being mopped up, danger emerged on other fronts. At 0700, 13 enemy tanks along with several self-propelled assault guns were spotted southeast of Hackenheim moving toward the positions of CCB. The Fourth Armored only had screening elements near the town (including some of the brand new M18s of C/704). With B/37 involved in the clearing of Bad Kreuznach, the Sherman tanks of A/37 and C/37 were dispatched to face the oncoming counterattack.

After preparatory shelling by the Germans, three enemy assault guns initiated the attack toward Hackenheim. The Shermans of Lt. Whitehill's A Company destroyed one of the assault guns while P-47 fighter-bombers took out another. The men of C/704 described it as "…the best piece of strafing of enemy troops we have yet seen. Sure glad we weren't on the receiving end when they let go with their .50s and rockets." But before making their retreat, the Germans managed to hit one of Whitehill's Shermans at a crossroad southeast of Hackenheim. The armored infantry suffered some casualties as well.

That wasn't the end of the German effort. At 0930, the bulk of the German force began a broader attack. But before the Germans could close in on the American defenses, fighter-bombers from the XIX TAC descended with a vengeance. Twelve enemy tanks were destroyed by the pilots while two of the assault guns were accounted for by gunners from the 37th Tank Battalion.

After the threat subsided, C/37 and A/10, along with C/704 and C Troop of the 25th Cavalry Reconnaissance Squadron, moved three miles south of Hackenheim to the high ground near Fürfeld. Their presence served to guard the approach leading north to Bad Kreuznach.

During the action, one of the M8 armored cars from C Troop was struck by an anti-tank round. In the turret was Lt. Art Irzyk (brother of Lt. Colonel Irzyk). The explosion killed the other members of the crew and threw the lieutenant out of the vehicle. He landed in a roadside ditch, seriously wounded. The troop commander, Captain Jack Keenan, crawled under enemy fire to the location of the destroyed armored car. He discovered that Lt. Irzyk had survived the blast but was far too seriously injured to move under his own power. Keenan managed to drag the lieutenant back down the line of the ditch and eventually was aided by others in moving Art to safety. He was rushed back to the 22nd Armored Field Artillery Battalion's aid station, where Dr. Iuppa, the battalion surgeon, worked feverishly to save both of Art's legs. (Art was soon evacuated to a hospital in the United States, where he underwent extensive treatment. Despite long odds, his legs were saved, and he regained nearly full use of them.)

Meanwhile, A/37 and C/10 advanced about two miles to take the high ground south of the town of Wöllstein. From this position, they had a clear view of the town and its approaches. The Germans were aware of their presence and hit them with heavy mortar fire.

Once B/37 and B/10 finished mopping up Bad Kreuznach, they moved into an assembly area between Hackenheim and Frei-Laubersheim, filling the gap between the other elements of CCB. This created a defensive arc guarding the approaches to Bad Kreuznach from the south and southeast.

The Germans launched another desperate counterattack, this time in the direction of Fürfeld where C/37 and A/10, along with the tank destroyers of C/704 and the armored cavalry of C Troop, stood guard on the far-right flank of the combat command. The battered remnants of two *Panzer Grenadier* regiments of the *2nd Panzer Division* were involved, which amounted to the equivalent of three companies of infantry supported by approximately 15 *Panzers*. P-47s took to the sky in response and put on a show in front of the men of C/704, strafing the enemy troops and slowing the pace of the attack. Despite the violent air cover provided by the P-47s, some of the Germans made it within close enough range of the American positions that Lt. Oliver of C/704 was able to use grenades to kill three of them. But in the end, the P-47s made the difference, destroying most of the *Panzers* and forcing the balance of the enemy armor and infantry to retreat to the southeast. The Americans didn't walk away unscathed: C Troop suffered seven casualties (two KIA and five WIA).

Having squelched the German counterattack with the assistance of XIX TAC, CCB resumed its attack. The plan called for the B Team to seize the town of Volxheim, midway between Hackenheim and Wöllstein. A/37 and C/10, already in possession of the high ground nearby, would then descend on Wöllstein.

The 66th Armored Field Artillery Battalion fired a preparatory barrage in support of the B Team's assault. The Germans hit back with counterbattery fire, which took out one of the 66th's ammo trailers and a halftrack. The B Team jumped off at 1600 and faced stiff resistance as they closed in on Volxheim. The approach was blocked by an imposing barricade defended by an enemy tank and some assault guns. American fighter-bombers were used to blast away the obstacle and suppress the fire of the armor, clearing the way for the assault team to enter the town. Elements of the *305th Regiment* of the *198th Infantry Division* and the *669th Assault Gun Brigade* offered some of the stiffest resistance the Fourth Armored had seen in weeks. Enemy mortar and artillery rounds were directed against the advancing infantry, and armor placed inside the town made it difficult for the American tanks to attack.

After heavy fighting, the infantrymen of B/10 made their way toward the center of the town, whereupon they discovered a German assault gun blocking the way forward. The armored infantry tackled the German armor on their own. S/Sgt. Robert Miller grabbed a bazooka and in the face of heavy machine gun fire, worked his way to within a few feet of the assault gun before taking his shot. Elsewhere in town, Captain Thomas J. Donnelly, after seeing one of his men wounded by fire from another enemy tank, moved to an exposed position to provide covering fire so that the soldier could be extricated. Donnelly then secured a bazooka and moved within 60 yards of the *Panzer* and opened fire, forcing it to withdraw. The captain then grabbed a grenade launcher and pursued the enemy tank through the town. His actions cleared the way for his platoon to advance behind him and continue the attack.

The battle in Volxheim raged until 1900. As stated in the division's combat history, "Much of the fighting was hand to hand as it was necessary to rout the enemy from his positions." Bravery was exhibited in many ways. When Private Nathaniel Lytle's squad leader was wounded by enemy tank fire, Lytle went forward and dragged him to safety. Nathaniel then exposed himself to fire when he went to get medical aid.

The fight was a tough one for the tankers of B/37 as well. Before daylight faded, a *Panzerfaust* took out another Sherman, reducing B Company to only six medium tanks. There were still two *Panzers* in the town and despite their best effort, the armored infantrymen couldn't get to them with their bazookas. By nightfall, the B Team cleared about three-quarters of Volxheim. Rather than continue the attack in the dark, they set up a defensive perimeter for the night.

Due to the difficulty encountered at Volxheim, A/37 and C/10 postponed their attack on Wöllstein and remained overnight on the high ground south of the town. C/37 and A/10 remained on the high ground southwest of Fürfeld. Abrams didn't make the progress he hoped for on March 18, but CCB destroyed seven assault guns and captured many prisoners from both the *669th Assault Gun Brigade* and the *305th Regiment*.

The Battle for Sankt Johann

On March 18, CCA moved out at 0630 from the high ground near Zotzenheim and Ippesheim. Their first task was to attack the larger town of Sprendlingen, three-and-a-half miles east-northeast of Bad Kreuznach.

The advance was led by the Sherman tanks of A/8, commanded by Captain Len Kieley. Only scattered German forces opposed them. By 0730, Sprendlingen was secure. B/8 and B/53 continued two miles farther to the southeast and occupied Gau-Bickelheim. With the capture of that town, the noose was tightened around the German forces remaining in Bad Kreuznach. The encirclement of the city by the Fourth Armored Division was complete.

C/8 and C/53 moved near the crest of the high ground a quarter-mile east of Sprendlingen. The guns of the 94th Armored Field Artillery Battalion were positioned only 100 yards behind them, concealed by the hill. To the northeast of the forward elements the village of Sankt Johann lay in clear sight. The houses on the edge of town were only a half-mile away.

Al Irzyk was eager to maintain CCA's momentum. Unlike the conditions he faced for so many weeks prior to this, the weather was ideal for offensive operations and cross-country movement. He was ready to go, but the command to proceed hadn't yet been given by Colonel Sears. As the minutes turned into hours, Al's mood shifted from eagerness to frustration. Irzyk grew concerned that the German troops at Sankt Johann were being awarded valuable time to prepare their defense. His mind raced back nearly three months to the Battle of the Bulge. He believed that the delays he experienced at Burnon had gifted the Germans valuable time to prepare a stronger defense at Chaumont. December 23 was seared in his memory. He dared not repeat it.

Rather than remaining idle, the 28-year-old tank battalion commander … a young man leading boys and men as many as 10 years his junior … went to the front and looked down upon Sankt Johann. The only road leading to the town ran straight downhill and was flanked on both sides by a vast vineyard. To Irzyk's right, approximately a half-mile distant, a high ridge ran parallel with the road all the way to the town and beyond.

Irzyk prepared a detailed plan in anticipation of receiving the green light from Colonel Sears. C/8 would make the main assault over the road and vineyards leading to the town. Sensing the importance of the high ground to the right of the road, he dispatched the tanks of A/8 to climb to the top of the ridge to support the eventual drive by C/8. B/8, already positioned farther south after capturing Gau-Bickelheim, advanced to a position southeast of Sankt Johann. This placed them in an ideal position to support the C Team when they eventually emerged from Sankt Johann and drove toward the next objective, Wolfsheim.

Lt. Colonel Irzyk watched Len Kieley's tanks lumber up the steep slope "like goats" toward the crest of the ridge. After a laborious ascent, A/8 reached the top of the ridge and was positioned to provide fire support for the attack. All that remained was for Al Irzyk to receive the "go" signal from the commander of CCA.

And then it came. At 1600, Colonel Sears radioed Irzyk with the command to proceed with the attack on Sankt Johann and then continue to Wolfsheim, less than a mile beyond Sankt Johann. Lt. Colonel Irzyk's biggest concern at that moment was the limited daylight remaining with which to conduct the attack. If he encountered significant resistance at

The road leading into Sankt Johann from the west. The town of Wolfsheim is visible in the background (photograph by author in 2019).

Sankt Johann, it might be dark by the time his leading elements reached Wolfsheim, making an attack against that town a greater challenge. But enough of those concerns for now. First things first. All else was moot until the C Team took care of Sankt Johann.

On Irzyk's order, the Shermans of C Company cranked up their engines and advanced in a spread formation, taking advantage of the firm ground. Until they came over the crest of the hill, the Germans would have no idea what was about to hit them.

It ended up being the Americans who were surprised. As the Shermans started down the slope toward the town, the specter of Chaumont enveloped the battlefield. The unmistakable screeching of 88mm shells assaulted Irzyk's ears. With his eyes, he saw five Shermans quickly hit and burning. The enemy onslaught was so fast and accurate, he was sure that the dual-purpose anti-aircraft guns had been zeroed-in beforehand. German air bursts struck the area where the M7s were staged. Observing from the high ground behind the assault company, Irzyk watched the remaining tanks of C/8 scurry for whatever cover they could find. The attack had come to an abrupt and devastating halt.

But what of the tanks of Captain Kieley's A Company? They were sent to positions atop Hill 271 for just such an event. Irzyk did not see or hear even a single shot fired from the hill in response. How could that be? He raised Kieley on the radio. The frustrated captain explained that the enemy guns were in positions tucked into the base of the very hill he was sitting atop. The grade of the slope was such that the Shermans' gun barrels could not be depressed low enough to draw a bead on the targets. The tanks of A Company were rendered helpless.

Irzyk had an ace up his sleeve. Using Captain Kieley as a forward artillery observer, he called upon Lt. Colonel Bob Parker's 94th Armored Field Artillery Battalion to hit the German guns with everything they had. The 94th also had a Piper Cub observer plane overhead, piloted by Lt. Bothwell. There was just one problem: B and C Batteries of the 94th were too close to the town and unable to establish the proper elevation for their guns. However, Battery A was able to fire along with the 276th Armored Field Artillery Battalion and the 179th Field Artillery Battalion (the latter packing the added punch of 155mm howitzers).

As the artillery pounded Sankt Johann, Lt. Colonel Irzyk contemplated his next move. C Company, now significantly understrength, was still disorganized and rattled from the disastrous initial attack. A/8 was rendered virtually useless, for the slope was too steep for Kieley's tanks to descend straight toward the town. If they were going to join the action, they had to retrace the route taken to reach their current positions. And as for the tanks of B Company, they were too far to the east and not in position to attack Sankt Johann.

Darkness was approaching, and he had little time to work with. Irzyk had but one dominating thought: he had to complete his mission. But how? The veteran tanker saw only one option: he and his tank crew would personally lead the attack.

Hopefully, Parker's howitzers had done their job. He would spur his M4A3E8 Sherman at top speed down the hill and carry out the assault single-handedly. Once within Sankt Johann, he would radio the C Team and tell them to close in on him (believing that his successful charge and leadership by example would be the catalyst they needed). Keenly aware of the personal danger he faced, he radioed Executive Officer Bert Ezell and Operations Officer (S-3) Sam Diuguid and reviewed their mission to and beyond Sankt Johann. If anything happened to him, they would be prepared to carry on the attack.

Irzyk briefed his tank crew on what they were about to do. Al later wrote, "Their lips clamped and they looked stricken, but they nodded and their eyes said, if you can do it we can too."

10. From the Moselle to the Rhine

On Irzyk's command, the tank driver buried the accelerator, sending the M4A3E8 down the hill at maximum speed. As Irzyk instructed, the crew members manning the bow machine gun and the .50 caliber co-ax machine gun spit out a constant stream of lead in front of the tank. The commander's hatch was unbuttoned and Irzyk, riding high, added the turret-mounted .30 caliber machine gun to the recipe. His initial descent toward the town received no response from the enemy. But when the Sherman reached the halfway point, smaller caliber German guns opened fire. The shells landed harmlessly behind Irzyk's tank as his driver continued at full speed. He was moving so fast that the German gunners must have had difficulty leading the Sherman.

As Irzyk's tank slowed and approached the first buildings in the town, he was astonished to see the Sherman of one of C Company's platoon leaders, Lt. Mandel Rubin. The tank was tucked up against one of the homes. Irzyk assumed that during the initial attack, Rubin must have skirted the enemy fire by going wide left of the road.

Rather than stop and calibrate with Lt. Rubin, Irzyk maintained his momentum and continued into Sankt Johann on the main road that leads straight through the town from one end to the other. He waved at Rubin with a command to follow him while keeping his own tank moving.

The sky grew darker with every passing minute. As Irzyk's tank drove down the main street, he noted that all the window shutters were closed. There were no lights lining the street. It was, in his words, an "abandoned ghost town." As he arrived at the center of the village, he came up against an imposing, eight-foot-tall road block built out of huge logs. Al wasn't going to let it stop him. His gunner fired the powerful 76mm gun at point blank range, first with a high-explosive round and then with an armor-piercing round. The sequence was repeated until the barricade was splintered enough for the Sherman to overrun the remains.

As Irzyk drew up to the far edge of town, he faced a similar roadblock. His gunner dealt with it in the same fashion as the first, and then Irzyk set his sights on Wolfsheim. Lt. Colonel Irzyk was bound and determined to complete his mission. He knew B Company had been positioned to assist once the main force moved toward Wolfsheim, and so they were probably not too far away.

Peering down the road in the increasingly dim light, the road to Wolfsheim looked wide open. It was only three-quarters-of-a-mile to the town, with more vineyards flanking the sides of the road. No other tanks had closed behind Irzyk's command tank. But he didn't see that as a reason to stop.

Irzyk's driver pushed the accelerator and started down the road. Irzyk remained standing atop his commander's seat with much of his body outside the turret. The tank had advanced about half-way to Wolfsheim when a "loud shattering explosion" ripped through the still evening air. A round from a *Panzerfaust* struck the side of the tank, bringing it to a jarring stop. Hot fragments sprayed the inside of the Sherman, creating cries of pain that reverberated within the confines of the steel cage. Shrapnel tore into Irzyk's lower leg. He felt the sharp sting immediately. Along with his gunner and loader, they bailed out of the turret and found the driver and bow gunner already on the right side of the road, "writhing in pain." Irzyk's leg began to throb. He knew he was bleeding, but he didn't consider it to be a serious wound.

After checking on his men, Irzyk mounted the tank to inspect the damage. The turret was jammed, rendering the main gun and co-ax machine gun virtually useless. And given the way the tank had come to such a jarring halt, he was sure that it was immobilized.

Irzyk dismounted again to further check on the seriousness of the injuries suffered by his crew. Right after hitting the ground, he heard the familiar sound of an approaching Sherman tank. By then, only a five-day-old moon provided illumination, but it was enough for him to make out the form of an American tank coming rapidly down the road from Sankt Johann. He thought that it must be Lt. Rubin finally joining him.

Irzyk was alarmed when the approaching tank didn't show signs of slowing down. He knew he could see *them*. Could they not see his tank blocking the road?

Before his eyes, the careening Sherman slammed into the back of his command tank. In Irzyk's words, "The blow was so sudden and violent that it not only bounced the crew members around but injured them as well." Out of the turret came not Lt. Rubin, but another C Company platoon leader, Lt. Joe Ike. "He threw up his hands as if to say that he had no explanation." Irzyk and the lieutenant both turned to the driver to find out what had happened, only to discover that he was dead. It appeared that as Ike's tank came down the road, another *Panzerfaust* had found its mark. In Irzyk's estimation, it must have immediately killed the driver and created a runaway tank.

Nine tankers, most of them injured and some seriously, huddled together in the roadside ditch beside the crippled tanks. Irzyk hoped that reinforcements would come at any moment on the heels of Ike's tank. But as they looked toward Sankt Johann, they saw nothing and heard only a still silence.

Realizing that the *Panzerfaust*-wielding enemy must not be far away, Irzyk's senses were on full alert. He kept an eye out in all directions. Suddenly, he thought he saw movement in the direction of Wolfsheim. He strained to see through the dim light. And then to his alarm, he made out a large tracked personnel carrier loaded with German soldiers. The vehicle moved slowly down the road directly toward his incapacitated tanks and their beleaguered crews.

What were they to do? A strand of woods lay not too far in the distance. But most of the tankers would be unable to make the trek due to their wounds. They could use their grease guns and .45 pistols to defend themselves. But in the open terrain, with only the shallow ditch and the hulls of their tanks for protection, that was not an appealing option.

As the German vehicle continued to creep toward them, Irzyk acted. The .30 caliber machine gun mounted outside of his commander's hatch was still operative and had a belt of ammunition already loaded. Believing this to be his best chance, Al mounted the tank and climbed into the turret. Setting his sights on the approaching vehicle, he squeezed off an initial burst. He then pulled tight on the trigger and watched the glowing tracer rounds light a path to the target. He could see the bullets hitting the vehicle, but the personnel carrier kept coming, slow and steady. As he squeezed off more rounds, he could see bodies slumping. He felt sure his fire was effective, but onward the carrier came. Then suddenly, to Al's great relief, the vehicle turned off the road to the left, seemingly out of control. The carrier kept moving until it disappeared down a slope.

Lt. Colonel Irzyk dismounted the tank and rejoined his men. He knew he had to get help. Presumably unable to raise anyone on either of the tank radios, he decided to single-handedly make the journey back toward Sankt Johann to bring up reinforcements. He hoped that his executive officer and S-3 were taking charge in his absence. But he couldn't leave it to chance that they would be on their way soon.

Al drew his .45 automatic pistol from its holster. With that as his only protection, he walked over to the woods, which paralleled the road back to Sankt Johann and eventually to Hill 271. He used the woods to maintain some semblance of cover, not knowing where the enemy might be. After making his way a fair distance, he heard movement and voices in the night. He moved closer to the edge of the woods, and thankfully, he saw a column of American tanks and men. Sam Diuguid, his S-3, was in the lead.

This was the B Team. Sam had called them back to replace the C Team for the finishing blow against Sankt Johann. After the B team pushed through the town, engineers from the 24th Armored Engineer Battalion came forward to destroy the German guns that escaped the artillery barrage. The tally of what held up the C Team was impressive: four 88s, nine 20mm anti-aircraft guns, and three other anti-tank guns.

Lt. Colonel Irzyk was back in command of his battalion, reunited with a team that was thankful to see him alive. Irzyk's first order of business was getting aid to the battered tank crews. Fortunately, the medical peeps were near the forward part of the column, so Irzyk had them quickly dispatched to help the wounded men huddled near the disabled tanks.

Irzyk, of course, was among the wounded. Leaving matters to Sam, he headed back to the aid station for treatment. Not until he arrived did he realize what had happened to him. Metal fragments from the *Panzerfaust* had sliced through his right boot and tore into his leg above the ankle. The medics removed the fragments and then cleaned and dressed the wound.

After getting a final briefing from Bert Ezell, Al curled up in a HQ halftrack. Unable to fall asleep due to his throbbing leg, he thought about the action he had just been through ... and of tomorrow's plans. Eventually, he fell into a hard sleep, not knowing that his actions that day had earned the coveted award of the Distinguished Service Cross.

CCB's Drive to the Rhine

On March 19, three of America's most powerful generals, Omar Bradley, Courtney Hodges, and George Patton, met at the headquarters of the 12th Army Group. Their shared concern: the U.S. First and Third Armies had been throttled back and placed on defense so that Eisenhower might shift divisions north to better enable Montgomery's upcoming assault on the Rhine. But in a turn of events that day, Ike authorized reinforcement of the Remagen bridgehead, bringing the allowance up to nine divisions. Accompanying the reinforcement was an instruction for the First Army to be on alert for an order to break out of the bridgehead anytime from March 23 onward.

Bradley piggybacked onto Ike's orders an approval for Patton to cross the Rhine on the run. Rather than assaulting the river near Koblenz, he suggested the Mainz-Worms area. After crossing, TUSA would make a push toward Kassel. This would result in a pincer movement executed by the First and Third Armies.

At daybreak, the elements of CCB holding the western section of Volxheim commenced their effort to clear the balance of the town. Perhaps the Germans had withdrawn during the night, for by 0700, the armored infantry of B/10 completed the job with ease.

It was finally time to assault Wöllstein. The tanks and infantry of A/37 and C/10 began the attack at 0745. Mortars and burp guns were the only substantive weapons encountered. The town was cleared by 0900.

With the infantry riding atop the tanks, part of the column advanced south to Siefersheim. At 0915, a preparatory barrage paved the way for C/37 and A/10. The tanks and infantry followed quickly on the heels of the exploding shells and entered the town at 0930. German small arms and mortars rang out as well as fire from an assault gun, which knocked out yet another tank of C Company. One hour later, the town was clear.

The column continued south toward Wonsheim, a little less than a mile away. At about noon, the HQ staff of C/704 moved to a position on high ground overlooking the town to watch their tank destroyers in action. From their vantage point, they observed what they later described as "one of the best battles we have ever witnessed."

P-47s initiated the onslaught, followed at 1400 by an artillery preparation conducted by the 66th Armored Field Artillery Battalion. The barrage didn't last long, as it was lifted when word was received that friendly troops might be in the town (but not before hitting a six-piece horse-drawn artillery column). As noted in the 66th's journal, "Excellent effect was reported on all targets by observers."

The observers from the 704th noted that the Sherman tanks charged the town across open ground with their machine guns blazing. When the tanks drew closer, they opened fire with their main guns and "blasted the hell out of the town." A German anti-tank gun hit one of the Sherman tanks but was in turn taken out by the M18 Hellcats of Sergeant Stasi and Sergeant Jesky (Stasi's gunner was Corporal Sorrentino). At 1530, C/37 and A/10 entered the town without meeting much more resistance (it turned out that no friendly forces were present).

As C/37 and A/10 advanced to the south, A/37 and C/10 headed east toward Gumbsheim, taking the town easily by 1300. A/37 and C/10 turned due south and drove three miles to capture Wendelsheim. Not far outside of Gumbsheim, Sergeant Stasi's tank destroyer hit two mines, blowing off both tracks. The crew was seriously rattled but fortunately escaped injury.

At the end of the day's action, CCB established their outposts on a three-mile line running generally north to south extending from Eckelsheim through Wonsheim and on toward the high ground east of Wendelsheim. More than 500 soldiers from the German *198th Infantry Division* were taken prisoner.

CCR Lends Support

During CCB's attack, elements of CCR drew closer to the front to support Lt. Colonel Abrams' combat command (CCR's B/35 and A/51 arrived the evening before). Colonel Blanchard's command would commence offensive operations on the right flank of CCB.

First into the fight was the task force commanded by Major Harry J. Rockafeller, comprised of B/35 and A/51. Advancing east from the vicinity of Fürfeld, he drove three miles to the east and planned on attacking Stein-Bockenheim from the northwest. En route to Stein-Bockenheim, he ran into strong anti-tank fire from three anti-aircraft guns and encountered a minefield at a key crossroads. The first two tanks passed through the minefield, but the third and fourth tanks struck mines, delaying the rest of the column behind them. The infantry deployed past the minefield to provide covering fire while the engineers cleared the mines. The recovery vehicles came forward to remove the two damaged tanks.

Rockafeller's attack resumed at 1430, but with adjustments to the original plan. A/35 and C/51 were brought up to attack Stein-Bockenheim. The combined arms team moved cross-country and attacked from the northwest. Wonsheim (not yet cleared by CCB) lay off their left flank, and it was feared that enemy forces there might present a threat.

Indeed, anti-tank fire rang out from the west edge of Wonsheim and knocked out one of the Shermans of A/35. The attack progressed over the crest of a hill that provided defilade cover from the direct fire coming from Wonsheim. Afforded that protection, the tanks assaulted Stein-Bockenheim. At 1525, they reported the town cleared, killing 14 Germans and capturing 40 in the process. The tanks and infantry then occupied the high ground southeast of town.

Farther back to the west (south of Fürfeld) CCR was charged with extending the American front two miles to the south. C/35 and B/51 were dispatched to clean out the towns of Neiderhausen and Winterborn, while a platoon each from B/35 and A/51 attacked Tiefenthal. All three towns were taken without casualties among the armored infantry or tankers. The Germans were not so fortunate, with seven killed and 87 taken prisoner.

The 704th Tank Destroyer Battalion received the task of protecting the division's lines of communication. A platoon of A/704, one platoon of B/35, and one platoon of B/51 were assigned this mission (all the other tank destroyer companies as well as the 704th HQ Company were committed elsewhere). The small force moved from Weinsheim and closed in on Fürfeld at 1120.

On March 19, the division had chalked up a gain of only 10 miles beyond the Nahe River. Along with the 90th Infantry Division, *Olympic* was ordered to change the direction of their attack to the southeast. Their general orders called for them to drive to the banks of the Rhine River in the area between Mainz and Worms. As night fell on March 19, *Olympic* was poised 18 miles northwest of Worms and only 11 miles southwest of Mainz.

CCB Reaches the Rhine

On March 20, Lt. Colonel Abrams renewed his drive for the Rhine. Striking out at 0700 from the vicinity of Wendelsheim, B/37 and C/10 swept into Erbes-Büdesheim on the heels of an artillery preparation provided by the 66th Armored Field Artillery Battalion. A/37 and C/10 continued into Heimersheim, a small town northwest of Alzey. From that position, CCB launched its attack on Alzey.

At 0815, the artillery delivered a preparation on the city. B/37 and B/10 followed behind the barrage at 0930. The only resistance they encountered was the familiar combination of a manufactured roadblock and a handful of soldiers defending it with small arms.

Following the capture of Alzey, CCB split into two columns, both of which drove to the southeast. One task force took on Dintesheim while the other attacked Eppelsheim.

German vehicles were observed fleeing toward the two towns. American fighter-bombers struck ahead of the 37th's tanks, devastating the German force before the churning Shermans caught up with them. With their vehicles and means of retreat destroyed, many of the German troops in the column surrendered. At 1215, CCB attacked Dintesheim and Eppelsheim simultaneously and cleared them both by 1445.

Abrams consolidated his command near Eppelsheim in preparation for the final drive on Worms, another 10 miles to the southeast. By 1530 the column entered Pfeddersheim, two miles from the outskirts of Worms. Only light resistance was encountered, but bad news arrived when it was discovered that both bridges spanning the Pfrimm River had been destroyed (one of which was blown up in their face).

In this region, the Pfrimm River flows generally west to east, eventually terminating where it flows into the Rhine River at Worms. Denied a crossing at Pfeddersheim, C/37 and A/10 headed east to the adjacent town of Leiselheim. They found a small stone bridge there and crossed over to the south bank. C/37 and A/10 advanced to the town of Pfiffligheim where they worked diligently to clear it of enemy troops, who returned fire with small arms

An M4A3E2 "Jumbo" passes through Alzey on March 20, 1945 (U.S. Army photograph, courtesy Darren Neely).

and *Panzerfausts*. As C/37 and A/10 attacked, A/37 and C/10 bypassed Pfiffligheim to the south and headed straight for Worms, entering the city at 1925. C/37 and A/10 cleared Pfiffligheim by 1700, and then joined A/37 and C/10 at Worms.

Worms is bisected by the Pfrimm River, with two bridges connecting the two unequal halves of the city. Both bridges were destroyed, which limited CCB's route to the Rhine. The Pfrimm is not a major river (only 25 to 30 feet wide where it flows through the city), so it didn't take long for the engineers to install a bridge over which a platoon of C/37 soon crossed. Meanwhile, B/37 and B/10 advanced farther south of the Pfrimm River. At 1730, they entered the town of Horchheim, southwest of Worms.

When the Sherman tanks of C Company reached the Rhine, they saw before them an exodus of Germans trying to flee across the river in boats. The tankers killed countless numbers of Germans on the river and along its banks as the enemy attempted to reach the far shore. They were sitting ducks.

Some of the Germans pressed against the river either surrendered voluntarily or were forced into submission. The tank of Paul Glaz, staged ahead of the balance of his company, was approached by about 50 Germans. Behind this contingent, another 150 or so of their compatriots were trying to make it to the river. While his gunner held the 50 willing prisoners at bay, Glaz turned his turret-mounted machine gun against the larger group. The bursts only injured a couple of Germans, but it stopped the rest in their tracks. With the entire cluster of 200 enemy soldiers frozen in the sights of his guns, he drove the tank to the far end of the enemy formation and paraded the entire group of prisoners back to the rear. At Worms, a total of 600 prisoners were taken, predominately from the *47th Volksgrenadier Division* and the *54th Nebelwerfer Regiment*.

The 35th Tank Battalion and 51st Armored Infantry Battalion, each now assigned to CCB, spent the day advancing along the combat command's far right flank. C/704 and elements of the 25th Cavalry Reconnaissance Squadron worked with the two battalions. During the morning, the tank destroyers and armored cars captured Nack, Offenheim, and Friemersheim (an advance of more than five miles to the southeast). C/704 inflicted heavy casualties and took a fair number of prisoners. In the C/704 journal it was noted that, "Sergeant Willard Fox and Danny Lamay put on a one-man blitz and took about 50 prisoners, eight pistols, Lugers, etc."

During the sweep along CCB's right flank, C/704 drew fire from enemy tanks and snipers at various places, but there were no casualties. In return, the gunners in Sergeant Jesky's and Sergeant Zamora's tank destroyers knocked out a German self-propelled gun and a light tank near Wahlheim (three other SPs apparently got away). The 25th Cavalry worked their 37mm cannons and machine guns. C/704's final attack for the day took place at Nieder-Flörsheim, seven miles southeast of Alzey.

March 20, 1945. German civilians hang white linen to signal their submission to the American advance near Worms (U.S. Army photograph, courtesy Darren Neely).

By the end of the day, the forces working CCB's right flank cut a swath 13 miles long before outposting the high ground near Pfeddersheim. Before the tank destroyer crews settled in for the night, they refueled, replenished their ammunition, and picked up a new supply of rations.

It was a great day for Captain Winkhaus and Private First Class Modlin, who left on furlough for the United States. While envious, their friends and brothers in arms from C/704 were glad to see anyone get a break. With the captain's departure, Lieutenant Richard Baudo was made acting commanding officer and Lieutenant Charles Callaway, executive officer. Lieutenant Harry Doughty now had the 1st Platoon and Lieutenant Feaux had the 2nd Platoon

During the drive to Pfeddersheim, the 704th experienced one of the great misfortunes of war: friendly fire. During the attack, crewmembers of the 35th Tank Battalion spotted the new M18s with the muzzle breaks. Thinking they were enemy tanks, they fired on the M18s and other nearby troops. The tank fire missed the Hellcats but knocked out one of the 25th Cavalry's M8 armored cars, killing one member of its crew and wounding two others. As compassionately noted in the unit journal, "It was an understandable mistake because these new tanks sure look like the enemy tanks."

CCA Follows Suit

CCA began March 19 near Wolfsheim. Lt. Colonel Irzyk was back in the saddle, his M4A3E8 Sherman returned to service by the swift work of his mechanics. They repaired the hydraulics, cleared the debris that jammed the turret, and patched the penetration spot made by the *Panzerfaust*.

Colonel Sears' combat command commenced their attack at noon, with A/8 and A/53 leading the charge to the east into the village of Vendersheim. Meeting no resistance, the column continued over two miles to the southeast and the day's main objective, the much larger town of Wörrstadt. Having received reports from air reconnaissance that the town was held in strength, Irzyk called for an artillery strike on the town and deployed all three of his medium tank companies for an assault.

C/8 moved to higher ground overlooking the town while Captain Ben Fischler's B/8 occupied positions from whence they would provide fire support. The A Team was assigned the task of making the assault on Wörrstadt. The Germans made a tough stand, but with only *Panzerfausts* and small arms as assets and the demoralizing strike by the artillery, it was just a matter of time before the town was cleared. By the time darkness settled in, it was done.

Once the B Team was no longer needed in support of the attack, the medium tanks and armored infantry were used to screen CCA's right flank. Their advance led them to capture the towns of Wallertheim and Rommersheim. They also cleared out Sulzheim, which lay directly west of Wörrstadt. Only light small arms resistance was met at each town, but unfortunately, Lt. Colonel Irzyk lost another platoon leader when Lt. Jenkins was evacuated after being hit by sniper fire. Late in the day, C/8 (though understrength from its losses the day before) and C/53 were pressed through the positions held by the B team and advanced two miles south-southeast of Wörrstadt to capture Spiesheim, which they outposted for the night.

As daylight approached on March 20, CCA's outposts near Spiesheim were a mere dozen miles from the Rhine. Having received the order for *Olympic* to change direction, B/8 and elements of the 10th Armored Infantry Battalion drove due south at 0600. Two hours later, Albig fell into their hands. From there, they slid southeast to bypass Alzey (that city being left to CCB) and subsequently captured Gau-Heppenheim, two miles east of Alzey.

CCB cut across two of the main roads leading east from Alzey. The Germans, likely sensing the trap, fled south from the city. As they emerged into the open terrain, they were hammered from the air by P-47s.

To clear out some of the enemy pockets remaining between CCA and CCB, A/8 and C/8, working with supporting infantry, seized the towns of Armsheim, Flonheim, Bornheim, and Bermersheim, all of which were west and southwest of CCA's primary axis of advance. During the day, Lt. Rubin, the tank platoon leader from C/8, became yet another casualty among the battalion's officers when he was struck by a sniper's bullet.

Captain Kieley's A/8 moved on to capture the towns of Dautenheim, Hochborn, Monzernheim, Westhofen, and Abenheim. When the Germans offered resistance, the formula applied by Kieley had by this time become routine. As he later described, he would dispatch tanks to each side of the town: "One to the left, one to the right, get it burning and let the infantry take care of it." As night fell, they cleared the town of Herrnsheim, a suburb of Worms (in stark contrast to the aforementioned tactics, a single halftrack dispatched by Kieley accomplished the task). The tankers of A Company were less than two miles from the Rhine River, having made an impressive advance of more than a dozen miles.

Meanwhile, B/8 and B/53 advanced on a route due east from Alzey and captured Dittelsheim and Bechtheim. From there, they darted two miles to the southeast and entered Osthofen. The Germans left a rear-guard force there, but it was not enough to slow down the American attack. The B team ended the night less than two miles from the west bank of the Rhine River. It was a spirited day for Colonel Hayden Sears' CCA.

The German Situation West of the Rhine

The German *7th Army* was finally given the order allowing them to conduct a wholesale retreat across the Rhine. But it was too late.

The German forces caught between the Fourth Armored Division and the Rhine River had run out of both real estate and hope. Pinned with their back to the unfordable river, with all the bridges destroyed by their own countrymen's hands, they had few options. The most prudent choice was to remain west of the river and flee south, but not all chose that route. The commander of the *2nd Panzer Division*, *Generalmajor* Meinrad von Lauchert, ordered his men to breakout to the east in small groups. Along with some of his staff, he swam across the Rhine. (After escaping the trap, he gave up the war and walked to his home in Bamberg, well over a hundred miles to the east. He was replaced by *Generalmajor* Oskar Munzel).

No matter how hopeless, the Germans fought on with the resources at hand. On occasion, they demonstrated that they still had the capacity to sting. On March 20, defying the notion held by many that American dominance of the sky was absolute, the *Luftwaffe* launched what historian Charles Province described as the "heaviest air attacks on the Third Army in the entire campaign." The Luftwaffe sent 314 enemy aircraft (including *ME 262* jets) skyward to conduct 61 raids (this according to a count made by Third Army anti-aircraft artillery observers).

In the Fourth Armored Division's zone, the Germans made a feeble attempt to create a defensive line stretching 18 miles from Bingen southeast to Alzey. But Sears and Abrams' combat commands had punched through this line before the Germans ever had a chance to formulate their defense. Perhaps the biggest show of force on the front of the Fourth Armored was the reappearance of the *Luftwaffe* over the Nahe River bridges as part of the aforementioned broader effort in the air. On March 20, thirty enemy planes attempted to hit the bridges. The anti-aircraft guns of the 489th Anti-Aircraft Battalion ensured that 14 of them did not return to their base. The 452nd Anti-Aircraft Battalion, providing additional support, destroyed a dozen more and scored another four probables.

Patton Brings on the Infantry

As the Fourth Armored ripped apart the German defenses west of the Rhine on March 20, Patton met with Major General Eddy at XII Corps headquarters near Simmern. Wanting to beat Montgomery across the Rhine, and having received Bradley's blessing just the day before, Patton urged Eddy to gain a crossing near Oppenheim the following day. Eddy asked for another day to prepare, to which Patton shouted, "No!" Eddy maintained his protest and won the debate.

On March 21, Eddy summoned to his headquarters Major General Irwin of the 5th Infantry Division. Irwin was on the verge of meeting with his own staff for the task of moving into reserve for XII Corps, but Eddy intercepted him. Revealing to Irwin that the 5th would have to make its crossing the following day, Irwin protested that he could not execute a "well-planned and ordered crossing" on such a short timetable. Eddy invoked the shadow of Patton to spur him on. "You've got to get across, Red. Georgie's been tramping up and down yelling at us." Thereafter, Irwin met with his staff, informing them that an assault on the Rhine was in their future. The prospect of enjoying the comfort of moving into reserve was no more.

Coiling Up Behind the Rhine

On March 21, the men of the Fourth Armored expected to pull the assignment of clearing the city of Worms. Perhaps they would even draw the honor of being the first unit of the Third Army to cross the Rhine River. But all of that changed when word was received from XII Corps that elements of the 5th Infantry Division had been given the responsibility for mopping up the city.

The transition was made in rapid fashion. By 1100, the relief of CCB was complete. Abrams' combat command shifted north of the city with the task of clearing out more than 10 towns in an area extending roughly 10 miles above the northern outskirts of Worms.

CCA advanced north as well, advancing in two columns on a path parallel to that of CCB. The net effect was the clearing of German remnants west of the Rhine. Each task force was commanded by one of the commanding officers of the two principle battalions: Lt. Colonel Irzyk (8th Tank Battalion) commanding one, and Lt. Colonel George Jaques (53rd Armored Infantry Battalion) the other.

Task Force Jaques entered Dexheim at 1400 with no resistance, and then at 1630, Oppenheim and Nierstein. Task Force Irzyk advanced on the right of TF Jaques. Led by the light tanks of D/8, they reached the town of Dienheim at 1445. Nestled on high ground less than a mile west of the Rhine, the town offered a magnificent view of the river. It also offered the sight of a treasure-trove of German barges and assault boats anchored along the far bank of the river. Irzyk brought forward his Sherman tanks and assault guns and jockeyed them to the edge of the ridge. From there, they pummeled the stationary targets.

After the day's action, CCA went into an assembly area near Dienheim. They were 14 miles north of Worms and directly south of Oppenheim. As the Fourth Armored moved into position, the 90th Infantry Division drew up to the Rhine and contacted the left flank of CCA. The only serious interference by the Germans came via the *Luftwaffe*. During the day, 20 enemy aircraft struck the Fourth Armored Division's assembly areas. The positions of C/704 were strafed by low-flying *ME 109s*, but no one on the ground was hit. The same could not be said for the Germans, as Sergeant Krewsky used his tank destroyer's ring-mounted .50 caliber machine gun to down one of the planes.

Some of the German troops trapped west of the Rhine filtered through the area. It wasn't unusual for Americans moving through the rear to come across individuals or small groups of Germans making their way toward the Rhine. Such was the case when men from C/704, traveling in two peeps, were returning to their unit after performing maintenance on their vehicles. They took three Germans captive on their way back and proceeded to leave their route in search of a prisoner of war cage. Thinking that the most probable location for such a cage would be in Worms ... and believing it had already been cleared ... they headed into the city. They came across more Germans in Worms, but they were not of the prisoner variety. Not a moment too soon, the two peeps (Sgt. Fox and Danny Lamay in one, Sgt. Robert Taylor and Cpl. Perrine in the other), "took off, but fast, expecting to stop lead any minute." They sped north, making their way back to the company position at Eich.

The 35th Tank Battalion and 51st Armored Infantry Battalion, both of which were supporting CCB, reverted to control of CCR. The 11th Armored Division, drawing up to the south of the Fourth Armored, relieved some of the division's units that had been screening the far-right flank.

The offensive in the Palatinate was nearly complete. All that remained was mopping up in the areas bypassed by the spearheads. That day (March 21) Patton reflected on the latest achievements of the Third Army:

> I really believe this operation is one of the outstanding operations in the history of war. We have put on a great show, but I think we will eclipse it when we get across the Rhine.

The relief by the 5th Infantry Division continued March 22. All elements of the Fourth Armored were alerted to pull back from the Rhine to an assembly area near the familiar town of Bad Kreuznach, now 25 miles behind the front line.

Colonel Sears' CCA moved out at 1300. Four hours later, they pulled into an assembly area near Sprendlingen. CCB was also alerted to move, but a last-minute change kept Abrams' command near Bechtheim, not much more than five miles northwest of Worms. The advantage gained was the ability to spend the entire day on the care of equipment and vehicle maintenance. As for CCR, they remained near Stein-Bockenheim where they served as a blocking force on the division's southern flank.

There was a celebratory moment that day for the 66th Armored Field Artillery Battalion. With the benefit of prolific record keeping, the battalion fired its 100,000th round since going into action in Normandy on July 17. At 1206, the battalion commander, Lt. Colonel Neil Wallace, pulled the lanyard, assisted by members of Battery A's first section: Chief of Section Sgt. Quinn, gunner Cpl. Bennick, driver T/5 Wilson, and gun crew members Pfc

Compton, Pfc Rhodler, Pfc Dunn, and Pfc Leichtman. The shell casing was preserved, inscribed, and placed within the battalion's archive.

Perhaps the most welcome news of the day, however, was the departure of 23 enlisted men and two officers for rest and recuperation back home in the United States.

The most critical action impacting the future of the Fourth Armored was happening on the front of the 5th Infantry Division. When the day started, Irwin's division was not yet fully assembled on the banks of the Rhine. By nightfall, they had drawn up to the river. Trailing behind the division came the abundance of matériel required for the impending assault across the river. It was no small task to move everything into place given the massive amount of engineering and bridging equipment required for the support and expansion of the bridgehead. Once the logistics were in order, the assault across the Rhine would follow.

11

Jumping the Rhine

Leave It to the Experts

In the 5th Infantry Division's zone, the width of the Rhine River ranged from 270 to 400 yards, making it not the mightiest of water obstacles but one of consequence nevertheless. The American position was enhanced by their hold on the high ground commanding the crossing sites.

In stark contrast, the terrain immediately east of the Rhine was flat and characterized by swathes of open fields punctuated by modest-sized towns and villages. Not until a dozen miles or so to the east does the elevation change. Roads and highways then begin their ascent toward communities carved into the side of the increasingly mountainous terrain. The Germans would take advantage of the more favorable defensive options offered by the high ground. But at the crossing sites themselves, the topography favored the Americans.

The 5th ID's assault pitted them against the German *7th Army*, commanded by *General* Ferber. The forces defending the river were a makeshift assembly of battered units and support personnel, hastily thrown together under the leadership of *General* Ralph Graf von Oriola's provisional *XIII Corps*. The most notable of Oriola's resources were the *559th Volksgrenadier Division* (at about 60 percent strength), the weaker *159th Volksgrenadier Division* (functioning at this stage primarily with four infantry battalions), and remnants of the veteran *2nd Panzer Division*. Given the paucity of resources, there was little the Germans could do to stop the Americans from gaining and reinforcing a bridgehead.

Commencing at 2200 on March 22, assault boats manned by the 204th Engineer Battalion carried two battalions of the 5th Infantry Division's 11th Infantry Regiment across the Rhine. There were two crossing points: Nierstein to the north and Oppenheim to the south. The Nierstein crossing was virtually unopposed. The boats crossing at Oppenheim drew machine gun fire when they reached the midpoint of the river. After a 30-minute fight, the defenders gave up. By sunrise, six infantry battalions were across. And best of all, the cost to Irwin's division stood at a modest 28 casualties.

Patton's assault over the Rhine drew Hitler's personal attention. At 0230 on March 24, with the river crossing less than 30 hours old, the *Führer* held a conference at his Berlin headquarters. He considered the bridgehead at Oppenheim to be the "greatest danger" (presumably as opposed to the bridgehead at Remagen). After reflecting on the relatively narrow width of the Rhine at this location, he bemoaned, "On a river barrier only one man has to be asleep and a terrible misfortune can happen." The best response the staff could muster at that moment was to dispatch five tank destroyers from a camp at Senne. Adolf Hitler, the commander of what was at the height of its powers the greatest army of its day, was reduced to directing the action of a platoon.

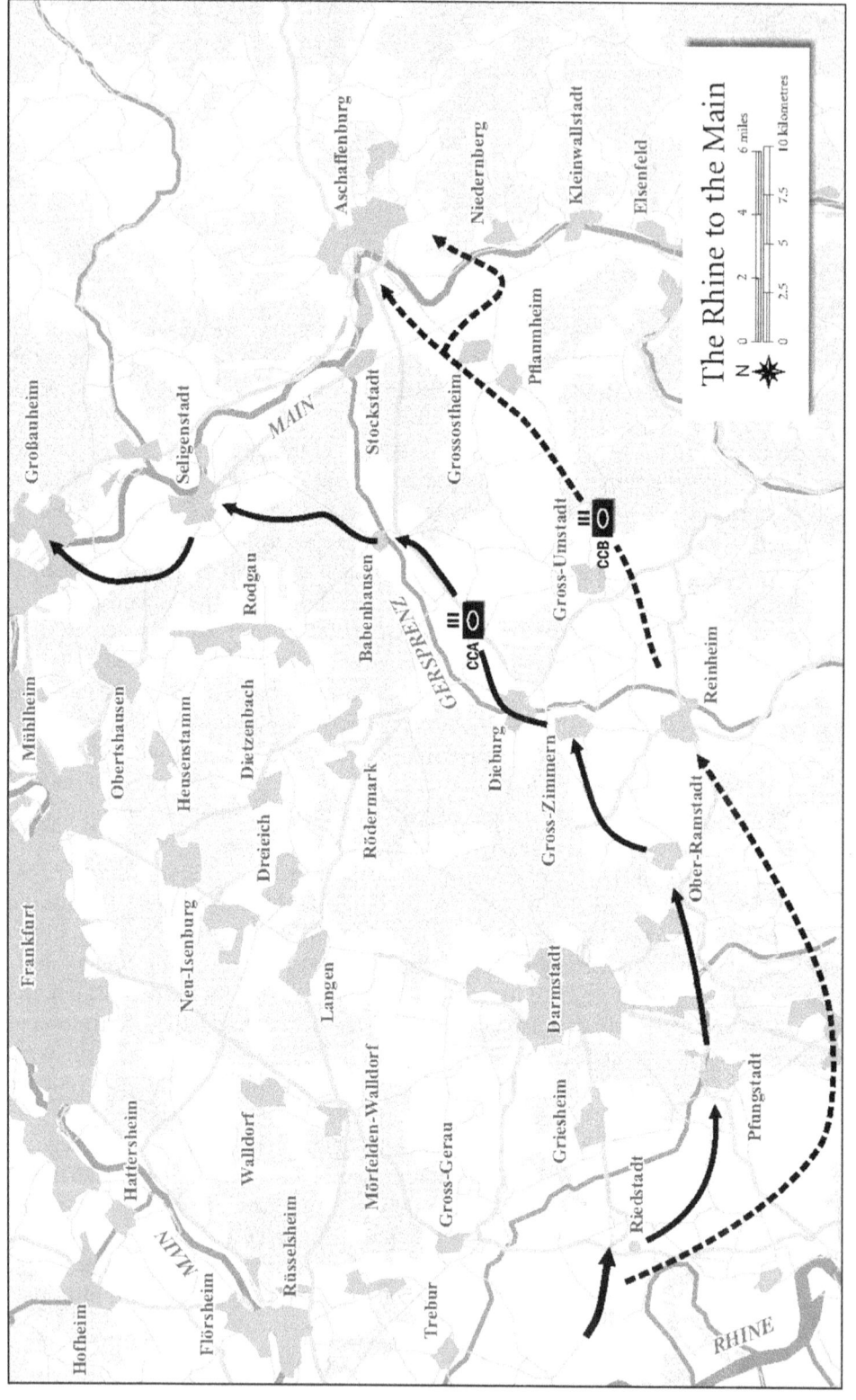

The Rhine to the Main (© Petho Cartography, 2020).

As for Patton's reaction, he was quick to send a congratulatory message to his troops:

Third Army General Orders 70, March 23, 1945
To the officers and men of the Third Army and to our comrades of the XIX TAC:
In the period from January 29 to March 22, 1945, you have wrested 6,484 square miles of territory from the enemy. You have taken 3,072 cities, towns, and villages, including…. Trier, Coblenz, Bingen, Worms, Mainz, Kaiserslautern, and Ludwigshafen…
You have captured 140,112 enemy soldiers and have killed or wounded an additional 99,000 thereby eliminating practically all of the German Seventh and First Armies. History records no greater achievement in so limited a time…
The world rings with your praises: better still, General Marshall, General Eisenhower, and General Bradley have all personally commended you. The highest honor I have ever attained is that of having my name coupled with yours in these great events.
Please accept my heartfelt admiration and thanks for what you have done, and remember that your assault crossing over the Rhine … assures you of even greater glory to come.

Patton wrote another compelling letter that same day to a much different audience: his wife, Beatrice. One fateful, unambiguous sentence spoke volumes. It would be the most compelling evidence for determining the true intent behind the controversial orders he would issue within the next 48 hours:

We are headed right for John's place and may get there before he is moved.

Changes in Command … and a Seed Is Planted

Patton's message to his army was an appropriate last hurrah for Major General Hugh Gaffey. The next commander of the Fourth Armored (now the fourth in its brief history) was Brigadier General William M. Hoge, formerly the commander of CCB of the 9th Armored Division. In his prior role, Hoge put two significant feathers in his cap: his inexperienced unit fought valiantly in a delaying action at St. Vith during the Battle of the Bulge, and more famously, it was his command that captured the bridge at Remagen.

Hal Pattison (the executive officer of CCA) later speculated about the factors leading to the transition from Gaffey to Hoge. From the moment Gaffey was assigned to replace Major General Wood, the Fourth Armored staff believed he (Gaffey) was being groomed for command of a new corps. When the Germans lashed out in the Ardennes, any such plans were upset and Gaffey continued in command for more than three months. The universal hope among the men of the Fourth was that Wood would return. Said Pattison,

In any case, it was not until the third week of March 1945 that XXIII Corps was activated and General Gaffey left the Division to assume command of it. By then Wood was commanding Fort Knox and Brigadier General William Hoge, who had captured the Remagen Bridge and was long past due for the reward of promotion and bigger command, became the fourth of the series of great commanders of the 4th Armored Division.

Brigadier General Hoge inherited responsibility for executing the division's latest orders. The Fourth Armored was alerted to cross the Rhine the following day (March 24) and then attack through the bridgehead established by the 5th Infantry Division. The objective thereafter was to seize a bridge over the Main River near Hanau, 32 miles to the northeast. The order of march was CCA, the 25th Cavalry Reconnaissance Squadron, CCB, and finally, CCR. But first, there was much to be done at the Rhine bridgehead.

Before *Olympic* could be unleashed, a bridge suitable for armor had to be installed. The engineers from the 150th Engineer Combat Battalion handled the task magnificently.

By late afternoon on March 23, a Class 40 M-2 treadway bridge, almost 1000 feet in length, was up and running. By the end of the day, the bridgehead was expanded to an area six miles deep and seven miles wide, providing ample room for *Olympic* to cross and begin maneuvering.

In advance of the Fourth's crossing, the 10th Armored Infantry Battalion's S-3 section and part of the recon platoon were sent to reconnoiter the area northeast of Oppenheim where the 5th Infantry Division held the bridgehead. The report brought back to the battalion commander, Lt. Colonel Cohen, was ominous: the recon party leader, 2nd Lt. Norman Hoffner, said that "he had never been under such tremendous artillery fire and the engineers were having a tough time repairing the damage."

The Fourth Armored Crosses the Rhine

The units of CCA moved from their assembly area at 0700 on March 24. To help protect the troops from enemy aircraft and artillery, engineers used artificial fog generators to mask the bridge. At 0900, the M5A1 Stuarts tanks of D/8, leading the way not only for the 8th Tank Battalion but for the entire division, started across the pontoon treadway bridge at Nierstein. The length and design of the bridge forced the tank drivers to limit their speed to only three miles per hour. Greeting each vehicle was a sign left behind by the enemy: "*See Germany and Die.*"

The first tank across the river belonged to Lt. Kaminsky, the commanding officer of D/8. His company was followed by the medium tank companies, A, B, and C. The last vehicle in the CCA column reached the east bank at 1250. The nearly four-hour transit time offers a sense of the sheer size of a combat command.

As CCA made its way across the bridge, Lt. General Patton arrived as a conquering warrior, eager to make the crossing himself. He walked to the midway point of the bridge and stopped in his tracks. A photographer was there to capture what happened next on the Nierstein pontoon bridge: Patton unzipped his trousers and famously pissed into the Rhine River. To Brigadier General Dager, Patton remarked, "Dager, I've been waiting three long years to spit in this creek." When he reached the opposite bank, exiting the bridge on foot, he deliberately stumbled, grabbed two handfuls of dirt, and shouted, "Thus William the Conqueror!"

CCA had little time for theatrics. The plan of attack called for the team to head southeast and bypass Darmstadt, a city of approximately 116,000 people. The column would swing around the city before setting out on the main axis of attack to the northeast. (As it turned out, *General* Felber of the German *7th Army* abandoned Darmstadt that day for fear that any forces committed to its defense would be destroyed.)

As Colonel Sears' command assembled in the southeast portion of the bridgehead, the Germans placed the point of the column under intense artillery and anti-tank fire. As stated in the journal of the 94th Armored Field Artillery Battalion, "The slightest movement, a puff of dust was sure to attract a German volley." The American Cub pilots were unable to spot the German guns from the air. Whenever the pilots attempted to fly beyond their own lines, they were chased away by withering machine gun and anti-aircraft fire. The battalion commander (Lt. Colonel Parker) did his best to estimate the German positions by using his map, a compass, and the direction and intensity of the sounds from the enemy guns. His estimates "were all on the nose" and the pilots were able to validate the gun positions from the air. The subsequent counter-battery fire silenced the enemy artillery, paving the way for CCA's advance.

The 8th Tank Battalion led the column on a four-mile run to the east-southeast through friendly territory. At Leeheim, the tanks of D/8 moved beyond the forward positions held by the 5th Infantry Division. With the column heading into enemy-held territory, Lt. Colonel Irzyk moved the B Team (B/8 and B/53) to the front.

The advance continued nearly due east until running into strong resistance at Wolfskehlen. Sensing that the fight would take some time, Irzyk sent the A Team toward Crumstadt via an alternate route while the B Team continued its attack at Wolfskehlen.

The A Team ran into its own difficulties when it came within a mile of Crumstadt. Heavy fire from artillery and self-propelled guns erupted from nearby Philippshospital. Attempts to maneuver into a better position to take out the enemy guns were foiled due to the muddy terrain. After a long duel, the guns at Philippshospital were silenced and the advance to Crumstadt continued.

The defenders of Crumstadt were well prepared with anti-tank guns, *Panzerfausts*, and small arms. Lt. Colonel Irzyk called for a TOT which softened up the German defenses. The A Team advanced into the town on the heels of the barrage, and after a spirited fight, sent the defenders into retreat. Behind them, the B Team finally cleared Wolfskehlen. A/8 suffered a significant loss when Captain Len Kieley was evacuated.

Months of combat and difficult living conditions had gotten the better of Kieley. He later described how awful the hygiene of the tank crews became while on the move day after day. Spent 75mm shell casings became the vessels of choice for urinating and defacating while in the tank. Dysentery was the norm. He suffered from a severe case of scabies, with multiple open sores on his skin. His teeth were in terrible condition and, by his own account, he was "mentally not in good shape." Kieley spent the next six weeks in a hospital in Paris. Irzyk assigned Lt. Ferguson to replace him.

After the first three strongpoints, the enemy didn't seem to have much left to put in the way of CCA. Sears' combat command turned to the east and tore through Eschollbrücken, Pfungstadt, Darmstadt-Eberstadt, and Nieder-Ramstadt. CCA took advantage of the approaching full moon and continued their drive well after dark. They made Ober-Ramstadt their final stop at midnight. From their starting point at the bridge, they had driven a little more than 18 miles as the crow flies.

Queued up behind CCA was Lt. Colonel Abrams' CCB, which didn't start crossing the bridge until 1600 on March 24. Their mission was to protect CCA from potential enemy counterattacks originating from the south.

C Troop of the 25th Cavalry Recon Squadron led the way across the bridge, followed by the tank destroyers of C/704. Then came the main combat elements, led by A/37 and C/10. The M7s of the 22nd Armored Field Artillery Battalion started across at 1730.

The Germans continued their attempt to take out the bridge by air. An estimated 154 aircraft participated in the latest round of attacks and as many as 33 were reportedly shot down by anti-aircraft crews.

The *Luftwaffe* had little impact other than rattling the nerves of those making the crossing. Wally Righton of the 704th Tank Destroyer Battalion said, "I was never so scared in all my life." The Germans also threw their artillery into the mix. By the time Captain Stanley Lyons of the 10th HQ Company crossed, it was night. Lyons noted that the German shelling around the bridgehead remained intense.

The threat presented by the attacking aircraft and artillery caused one driver to buckle.

Pfc Charles Wilson, driver of a chaplain's peep, suddenly found himself stuck on the bridge when traffic ground to a halt. Ahead, the driver of another vehicle abandoned his position and started back across the bridge on foot. Two officers, one wielding his .45, compelled the distraught soldier to return to his vehicle. As they passed Wilson's peep, he heard the driver's "stifled weeping, and muffled swearing." The column began to move again as anti-aircraft fire bristled overhead.

Cavalrymen of C Troop, 25th Cavalry Reconnaissance Squadron in action (courtesy Jim White).

11. Jumping the Rhine 165

Once across the bridge, CCB travelled the first few miles using the route taken by CCA. Abrams' column split off on its own at Erfelden. Moving south to Stockstadt am Rhein, CCB encountered resistance akin to what CCA experienced at Wolfskehlen. It appeared likely that the Germans had cobbled together what forces they could in a last-ditch defense anchored on the barrier towns close to the river.

A/37 and C/10 entered Stockstadt and cleared it by 1900. The tanks of C/37 and infantry of A/10 then drove east on a route parallel and to the south of that taken by CCA. At 1930, they attacked Hahn, where they faced only light resistance and made quick work of it. The column roared past the tightly-packed two and three-story homes with their steeply pitched roofs pointing to the sky in uniform fashion.

Once outside of Hahn, the armored vehicles picked up one of the excellent *Autobahnen* and sped four miles south to Hähnlein. The tanks and infantry entered the town under cover of darkness and dispensed with several *Panzerfaust* teams that sought to protect the obligatory barricade at the main street heading into the town. It was fortuitous for Abrams that resistance was light, since just one knocked out Sherman on the narrow main road in Hähnlein was likely to block the passage of the trailing vehicles. Backing up or turn-

March 9, 1945. American infantrymen from the 318th Infantry Regiment, 80th Infantry Division, scale a road block in Kyllburg, Germany. This is a good example of the type of roadblocks faced by the Fourth Armored during their drive across Germany (U.S. Army photograph).

ing around the column was nearly impossible within the confines of the town; the advance would likely come to a halt until the obstacle was cleared out of the way.

By midnight, the spearhead of CCB was located about 10 miles southwest of the lead elements of CCA. Abrams continued driving his tanks forward through the early morning hours of March 25.

CCR, being last in the division column, didn't start across the Rhine until 2345. The last vehicle crossed the bridge at 0300 on March 25.

It took 18 hours for the division to cross the Rhine. With approximately 2500 vehicles, putting an entire division across the river was no small task (especially given the attempts by the *Luftwaffe* to inflict damage on the bridge).

CCA's Race to the Main River

When the lead elements of CCA moved out at 0615 on March 25, they were already 18 miles beyond the Rhine. The once daunting water barrier guarding the approach to the heart of Germany was now not much more than an afterthought.

The Sherman tanks of C/8 led the column away from the town of Ober-Ramstadt. Their first objective was Hill 214. The tanks ascended the hill, and upon reaching the crest, their commanders were greeted by the sight of a freight yard near Groß-Zimmern. A large group of boxcars and flatcars sat idle, loaded with personnel carriers and 105mm howitzers. The tankers unloaded on the stationary targets. It was akin to target practice.

There was little opposition as the combat command moved northeast for nine miles through the towns of Roßdorf, Georgenhausen, Groß-Zimmern, Dieburg, and Altheim. The medium tank companies alternated when attacking the towns, one leap-frogging past the other. The absence of German defenses changed significantly three miles farther to the northeast at Babenhausen, where a nest of anti-aircraft guns gave the Americans considerable trouble. At 0900, the defenders reported being under attack, which prompted the commander of the German forces at the city of Aschaffenburg (eight miles to the east on the Main River) to issue an order to burn all secret documents. After the enemy position was silenced, the column turned north, cutting across a heavily wooded area and emerging five miles later in the open plain overlooking the Main River and their next objective: Seligenstadt.

Before the assault on Seligenstadt took place, Cub pilot Lt. Billy Wood spotted an intact railroad bridge spanning the Main four miles to the northwest, just outside of Klein-Auheim. On the opposite shore of the river was Großauheim. The rail line skirted the west side of that town, with a light industrial area lining the west side of the tracks. The buildings on the edge of Großauheim bordered the east side of the tracks, while the south edge of the town traced the line of the river.

The plan underwent an immediate change. CCA would forego an assault on Seligenstadt in favor of a drive for the bridge.

Lt. Wood also observed German engineers at work near the bridge site. Something had to be done to disrupt them if the span was going to be captured intact. To buy time for CCA's tanks and infantry, the six M7s of Battery A of the 94th AFAB set up as rapidly as possible, and with Lt. Wood serving as the spotter, fired furiously to disrupt the engineers. When the battery exhausted its 105mm ammunition, shells from B/94 were cannibalized to keep the interdiction fire going.

Passing ammunition into an M7 of the 22nd Armored Field Artillery Battalion (courtesy John Harris).

When the Sherman tanks of C/8 arrived on the scene, they added their direct fire to the effort. In combination with the artillery, the tanks pinned the Germans in place while a company of armored infantry made their way toward the bridge.

When the men of the 53rd AIB reached the railroad bridge, they found that an appendage had been added for vehicle traffic. The Germans had set off demolitions which blocked the railway portion of the bridge, but the appendage, while damaged, remained in place. It was now up to the doughboys to grab it.

The liaison officer from the 94th, Captain Temple, observed from the river bank. He lifted the artillery fire at the last possible moment before the infantry began their charge. The Germans prepared their defenses well, as evidenced by the small arms and 20mm AA fire that raked the approaches. Mines and booby traps combined with the enemy fire claimed six American lives and wounded at least 10. When the attack faltered, Lt. William E. McInerney of C/53 moved to the front of his company and led a charge across the bridge, which inspired his men to follow. Despite their losses, the armored infantry pushed across the damaged span.

C/53 and A/53 made it to the other side of the river. The light tanks of D/8 were brought to the river with hopes of crossing, only to discover that the bridge was impassable for vehicles. Things became even more serious when the bridge was further damaged, so much so that additional infantry couldn't cross. C/53 and A/53 were left to their own devices, save for direct and indirect fire support delivered from the other side of the river.

The Germans holding positions on the upper floors of the houses and churches nearby had a clear view of the bridge and its approaches. There was also an unobstructed view at ground level looking down the line of the railroad track. If a bridgehead was going to be established, it meant that Großauheim had to be cleansed of the enemy.

C/53 and A/53 began the arduous task of clearing the buildings. Additional infantrymen attempted to cross the river by boat, but German infantry, supplemented by snipers occupying at least one of the two churches and other buildings along the river, placed the boats under fire. The reinforcements were forced to turn back. The snipers also made their presence known to the armored infantry clearing the town. 1st Lt. John E. Olson, one of the officers leading a platoon inside Großauheim, hid his officer insignia to reduce the likelihood of being targeted by the enemy marksmen.

One of the German snipers turned to another target. Pfc Stevenson Moomaw, a medic with the 53rd, went to the aid of a wounded G.I. laying in the middle of a street swept by gunfire. Upon reaching the soldier, he began rendering aid. A sniper's bullet struck Moomaw, but he kept working on the wounded man. Two more shots rang out, mortally wounding the medic. (Moomaw was awarded the Distinguished Service Cross posthumously.)

The railroad bridge crossing the Main River into Großauheim as it appeared in 2019. The church visible in this photograph existed in 1945 and provided excellent observation and fields of fire for the Germans (photograph by author).

After Sergeant Nick Alexander's unit crossed the river, they set up defensive positions in the houses within Großauheim. As evening fell, Alexander took some time to wash up. While he was in the midst of cleaning himself, a jeep came to pick up platoon sergeant Lou Tomillo for a patrol. Tomillo wanted Nick to go with him, but seeing he was preoccupied, Lou took Charlie Metzler with him instead. It was the last that Alexander would ever see of Tomillo and Metzler.

Not long after dark, the situation changed abruptly when a train pulled into the rail station on the edge of town. Twenty-five railroad cars rolled in. They were loaded with German troops and mounting four 150mm guns and several anti-aircraft weapons.

Lt. Olson and his men opened fire as the train came to a halt. Young soldiers from an engineer officer candidate school piled out of the opposite side of the railroad cars and returned fire while using the train for cover. At 2000, the Germans mounted a counterattack. As author Charles McDonald wrote in the official U.S. Army history, "Men of both sides soon were so intermingled that for a while American artillery dare not risk firing on the German guns."

The men of the 53rd Armored Infantry Battalion fought deliberately but were forced back closer to the bridge. As the battle progressed, American engineers worked under enemy fire to complete a temporary bridge. More armored infantry from B/53 finally managed to cross the river and joined the battle. During the melee, an enemy round (probably from a *Panzerfaust*) struck the ground near Lt. Olson, wounding him.

The fight went on so long and with such intensity that the armored infantry's ammunition ran low. Unable to be resupplied as soon as they needed it, their only recourse was to call for artillery support. Forward observer 1st Lt. Sherman R. McGrew and S/Sgt. Richard Lane instructed the infantry to pull back 60 yards from the railroad so that the M7s had a safety buffer between friend and foe. Under McGrew's guidance, three artillery battalions (including a battalion of powerful 155mm howitzers attached to CCA) worked over the train and surrounding area. Five of the cars, loaded with munitions, disintegrated as catastrophic blasts engulfed them. Said McGrew, "Those explosions damn near knocked me flat each time a car went up, and I was 500 yards from the railroad." As the engagement continued into the night, McGrew shifted the artillery fire into a lumber yard where it appeared the Germans had taken refuge. After a harrowing battle lasting until midnight, the Americans finally gained control of the town. The engineers continued to work on the bridge in preparation for heavy vehicles to cross. The next morning, 75 German bodies were found in the lumber yard.

CCA's drive to the Main River was an impressive feat. They covered well over 20 miles that day and capped it off by gaining the bridge at Großauheim.

The crossing of the Main caused rancor within the leadership ranks of the German Army. The following day, *Generalfeldmarschall* Kesselring sacked the commander of the *7th Army*, the evasive *General* Felber. The commanding *General* of *LXXXV Corps*, *General* Kneiss, was dismissed three days later.

CCB Strikes East

On March 25, CCB's mission was to block any enemy attacks emanating from the south that might threaten the flank and rear of CCA. Lt. Colonel Abrams had his work cut out for him if his command was going to keep pace with Colonel Sears' CCA.

All signs early on pointed to that not being a problem. Abrams spurred his combat command through the night of the 24th and on through the morning of the 25th, catching the enemy by surprise (so much so that the Germans were forced to destroy several supply dumps). The column rolled seamlessly through the first few towns.

At daybreak, A/37 and C/10 ran into resistance at Jugenheim, the first town along the route that was carved into the higher terrain above the Rhine Plain. After the lead tank was knocked out by a *Panzerfaust*, the armored infantrymen became disorganized. Captain Kenneth L. Hoffman (C/10) dismounted and went forward to reorganize his men. A German sniper struck him in both legs, but Hoffman refused to be evacuated. Instead, he had two soldiers carry him about as he issued orders. Only after the attacked renewed did he agree to be evacuated. During the time spent clearing the town, the Americans discovered a hospital where 300 enemy soldiers were being treated (all of whom were taken prisoner).

The advance continued. B/37 and B/10, working to the south to guard the right flank of CCB's advance, entered Ober-Beerbach at 0745. They captured 400 Germans without a fight.

D/37 was placed at the head of the column and the pace picked up. When the tanks required gas, servicing was done as quickly as possible while on the road. The column jogged to the northeast and entered Reinheim at 0930. At that point, Abrams was only 15 miles southwest of his objective on the Main River.

Abrams' tanks reached the Main River south of the city of Aschaffenburg at 1220. They were approximately 11 miles southeast of where CCA achieved its crossing (a gap of this size between the two combat commands was atypical, but it came about in large part due to the opportunistic shift of CCA toward the railroad bridge).

D/37 was dispatched in search of a bridge near the town of Niedernberg (four miles south of Aschaffenburg). Not finding one there, the column drove northeast along the west bank of the river by way of the primary road paralleling the waterway. A company of armored infantry, coupled with a platoon of the light tanks, covered the ground between the road and the riverbank. As the column moved north alongside the waterway, they observed a ship bristling with 20mm anti-aircraft guns. After spotting the American infantrymen, the flak guns opened fire, inflicting serious casualties on one of the platoons. The enemy fire interfered with the movement of the main column, so the route was changed to some minor roads and trails that were out of the line of fire.

The enemy vessel was not forgotten. A section of tanks quickly approached and worked over the ship, eventually sinking it. Some of the survivors made it to shore, and 20 to 25 of them were collected. To the amazement of Captain Lyons, they were all women. The battalion commander, Lt. Colonel Cohen, realized that taking females as prisoners of war might cause some complications (Lyons described the situation as a "sticky wicket"). Through an interpreter, Cohen told the women to go to their homes.

Captain Lyons stood on an embankment and watched his HQ Company pass by in column formation. He later recounted the scene:

> Along came Lt. Pluff in his assault gun. He was grinning like a Cheshire cat and pointing down at the front of his tank. I didn't understand what it was he was pointing at until I spotted a 75mm solid shot stuck in the housing of the tank's final drive. He later told me that he had been shot at and hit by a German anti-tank gun which his gunner destroyed. It was a unique thing because not only was the tank fully operational, but not a single drop of oil had been lost from the final drive.

As they continued to press forward along the riverfront, the light tank crews found an intact railroad bridge three miles north of Niedernberg, close to the town of Nilkheim. When 2nd Lt. William Weaver approached the bridge in his M5A1 tank, he spotted two

500-pound bombs strapped to the structure. Before going another step forward, he radioed Abrams to report the find and asked for instructions. Abrams replied to the tank platoon leader (who was in his first day in that role), "You've done an excellent job—proceed." Contemplating the consequences, Weaver asked for clarification. Abrams' response couldn't be misunderstood. "Get your ass over the bridge, sonny."

Elements of the 10th Armored Infantry Battalion's reconnaissance platoon maneuvered onto the bridge and disconnected the bombs. The balance of D/37 and the 10th Armored Infantry Battalion were the first to cross. Lt. Donahue's light tanks outposted the high ground east of the bridge.

Crossing on a naked railroad bridge made for a slow and rough ride. As Captain Lyons pointed out, "It seemed that the further you went the higher you bounced until you had to come to a complete halt and start all over again." Eventually, the engineers placed boards along the tracks and used a bulldozer to push dirt in between the rails, making it possible for vehicles to ease their way across the bridge with less difficulty.

While the railroad bridge was being secured, Lt. Whitehill's A/37 led the main column of CCB directly toward Aschaffenburg with the hope of finding the main highway bridge there intact. When the lead elements arrived at the bridge site, they found the approaches unguarded and sped toward the crossing. Accounts vary in regard to what happened next. According to the 10th Armored Infantry Battalion journal, six tanks and a peep made it to the other side. As the seventh tank was in the process of crossing, the bridge was suddenly blown. However, in the 37th Tank Battalion journal, no mention is made of this. Instead, it states that the bridge was blown when the Shermans of A/37 had closed to within 300 yards. Clouding the situation further is a German account that describes combat that resulted in

The railroad bridge near Nilkheim, as it appeared in 2019 (photograph by author).

the lead American tank being knocked out as it crossed the bridge, and that the bridge was subsequently destroyed at 1326.

In any event, all accounts agree that the crossing was foiled. The bulk of CCB was routed to the railroad bridge. By 1600, the tank and infantry teams were across and carved out a bridgehead in an area nestled between Aschaffenburg, Schweinheim, and Obernau. Soon thereafter, enemy troops (likely from the *9/2 Pioneer Battalion)* were spotted at the edge of woods close to the vehicle assembly area. The Roadquarters Detachment fired .50 caliber machine guns at the tree line. One hundred and fifty Germans surrendered.

The really hard work began at 1730 as A/10, B/10, B/37, and C/37 commenced their attack into Aschaffenburg. The remainder of the units of CCA stayed within the bridgehead. Only 20 minutes after commencing the operation, orders were received to halt the attack and for all units to consolidate within the bridgehead and dig in for the night. The tanks of D/37 outposted the high ground east of the river.

Twenty miles to the west, the city of Darmstadt, now well to the rear, presented another set of challenges. Though the city was bypassed by the primary combat commands, it could not be ignored. CCR drew the assignment of clearing the city. The effort began with the aircraft of XIX TAC, which delivered a thorough pounding of the city. At 1330 a task force composed of units from CCR's 35th Tank Battalion and 51st Armored Infantry Battalion entered Darmstadt. They discovered that the Germans had abandoned the city, and the Americans declared it clear just an hour later.

On this same day, in another letter to his wife Bea, Lt. General Patton confided, "Hope to send an expedition tomorrow to get John." He was on the verge of making one of the most disastrous decisions of his military career.

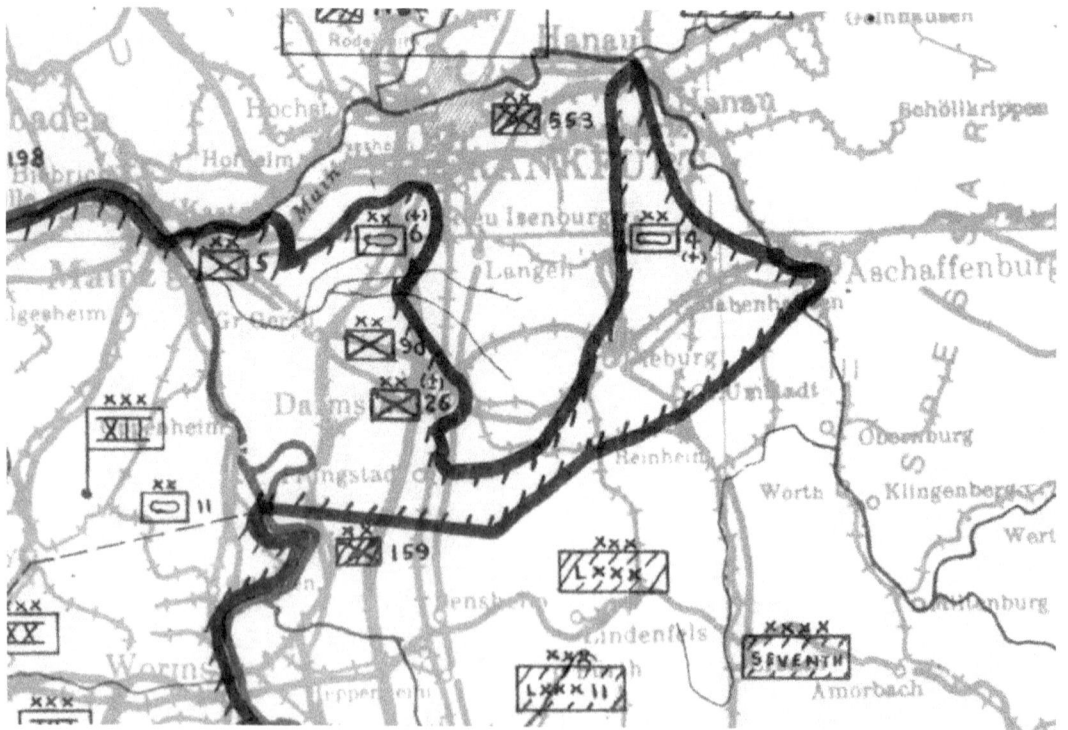

The 12th Army Group situation map for March 26, 1945 (U.S. Army digital archives).

In pursuit of 900... or one

The sequence of events leading up to the commission of what became known as the "Hammelburg Raid" is not entirely clear. There are conflicting accounts and testimonials from the participants as well as several authors and researchers who have reconstructed it. But it is most likely that first seed planted for the mission was a visit paid to Major General Eddy's command post on the evening of March 25. The visitor was Patton's aide, Major Alexander Stiller.

Stiller came to the Fourth Armored HQ to personally relay a directive from his boss: Patton wanted a special task force assembled to liberate a prisoner of war camp located 36 airline miles behind enemy lines. More precisely (though the exact location was not known to the participants at the time), the camp was located a little over a mile due south of the town of Hammelburg. *Oflag XIII-B* was thought to house approximately 900 American officers. Major Stiller informed Eddy that he (Stiller) would accompany the mission but would not be in command.

The estimate of the number of prisoners believed to be at *Oflag XIII-B* is an important element in the story about to unfold. It is known with certainty that Patton believed the number to be 900, as that is what he recorded in his diary. Referring to the subsequent visit he made to Eddy's headquarters on March 26, he therein wrote:

> directed Eddy to send an expedition to the east about 60 miles for the purpose of recapturing some 900 American prisoners alleged to be in a stockade there.

He also expressed this number in a letter to his wife on March 27:

> Last night I sent an armored column to a place 40 miles east of Frankfurt where John and some 900 prisoners are said to be.

At a press conference on March 30, Patton said in part:

> There was a prisoner of war camp containing at least 900 Americans—mostly officers, both ground and air.... I felt that I could not sleep during the night if I got within 60 miles and made no attempt to get that place.

Patton specifically mentioned 900 prisoners in another letter to his wife on March 31. Lest that not be enough, on April 5 Patton expressed his foreknowledge of the prisoner count in a letter to his sister Nita:

> An expedition I sent out actually rescued Johnny and then got recaptured itself. When I sent it out, I did not know that Johnny was in the camp but did know that there were 900 American officers there. Actually, there were 1200. I am hoping that some of them got away.

After Major Stiller's meeting with Eddy, it appears likely that Eddy in turn telephoned Brigadier General Hoge to explain what Patton had asked of them.

Brigadier General Hoge, though brand new to his role as commander of the division, thought the order impossible to obey and said as much to Eddy. Given that Hoge's existing orders for the division called for a drive to the north after crossing the Main River, it made little sense to him to send a task force nearly 90 degrees to the east. Additionally, with the Fourth Armored Division's turn to the north, the task force would be moving into the zone of the U.S. Seventh Army.

The commander of XII Corps was sympathetic to Hoge's concern and informed him that he (Eddy) would take the matter up with Patton. When the conversation ended, Hoge believed that was the end of it, and he made no further plans to execute the mission.

What was at work here? *Oflag XIII-B* was carved out of the *Lager Hammelburg*, a prominent military training facility built in 1873. *Lager Hammelburg* included a sprawling training ground that extended in some directions more than four miles from the main facilities. At the south end of the training ground, there was an unoccupied hamlet, and the west side was hemmed in by a string of densely wooded hills, the most prominent portion being the Reussenberg.

Prior to the Battle of the Bulge, *Oflag XIII-B* held not 900 American prisoners of war, but somewhere between three and four thousand Serbian officers of the Royal Yugoslav Army taken prisoner in 1941. The even larger *Stalag XIII-C*, where up to 10,000 or more prisoners were held, was located on the east side of the camp. The enlisted men and non-commissioned officers held at *Stalag XIII-C* were of British, American, and Soviet origin.

During January 1945, the Serbs at *Oflag XIII-B* were joined by 800 American prisoners. Many of the new arrivals were officers captured during the Battle of the Bulge. Among the prisoners was 1st Lt. Lyle Bouck, Jr., commanding officer of the 99th Infantry Division's I&R Platoon, which played a critical role during the opening hours of the battle on December 16. The most senior among the officers was Colonel Charles C. Cavender, a regimental commander from the 106th Infantry Division, which had surrendered two of its three regiments in the Schnee Eifel during the early days of Hitler's winter offensive.

On March 8, 430 additional Americans arrived after an arduous trek from *Oflag LXIV*, an officers' prisoner of war camp near Szubin, Poland. The prisoners marched through terrible winter conditions for the better part of five weeks. On February 26, those who survived the march were loaded into boxcars for a trip by rail that lasted an agonizing 10 days before reaching the town of Hammelburg.

The transplanted Americans were under the command of Colonel Paul Goode. His chief of staff was Lt. Col. John Knight Waters. Captured on February 14, 1943, during the battle of Kasserine Pass in North Africa, Waters became POW number 4161 at *Oflag LXIV*. There was one other very distinguishing characteristic about Waters: he was the son-in-law of Lt. General George S. Patton. Lt. Colonel Waters was the "John" Patton referred to when writing to his wife on March 23.

While it was not known with 100 percent certainty that Waters was among the prisoners currently at *Oflag XIII-B*, it was more likely than not. It *was* known with certainty that he had been held at the camp in Poland. It was *also* known with certainty that many of the officers previously held at Szubin had been transferred to Hammelburg before advancing Russian forces liberated *Oflag LXIV*. The news of

Lieutenant Colonel John Waters, just a few days before his capture on February 14, 1943, in North Africa. He would spend more than two years as a prisoner of war (courtesy George Patton Waters).

Waters' movement came via a report from Major General John R. Deane, head of the U.S. Military Mission to Moscow, who learned of this from Soviet intelligence earlier in the year. The information then flowed to Patton. Also, the prisoners at *Oflag XIII-B* used a secret radio to report the arrival of prisoners from Poland.

Had John Waters survived the trek from Poland? It was a difficult, dangerous trip of over 300 miles in distance. It was a trip which hundreds of prisoners failed to complete. But if Waters had indeed survived the march, *Oflag XIII-B* was his likely home. Granted, there were dozens of *Oflag* camps (these were reserved for officers, while *Stalags* were restricted to enlisted men). But the odds were slim that officers would have been siphoned off from the march and parceled off to other camps.

As this drama played out, a war remained to be fought. As the hands of the clock ticked beyond midnight and March 26 arrived, the Fourth Armored Division was fighting hard to maintain their two bridgeheads over the Main River. They couldn't have imagined being asked to siphon off valuable tanks and armored infantry for a mission that no reasonable or responsible commander would have commissioned. But in this case, nepotism and personal interests were about to trump all else. The only other explanation to emerge would come from Patton himself. And his account of events would be rife with self-serving revisionism embraced only by those not wishing to see his reputation tarnished.

A Tough Nut to Crack at Großauheim

On the morning of March 26, Colonel Sears' units continued to hold a small bridgehead at Großauheim. At 0530, the Germans launched another counterattack but could only muster 50 soldiers for the effort (though they did manage to support the attack with artillery). The men of the 53rd Armored Infantry Battalion, still fighting without armor support within the bridgehead, relied on machine guns and small arms to repulse the attack.

With CCA facing tough resistance in the bridgehead, Colonel Sears received reinforcements culled from CCR. A task force consisting of one company each from the 35th Tank Battalion and 51st Armored Infantry Battalion was dispatched to Zellhausen, a town located about six miles southeast of CCA's bridgehead. This helped close the substantial gap that existed between CCA and CCB.

The Germans applied accurate artillery fire near the crossing site at Großauheim, which hampered the engineers' efforts to repair the bridge. When the structure was finally complete, the first vehicles to cross the river were two platoons of light tanks from D/8. Not long after leaving the bridge site, one of the platoon leaders (Lt. Kaminsky) and the other members of his tank crew were killed when a *Panzerfaust* destroyed their M5A1 tank.

To expand the bridgehead, a combat team from the 26th Infantry Division was inserted. The infantrymen from the *"Yankee Division"* pushed through the positions of the 53rd Armored Infantry Battalion, and with the support of guns from CCA, attacked Großauheim. The Germans continued their staunch defense of the town, forcing the American infantry to pry them out of the cellars with the use of hand grenades.

As the intense fighting continued, Lt. Colonel Irzyk's 8th Tank Battalion waited impatiently on the other side of the river. The tank companies outposted numerous towns along a front stretching for six miles south of Großauheim. Southwest of Hainstadt, the tankers captured a large supply depot containing a stash of medical supplies valued at an estimated two-and-a-half-million dollars.

CCB's Bridgehead over the Main

While *General* Felber may have lost his command because of CCA's capture of the bridge at Großauheim, CCB's bridgehead south of Aschaffenburg had certainly not escaped the German's attention either. During the early morning hours of March 26, the Germans threw as much as they could muster at CCB. The attacks came not only against the bridgehead but against the right flank of Lt. Col Abrams' combat command on the west side of the Main.

The Hellcat tank destroyers of C/704, working in tandem with C Troop of the 25th Cavalry Reconnaissance Squadron, were positioned near Großostheim, west of the Main River and some three miles southwest of the bridgehead near Nilkheim. Their assignment was to guard the rear and right flank of CCB. Throughout the night, enemy aircraft bombed and strafed the area.

Shortly after 0100, in what would turn out to be one of the most damaging attacks of the war against C/704, eight to 10 enemy tanks and another three to five assault guns attacked near the 1st Platoon outpost (the enemy armored vehicles were stalking the rear of an American column moving through the area). A German self-propelled gun fired on a Sherman tank at the rear of the column, setting it aflame.

The tank destroyers were only partially manned when the attack started. Those in the turrets quickly traversed their guns to the rear while the sleeping crewmembers, awakened by the gunfire, sprung to life and climbed into their vehicles. But before they could halt the German assault, the Hellcats of Sergeant George Kachline and Sergeant Pat Mascara were both knocked out and burned.

The injuries suffered by the crews were severe. Pfc Erwin Lanzendorfer, who had been with the company since before the battalion left the U.S. for England, was instantly killed. Sergeant Mascara, who joined the company as a new replacement in December, lost a leg and suffered other severe wounds. Corporal Michael Dawda, with the company since 1942, and Pfc James Kingery, who joined shortly before leaving the States, were both severely burned. Corporal George Zeljak, a veteran since 1942, received serious wounds when he was struck by machine gun fire. Corporal Aita, one of the newest replacements, was also wounded. Pfc Fred Wright, who joined as a replacement in November 1944, was slightly wounded. At 0200, the security vehicle was also hit. Pfc Albert Gordon was mortally wounded, living only a short time. Pfc Horace I. Marshall, the security vehicle driver who only recently joined the company, was killed instantly. Sergeant Bronislaw Dlugosz was wounded for the second time in six months. Both the 1st and 2nd Platoon security vehicles were disabled, as was Lieutenant Fieux's peep. Corporal Dreiswerd was hit by shrapnel. Pfc Solomon Tone was wounded but not evacuated. Despite the carnage, Corporal Stephenson, the gunner with Sergeant Jesky's crew, knocked out one of the assault guns and managed to drive off the rest.

In total, C/704 claimed three self-propelled guns destroyed and 10 of the enemy killed. But it was small consolation for their own losses. Fortunately for the elements of CCB holding their position in the bridgehead, the attack against their rear was repulsed. Their work done, C/704 moved out at noon and took up new positions at an outpost in the woods near Großostheim.

At 0300, all companies of the 10th Armored Infantry Battalion east of the Main River were ordered to prepare for a German counterattack. When C/10 received the alert and an accompanying message for redeployment of the company, T/Sgt. Edwin D. Beaghler personally contacted each platoon leader and delivered the message. When attacked by an enemy patrol, he fought his way back, preventing the enemy from capturing the message.

Before the German attack commenced, the *Luftwaffe* tried to destroy the bridge from the air. At dawn, the distant drone of aircraft filtered into CCB's rear positions near the bridgehead. Shouts of "Air, Air" brought everyone's attention to the fog-shrouded sky. The ceiling was very low with rain falling during the morning, masking the approaching aircraft.

Standing in the turret ring of the supply vehicle was Mess Sergeant Theodore H. Behney of the 10th Armored Infantry Battalion. Manning the .50 caliber machine gun loaded with a combination of tracer, armor-piercing, and incendiary rounds, he directed his aim in the general direction of the sound of the aircraft motors. Suddenly, a German twin-engine bomber broke out of the fog at a height not more than 150 feet. He opened fire, and his rounds quickly swept across the bomber's left wing, through the left engine, and then shattered the Plexiglas cockpit. The bomber rolled to the left and disappeared beyond a nearby ridge, exploding on impact. A second bomber and several enemy fighters appeared as well, but they quickly departed without doing any damage.

After the failed attack from the air, enemy armor made a strike against the bridgehead. The Germans assembled a force of 11 assault guns and two tanks for the attack. As the armor advanced through the morning rain, the 37th Tank Battalion destroyed three of the assault guns. The rest of the German armor withdrew to the south.

Later that day, Captain Lyons, along with Newton and Lt. Andrew Pluff, went forward to observe Aschaffenburg from a ridge overlooking the city. As they observed through binoculars, they had their first sighting of a German *ME 262* jet fighter. They took note of the unusually large engines, one mounted beneath each wing. And when the plane flew across the ridge, they observed the absence of propellers. Newton left the group to report the sighting back to the battalion command post. Captain Lyons and Lt. Pluff remained crouched on the ridge to continue their observation of the Germans as they prepared their defenses in the city. Pluff stood up, and just a moment later, a bullet struck the ground close to his feet. Just as Lyons warned him to get down, a second round was fired, striking and killing the lieutenant.

It was tragic whenever a man was killed in action. But for the 10th AIB, the loss of a man like Lt. Pluff, who fought so valiantly throughout the campaign, was especially hard to take. But no matter how difficult it was for his brothers-in-arms, it was surely harder for his family. Pluff, just 26 years old, left behind his wife Lavern and a young son, Charles.

At 1500, Lt. Colonel Abrams informed the battalions that elements of the 26th Infantry Division would relieve them, and that the U.S. Seventh Army was taking over their zone. CCB would shift to the north and use the bridgehead gained by CCA to carry on the attack along with Colonel Sears' combat command.

But before CCB departed, there was one more task to undertake. At 1700, the 37th Tank Battalion was informed that they were to furnish a company of medium tanks and one platoon of light tanks for a raid to rescue some American prisoners of war. At 1800, Lt. Colonel Abrams and Lt. Colonel Cohen met with Major Hunter at the 37th Tank Battalion's command post to plan the details. What the raiders were not aware of was the true underlying motivation for the task force: to bring back one man, Lt. Colonel John K. Waters, the son-in-law of Lt. General George S. Patton.

12

Task Force Baum

Subterfuge

On the morning of March 26, Lt. General Patton traveled to the headquarters of XII Corps to visit with Manton Eddy. Upon his arrival, he was informed that Eddy wasn't there. In his absence, he instructed Eddy's chief of staff, Brigadier General Ralph Canine, to phone the commander of the Fourth Armored Division and issue him (Hoge) the order to launch the task force.

Eddy must have anticipated Patton's visit as well as his intent. Canine replied to Patton, "General, the last thing Matt told me before he left was that if you came by and told us to issue that order I was to tell you I wasn't to do it."

One would think that such a response would provoke a stern retort on Patton's part. Instead, Patton reiterated the instruction for Canine to get Brigadier General Hoge on the phone.

Canine made the call, but Patton took hold of the phone and personally issued the order to Hoge who, despite his short tenure as the commander of the Fourth Armored, protested for lack of resources. Patton's response was unusual. "I promise I'll replace every man and every vehicle you lose." To some, such an assurance reflected a lack of concern for the fate of the men that would comprise the task force. In every sense of the word, they were expendable. But for what greater cause?

In his diary, Patton confided that Eddy and Hoge "were reluctant to do this because they said if I failed, I would be severely criticized. However, I do not believe that fear of criticism should prevent my getting back American prisoners, particularly as in the last death struggles of the Germans, our men might be murdered."

Protecting Patton's reputation could hardly have been at the forefront of Eddy and Hoge's thoughts. Undoubtedly, their concern was for the men under their command. This was an unprecedented mission and a request that invited disaster. Complicating the situation even further for Hoge was the fact that he would be sending the task force in one direction (east) while the rest of the division headed another (north). Should the mission not go as planned, Hoge had little to no capacity to go to the rescue. The task force would be, for all practical purposes, on its own.

From the outset, there were cracks in the cover story for the mission. In a side conversation, Major Stiller (who was apparently at Hoge's command post when Patton called) explained to Hoge that Patton was personally bent on liberating the camp. He also revealed to Hoge that he (Stiller) wanted to go on the mission "only because General Patton's son-in-law Colonel Waters, was in the prison camp." As the historian Martin Blumenson wrote. "…Patton asked him whether he would like to accompany the task force. Stiller understood this to be an order." Blumenson quoted Stiller, "a request by a general is an order."

12. Task Force Baum

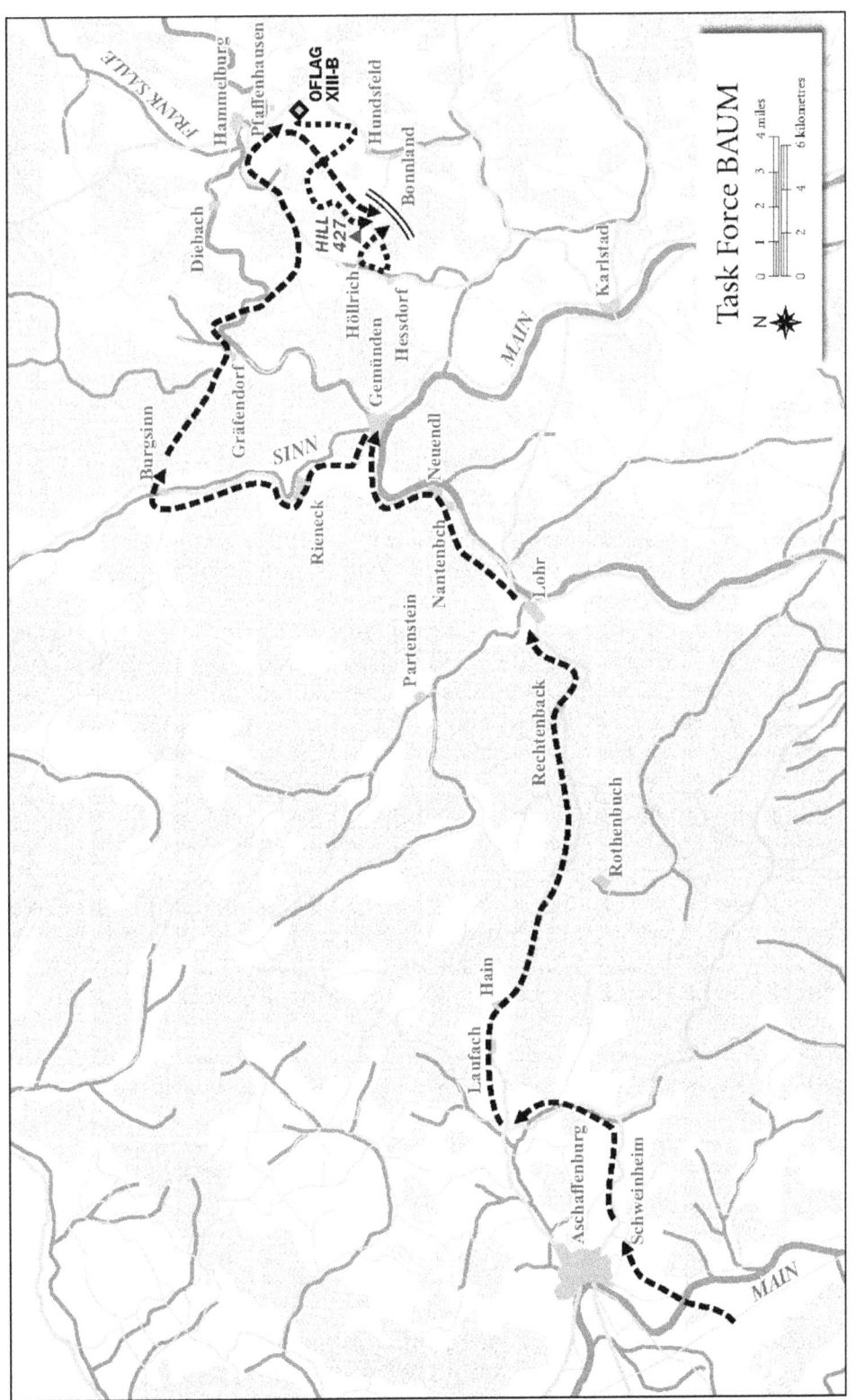

Task Force BAUM (© Petho Cartography, 2020).

After taking the call from Patton, Hoge was left no choice in the matter. And so, the wheels for the raid were set in motion.

Colonel Roberts (the new assistant division commander) met with the commander of CCB. When informed of the order, Lt. Colonel Abrams joined the chorus of those who believed the very idea of the mission to be folly.

Abrams called Hoge to protest. He believed that if the mission were to be executed, the full weight of CCB should be utilized. In his estimation, a combat command could go *anywhere*, with no fear of defeat. Indeed, they had been doing so for days on end! Hoge, having already made and lost this argument with his superiors, informed Abrams that the task force must be no larger than two companies. Abrams felt certain that such a small task force, driving that far behind enemy lines, would not have the means to support itself. It would be wiped out.

Abrams expressed that he would like to speak with Patton directly and plead his case. Hoge told him that he would have the opportunity, as Patton would be visiting with him later that morning.

Selecting the Task Force Commander

While waiting for Patton to arrive, Abrams took steps to ready for the mission. He contacted Lt. Colonel Harold Cohen, commanding officer of the 10th Armored Infantry Battalion, and instructed him to prepare.

Patton, Stiller, and Hoge arrived at Abrams' command post. The Third Army commander asked who would be leading the task force. When Abrams asserted that he was going to lead the raid with his full combat command, Patton replied, "You are not going and neither is your combat command. This is to be a small force. Now, answer my question. Who is going to lead it?"

Abrams adjusted his response and informed Patton that Hal Cohen would be leading the task force ... if he was well enough.

What was Cohen's affliction? The battalion commander had a severe case of hemorrhoids.

Patton asked to have a doctor brought in. When the battalion surgeon arrived, the entire entourage.... Patton, Stiller, Hoge, Abrams, and the surgeon ... went to Cohen's command post. There, they found Cohen consulting with his S-3 (Captain Abraham Baum), the 37th Tank Battalion commander Major William Hunter, and Hunter's S-3, Captain William Dwight. Patton and the surgeon pulled Cohen aside and had him drop his pants. Without hesitation, Patton agreed that Cohen was in no shape to go on the mission.

So, if not Cohen, then who?

Cohen immediately recommended 24-year-old Captain Baum to lead the task force. A seasoned veteran of the 10th Armored Infantry Battalion, Baum had been in harm's way on plenty of occasions. He was no stranger to combat and rapid advances.

All parties agreed with the choice of Captain Baum as the task force commander. Patton then shared some private words with Baum, after which he headed for the door. Patton's last words before departing were, "Major Stiller will fill you in on the details."

A Recipe for Disaster

Lt. Colonel Abrams asked Stiller, "What's so special about Hammelburg?" Stiller replied, "There's a POW camp there with **300 American officers** (emphasis added) in it. Patton wants them liberated."

Why did Stiller set the expectation that only 300 officers were held prisoner, when Patton believed the number to be *900*? And why is this important? We will likely never know the answer to the former question. But as for the latter, the importance is clear and obvious: if the task force was created with the capacity for 300 prisoners as opposed to three times that number, Captain Baum was destined to have a serious issue on his hands. The vehicle capacity of the eventual task force was enough to bring back 300 (plus the task force members themselves) without too much difficulty. But even jammed to the gills, with men clinging to the exterior of every vehicle, there was not enough for 900.

Major Stiller removed a map from his briefcase and highlighted the route to Hammelburg. Abrams and Cohen focused on the fact that the tanks and halftracks would not have the range to get there and back. In response, Stiller recommended they carry as much extra fuel as possible. He also suggested that the task force should be able to capture fuel and extra vehicles. Some might say that it was folly to predicate the success of the mission on the unknown availability of fuel and transportation.

Captain Baum leaned in and studied the map as the conversation continued. He asked Stiller, "Where is the POW camp in relation to the town? It's not indicated on the map." Stiller didn't know. But he relayed that Lt. General Patton believed that local civilians could be forced to reveal that information. This was yet another loose end left to chance.

The Combat Command Debate

A lingering subject of controversy has been the decision to send a small task force instead of a full combat command. Of all the participants, Abrams was the most vocal about the need for a larger force. The role that others played in the final decision is not entirely clear. It does seem that Hoge agreed with Abrams. Eddy, on the other hand, appears to have believed that the commitment of an entire combat command would have compromised the strength of XII Corps' thrust to the north, perhaps jeopardizing its success (though it is unlikely that a negative consequence would have resulted, given that the Fourth Armored *routinely* used only two of its three combat commands at a given time). Patton later lamented that he let Eddy and Hoge talk him out of sending a combat command. There seems to be some evidence of Eddy voicing that opinion, but no supporting evidence that Hoge expressed that point of view in his conversation with Patton.

Adding to the controversy was Patton's diary entry on March 31:

> *I made* [the raid] *with only two companies on account of the strenuous objections of General Bradley to making any* [effort] *at all. Had I sent a combat command as I had first intended to do, this mistake would not have occurred.*

It is noteworthy that Bradley *clearly* stated in his own memoir that he knew nothing about the raid in advance of its execution. According to his own account, his knowledge was gained after the fact.

There was also the viewpoint of Major Stiller. At some point along the line, Hoge informed Stiller of the size of the task force. As Blumenson wrote, "He (Stiller) was somewhat surprised when Hoge asked him what he thought of it." In Stiller's opinion, the force was too small. Blumenson also wrote,

> *Stiller anticipated dropping off some men to guard each bridge to keep it open when the force returned. He thought that the group was strong enough to get to Hammelburg but not strong enough to return.*

As for the division commander, Blumenson offered, "Hoge said he did not expect the task force to get back. He was opposed to sending anything."

In any event, the use of a full combat command was denied. No matter the explanation, responsibility for the mission and the size of the task force rested squarely with Lt. General Patton.

The Men and the Mission

Back at the command post of CCB, Abrams laid out the mission for his team. In its simplest form: break through the German lines, drive northeast to liberate *Oflag XIII-B*, and return with the American prisoners Lt. General Patton believed to be held there.

The formation of Task Force Baum was completed by 1700. The core elements were a company each of armored infantry and medium tanks. A/10 was 173 men strong (including four officers) and was equipped with 15 halftracks. C/37 had 10 of its normal complement of 17 Sherman tanks. The medium tank company also had an M32 tank recovery vehicle (built on a Sherman tank chassis), a peep, and a WC 52 Dodge truck for transporting cargo. A platoon of five M5A1 light tanks were provided by D/37.

The 10th AIB supplied several important components above and beyond the company of armored infantry, including a portion of the reconnaissance platoon, one M5A1 (used as a command tank), three halftracks, and three 105mm Sherman assault guns.

Rounding out the task force was a medical attachment with two peeps and an M29 "Weasel" (a small, fully tracked cargo carrier also used for transporting casualties over difficult terrain).

The M29 "Weasel," a fully-tracked cargo carrier also used for transporting casualties over difficult terrain (U.S. Army photograph).

12. Task Force Baum

In the absence of artillery support, the assault guns could be critical for providing both direct and indirect high-explosive fire support, as well as offering rapid deployment of smoke rounds. The key difference between the assault gun Sherman and a regular Sherman (other than the main armament being the 105mm howitzer in place of the usual 75mm gun) was the lack of a gyrostabilizer for the gun and a manually operated turret traverse as opposed to the faster hydraulic system found on the regular Sherman.

According to research conducted by Peter Domes and Martin Heinlein (the preeminent post-war experts on the mission), there were also 15 enlisted men from B/10 and C/10 who crewed the nine additional halftracks assigned to carry extra fuel and ammunition. These were also the halftracks that would accommodate the liberated prisoners on the return trip.

In total, there were 314 enlisted men and officers. Captain Robert F. Lange led A/10. He was a highly effective company commander, having received the Silver Star for his actions during the Battle of the Bulge. 1st Lt. George W. Casteel (the 10th AIB executive officer) accompanied Lange. The platoon leaders from the 10th Armored Infantry Battalion were 1st Lt. Allan I. Moses and Elmer C. Sutton. The reconnaissance patrol leader was 2nd Lt. Norman E. Hoffner. The assault gun platoon was led by T/Sgt. Charles O. Graham (having just assumed command after the death of Lt. Pluff).

The Sherman tanks of C/37 were led by 2nd Lt. William J. Nutto, accompanied by 1st Lt. Walter W. Wrolson (currently the maintenance officer, but he was an experienced platoon leader prior to that assignment) and platoon leader 2nd Lt. Raymond W. Keil. 2nd Lt. William G. Weaver Jr., commanded the platoon of light tanks from D/37.

There was one more officer on the task force: Major Alexander C. Stiller, Third Army HQ. He was supposedly just along for the ride.

One officer who expected to go on the mission was Captain Lyons, the commanding officer of the 10th Armored Infantry Battalion's HQ Company. It was his unit that provided the assault gun platoon, reconnaissance platoon, and command track. As the task force elements were forming up, Lyons was standing in the turret of the command track when Lt. Colonel Cohen approached and asked him, "What the hell are you doing?" Lyons replied that since half of his company was assigned to the task force, he was going on the mission. Despite an argument that ensued (the two officers were friends since 1942 and could speak frankly), Cohen insisted that Lyons dismount and remain behind.

As it turned out, Lyons did gain an assignment related to the mission: he was to remain behind with the S-2 command halftrack and attempt to maintain radio communication with the task force. For security, Lyons retained a section of the machine gun platoon mounted in two halftracks.

As for Captain Baum, he was none too happy about the presence of Major Stiller. What was his function to be? How was he to add value to the mission? Of greatest concern to Baum was the fact that the major outranked him. Under normal circumstances, Baum was subject to Stiller's commands. The captain's concern was dismissed cavalierly by Stiller when he proclaimed, "I'm going for the laughs and thrills." But the truth of the matter was revealed when Stiller confided to Lt. Colonel Abrams (but not to Baum, who remained unaware), "I think Patton's son-in-law is in there." Obviously, his mission was to personally ensure the safe return of Lt. Colonel Waters. Having served as Patton's bodyguard, he would play that role for Waters once he located him at the camp.

Abrams fleshed out the plan to a greater degree. Under cover of darkness later that night, other elements of CCB would open a route for Task Force Baum at the village of

Schweinheim. As recent events had shown, there was no way of knowing what resistance the Germans might muster once the breakthrough occurred. If all went well, Task Force Baum would arrive at *Oflag XIII-B* during the afternoon of March 27 and be back behind American lines that same night. Hopefully, the entire mission would be completed within little more than 24 hours.

Opening the Door at Schweinheim

1st Lieutenant Richard Pancake (the new commander of B/37) and Captain Adrian Tessier (Pancake's counterpart with B/10) drew the assignment of clearing the way for Task Force Baum. They briefed their team at 1700 and an hour later they were moving toward Schweinheim.

As was so often the case in recent weeks, the medium tanks led the way with infantry riding atop and the balance of the infantry riding farther behind in halftracks. Lt. Pancake divided his under-strength company into three platoons. The lead platoon consisted of four tanks, the second platoon three tanks, and the third platoon, only two. The first two platoons had the responsibility of clearing obstacles and securing the numerous cross streets from one side of town to the other (about a half-mile stretch). The third platoon would be held in reserve. Once the route was deemed secure, Task Force Baum would barrel through and be on its way.

Corporal William W. Smith, the driver in one of the Sherman tanks, had never gone into battle after dark before. The prospect of receiving his baptism in night warfare added to his nervousness. That wasn't the only reason for his concern. He later said, "The town was reported not to have too much resistance, but when you hear that, watch out!" There was no telling what to expect. Would this be another one of the many towns where resistance was nil? Or would the Germans be prepared to make a fight of it? They would find out soon enough.

At 2030, three artillery battalions (the 22nd AFAB, 66th AFAB, and 191st Field Artillery) placed a preparatory TOT barrage on the town, unleashing 10 volleys each (540 rounds in total). After 30 minutes of pounding by high-explosive shells, Pancake's tanks ... each carrying a squad of Tessier's armored infantry ... began advancing toward the town.

The Germans were ready for them. Among the troops prepared to stop the attack were young reserve officer candidates from Aschaffenburg, hastily assembled and dispatched by Major Emil Lamberth. Pancake and Tessier didn't know it yet, but they were about to poke a hornet's nest.

When the lead tank drew close to the first buildings on the edge of town, a round from a *Panzerfaust* ripped through the night, bringing the Sherman to a dead stop on the narrow street. Rather than wait for the rest of the tanks, Tessier's leading infantrymen moved forward and worked their way into the town. They started clearing the houses but hesitated to move too far without the tanks.

Lt. Pancake attempted to reach the disabled tank by radio. Unsuccessful, he left his own tank and moved forward to see what could be done. When he came across Corporal Lester Powell, he ordered him to move the tank.

Powell drove his peep to the front of the column. He scaled the tank and lowered himself in through the turret hatch. He found four of the crewmen dead. The fifth was still alive but unconscious with one of his legs blown off. Powell worked his way into the driver's seat and moved the tank to the side of the road. He then grabbed the surviving tanker, muscled him out of the hatch and lowered him to the ground. Powell was hit by enemy fire as he left the tank. Despite his own serious injury, he placed the wounded man across the hood of the peep and sped back to the rear.

With the damaged tank out of the way, the three remaining tanks of the lead platoon moved forward and resumed their support of the infantry. Once the first tank platoon was far enough into the town, Pancake ordered the three tanks of the second platoon to move in and seal off the side streets. Before the entire second tank platoon and supporting infantry joined them, the Germans hit the rear part of the column with mortar fire, which sent the infantrymen in search of cover. Another Sherman farther back in the column was hit by a *Panzerfaust*. The road was blocked once more, but the crew managed to recover their senses and discovered they could back the tank out of the way.

One of the Shermans turned off the main road onto one of the narrow side streets. An explosion rocked the tank. Fearing they had been severely hit, the crew bailed out (not an uncommon reaction). While the tankers gathered themselves, a German soldier dropped into one of the hatches and commandeered the tank. After driving it down the street, the thief managed to turn the tank around. The new owner then employed the Sherman's guns against the American infantry.

Meanwhile, Tessier compelled his men to move forward in the face of the mortar fire. Many of the infantrymen had taken refuge in a small field on the edge of town. Tessier, having moved back to the rear of the column, grabbed six men and executed a flanking maneuver down an alley. They came upon a four-man German mortar team, and after taking them by surprise, marched them to a nearby wall. Among the Germans was a lieutenant who, when face to face with Tessier, spit in his face and said, "*Amerikanisch Schweine.*" In an instant, Tessier pulled out his knife with one hand and grabbed the German by the hair with the other. A quick, blood-letting, deadly slash across the throat was all that was needed to subjugate the three other Germans to Tessier's band of men.

Tessier and Pancake urged their infantrymen and tankers deeper into the town. The main street had several curves and intricate crossroads to negotiate. It was slow going, and after more than two hours, the B Team hadn't pushed completely through Schweinheim.

At 2330, Captain Baum decided he could wait no longer. He was counting on the cover of darkness as a shield for his drive to Hammelburg. Every minute delayed at Schweinheim was a minute of stealth stolen from him.

Baum drove his peep from the task force assembly area toward the sound of battle. He soon found Lt. Pancake, who was directing the attack on foot. The tank commander advised Baum of the status of the attack. After some heated words between the two officers, Baum told Pancake to move his tanks to the sidewalks. He was going to bring his task force through whether the B Team had finished the job or not. Baum then found Tessier and told him the same thing.

Baum returned to his column and issued his final orders over the radio. No lights were to be used except for the blackout lights on the rear of the vehicles. The sirens were to be used as they moved through the town. They were not to stop to shoot, and if they encountered any vehicles blocking the way, they were to either bypass them or ram them. The drivers were instructed to stay close and follow the vehicle in front of them.

The column plunged into Schweinheim with the Shermans in the lead. The light tanks came next, followed by Baum's peep and the other light vehicles. Then came the long series of halftracks, the three 105mm assault guns, and finally, the service vehicles.

With siren blaring, the lead Sherman entered the town. Following right behind came the entire column strung out in line with all vehicles adding their sirens to the chorus.

Tessier and Pancake's men ceased firing as the task force barreled down the street. At first, the German fire slackened as well. But as the column moved farther down the half-mile stretch, some of the enemy troops regained the presence of mind to fire their weapons. Despite the late German response, the lead tanks made it through the town unscathed and burst into the open terrain on the east edge of Schweinheim. The other vehicles followed in a steady, unbroken stream. Once in the clear, Captain Baum moved the light tanks of D/37 to the front.

The D Company platoon leader, 2nd Lt. William G. Weaver Jr., occupied the assistant driver's seat of the lead tank. The other three crew members barely knew him, since he had just taken command of the platoon a few days prior. In the driver's seat to Weaver's left was T5 James Mabrey. Above him in the turret was the gunner Pfc Frank Malinski and the platoon sergeant of D/37, S/Sgt. Robert Vannett.

The commanders of B/37 and B/10 now had the task of extricating their men and vehicles from the town. When they returned to their lines, they brought 35 German prisoners with them. By 0230 on March 27, the two companies had returned to their outposts guarding the bridgehead.

In the morning, CCB and the rest of the Fourth Armored Division left Task Force Baum behind. Once relieved by the 26th Infantry Division, Lt. Colonel Abrams' combat command moved north and followed CCA across the Main River near Hanau. With the 37th Tank Battalion and 10th Armored Infantry Battalion both reduced in strength by one-third, they were assigned to CCR. The well-rested 51st Armored Infantry and 35th Tank Battalions replaced the 10th and 37th in CCB.

The 314 intrepid men of Task Force Baum were, in almost all respects, on their own. However, one small band of soldiers remained behind to assist the task force. Captain Lyons, whose orders were to maintain radio contact with the task force, moved his men and radio gear back behind the river to the outskirts of Niedernberg. He set up shop at a farmhouse that had previously served as the battalion command post. For now, Lyons and a Piper Cub liaison plane were the only connecting threads between Captain Baum and the Fourth Armored Division.

13

The Road to Hammelburg

The Task Force Unleashed

By air, the distance from Schweinheim to Hammelburg was 35 miles. By road, depending upon the route taken, getting to *Oflag XIII-B* would be more on the order of a 45- to 50-mile trip. Captain Baum hoped his task force would arrive at the camp prior to sunrise. But with the delay incurred at Schweinheim, the timetable was in jeopardy.

Free of Schweinheim, Baum wasted no time. Lt. Weaver's tank picked up speed and set the pace for the column. The task force drew minor small arms fire as the vehicles raced single-file through the nearby towns of Haibach and Grünmorsbach. The enemy inflicted some casualties among the armored infantry riding in the halftracks and atop the medium tanks, but Baum didn't allow the losses to delay the mission. As they exited Grünmorsbach, the lead tank was a little over two miles beyond Schweinheim.

Straßbessenbach, slightly over a mile to the east beyond Grünmorsbach, presented the next likely obstacle. A sharp, tight left turn was required inside the town, and Baum drove his peep to the front of the column to ensure Lt. Weaver followed the proper route. If each driver kept his eyes on the specks of light mounted above the rear fenders of the vehicle in front of them (the "cat's eyes"), the column would remain intact.

Baum parked his peep at the intersection and watched as each vehicle came through and made the turn. Satisfied that the task force was whole, he drove back toward the front of the column and inserted his peep behind Weaver's tank. By the time the maintenance and service vehicles rounded the turn, the lead tank was driving down the main street of Keilberg.

After less than three-quarters of a mile, the column passed uneventfully through the tiny village of Unterbessenbach. Eight-tenths of a mile later, a hard-right turn put the task force on a road leading to Weiberhof, another quarter-mile away. It was here, at 0230, that Task Force Baum made another right turn onto Highway 26, the principle route toward Hammelburg. Unless the Germans denied them access, Highway 26 would take the task force within a dozen miles of their objective. Another quality road (Highway 27) would then carry them the balance of the way.

The task force continued through the dead of night along Highway 26. To help prevent the local citizens from reporting his presence and direction, he ordered the lead tanks to knock over the telephone poles lining the road. The poles were not much higher than six feet, so taking them down wasn't difficult, even for the light tanks. Soldiers from other vehicles farther back in the column dismounted and cut the lines by hand, just in case the wires were still intact.

The task force passed without incident through the south edge of Frohnhofen. Just before reaching Laufach, Lt. Weaver's tank came upon a small group of German troops

Hammelburg as it appeared in 2019 from the high ground to the south (photograph by author).

assembled for morning exercises on a field adjacent to the road. When the M5A1 came within range, Sergeant Vannett opened fire with the tank's machine gun and kept firing as the spry Stuart rolled by the field. T5 George Wyatt, the gunner of the M5A1 commanded by Sergeant Donald Yoerk and next in line in the column, unleashed his machine gun as well. Some of the Germans grabbed their small arms and returned fire, but they could do little to slow down the American column. Other tanks fired as they passed the field, and by the time the halftracks came down the highway, five Germans were dead.

Farther down the highway, Lt. Weaver encountered other German soldiers marching toward him. Realizing they were face to face with American tanks, the Germans threw their hands in the air. The tankers had the Germans lay down their arms on the pavement and then crushed the weapons under the treads of their tanks. With the help of Pfc Malinski (who spoke some German) they instructed the prisoners to continue marching down the highway and surrender to other American forces that were following behind them. The column then headed into the southern section of Laufach. According to reports by German witnesses (but not noted in American accounts) a *Panzerfaust* team lurking farther down the road hit and disabled one of the light tanks. One of the tankers was killed and his body left near the scene. The Stuart was hooked up to the recovery vehicle and continued with the column (it was abandoned not too much farther on the route).

Baum moved the medium tanks into the lead. Lt. Nutto spurred the 10 Sherman tanks of C/37 to the front of the column. He placed his command tank, the M4A3E2 assault tank *Cobra King*, into the fourth spot in line. (*Cobra King*, having been the lead tank that relieved the 101st Airborne Division at Bastogne, became what is arguably the most famous tank in American military history. In 2019, *Cobra King* went on display at the United States Army National Museum located near Fort Belvoir, 15 miles south of Washington, D.C.)

The original *Cobra King*, the M4A3E2 Sherman tank that led the relief of Bastogne and was eventually abandoned during the Hammelburg Raid. The restored tank was delivered to the site of the National Museum of the United States Army in 2018 (photograph courtesy Design and Production Incorporated, © Duncan R. Miller).

The town of Rechtenbach in 2019 (photograph by author).

About one-and-a-half miles east of Laufach, the task force (still on Highway 26) passed through the south edge of Hain and then began its ascent into the *Spessart*, a heavily forested mountain range dominating the area. The road was carved into the hillside with trees pinned to the shoulders. There was no other choice than moving single file and keeping their fingers crossed that the forest would be clear of the enemy. A single *Panzerfaust* could bring the column to a dead stop.

For the next five miles, the task force followed the twisting and turning highway through the dense Hain Forest. The route carried them to the east-southeast, past the village of Rothenbuch. The roadway then entered the Rothenbucher Forest, which blended seamlessly into the Lohrerstraße Forest. Four-and-a-half miles after Rothenbuch, the highway passed through the town of Rechtenbach. Throughout the entire stretch from Hain to Rechtenbach, the column advanced unopposed.

The Road to Lohr

Beyond Rechtenbach, Highway 26 descended into a densely wooded valley extending three-and-a-half miles toward the town of Lohr. The pavement was carved into the north wall of the valley, leaving no room for maneuver other than straight ahead.

As the column approached a section of the highway known as "Waterhouse Curve," there was an encounter with a truck and its four occupants. As the vehicle approached from the opposite direction, the forward elements of the column opened fire. One of the Germans (a *Nazi Youth*) was killed and the driver wounded. The advance then continued through the forest along Highway 26.

As the column exited the woods, they could see in the distance the first signs of Lohr, a commercial center sitting astride the Main River. Lohr's population was much larger than the small towns and villages they had breezed through up to that point. It had the potential to be the task force's first major obstacle.

Captain Baum would not seek a river crossing here. Instead, he would stay on Highway 26, which runs through the northern section of Lohr and then continues to the northeast, tracing the west bank of the river toward the town of Gemünden. Baum's intent was to slip through Lohr without engaging the enemy.

Baum placed the light tanks back at the front of the column. Weaver's tank led the way into the outskirts of town and lucked out when they came to a roadblock that had not been closed. The column proceeded along the more constricted roads of the town but made it through without drawing fire (unfortunately, at least one German woman dressed in service attire was fired on and killed).

The task force continued to the northeast along Highway 26. Not far outside of town, they came face to face with a truck from the TOTE company, which they fired upon and destroyed (they probably didn't distinguish it from a military vehicle). A more valuable target was spotted on the river: a tugboat towing five barges. The platoon of Stuart tanks opened fire on the figurative sitting ducks.

Highway 26 ran parallel with a railroad track, and together they traced the west side of the Main River all the way to the town of Gemünden. Approximately four miles from Lohr, Weaver's tank approached an "ack-ack" train, 30-cars long and bristling with anti-aircraft guns mounted on concrete pillboxes.

Weaver's gunner opened fire on the locomotive. The train track was above the grade of the road and the German gunners were powerless since they couldn't depress their guns low enough to fire back. As the rest of the American column sped by, they added to the carnage. When the armored infantrymen drew close enough, they used thermite grenades to destroy the cars mounting the anti-aircraft guns.

Gemünden

Task Force Baum continued north along Highway 26 toward Gemünden, where the highway crossed the Saale River (which flowed south into the Main River). Capturing the bridge at this location was critical. If the task force succeeded in crossing the Saale at Gemünden, they had access to the most direct route to Hammelburg. From there, only three-and-a-half miles remained before accessing Highway 27, and then it was only eight miles to Hammelburg.

The task force continued toward Langenprozelten (a smaller town just west of Gemünden). At Langenprozelten, the Main River makes a sharp turn to the east, as does Highway 26. At the bend in the river, the heart of Gemünden is about two miles away. It may have been in this area that Baum lost his first medium tank to enemy fire. (The exact location is uncertain. Some accounts suggest it was hit closer to Lohr in tandem with the clearing of a roadblock.)

From this vantage point, Captain Baum saw an even more inviting target: cradled between the Main River and Gemünden was a railroad yard. Time was of the essence, so rather than set the sights of his guns on the rail cars, he sent a radio message requesting an airstrike. Baum maintained his focus squarely on acquiring the bridge over the Saale River.

The view facing east across the bridge in Gemünden in 2019 (photograph by author).

Rather than send the task force headlong toward the bridge, Baum dispatched his reconnaissance unit to scout the area. Lt. Norman Hoffner led his team of three peeps through the west side of Gemünden. Once at the west end of the bridge, he identified enemy positions in two three-story houses. The buildings stood like sentries at the other end of the span. An imposing, ominous castle, perched upon a hillside on the German side of the bridge, overlooked the scene.

When Hoffner saw some mines on the approach to the bridge, his men threw smoke grenades for cover and then moved the mines off the roadway. They drew gunfire, but no one was hit. Hoffner raced back to update Baum on the situation.

Captain Baum instructed Hoffner to test the German defenses. The lieutenant returned to the bridge with his team and commenced fire. The recon unit unleashed streams of bullets from the .30 caliber light machine guns mounted on their peeps.

No matter the response from the Germans, the reality was that Baum had no choice but to cross the bridge. He ordered an attack by a combined force of tanks and infantry. The M4A3E8 of platoon leader 2nd Lt. Raymond Keil was the first tank in line. Nutto placed *Cobra King* with its thicker armor plate behind Keil's tank. A platoon of infantry led by Lt. Elmer Sutton would do the heavy lifting. Their protection was little more than the wool of their uniforms.

The tanks crept toward the entrance to the bridge, which was hemmed in by the tightly-packed homes. The infantry followed suit. The assault team drew sporadic small arms fire as they advanced.

When Lt. Keil's tank came within 15 feet of the bridge, the Germans responded with a level of force not previously revealed by Hoffner's reconnaissance. Multiple *Panzerfausts* were unleashed. Nutto, inside the turret of *Cobra King*, thought he heard an anti-tank gun fired from across the river. But the most dangerous threat was likely much closer, as it appears that the Germans occupied the buildings on both sides of the river.

A *Panzerfaust* round struck Lt. Keil's tank, bringing it to a dead stop. The wounded crew bailed out, as did the lieutenant. With the road blocked by the damaged tank, Lt. Sutton's infantrymen continued without tank support toward the bridge.

Nutto was desperate to get the abandoned tank away from the entrance to the bridge. He dismounted from *Cobra King* and attempted to persuade one of the tankers to return to the Sherman and move it. At that moment, Captain Baum appeared. He had just arrived at Nutto's side when a *Panzerfaust* round struck the pavement in front of them. The shrapnel hit Nutto squarely in the chest, neck, arms, and legs. Baum was hit in his right knee and hand. Nutto, though bleeding badly from multiple wounds, was still able to walk. One of the medics took him back farther in the column to render aid.

Lt. Sutton and several others from his platoon made it across the bridge. Two infantrymen sprinted onto the span to join them, and two more were poised to follow. One of the men racing across was T/SSgt. Freddie G. Humpick. Before they reached the other side, the German engineers set off the charges they had placed underneath the span. A huge explosion rocked the center of the masonry bridge, sending up a cloud of dust and flying stone. A gaping hole was left in the middle of the span. The two brave infantrymen were killed instantly.

To Find a Bridge

The fighting in Gemünden was intense. Baum lost at least one other medium tank to enemy fire, and perhaps as many as 25 to 30 armored infantrymen were either killed in action or captured. But what was of greatest significance relative to the mission was the destruction of the bridge spanning the Saale River. The planned route to Hammelburg was no more.

With no bridging equipment available, Baum had to find another way to get to Hammelburg. Unable to cross the Saale, he would have to advance north along a route to the west of the Sinn River and hope to find a bridge across *that* river. Unfortunately, his map didn't show evidence of a bridge across the Sinn. He could only hope to find one. Baum sent one of his men to find the best place to pick up a road to the north while he got to work on the difficult task of backing up the column and changing its direction.

Lt. Hoffner's recon unit covered the withdrawal of the remaining tanks and infantry closest to the bridge. Most of the column was out of sight of the enemy, so moving them into the right position was a little bit easier … but it wasn't easy by any stretch of the imagination.

Captain Baum kept the column as close to the Sinn River as possible, constantly on the watch for a bridge. After advancing a few miles, the lead M5A1 commanded by Sgt. Yoerk came to a fork in the road. The road to the right wrapped around the base of a large hill, while the road to the left ascended it. Not sure which route was the best, Baum sent Yoerk's tank to scout the route to the left. The task force would hold in place until they returned.

Yoerk's M5A1 climbed the hill, only to discover that the road came to a dead end. As he ordered his driver to back up the tank and turn around, they threw a track. Yoerk and his three crewmembers dismounted and walked down the hill to rejoin the task force. But before they left, Sgt. Yoerk spiked the tank by tossing an incendiary grenade inside the crew compartment followed by a thermite grenade placed down the barrel of the main gun. Once back at the column, they took their place in one of the halftracks.

As Baum waited for the return of Yoerk and his crew, he faced one of his toughest decisions. There were four men with severe wounds that needed attention beyond what his medical team could provide. Baum instructed the medics, "Put them on the road. Stick a rifle in the ground and a white bandage on it. The Germans will pick 'em up." These weren't the only men left behind during the mission. It was a gut-wrenching course of action.

As the task force continued beyond the town of Rieneck, a motorcycle came speeding down the winding road. The motorcyclist—a German officer named Karl Stübinger—found himself face-to-face with the lead American tank. Stübinger told Baum that he was on leave and wished to surrender. After pressing Stübinger for more information, the German revealed that he lived in Hammelburg. Brandishing a knife for added incentive, Baum demanded through his interpreter that Stübinger tell where the nearest bridge was. The German said that there might be a bridge farther upstream at the village of Burgsinn (another three miles to the north). Baum plunked the prisoner on top of Weaver's tank. The task force continued north with Stübinger as their guide.

A greater prize fell into Baum's hands when a German *General*, riding in a *Volkswagen*, drove into the face of the column and was captured along with two of his staff members. Baum loaded the general onto one of the halftracks and continued his advance.

As indicated by Stübinger, there was indeed a bridge at Burgsinn. The structure was small, and Baum was concerned that it might not bear the weight of the armored vehicles. The vehicles crossed one at a time to keep the stress on the bridge as low as possible. Fortunately, the span held, and the entire column continued east beyond the Sinn River.

Task Force Baum now depended upon a winding secondary road leading to the east. For the next seven miles, the road weaved through dense woods and hilly terrain. When the pavement finally exited the woods, it descended sharply into the town of Gräfendorf nestled in the Saale Valley.

This view is typical of the nature of the woods that *Olympic's* armored infantrymen fought in during the winter and early spring of 1945 (photograph by author).

The town of Gräfendorf in 2019 (photograph by author).

Near Gräfendorf, the Americans saw hundreds of ragged prisoners marching down the road. Their German guards didn't oppose Baum's advance and the lot of them surrendered. Baum discovered that the prisoners were Russians. Suddenly enjoying a taste of freedom, the liberated men relished the opportunity to go after the German guards. Baum turned the Germans over to the Russians, along with about 200 prisoners taken up to this point in the journey. The captives became the captors. The Russians proceeded to loot Gräfendorf, primarily confiscating food and liquor.

Upon arriving at Gräfendorf, Lt. Stübinger claimed that he was no longer familiar with the area. If that were true, his value to Captain Baum had vanished. After speaking with the Americans, the mayor of the town offered up one of their citizens. Fifty-seven-year-old Anton Försch became Baum's new guide.

Back at his base outside of Niedernberg, Captain Lyons had lost radio contact with the task force. Despite his continued attempts to raise Baum on the radio, there was no response for the balance of the mission. Lyons and his team, ever hopeful of regaining contact with the task force, didn't rejoin the 10th Armored Infantry Battalion until April 4.

The Jig Is Up

The American column followed a road tracing the north bank of the Saale River. A little less than two miles from Gräfendorf, they found a small bridge that led into Michelau. The road then continued to trace the river along its south bank until splitting off toward Weickersgrüben.

At 1400, a German liaison plane spotted the column. The Americans turned their .50 caliber machine guns skyward but failed to erase the prying eyes. Baum sensed that the Germans were aware of his position and strength. But he remained confident that he would reach *Oflag XIII-B*.

At that point, Försch told Baum that he was unfamiliar with the area ahead. Baum pressed him for information. Rather than stand pat on his claim of not knowing the way to Hammelburg, Försch pointed Baum toward a road leading up a steep hill northeast of Weickersgrüben. Accepting it as the best route to follow, the task force climbed the heavily wooded slope. A half-mile later, they reached the top only to find that the road hit a dead-end at a mining quarry.

More valuable time had been lost. Seeing that Anton Försch's value had been exhausted, Baum dispatched his driver and his interpreter to return to the village of Weickersgrüben in search of another civilian guide. They returned with a reluctant Karl Stürzenberger. The new guide told Baum that the column would have to return to Weickersgrüben. From there, another road would take them to Route 27 and Hammelburg.

Once turned around and back on the main road, the task force sped south along the road leading out of Weickersgrüben. The road eventually emerged from the woods and came to an intersection that provided a panoramic view unlike anywhere else along the route. After making a sharp left turn, the lead tank was on its way east for another seven-tenths of a mile before coming to a "T" intersection with Highway 27. For that entire stretch between the intersection, the view to the east had been spectacular. What Baum didn't know was that the Germans had an even better view from atop Hill 427, one-and-a-half miles from where the entire column was parading in front of them.

The task force was within five miles of *Oflag XIII-B* (though Baum still did not know

Hill 427 as it appeared in 2019. Task Force Baum met its fate on the opposite side of the hill (photograph by author).

the exact location of the camp). With the route to Hammelburg now clearly known, Baum released Stürzenberger, who retreated to his home in Weickersgrüben.

Task Force Baum turned to the northeast along Highway 27. After slightly less than two miles, the highway skirted the west end of the village of Obereschenbach, its humble homes visible off to the right of the highway. The task force continued along Highway 27 toward Untereschenbach, another mile to the northeast. From there, the column would turn almost due east toward Hammelburg.

The Hetzers

Several *Hetzer* tank destroyers from the *251st Heavy Tank Destroyer Battalion* lay in wait in anticipation of Baum's arrival. Commanded by *Hauptmann* Richard Köhl, the small but effective tank destroyers had been transported approximately 20 miles by rail from Schweinfurt to Hammelburg. Arriving on the same train was the *10th Signal Training and Replacement Battalion,* which remained at Hammelburg to defend the town. They had arrived at the station at 1200, and Köhl quickly unloaded the *Hetzers* and moved them into positions in between Hammelburg and the neighboring town of Diebach.

As the American column made the turn to the east, they exposed their flank to the *Hetzers.* Despite Köhl's favorable position, his gunners failed to hit any of the American tanks. Baum's tank gunners fired back furiously but drew no blood either.

TF Baum continued to move along the road carved into the base of the high ground

A *Hetzer* tank destroyer (courtesy Erwin Verholen).

The view from the Hetzers' firing positions. The steep road near the center leads toward the site of *Oflag XIII-B* (photograph by author, 2019).

overlooking the Saale River. At least one tank turned off the road and went north toward Hammelburg. After drawing fire, it returned. But this wasn't the direction the task force would take. Instead, Baum turned the column south. The vehicles began a steep, laborious ascent up the hill that faced Hammelburg.

As the tanks and halftracks struggled with the steep grade, Köhl's *Hetzers* opened fire again. This time, the German gunners found their mark, damaging one of the Shermans (the American crew managed to move the tank into a field out of the line of enemy fire). The other Shermans returned fire.

To help stem the onslaught of the German anti-tank guns, Baum directed two of T/Sgt. Graham's Sherman assault guns to a position on a tourist overlook. It was a vulnerable spot, but it provided the gunners with a better vantage point for returning fire against the *Hetzers*. S/Sgt. Morrison Westberry held his squad of armored infantry below the crest of the hill in an exposed position from where they provided covering fire as the task force continued past them. While the medium tanks and two assault guns dealt with the *Hetzers,* Captain Baum dispatched the light tanks, the remaining assault gun, a platoon of armored infantry, and most of the halftracks to secure the high ground.

The assault gun commanded by T4 Alfonso Casanova scored a hit on one of the *Hetzers,* which scurried for cover (Pfc Jack Stanley was his gunner, and Pfc Lawrence White was the loader). Graham's gunner, Pfc Herbert E. Reynolds, fired several rounds of smoke to help conceal the movement of the column as it continued up and over the hill. When a column of tightly-bunched German trucks was observed, Reynolds placed the vehicles under fire. He adjusted the elevation of the gun to account for the longer range and lobbed 105mm HE rounds at the column until he was zeroed in. When one of the shells hit its mark, the cargo of ammunition and fuel (intended for *Hauptmann* Köhl's tank destroyers) erupted and created a chain-reaction of explosions.

S/Sgt. Westberry and his squad had their hands full as well. In addition to providing covering fire, he assisted the medics in caring for casualties on the forward slope. He may have come to the assistance of Major Stiller. The 10th AIB unit diary provides details of the action:

> *When the peep of an officer who had a mission to accomplish received a direct enemy hit—turning the vehicle and mortally wounding the driver, S/Sgt Westberry unhesitatingly and daringly went to the assistance of the officer, righted the peep and provided a driver so he could finish his vital mission.*

Several halftracks were hit as they struggled to climb the hill. The armored infantrymen scrambled for cover. Among them was Sgt. Yoerk and his gunner, George Wyatt. Without a tank ever since their M5A1 threw its track earlier in the day, they came across the Sherman that had been hit moments earlier. Of that crew, one was dead, two were wounded, and two were uninjured. The crew was struggling to remove the body of their dead comrade, so Yoerk and Wyatt went to their aid. They extracted the fallen tanker and set his body on the ground beside the tank. They helped the two wounded soldiers to a halftrack and then returned to the Sherman along with the able-bodied crewmembers. With the help of a maintenance sergeant, they got the Sherman running again. Yoerk was back in action with a blood-soaked but more powerful tank than his old M5A1. It was a good thing because Task Force Baum needed every tank it could muster.

Hauptmann Köhl decided to withdraw his *Hetzers* and sent them circling to the east of *Lager Hammelburg* (Baum believed his tankers had knocked out a total of three *Hetzers* during the exchange). Köhl was sure that the *Lager* was the American task force's destination. In need of resupply, he reorganized out of sight of his enemy and eventually assembled near the town of Fuchsstadt.

Once Captain Baum gained the high ground, he found what he was looking for: *Oflag XIII-B* (i.e., *Lager Hammelburg*). Baum had an excellent view of the military complex and moved his task force into a position overlooking the camp from the north. Peering through his binoculars, he saw that the facility was ringed with a double row of barbed wire fencing and a series of watch towers. By his estimate, there were two companies of Germany infantry dug in on the high ground fronting the *Oflag*.

The Germans had suffered losses during Baum's approach to *Oflag XIII-B*, but Baum's task force had been injured as well. He was now down to six Shermans and four light tanks. He also lost one of the 105mm assault guns. Among the five halftracks that had been hit was the one that carried the extra gasoline for their return trip. The halftrack carrying the extra ammunition for the assault guns was destroyed as well. Three of the peeps were hit and destroyed, including the medical unit's vehicle. And the most impactful human loss was that of Captain Lange, commander of A/10, mortally wounded when his halftrack was hit.

The Assault on Oflag XIII-B

Baum organized his assault force behind the crest of the hill, out of sight of any Germans who might be peering back at him. He decided to employ a desert formation for the attack. His four light tanks and the half dozen remaining mediums would spread out side by side, leaving 50 to 100 feet between them. Lt. Nutto was fit enough to resume command of the medium tanks. The infantry (save for a platoon that Baum would hold back in reserve behind the hill with the halftracks) would march behind the tanks as they advanced across the open terrain leading to the camp. A/10 was now under the command of Lt. George Casteel (the 10th AIB executive officer). The two assault guns would remain at the crest of the hill to provide fire support with their 105mm howitzers. The peeps remained behind the hill, standing guard in the event enemy troops appeared on their flanks or to the rear.

Major Stiller ... who had been a virtual non-factor throughout the operation ... suddenly became involved. He asked Baum if he could take one of the armored infantry squads with him. Baum acquiesced to his request, even though his resources at that point were meager.

It was about 1630 when Baum gave the order to attack. The tanks moved down the hill, advancing at a speed that allowed the infantry to use them for cover. The assault guns opened fire on targets in front of the advancing Shermans and Stuarts. A round from one of the 105mm guns set a large straw barn on fire, creating a billowing cloud of smoke that obscured the camp from view.

The Germans were better prepared than Baum had imagined. A company of combat engineers (part of the command led by *Oberst* Höppe) held well-orchestrated positions that included a line of foxholes outside the wire fencing. When the American tanks came within 200 yards, the enemy opened fire with small arms and *Panzerfausts*.

The tanks and armored infantry worked diligently to uproot the German engineers from their prepared positions. Lt. Nutto received directions over the radio from Baum regarding the defensive hot spots that required attention from the Shermans. Some of the strongest enemy outposts were in outlying buildings, ranging from sheds to sturdier masonry buildings. A round from one of the tanks hit a guard tower on the north end of the camp, killing the lone German holding his ground there.

Sergeant Graham observed the battle from his firing position on the hill. Later he described part of the action:

> The hottest spot for the infantry guys was around the stockade. We were receiving machine gun and sniper fire from there. We knocked out all we could. When we stormed the stockade I saw one of our men get hit by machine gun fire, fall down and raise up and fire at the gun that hit him. He was on foot and got hit quite bad. He got to his knees and fired until they mowed him down.

At one point, Baum asked the Germans to surrender. This was out of the question for Höppe, and the battle not only continued, but intensified. After the Germans lost a 20mm anti-aircraft gun and Nutto shifted his tanks to conduct a flanking maneuver, the tide began to turn. Slowly but surely, the German positions were reduced, and the Americans drew closer to the prison wire.

Lieutenant Colonel Waters

The American prisoners within the camp heard the battle raging outside the perimeter and watched as the German guards took up defensive positions. Prisoners observing from the second story of the camp infirmary saw the attack unfolding before them. The sound of battle grew closer. Eventually, shells were falling within the compound itself. The American tanks' machine guns raked the barracks housing the Serbian prisoners (likely a consequence of the Serbs' unfamiliar uniforms being mistaken as German). Red-hot tracer bullets set a roof on fire.

The commanding officer of the prison camp, *General* von Goeckel, faced difficult choices. *Oflag XIII-B* was nearly adjacent to *Stalag XIII-C*. At that compound (commanded by Oberst Hans Westmann), there were another 10,000 prisoners. The standing order from Berlin was that if a camp was threatened with liberation, the prisoners were to be marched out and transported to another camp. Goeckel put the wheels in motion to evacuate the camp, but he soon realized that the opportunity to remove the prisoners from *Oflag XIII-B* had passed. There remained time, however, to move the prisoners from *Stalag XIII-C*.

General von Goeckel decided to surrender *Oflag XIII-B*. But before doing so, he ordered his guards to vacate their positions inside the camp and relieve the guards at *Stalag XIII-C* so that they were free to march the prisoners away. Goeckel also turned over the facility's extra arms and ammunition to Captain Dragon Yosefovitch, a Royalist officer from the Serbian portion of the camp (as opposed to a Communist who would be decidedly less friendly to the Germans should they arm themselves before the German soldiers departed). Yosefovitch armed 50 of his most trusted men. His plan in motion, *General* von Goeckel entered Colonel Goode's office and surrendered the camp to the Americans.

Colonel Goode and his staff contemplated their next move. Lt. Colonel Waters volunteered to leave the camp to contact the American forces. They would try to secure a cease fire that would halt the shelling of the compound, which continued to put both American and Serb lives at risk.

Along with three other American officers and a German interpreter (*Hauptmann* Fuchs, who served as the compound commander for the American section of the camp), Waters exited the main gate. Waters and Fuchs took the lead, with the three others following behind. One of the officers carried an American flag, the other a white sheet on a pole: the universal sign of surrender. The small band of men exited the prison gate and had not gone far when a lone German soldier suddenly appeared, brandishing a rifle. Waters had barely shouted "*Amerikanish*" when the German fired. The bullet struck Waters in the thigh and exited near the buttocks, coming close to hitting the base of his spine. He went down immediately, falling into a ditch and unable to walk. The German soldier advanced toward them and threatened to shoot the rest of the party. *Hauptmann* Fuchs, after some harrowing moments, managed to talk him down.

The German soldier marched the party back into the compound. The American officers retrieved a blanket and used it as a makeshift litter to move Waters. Serbian Captain Yosefovitch ordered some of his men to bring forward a stretcher. They carried Waters back to the POW hospital where a Serbian surgeon, Colonel Radovan Danic, went to work on Waters' wound. It was not certain at that moment that he would survive.

Freedom… For Now

After more than two hours of pitched battle, and with the camp now surrendered to the prisoners, the German engineers made an organized retreat (in the German after-action report, it states the *Lager* was lost at 1945). As the enemy fire subsided, Captain Baum ordered his small infantry reserve to move forward. Lt. Weaver, observing from his Stuart tank at the point of attack, saw some prisoners inside the compound lowering the Nazi flag from the main pole. In its place they raised a crude home-made American flag (the same flag that Waters' party carried with them during their failed attempt to bring about a cease-fire).

Weaver's tank charged and burst through the prison wire into the compound. Other tanks followed while the Sherman commanded by Sgt. Yoerk ran laterally across the line of the fence, stamping it down with the tank's treads.

Americans and Serbs alike rejoiced. Hundreds of prisoners swarmed around the tanks. The celebration may have been less vibrant had the prisoners known how far they were from American lines. And their mood would have certainly been dampened if they knew that their rescuers were in no position to load up the nearly *1300* American prisoners for a return trip to American lines … not to mention the 3000 Serb officers. They would discover those things soon enough. (Among the American prisoners was Captain William Marshall of the 8th Tank Battalion. He was captured during the Battle of the Bulge when in his role as liaison officer with CCB, he took a wrong turn with his peep while carrying the attack orders for December 23.)

In the wake of the battle, Baum's medics tended to the wounded. There was only so much that Zeno and Demchak could do on their own, and many of the task force members pitched in to help them. There were wounded Germans on the battlefield as well. When an enemy soldier approached 1st Sergeant Mackin and asked about receiving medical aid for his men, Mackin told him they would be "next in line" after his own men were cared for.

Captain Baum went to his command halftrack and instructed T/4 John Sidles to send a radio message, "Mission accomplished. Request air cover." Of course, the mission was far from complete. Baum still had to make his way back to American lines.

As for Major Stiller, his mission had just begun. As Baum's men regrouped, Stiller went into the camp in search of Lt. Colonel Waters. He eventually found him at the hospital, and after spending some time learning from Waters the details of what had happened, he returned to the task force. Stiller knew that Waters couldn't be moved due to the severity of his wound, and he must have felt a surge of disappointment over not being able to come through for Patton.

Baum eventually came face to face with Colonel Goode, and the two officers discussed their options. Goode was surprised to learn of the size of the task force and how far they were from the American front lines. Baum in turn was surprised and overwhelmed to learn that he had on his hands far more than the 300 prisoners he expected based upon the pre-mission briefing from Major Stiller. He later commented, "I could have thrown up when I saw them." He told Goode that it was up to him (Goode) to determine who among the prisoners would leave with the task force, and who would stay. (Many of the prisoners, after lengthy captivity, were in poor physical condition. 1st Lt. Bouck, who had been a prisoner for a little over three months, weighed less than 120 pounds.) He also left it to Colonel Goode to establish a semblance of order among the POWs. As for Baum, he went about completing the reorganization of his task force.

Many of the prisoners gathered their belongings and provisions and marched out of the camp through the darkness to join the task force. Some of the American officers grabbed weapons that were left on the battlefield by the dead and wounded. As described by Captain Shelden L. Thompson (one of the POWs), German weapons were passed around as well, including looted souvenir pistols.

Baum sought out Colonel Goode once again to see how he had organized the prisoners. He was dismayed to find Goode mired in indecision. The task force commander took matters into his own hands. He broke the news to the assembled prisoners that he had very limited capacity on his vehicles. Those that could not find a place on a halftrack or tank would have to walk.

Several hundred dejected prisoners limped back to the camp. Those that remained with the task force tried to find room on one of the vehicles (among them, Lt. Bouck who, along with his friend Lt. Matthew Reid, grabbed a spot on the second Sherman tank in the column). They covered the tanks and halftracks like a swarm of locusts, holding on to every surface area they could. Liberated prisoners sitting on the hood of a halftrack were shooed away from the windshield. Tank commanders rejected some of the riders when they interfered with the traverse of the turret. Each tank normally carried 10 to 12 men riding on the hull. The halftrack's normal capacity was a dozen infantrymen, plus the driver and an assistant in the cab. Under normal circumstances, perhaps an additional half-dozen could be squeezed in. But with men taking up every available inch and clinging to every part of the vehicle possible, the number of passengers per vehicle was greater. Still, not much more than 200 prisoners found a spot with the column. Those that could not find a place retired to the camp or took their chances escaping on foot (either with the column or by following their own course).

Captain Baum brought together a council of his officers. Spreading his map out over the hood of his peep, he reviewed the route. The task force would head south over secondary roads and make its way to Highway 27. Baum believed it promised the best odds of gaining an element of surprise and stealth.

Before launching the entire task force into the night, Baum drew up a plan to have Lt. Nutto make a reconnaissance to see if the road to the south was free of the enemy. Nutto's probe would consist of all six of his Sherman tanks and three halftracks laden with armored infantry. If Nutto ran into the enemy in strength, he would be equipped to deal with it. If he found that the road was clear, Baum would follow with the rest of the task force advancing in a column. Since the vehicles conducting the reconnaissance wouldn't be returning to the task force assembly area, the ex-pows remained on board.

Major Stiller, who had not been part of Baum's circle of officers, suddenly appeared on the scene. He brought Baum up to speed on Waters' condition, including the fact that Waters couldn't join the column. None of this was of any consequence to Baum, and he shrugged it off. The captain then reviewed for Stiller's benefit the route about to be taken.

Stiller asked why the task force couldn't head north. In his opinion, they should move in that direction with the hope of catching up to Patton's Third Army. For his part, Baum was sure that heading away from the camp using the same route they approached from was an invitation for contact with the enemy. The portion of Highway 27 Stiller wanted to use was exactly where they had waged the pitched battle with the *Hetzers*. The Germans were likely to have maintained a presence there. With his tanks and other vehicles blanketed with men, Baum would be placing them in danger if he knowingly advanced into the teeth of the enemy. Intentionally fighting his way through enemy positions would be too dangerous a proposition.

Stiller protested by saying that they didn't know where the U.S. Seventh Army was located (but truth be told, he didn't know where Patton's Third Army was either). In Baum's favor, the Seventh Army should be advancing *toward* the task force, whereas the Fourth Armored was moving away.

Baum had enough of it. He told Stiller,

> *I said we're moving south. For God's sake, stop challenging me. I have enough on my mind. And I'm still running this show. Nutto, get going. Find me a clear route.*

No one within American lines was aware of the dire situation faced by the members of Task Force Baum. Not their combat commander, Lt. Colonel Abrams. Not their division commander, Brigadier General Hoge, nor the corps commander, Major General Eddy. And the man with the biggest stake in the mission … the man who commissioned it … was in the dark as much as anyone. Before the end of the day on March 27, Patton, having not received any news, wrote to his wife:

> *Last night I sent an armored column to a place 40 miles east of Frankfurt where John and some 900 prisoners are said to be. I have been nervous as a cat all day as everyone but me thought it too great a risk. I hope it works. Al Stiller went along. If I lose that column, it will possibly be a new incident, but I wont (sic) loose (sic) it.*

In his diary the same day, he wrote:

> *I was quite nervous all morning over the task force I sent to rescue the prisoners, as we could get no information concerning them. I do not believe there is anything in that part of Germany heavy enough to hurt them, but for some reason I was nervous—probably I had indigestion.*

Perhaps his nervousness and indigestion were brought about because, deep down, he could not stomach the thought of what he had done.

14

The Only Mistake

The Return Trip Begins

As Lt. Nutto prepared for his reconnaissance mission, Captain Baum began organizing the rest of the task force. He decided to form up a column with the intent of being ready to depart the camp as soon as he knew the route to the south was clear. He placed Lt. Weaver's light tank at the point, followed by the assault guns, the reconnaissance peep, and then the halftracks.

Nutto ordered his men to start their engines. The drivers responded, and the stillness of the night was broken by the sound of American hardware firing up in unison. Exhaust spilled into the cool spring air. The lead tank crept into the darkness as it started down a trail that headed south from the camp. The rest of the tanks and halftracks formed a column and followed.

Nutto's column had barely left the assembly area (according to Baum, they had not gone more than 50 yards) when two or three *Panzerfausts* cut through the dark of night. One *Panzerfaust* blasted the last tank in line. Another round missed its mark but struck a nearby haystack, "lighting up the countryside for several hundred yards in all directions." The enemy lurked in the night, their numbers unknown. But no additional rounds were fired.

Baum immediately changed his plan. Rather than have the main elements of the task force form into a column, he instructed his men to take up defensive positions. The main body would maintain their vigilance and a defensive posture until Nutto completed his reconnaissance and reported back.

Unknown to Baum and Nutto, their opponent, *Oberst* Höppe, had placed his troops in positions sealing off the main exits from *Lager Hammelburg* and its sprawling training ground. The Germans were familiar with the terrain because they had trained there. Höppe's men had the task force under observation and were aware of virtually every move the Americans were making … including the departure of Nutto's tanks and halftracks.

Now minus a tank, Nutto's force pushed away from the main body of the task force and headed south. A full moon would rise higher into the sky as the night progressed. This made the advance easier in some respects, but also more dangerous since they could be more easily seen by the enemy (though a high overcast likely cut down on some of the moonlight).

Not wanting to steer into an ambush, Nutto exercised caution whenever the terrain in front of him offered the enemy an opportunity for concealment. He would leave his tank and conduct a reconnaissance on foot before allowing the lead Sherman to continue. (Nutto personally rode in the Sherman tank commanded by Sergeant Kenneth Smith. *Cobra King* was hit and immobilized earlier in the mission. A fire inside the tank, generated either by the enemy round or the crew intentionally spiking the tank, cooked off the machine gun ammunition.)

After a slow crawl for one-and-a-third miles, Nutto's lead tank arrived at a small village about a half-mile north-northeast of Bonnland. There was no sign of life as he passed through. The lead tank then approached an intersection just north of Bonnland. Looking south toward the town, perhaps 200 yards beyond the intersection, he spotted a roadblock consisting of a healthy stack of logs. The Germans had sealed off the road leading south … and the most direct route toward American lines.

Nutto radioed Captain Baum and informed him of the roadblock. Baum climbed into his peep and sped down the trail to see it for himself. Peering at the obstacle in the moonlight, he felt confident that the Germans had defenders at the roadblock. It would be folly for him to send the tanks crashing through the barricade. The prisoners wishing to escape with the task force were still mounted on the tanks and halftracks in Nutto's probe, leaving them vulnerable to enemy fire. Instead of advancing toward the roadblock, Baum issued new orders to Nutto: "Go back to that intersection and try that road. If it's open we can probably hit the highway from there." Baum added, "While you're doing that, I'll send the recon platoon up that road. You follow us as soon as you can."

Baum took off through the darkness and returned to the main body of the task force. Lt. Hoffner got underway with elements of the reconnaissance platoon on the route dictated by Baum. After Nutto got his tanks and halftracks turned around, he followed Hoffner's route.

Oberst Höppe's proxy eyes watched all this activity from the observation tower atop Hill 427.

Things didn't turn out well for the recon group. When Lt. Hoffner's peep reached the vicinity of Hill 340, he encountered a defended roadblock. The gunfire from the German engineers was heard by Lt. Nutto, who stopped the column in place at the sound of the fighting. Hoffner sped back and informed Nutto and Baum (who had since rejoined Nutto's small column) about the roadblock. Hoffner also opined that the German position on the high ground made the route too dangerous to use.

An alternative route existed in the form of a trail that split off to the west and carved its way through the base of the Reussenberg Mountains. Much of the trail ran through a very heavily wooded area. Some comfort was gained with the prospect that woods might offer some concealment from the increasingly bright moonlight. Nutto's probe took off in that direction.

After two miles, Nutto found that the trail tapped into a better road, which he followed for another two-and-a-half miles. When he next radioed Baum, they mutually determined that Nutto was at the base of Hill 427. Baum ordered Nutto to continue down the road to the village of Heßdorf, which is bisected by Highway 27. If Nutto radioed that it was clear, Baum would crank up the main column and advance from the camp to join him.

Nutto's column of eight vehicles moved slowly away from Hill 427. After advancing less than a thousand yards to the southwest, he came to an intersection. A turn to the right would lead to Höllrich (also bisected by Highway 27). Instead, he continued straight toward Heßdorf, less than two miles away.

Just outside the north edge of Heßdorf, the column crossed a small creek. Nutto turned south on Highway 27 and quickly encountered two road blocks that prevented him from going farther into town. The citizens of Heßdorf, awakened by the clamor of the armored vehicles, hung white sheets and towels out the windows to prevent their homes from being assaulted. Rather than try to break through the roadblocks, Nutto turned his small column north on Highway 27 and headed directly for Höllrich.

Unbeknownst to Lt. Nutto, lying in wait at Höllrich were 100 cadet officers led by *Hauptmann* Franz Gehig. The improvised force, armed with rifles, machine guns, and *Panzerfausts*, was attached to the *413th Infantry Division*. The team was sent north to help deal with the American penetration (they passed through Gräfendorf just two hours after TF Baum's departure from the town). After Gehig's arrival at Höllrich, he received an order to block the roads leading from *Lager Hammelburg* to Highway 27. After erecting the roadblocks, he established ambush positions that favored his *Panzerfausts*.

Nutto's lead Sherman drew up to the first houses on the south edge of town. Nutto left the tank behind and went on foot to scout the way forward. Not a soul was in sight, nor a sound to be heard within the town. He made his way back to his tank and reported his progress to Baum via radio.

Believing that Nutto had secured a way out, Baum gave the order for the main task force to form up. His column was now several hundred escapees lighter, for as the hours passed since Nutto's departure, many of the men grew disenchanted with the prospect of making it out with the task force and opted to return to the camp. It was not a source of disappointment for Baum, as it made his job easier.

Back at Höllrich, Nutto moved the column forward. The second tank in line remained a fair distance behind the lead Sherman. The other tanks and halftracks followed.

As Nutto's tank entered the town, the scene changed in a flash. A *Panzerfaust* opened fire, finding its mark on Nutto's tank. The American tank gunner got off a single round before a second *Panzerfaust* struck. The Sherman following behind Nutto's, which had been moving toward the highway when the enemy fire erupted, continued forward until it too was hit by a *Panzerfaust*, sending the passengers tumbling onto the pavement (one of the Americans sitting next to the turret was killed). The tank caught fire, illuminating the scene. Machine gun bullets cut through the night, the thread of intermediate red and yellow tracers providing guidance for the men squeezing the triggers.

Bedlam ensued. Someone pushed Nutto out of the turret hatch, sending him tumbling to the ground. The able-bodied crew members bailed out of the lead tanks and scrambled to get away. The prisoners that survived the blasts scattered for cover. Machine gun bullets stopped some of the men in their tracks. Lieutenants Bouck and Reid, each armed with an M3 sub machine gun, sought cover in a nearby ditch. As Nutto lay dazed near the tank, he heard Germans close by, some of whom mounted his tank and seized control of it.

The third Sherman in the column fired a round in response. When a German raised a *Panzerfaust* and took aim, a machine gun from the Sherman cut him down. Bouck and Reid, hearts pounding as they watched the scene unfold, spotted a *Panzerfaust* team illuminated by the burning tank. Reid said to Bouck, "Let's go get them." They crawled to within a short distance and opened fire with their grease guns. Confident that the bullets found their mark, they hurriedly made their way back to the other tanks.

The remaining Shermans, along with the three halftracks, managed to reverse their direction. Battered and bruised, they made their way back the way they came, hoping to return to the main task force.

Before the start of the skirmish at Höllrich, Baum had formed up his column and placed Lt. Hoffner in charge of leading the way to Highway 27. He then raced ahead in his peep to connect with Nutto. He would wait with Nutto's group while Hoffner and the task force caught up.

As Baum approached Höllrich, he was dismayed by the sound of tank fire. And then coming up the road toward him he saw a Sherman, followed by the two remaining medium tanks and the halftracks. He was angry at having lost more tanks, but he was even more upset over the loss of Nutto, the trusted and competent commander of C/37.

It was now 0300. Having been rebuffed on every route, Baum decided that enough was enough. They would reorganize and wait until daylight to make their way out toward American lines.

Baum ordered the task force to assemble near the base of Hill 427, where the densely wooded hillside at his back offered a modicum of protection. Once they arrived there, they would siphon off gasoline from some of the halftracks to fill the Stuarts, assault guns, and remaining Shermans. The respite would also give the medics an opportunity to tend to the wounded.

As Baum went over the plan with his team, Major Stiller revealed to Baum that many of the prisoners felt their best odds lay with their return to *Oflag XIII-B*. Baum responded, "I'll take those who want to fight. Tell that to Goode."

Only a dozen officers proved willing and stayed with the task force. Among them were Lieutenants Lyle Bouck and Matthew Reid. All of the rest … some two hundred men including Colonel Goode … opted to march back toward *Oflag XIII-B*.

At 0500, Colonel Goode lined up his men two by two and began the long trek back to the camp. Goode hoisted the white flag at the front of the column. Fifteen minutes after leaving the task force assembly area, some of the prisoners heard the rumble of tanks. A G.I. wondered aloud if it was the sound of the task force getting under way. One of his compatriots didn't think so. To him, the sound seemed to be coming from another direction.

He was correct. The enemy was closing in.

The Finale

Task Force Baum had been whittled down to about 110 able-bodied men, plus the dozen prisoners willing to fight their way out. Baum's medium tank company stood at only three Shermans, but he still had four of the light tanks and two of the Sherman 105mm assault guns. There were 22 halftracks. Gasoline was a major problem; not all the vehicles could make it back to American lines with the available fuel.

Baum ordered the crews to empty the gas tanks of eight of the halftracks to fill the remaining vehicles as best they could. The abandoned vehicles were set on fire. A final radio message announced that the mission had been accomplished and the task force was returning.

The wounded soldiers unable to continue were placed inside a nearby barn marked with the Red Cross insignia. Lt. James Cook, a POW from the 35th Infantry Division, was among the wounded. While in the barn nursing the leg and foot wounds he received during the melee at Höllrich, he overheard that the injured were going to be left behind. Unwilling to resign himself to that fate, he summoned the strength to fight on and found a spot in one of the halftracks.

Baum rallied his men and briefed them on the task ahead. They would fight their way through to friendly lines, no matter what. They would avoid towns. If they had to cross a stream and couldn't find a bridge, they would drive a halftrack into the water and use it as an improvised bridge.

At 0810, the exhausted men of Task Force Baum mounted their vehicles. Baum's next command was, "Turn 'em over!!"

Just as the lead tanks started to move, a torrent of enemy fire descended upon them. All hell broke loose. Where was the enemy firing from?

During the night, a platoon of German infantry armed with *Panzerfausts* slipped into the heavily forested slope above the clearing where the task force vehicles now idled. They were only 50 yards away. But the nearby *Panzerfausts* weren't the only threat. Far from it. Baum observed enemy armor and infantry closing in from several directions.

Once again, Baum faced the *Hetzers* from the *251st Heavy Tank Destroyer Battalion*, which after refueling and replenishing their ammunition had assembled at Fuchsstadt. The *Hetzers* fired from positions south and southeast of the American's assembly area. Baum reported six *Panzers* advancing from the southeast along with some of the *Hetzers*. He also thought he saw a half-dozen *Tigers* firing from positions to the northeast, and he reported a column of *Panzers* approaching from the direction of Weickersgrüben. Every possible avenue of escape for Task Force Baum was closed off (German records, however, show no evidence of armor other than the *Hetzers*).

The veterans of the Fourth Armored Division fought back out of desperation. The assault guns attempted to lay smoke and followed with high-explosive rounds. Alfonso Casanova and his crew fought as gallantly as one could expect. A direct hit on the Sherman wounded Casanova, his gunner Pfc Jack Stanley, and the assistant gunner Pfc Lawrence White. They kept firing until a second round struck the tank. Both Stanley and White were incapacitated … but Casanova took over the 105mm gun, loading and firing on his own. He shot three more rounds before a third and final enemy round slammed into his assault gun. Miraculously, the crew members were able to abandon the tank and made it to safety.

Sgt. Graham's assault gun held out a little longer. The Sherman took several blows both direct and glancing while spitting out 105mm shells. But it was just a matter of time before his crew joined the others and ran for cover in the woods. (Graham became one of the few members of the task force to avoid capture. It took him six days before he found his way back to American lines. The final day of his journey was particularly harrowing, as he came face to face with Germans before eventually encountering disbelieving infantrymen from the U.S. 45th Infantry Division).

The Shermans and Stuarts got off some shots, but within less than three minutes, all of them were hit and out of action, their crews scrambling for cover. Lt. Weaver, already mounted up in his M5A1, realized immediately that his 37mm gun was no match for what they were facing. He ordered his crew to abandon the tank and seek cover.

Sgt. Yoerk, whose inherited Sherman was positioned closer to the front of the column, saw enemy shells slam into the barn that had been set up as a medical aid center. The stone walls and roof collapsed, likely killing all within. Lt. James Cook, who had vacated the barn earlier for fear of being left behind, managed to get away from the halftrack he was in and sought cover behind the barn. In an account relayed to his son, he described the screams coming from within the building after its collapse. He and others made several unsuccessful attempts to rescue those inside.

The Germans held an insurmountable upper hand. As Baum took stock of the situation from his vantage point farther back in the column, it appeared that every vehicle had been hit and put out of action. Bedlam and chaos painted the base of Hill 427. Baum's next command was, "Every man for himself." Of course, given the expanse of the assembly area, not everyone could hear him. But they didn't have to. Many had already chosen flight as their only means of survival.

Halftracks were ablaze, with dozens of armored infantrymen trying to find cover near the open field. Some made their way to the woods on the slope above the clearing. Some were struck by enemy fire while trying to escape.

As Robert Zawada tried to flee his halftrack, a *Panzerfaust* round took his leg off below the knee. Though shocked and dazed, he maintained the presence of mind to fashion a tourniquet out of his belt. He managed to work his way to some cover, tucking himself within the crook of a fallen tree. When a retreating American solider stopped at his side and offered to help him, Zawada waved him on. He thought he would pass out, perhaps mercifully. But then another soldier (likely one of the POWs) came along and moved him closer to the cover of a halftrack. As he lay on the battlefield, he maintained consciousness and watched the German assault play out in front of him. The enemy armor drew closer, eventually pulling into the clearing alongside the burning American vehicles. German infantry came through with the *Hetzers* and started rounding up the Americans. As Zawada watched, a German approached and shot an American soldier at point blank range (Zawada believed the G.I. to be black). The Germans picked up Zawada and placed him in the back of one of the undamaged halftracks. Finally, he passed out.

Such scenes were in Abe Baum's rearview mirror. When he entered the woods, he drew the company of radio operator John Sidles and none other than Major Stiller. Baum issued an order to those within earshot to break up into groups of twos and threes and head west in search of American lines.

Baum and his two companions headed deeper into the woods and moved west up the slope of the Hill 427. Given Baum's injured knee, he struggled to keep up with Stiller and Sidles. The baying of dogs echoing through the woods provided extra incentive to forge ahead. When the trio reached the hilltop, they took a short breather before starting their descent to the west. As they got closer to the west edge of the woods, they saw six American soldiers emerge from the woods. Baum watched as the half-dozen G.I.s started down the open slope, only to have a group of German soldiers appear and take them prisoner.

Fearing a similar fate, Captain Baum thought better of going farther. Instead, he and his companions retreated into the forest. They started burrowing under a bed of leaves, planning to wait for nightfall before continuing their attempt to reach American lines.

As the three Americans worked on creating their hiding place, Sidles spotted a German soldier approaching. He warned Baum of the danger and then scurried up an incline, where he took cover behind a tree, carbine in hand. Baum and Stiller remained frozen in place, no doubt hoping they had not been seen.

The German brandished a rifle as he approached. He walked up to the two officers. Stiller reacted by raising his hands above his head in surrender. Baum, with no desire to become a prisoner, got to his knees and fumbled underneath his coat for his .45 automatic. His bandaged hand prevented him from quickly drawing it. The German casually set down his rifle, drew his own pistol, and just as casually shot Baum below the waist, burning the side of his scrotum and striking him in the inner thigh. Baum reacted by saying, "You son of a bitch, you shot my ball off." The German soldier laughed and revealed to Baum and Stiller that he spoke English. He told them that he used to live in Bridgeport, Connecticut.

Sidles watched from farther up the slope. He thought about shooting the German with his carbine. But instead, he revealed himself and surrendered. The soldier was distracted by Sidles' sudden appearance, and Baum took the opportunity to discard his dog tags (he was

Jewish). The German collected the Americans' pistols and proceeded to march them out of the woods. Stiller, being of higher rank, was separated from the others.

Baum and Sidles started the long, forced march back to *Oflag XIII-B*. Baum found it difficult to continue because of his wounds. Sidle didn't want to leave Baum's side, but the captain insisted that he go on without him.

The prisoners able-bodied enough to make it back to *Oflag XIII-B* were herded into an equestrian riding ring within the compound. Among them were Lt. Bouck and Lt. Reid.

They had a long trek in front of them. Some of the prisoners were marched out on foot, while others, for the initial leg of their journey, were loaded into cramped boxcars at Hammelburg. On April 5, those on the train were unloaded at Nuremberg and continued by foot from there. One member of A/10, Milton Koshiol, recounted how he was forced to march for two weeks before arriving at a prisoner of war camp at Moosburg, 150 miles to the southeast (American forces liberated the camp on April 29). As for Captain Baum, he was picked up and taken back to the camp. He joined the other injured men incapable of making the trek to Moosburg.

Waiting for News ... and Crafting a Story

Perhaps the first insight into the fate of Task Force Baum came via German radio on March 30. The announcer proclaimed that an American armored division had been captured and destroyed near Hammelburg.

Word leaked out about the mission. At a press conference that day, Patton addressed the issue.

> felt that I could not sleep during the night if we got within 60 miles and made no attempt to get that place.

Patton grew increasingly concerned about the fate of the task force. By the morning after the German radio broadcast, he seemed to have resigned himself to the mission being a failure. He even started to consider the impact the raid would have on his legacy, as evidenced by his diary entry on March 31:

> So far I have made only one mistake, and that was when I lost two companies of the 4th Armored Division in making the attack on Hammelburg. I made it with only two companies on account of the strenuous objections of General Bradley to make any (effort) at all. Had I sent a combat command as I had first intended to do, this mistake would not have occurred.

When Patton penned this reflection, he engaged in revisionist history less than a week after the fact. Unless Bradley lied in his own memoirs (of which there are two, hence doubling down when taking the second opportunity), Patton never gave Bradley the opportunity to object to the mission. In Bradley's words:

> I did not learn of the expedition until it had been on the road for two days. But by then the angry mutterings of division and corps had traveled the grapevine to Army Group. Out of them came the story of as brash a venture as Patton dared during the entire war. It was a story that began as a wild goose chase and ended in tragedy.

In fairness to Patton, there is some contradictory evidence indicating that Bradley *was* aware. Bradley's aide, Colonel Joe Hensen, wrote in his diary on March 28:

> When Patton ran off on his mission the other day, Brad told him he would allow it provided Patton did not become involved. He was ordered to withdraw if he did to prevent him from becoming entangled in the wrong direction.

14. The Only Mistake

What isn't entirely clear from Hensen's entry is just how Patton may have positioned "his mission." Was it presented to Bradley as a rescue operation? Or as a diversionary attack as Patton later claimed? The full truth of the matter will likely never be known.

Over the days to come, 15 men from Task Force Baum reached American lines. Among those who avoided capture were 2nd Lt. Norman Hoffner (commander of the reconnaissance platoon) and T/Sgt. Graham (commander of the assault gun platoon). Nine men were eventually listed as KIA, 32 wounded, 16 missing, and all others captured.

From the time the first men returned, details of the raid began to emerge and made their way up the chain of command. On April 4, "Hap" Gay, Patton's Chief of Staff, wrote in his journal:

> Two officers who had been at Hammelburg and liberated by Task Force Baum entered Third Army lines and told what happened. This narrative is of particular interest to the Army Commander because this was the first time he had news that his son-in-law, Colonel Waters, was one of the prisoners in the camp.

The two officers were brought before Lt. General Patton. Patton did not record what they said to him. However, Colonel (later General) Paul Harkins (who annotated Patton's memoir) noted that the two officers reported that Lt. Colonel Waters had also been a prisoner and had been shot. Patton then added that, after the visit with Graham and Hoffner, General Patch called him to report that three other escaped officers had made it to his headquarters. They too reported that Waters had been badly wounded. Patton wrote, "Patch said he would do everything in his power to capture the camp on the fifth."

That same day, Patton received word from other sources as well. He summed it all up in his diary on April 4:

> Patch called.... Three other officers who had escaped had reported to his Army and stated that Johnny Waters ... had been badly wounded and recaptured. Apparently the wound is serious but not dangerous as it is in the leg. I believe that the Seventh Army will probably relieve the camp today or tomorrow. I felt very gloomy over the fact that I may have caused Waters' death, but I believe I did the right thing, and I certainly could have never lived with myself had I known that I was within 40 miles of 900 Americans and not made an attempt to rescue them.

The following day, while still waiting for final confirmation of Waters' status, he wrote to his wife, repeating what he expressed in his diary several days before regarding Bradley's knowledge of the raid and the impact he (Bradley) had on the composition of the task force:

> My first thought was to send a combat command, but I was talked out of it by Omar and the others...
> I feel terribly. I tried to save him and may be the cause of his death. Al Stiller was in the column and I fear he is dead. I don't know what you and [little] B will think. Don't tell her yet ...We have liberated a lot of PW camps but not the one I wanted.

On April 6, a task force from CCB of the 14th Armored Division liberated *Oflag XIII-B* once and for all. They found only 75 Americans at the camp. The rest, including Major Stiller, had been marched farther into Germany.

Patton arranged for special treatment for his son-in-law. He dispatched Colonel Odom (the assistant Army Surgeon) to evacuate Waters from the prison camp. After Odom reported on Waters' condition, Patton arranged for two Cub planes (one of which was modified to carry a litter) to fly to the vicinity of Hammelburg. Accompanied by Odom, they flew Waters to Frankfurt. From there, he was transported to the nearby 34th Evacuation Hospital.

Patton visited his son-in-law at 1100 that morning (April 6). The first thing Waters asked his father-in-law was if Patton knew he (Waters) was being held prisoner at Hammelburg. Patton replied "No, I did not. I knew there were American PWs in the camp and that's why I went in."

On April 7, Patton wrote a letter to his daughter, within which he provided a revisionist account of the mission. He also described in detail the nature of Waters' injuries and his prospects for recovery.

On April 9, Patton returned to Lt. Colonel Waters' bedside and presented him with the Silver Star with Oak Leaf Cluster (an award that had been approved during Waters' captivity).

By this time, Captain Baum had also arrived at the 34th Evacuation Hospital for treatment. His wounds were healing well, and he yearned to return to his unit. Before departing the hospital, Patton visited with him. After the captain expressed his desire to return to the Fourth Armored, Patton arranged for a Cub plane to fly him back the following day.

Word of the disastrous raid continued to spread. During a press conference held on April 13, Patton embellished his tale:

> The force which we sent over ... was for the purpose of misleading the Germans and make them think we were going to Nuremburg, but actually (the task force) went to rescue 900 American prisoners there, got to its objective. They met the 2nd Panzer Division and two other divisions, which showed that our effort to mislead the enemy had its effect, because (had) he put these divisions up north, our efforts would have been much slower.

A week elapsed before there was any other recorded mention of the raid. The death of President Roosevelt on April 12 and the press coverage it received probably went a long way toward diverting public attention from the Hammelburg debacle.

The affair did not escape the attention of General Eisenhower. On April 15, the Allied Supreme Commander was inclined to update General Marshall on Patton's actions. Embedded within a three-page letter that served as a general update on the progress of the campaign and condition of the Army, Eisenhower wrote:

> In Army command, there is no weakness except for the one feature of Patton's unpredictability so far as his judgement (usually in small things) is concerned.

Later in the letter, Ike elaborated:

> Patton's latest crackpot actions may possibly get some publicity. One involved the arbitrary relief of a censor.... I took Patton's hide off, but there is nothing else to do about it. Then again, he sent off a little expedition on a wild goose chase in an effort to liberate some American prisoners. The upshot was that he got 25 prisoners back and lost a full company of medium tanks and a platoon of light tanks. Foolishly, he then imposed censorship on the movement, meaning to lift it later, which he forgot to do. The story has been released and I hope the newspapers do not make too much of it. One bad, though Patton says accidental, feature of the affair was that his son-in-law was one of the 25 released. Patton is a problem child, but he is a great fighting leader in pursuit and exploitation.

It wasn't long before the topic resurfaced in Patton's personal correspondence. The relative importance of the recovery of his son-in-law was further evidenced in a letter Patton sent to his wife on April 17:

> Some times I feel that I may be nearing the end of my life. I have liberated J. (John Waters) and licked the Germans, so what else is there to do?

That same day General Patton (he had officially received his fourth star just three days prior ... though he was not aware of it until April 18) flew to Paris to see Lt. Colonel Waters, where the two had a long talk. He found his son-in-law's condition to be much improved. He visited with him again the following morning before flying back.

And then on April 28, in another letter to his wife, Patton again mentioned Waters in a manner illustrative of how his son-in-law's plight and subsequent rescue occupied his thoughts.

> I have not heard from you since John was rescued so I suppose that having done that, my usefulness has ended.

Patton's desire for compliment and recognition—something he sought openly and perhaps even desperately from Eisenhower—extended to his own family.

Major Stiller was finally set free on April 29, when the Moosburg POW camp was liberated. On May 1, Patton visited the camp and wrote about the experience in his diary. Thirty thousand prisoners, mostly officers, awaited repatriation. The executive officer at the camp was the familiar Colonel P.R. Goode, who Waters had reported to when in captivity. In what seems to be an attempt to protect Waters' reputation, Patton claimed that Goode's illness during the march from Poland was the reason Waters never tried to escape. Other than the polished account Patton wrote later for his memoir, this represented the last notable mention of the Hammelburg affair.

As for Captain Baum, he returned to the 10th Armored Infantry Battalion on April 10, the day after Patton visited him at the hospital. Abe was ready and eager to resume his role as S-3. On April 18, he was promoted to the rank of Major. On April 27, Baum left for the French Riviera on a well-deserved leave. Though it was supposed to be for seven days, he did not return until May 13 (the cessation in hostilities occurring during his absence might explain the extension).

While Baum was away, it was announced to his battalion on April 30 that he had been awarded the prestigious Distinguished Service Cross (second only to the Medal of Honor). Baum was a worthy candidate for the latter. The likely reason his name was not submitted for the Medal of Honor: the nomination would have drawn more attention to the raid itself (inclusive of Congressional review … and in this case, scrutiny).

Postscript

After the war, Patton wrote about his decision to send the task force:

> On March 26, I crossed the Rhine with Codman and directed Eddy to send an expedition across the Main River to Hammelburg. There were two purposes in this expedition: first, to impress the Germans with the idea that we were moving due east, whereas we intended to move due north, and second, to release some nine hundred American prisoners of war who were at Hammelburg. I intended to send one combat command of the 4th Armored, but unfortunately, was talked out of it by Eddy and Hoge, commanding the 4th Armored Division, so I compromised by sending one armored company and one company of armored infantry.

Patton's post-mortem was another attempt at revisionism to cover what was certainly his primary intent behind the mission. Conspicuous by its absence at that time was any reference to Bradley.

In his memoir, Patton recites the details of the raid as he had apparently learned them from Major Stiller. He acknowledged that Stiller was on the raid but not in command (but he makes no mention of why Stiller was there). He mentions that Stiller had suggested that after the camp's liberation, the task force head north rather than south along the route it had come, and that Baum had refused that advice. At no time did he mention his son-in-law (another aspect that is conspicuous by its absence).

Major General Eddy's biographer, Henry Gerard Phillips, made an excellent observation about Patton's approach to his personal diary:

> Patton was clearly writing for posterity and frequently took pains in his diary to cover his tracks, justifying some action he had taken.

As for the men who served on the raid, they became members of an exclusive club, bound together by the common experience of doing what no other American soldier had ever been asked to do during the war. While Patton's underlying motivation for the raid could have created great animosity toward the Third Army commander, as a group, the participants in the raid were never so inclined. Even in the division's own post-war history, there is no mention of the raid's connection to Patton's son-in-law. Patton's error in judgment on this occasion was not enough to outweigh the respect he had earned on other fronts.

15

Breakout from the Main River Bridgehead

Preparing for the Next Phase

The next phase of the offensive called for the Fourth Armored to break out of the bridgehead at Großauheim and drive north as part of a trap to encircle the enemy units facing the American Third and First Armies. Specifically, *Olympic's* next objective was the high ground near Grünberg, 33 miles north of the Main River bridgehead at Großauheim.

Several things had to happen before *Olympic* could proceed. First and foremost, the bridgehead at Großauheim had to be expanded and a bridge installed that could support the Fourth Armored's vehicles. As that was transpiring, the 26th Infantry Division would relieve the elements of CCB operating in the Main River bridgehead south of Aschaffenburg. CCB would then be reconfigured and assemble south of CCA.

Clearing the town of Großauheim was beyond the capacity of the 53rd Armored Infantry Battalion, so assistance was brought to the fore in the form of the 328th Regiment of the 26th Infantry Division. On March 27, the infantry advanced through the bridgehead to clear out Großauheim as well as the neighboring city of Hanau, less than two miles to the northwest.

The Germans were reluctant to yield Großauheim and the bridge site. With their enemies closing in on all fronts, the desperation felt throughout the German command was palpable.

Artur Axmann, leader of the *Hitler Youth* since 1940, tried to rally the growing contingent of young boys fighting for the *Reich*: "It is your duty to watch when others are tired; to stand fast when others weaken. Your greatest honour, however, is your unshakeable faithfulness to Adolf Hitler." The presence of German youth became increasingly evident to the men of the Fourth Armored Division. It was also apparent that older citizens were being pressed into battle in greater numbers. After crossing the Rhine, Captain Lyons noted that,

> ...the German soldiers are getting younger and younger, some of them only in their early teens. Others were quite a bit older, in fact they could have well been grandfathers of the younger soldiers. It made little difference to us, the enemy was still the enemy, a trigger finger knows no age.

As demonstrated at the Main River, there remained a well of resistance which could be drawn from, even if sparingly.

The infantrymen of the *Yankee Division* pushed slowly through and beyond the positions of the 53rd Armored Infantry Battalion. At 0800, the Germans demonstrated their resolve by launching another counterattack. The men of the 328th Infantry were forced back into the lines of the armored infantry but brought the situation under control by 0915.

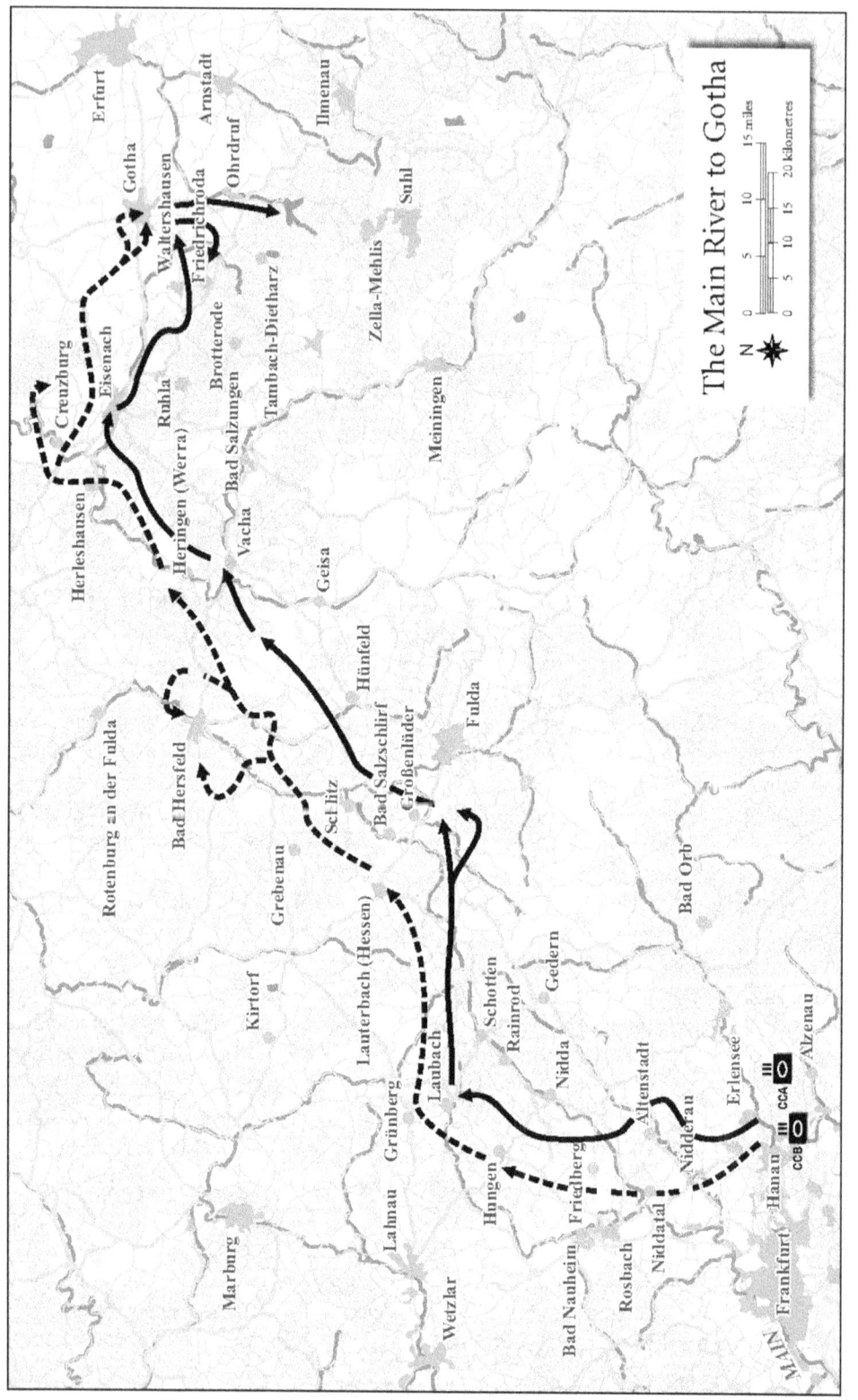

The Main River to Gotha (© Petho Cartography, 2020).

Captured members of the *Hitler Youth* (U.S. Army photograph).

Meanwhile, the engineers worked around the clock under the dual threat of artillery fire and counterattack and completed the installation of a treadway bridge at 1500.

Other elements of the 26th Infantry Division moved into position to relieve CCB near Aschaffenburg. At 0900, the infantry began taking over the positions of the 10th Armored Infantry Battalion which along with the 37th Tank Battalion was reassigned to CCR (both battalions were significantly understrength due to their donations to Task Force Baum).

The constitution of Abram's CCB was updated to include the rested 51st Armored Infantry Battalion (commanded by Lt. Colonel Dan Alanis) and Lt. Colonel Delk Oden's 35th Tank Battalion. The artillery available to Abrams remained strong, with the 66th Armored Infantry Battalion, 22nd Armored Field Artillery Battalion, and 191st Field Artillery Battalion still assigned to CCB. The combat command assembled near Babenhausen, 10 miles south of CCA's bridgehead.

While the Fourth Armored Division reorganized for future operations, so too did Lt. General Patton. The Third Army HQ moved from Luxembourg to Idar-Oberstein, Germany, 80 miles behind the front held by the Fourth Armored Division. It was the first time that TUSA would command operations from German soil.

It was also time for a new plan from SHAEF. On March 28, Eisenhower announced that after the encirclement of the Ruhr was complete, the Ninth Army would come under the control of Bradley's 12th Army Group. Thereafter, the primary thrust by the Western Allies would be carried out by Bradley. Montgomery's role would be reduced to protecting Bradley's northern flank. General Devers' 6th Army Group would protect Bradley's southern flank. Eisenhower also communicated the plan to his Russian military counterpart, Marshal Stalin.

The direct communication between Ike and Stalin, while justified, did not sit well with the British. Their discontent wasn't limited to the new communication protocols between the Allied and Russian military commands. Prime Minister Churchill was upset with Ike's change in strategy and was adamant about allowing Montgomery's 21st Army Group to carry the fight to Berlin. His protests were to no avail.

As Hoge's men prepared for the next leg of the conquest of Germany, they were not aware that their past deeds had been recognized at the highest level of authority within the United States. On the morning of March 28, SHAEF announced via *Stars and Stripes* that the War Department, by direction of the President, had cited the entire Fourth Armored Division for "extraordinary tactical accomplishment during the period from December 22 to March 27, inclusive."

CCA's attack from the Main River Bridgehead

On March 28, with the bridge over the Main River finally ready to accept vehicle traffic, Colonel Sears' Combat Command A was unleashed in all its fury. Even though the 26th Infantry Division had not cleared the enemy completely from Hanau, at 0300 the leading elements of CCA pushed across the bridge under the cover of darkness and moved into the eastern section of the city. As they progressed into the northern part of Hanau, the lead tanks of B/8 came upon a series of roadblocks that delayed the advance. While under enemy small arms fire, engineers came forward with the tanks to reduce the obstacles. Meanwhile, A/8 discovered an alternate route and by 0900, the lead tanks of Lt. Colonel Irzyk's 8th Tank Battalion reached the town of Roßdorf, six miles north of the bridgehead. After some initial resistance, the defenders, seeing the size of the attacking combat command, collectively surrendered.

The defenders of Ostheim, less than two miles to the north, were not as inclined to give up. Enemy troops brandished *Panzerfausts* and fired from within the buildings. The armored infantry often relied on hand grenades to flush out the stubborn enemy. After working methodically through the town, they declared it clear at 1145.

After CCA departed Ostheim, they only encountered light resistance the balance of the day. Irzyk's tanks charged north through the towns of Eichen and Altenstadt. After a clash near Florstadt with elements of their old foe the *11th Panzer Division*, the advance resumed at a torrid pace through Staden, Bingenheim, Berstadt, and Hungen … an 18-mile surge after leaving Ostheim. Near Hungen, Irzyk's tanks overran a huge column of enemy vehicles that extended for two miles. Much of the German equipment was destroyed and a significant number of prisoners taken.

An M7 from C Battery, 22nd Armored Field Artillery Battalion crosses the Main River near Hanau (U.S. Army photograph, courtesy Darren Neely).

The advance didn't stop there. After another dash of nearly nine miles, CCA reached their primary objective of Grünberg at 1800. It was an incredible advance of 33 airline miles in a single day.

CCB Follows Suit

Combat Command B, now consisting of the 35th Tank Battalion and 51st Armored Infantry Battalion as its primary maneuver units, departed its assembly area at 0545 on March 28. Lt. Colonel Abrams' command, led by A/35 and A/51, followed Colonel Sears' CCA over the Main River bridgehead. He then attacked along a parallel route about five miles to the west of CCA. Most of the infantry traveled aboard the tanks, and the empty halftracks were used to haul extra gas and ammunition in anticipation of the lead units outpacing their supply trains.

At Mittelbuchen, three miles northwest of Hanau, the Germans offered light resistance. The Shermans of the 35th Tank Battalion took care of most of the opposition while the infantry dismounted and mopped up the remaining elements.

CCB continued driving north, sweeping up prisoners and small towns along the way. Closer to Giessen, 88mm fire struck the Sherman tank of the 35th Tank Battalion's commander, Lt. Colonel Delk Oden. It was a devastating strike, killing his gunner and setting the tank on fire. The force of the shell blew Oden out of the turret. Though still nursing a wound from several days prior, he mounted another tank from which he continued leading the attack from the front. Oden received the Distinguished Service Cross for his actions.

Abrams' command moved with impressive speed. The battalion diary for the 51st Armored Infantry Battalion described it this way:

> *The remainder of the march to the vicinity of Harbach was merely a series of skirmishes in which the enemy would offer a slight amount of resistance, but would quickly surrender. Many prisoners were taken, and many vehicles including three self-propelled guns were destroyed. Fifty enemy were killed, one hundred and fifty were wounded, and over a thousand were taken prisoners of war. Our infantry casualties for the day were two men killed.*

Alexis Sommaripa, the psychological warfare agent who spent most of his time with the 37th Tank Battalion, continued to work his craft, demonstrating mastery at influencing enemy soldiers to lay down their arms. With the 37th Tank Battalion assigned to CCR, he now worked in tandem with the 35th Tank Battalion in CCB. At the town of Göbelnrod, 30 miles beyond Mittelbuchen, Sommaripa put his skills to work once again. As a task force of CCB waited 1200 yards outside the town, Alexis and his crew drove his specially equipped Stuart tank down the main street. He kept up a constant chatter over the two loudspeakers mounted to the tank, instructing the Germans to cease fire and surrender.

Alexis eventually left his tank on foot and continued to call out the German defenders. Amazingly, he did not draw any fire. But he did draw a response, as a garrison of more than 1000 enemy soldiers emerged from the buildings. Sommaripa instructed them to stack up their weapons and then form up into a column, hands raised over their heads. He then ordered them to march off toward CCB's positions outside of town. Always inherent in his message was the assurance that, as prisoners of war, they would be treated humanely in accordance with the Geneva Convention.

Not long after his success at Göbelnrod, Sommaripa met a tragic end. After continuing north, his tank was strafed by an aircraft. The driver was hit and the M5A1 went out of control, veering sharply off the road and overturning in a bomb crater. Sommaripa was thrown out of the tank, which then landed on top of him, crushing him to death.

By the end of the day, Lt. Colonel Abrams' lead units had advanced slightly farther north than CCA. At 1600, they arrived near the high ground outside of Beltershain, two miles north-northwest of CCA's eventual forward positions. A company each of tanks, infantry, and some supporting tank destroyers were left to hold the road center of Lich, about eight miles to the southwest, where they guarded approximately 2000 prisoners taken that day.

The Prisoner Dilemma

One of the obstacles faced by Abrams' troops became the number of Germans surrendering as his tanks and halftracks roared through the countryside and small towns.

Some German soldiers, tired of the war and unwilling to surrender, attempted to blend into the civilian population. A report from the G-2 of VII Corps on March 27 focused on the problem.

> *Every German guards his identity documents as he would his life. Since 1933 at the advent of Adolph [sic] Hitler, his New World, and his ruthless policies, the possession of an identity document has generally meant the difference between freedom and prison. The habit has been ingrained and it can be assumed every German will carry with him some sort of identity document if he has one. Therefore it can be assumed also, until proven otherwise, that a man carrying no such document is attempting to hide his identity or military-civilian status.*

The report went on to itemize the type of identity documents that "any healthy male 17 years of age or older (military age) probably will carry":

1. The *Wherspasz* (an identity booklet issued when a male turns 17 and is not yet in the military).
2. The *Soldbuch* (the booklet that replaces the *Wherspasz* when the soldier is inducted).
3. The *Entlassungschein* (discharge papers issued upon leaving the military, which the Americans recognized as a form of identification).
4. The *Ausmusterungschein* (a red piece of paper with the man's photo, indicating that he was not physically fit for military service).

Any man not capable of producing a document was assumed to be an active member of the *Wehrmacht*.

As town after town fell to the Americans, a common tactic for organizing those willing to surrender was the placement of posters instructing German soldiers to turn themselves in at a specific location. The posters emphasized that the German soldier would be treated in accordance with the Geneva Convention. If a German soldier dressed in civilian clothes turned themselves in, they were treated the same as an ordinary prisoner of war and evacuated to the nearest POW camp.

Not all prisoners made it back to a POW camp. For the G.I., the prospect of being separated from one's unit while escorting prisoners to the rear could be enough to bring a soldier to handle the situation in other ways. Sometimes, it was simply a reflection of the savagery inherent in warfare. A son of one of the officers from the 10th Armored Infantry Battalion described his father's viewpoint after his unit captured some Germans while the Fourth Armored was well out in front of the rest of the Third Army.

> *They were led into the forest by some of his fellow soldiers. "I never asked questions" he harrumphed at the dinner table once. Obviously they were shot. He said American soldiers would cut off the fingers to get the rings of dead German soldiers. He admired the SS, and thought they were the best fighters. "We had to kill 'em all," he told me.*

Screening the Left Flank

During the advance by the main body of CCA, a task force comprised primarily of elements of the 704th Tank Destroyer Battalion and 25th Cavalry Reconnaissance Squadron screened the left flank of Colonel Sears' column.

As CCA drew closer to its final objective at Grünberg, a spotter plane identified 20 German tanks in the area near Giessen, 12 miles west of CCA's vanguard. Wary of the enemy armor's intent, an outpost patrol was formed consisting of one M18 Hellcat, one M8 armored car, and two squads of men from the 25th Cavalry. The patrol positioned itself on both sides of the road leading into a nearby town. The Hellcat took its place to the left of the road, the M8 to the right.

At 1745, the patrol heard a column of vehicles approaching, but the sounds came from an unexpected direction opposite where the enemy tanks were previously spotted. The patrol had little visibility in the direction of the sound. One of the Hellcat crew, Phil Hosey, dismounted to find a more favorable position. No sooner had he left the Hellcat when the enemy column drove into their outpost.

The lead German vehicle came as close as six feet to the outpost before the Americans opened fire. A hail of bullets erupted from the machine guns mounted on the two cavalry peeps. The Hellcat opened fire with its 76mm main gun. The German vehicle at the head of the column was immediately brought to a stop by the thunderous fire. The wreckage blocked the road and bottled up the rest of the enemy force. German troops spilled out of the other vehicles, weapons drawn and ready to engage.

In midst of the confusion, Hosey, who was farther away from the outpost on his scouting mission, suddenly came face to face with a German soldier armed with a P-38 pistol. Armed only with his own .45 auto, Hosey found himself in a Mexican standoff. Both men froze, neither of them seemingly able to pull the trigger at point blank range. As Hosey recounted, "Luckily, he dropped his gun and said, '*Kamerad!*'" At that moment, the German ammo carriers in the column began to explode. Hosey declined the opportunity to take a prisoner and raced back to his Hellcat.

The exploding ammunition illuminated the scene. Hosey saw that the M8 had run into a ditch and was immobilized "with all six wheels off the ground." The crew of the M18 grabbed their tow cable, attached it to the rear of the armored car, and attempted to pull it out. Just as that was done and the M18 was backing off the road, "the ammo carriers went sky-high." Hosey, still dismounted, was hit by shrapnel. He later recounted:

> *I can still remember breathing through my mouth, only to lose it through a hole in my back. We had no medic, hence no morphine. The head of our band, a tech sergeant, ordered me strapped to a stretcher on the back of a jeep. We couldn't go through town as collapsed buildings and burned vehicles blocked the road. So we exited over plowed fields on one side of town.*

Caring for the Wounded

Phil Hosey may have been transported to the 704th Tank Destroyer Battalion aid station. The aid station was usually the first stop for the wounded. It was the job of the front-line medic to administer what aid they could on the battlefield and then help get the wounded back to the aid station, usually calling on a peep for transport.

When S/Sgt. Nick Alexander first arrived in France in July as a replacement for the mortar squad of A/53 (at the time, a private in rank), his role was that of a medic. He later described his primary responsibilities:

> *We injected morphine at the scene of combat, sprinkled sulfa drugs on the bleeding wound and if necessary, stopped the bleeding with a tourniquet. In addition, applied a splint to a fractured limb, while waiting for the peep to arrive, after which we loaded the man onto a stretcher that was transported back to the battalion aid station. There was one medic per company of about 200 soldiers. The online medics were with the advancing troops and underwent exposure to all of the incoming artillery and small arms fire. One medic actually performed a tracheotomy with a pen knife on the field.*

At the battalion aid station, the wounded were stabilized, bandaged, and given some form of pain relief.

Normally, the transport of the wounded from the aid station was carried out by ambulance. But before the Fourth Armored arrived in France, the decision was made by higher headquarters to strip the units of their ambulances. The belief was that the high profile of the vehicle would draw enemy fire. Instead, the medical teams were instructed to convert their weapons carrier (used by the medical units to transport medical supplies instead of munitions) into a makeshift ambulance. In the case of the 704th, they also employed captured enemy vehicles to evacuate the wounded.

If more treatment was required, the soldier was transported from the battalion aid sta-

February 28, 1945. A wounded infantryman of the 94th Infantry Division is removed from a jeep to an aid station near Trier, Germany, in the Third Army sector. 419th Medical Battalion (U.S. Army photograph).

tion to the collecting station at the regimental level, and then the division clearing station (operated by the division's medical battalion). The soldier would then be transported to either an evacuation hospital (a capacity of 400 beds) or a field hospital (also with a 400-bed capacity).

The evacuation hospital would retain patients for up to 10 days, with the intent of returning the soldier to his unit or sending them on for further care or rehabilitation. There were slightly more evacuation hospitals than there were divisions, so typically, each division was married to one (there were 50 evacuation hospitals available to support 45 American divisions).

The field hospitals were less common (19 in total). But unlike the evacuation hospital, the field hospital was comprised of three platoons, each of which could operate independently (though their bed capacity was reduced to only 100 per platoon). A platoon would typically work directly adjacent to the division's clearing station, handling severe cases that could not be transported beyond that point. The staff of the field hospital were also charged with operating combat exhaustion centers.

Once the proper care was allocated at either the evacuation or field hospital, the next stop (if necessary) was either a holding unit or a convalescent hospital within the theater. If the latter, they would eventually return to their unit or be placed in a reinforcement depot. If placed in a holding unit, they were on their way to a general hospital in the theater. After treatment, it was either back to their unit or a ticket to England or the United States for additional treatment.

Even though the Fourth Armored's casualty rate after January 1 was less severe than the division's first six months in combat, it was still plenty for the medical units to deal with.

During the period from January through April, monthly battle casualties handled through the division's clearing stations ranged from a low of 294 in January to a high of 784 during March. Non-battle casualties ranged from 582 in April to 673 in January.

Members of the Fourth Armored were not the only patients that received treatment at the field hospitals. During the four-month stretch, 771 prisoners of war were treated along with 41 civilians. Soldiers from other units were treated as well, to the tune of 403 between January 1 and the end of May. Thankfully, for the men of the Fourth Armored, only four battle casualties received treatment from the medical battalion during the month of May, along with a modest 125 non-battle casualties. The numbers reflect the more advanced care given by the 46th Armored Medical Battalion. There is no telling how many soldiers on both sides of the battlefield received care from the front-line medics, nor is there an accounting of how many civilians may have received treatment.

CCR Remains South of the Main

March 28 was a typical day for Colonel Blanchard's combat command. CCR functioned in its usual role, protecting the rear or flanks while maintaining readiness to provide reinforcing firepower to either CCA or CCB, should the need arise.

February 1, 1945. Medics of the 94th Infantry Division are being issued with vest-like red cross markers, in answer to the German claim that they cannot tell the difference between medics and regular troops because of insufficient markings (U.S. Army photograph).

The 704th Tank Destroyer Battalion's headquarters, with attachments consisting of one platoon from A/704, a platoon from the 37th Tank Battalion, and a platoon from the 10th Armored Infantry Battalion, moved from Leeheim at 1630 and closed in on Roßdorf at 1830. The town, 18 miles south of the Main River, was outposted and a security patrol established.

At 1430, the remainder of the 10th Armored Infantry Battalion (minus the men and vehicles assigned to Task Force Baum) moved out of its assembly area near Babenhausen and headed north. But there was one element of the 10th AIB that remained behind. At 1015, Captain Lyons and the 10th Armored Infantry Battalion's S-2 halftrack left for the vicinity of Aschaffenburg with the hope of maintaining radio contact with Task Force Baum.

The casualties inflicted on the enemy this day were substantial (primarily due to the ambush of the column near Hungen): 325 Germans were killed and 455 were wounded. Seventy-six trucks, 356 assorted motor transports, a variety of 10 different field guns, three armored vehicles, 10 *Nebelwerfers*, and 284 other vehicles of all shapes and sizes (202 of which were horse-drawn, which speaks to the state of the *Wehrmacht* in terms of their capacity to move troops with any sort of rapidity) were accounted for. The division report for the day stated that 406 prisoners were taken. However, the individual battalion journals cumulatively put that number in the range of several thousand (including those rounded up by the physiological warfare unit at Göbelnrod). In stark contrast, losses for the Fourth Armored were seven men killed and 24 wounded.

There was a sidebar for Brigadier General Hoge, and it involved George Patton, whose son-in-law wasn't the only prisoner on the Third Army commander's mind on March 28. As Patton and Bradley discussed the boundaries between the First and Third Armies, a reference was made to General Henri Giraud of the French Army (Giraud was famous for, among other things, escaping German captivity three years prior). Giraud had stated that members of his family (Patton believed them to be his wife and two daughters-in-law) were being held in captivity somewhere near Weimar. Patton suggested that Giraud's aide accompany the Fourth Armored Division, which he believed to be the American unit likely to get there first.

Little More than Road Marches?

In the official Army history of the campaign, *The Last Offensive,* historian Charles McDonald described the Fourth Armored Division's advance on March 29 and 30 as "little more than road marches." There was some truth to that assessment. But one's perspective might differ if you were among the men of the Fourth Armored who came face to face with the enemy during the waning days of March.

Following up on its magnificent advance made the day prior, CCA set out from Grünberg at 0630. Colonel Sears' mission was to capture the road center of Großenlüder, 26 miles due east of the combat command's point of departure.

During the advance toward Großenlüder, the usual roadblocks were encountered at many of the towns. But increasingly, they were undefended. The enemy often surrendered without offering resistance, but the occasional *Panzer* could still present an obstacle. As the day progressed, the most significant delays came about due to the weather. A morning mist turned into a heavier rain as the hours ticked by. An exceedingly heavy fog followed the rain, limiting visibility at times to only 20 yards.

While en route to Großenlüder, Lt. Colonel Irzyk received an order to change direction toward Herbstein. Irzyk selected D/8 to lead the attack on the town while the rest of his task force remained in place. Much to Irzyk's surprise, he received a follow-up order instructing him to switch direction back toward Großenlüder. The foray to Herbstein cost him time. But of greater concern to him was the loss of another platoon leader from D/8, Lt. Naddy. When his tank was destroyed, Naddy was wounded and the other three crew members killed.

The 94th AFAB also suffered a significant loss when A Battery passed through the town of Blaukenen. A civilian attacked the column with a *Panzerfaust*, striking one of the battalion's halftracks. T/4 Gordon Huff and Private Bow Smith were killed, and Private Behrens was wounded. After Pfc Thurnon C. Walden killed the civilian, the Americans burned the village to the ground during the ensuing battle.

CCA's advance for the day concluded at Großenlüder. After an artillery barrage, the tanks and armored infantry attacked and secured the town by 1930.

The Fourth Armored was a victim of its own success. In some respects, the advance made after breaking out of the Main River bridgehead was *too* good, as the other elements of XII Corps were trailing far behind. To allow the infantry divisions to close on Hoge's armored columns, both CCA and CCB were held in place for several hours on March 30.

CCA didn't move out until 1420. Their objective for the shortened day was the high ground near Bad Hersfeld, 20 miles to the north-northeast. As the tankers rolled into towns along the route, they noted that the barricades they encountered were often under the early stages of construction (they believed that their advance was so rapid, the enemy didn't have time to complete their work … and they were probably correct). For the first time in several days, small detachments of enemy armor were encountered. Near Sieglos, D/8 encountered five *Mark IVs*. The M5A1 tanks, though outgunned, took immediate action and knocked out one of the *Panzers*. Irzyk dispatched the more powerful Shermans of C/8, whose drivers quickly jockeyed their tanks into position. The gunners accounted for three more of the *Mark IVs* before the lone remaining tank fled the scene. C/8 lost two Sherman tanks, not to the *Mark IVs*, but to the seemingly ever present and dangerous *Panzerfausts*.

Elsewhere along the route, three more *Mark IV Panzers* were destroyed by American artillery fire. A few miles north of Schlitz, the gunner in the Sherman commanded by Lt Davis (an observer for the 94th) knocked out a *Panther*.

As daylight faded, the 8th Tank Battalion came upon a lucrative target when one mile south of Motzfeld, A/8 ran head-on into a column of enemy vehicles transporting gas, ammo, and troops. The Shermans placed the column under fire, quickly setting the vehicles ablaze. The ammunition cooked off in a series of explosions. The German troops didn't stand a chance, and all were either killed, wounded, or captured.

At 2300, the lead elements of CCA reached the high ground between Bad Hersfeld and Vacha. The combat command also outposted the towns of Gethsemane and Hillartshausen.

Several hours after darkness settled in, the 94th, which had moved into position near the town of Hilmes, also had an encounter with a column of ammo trucks. The German vehicles stumbled into the battalion's positions, and according to the battalion history, "a few bursts of machine guns left the trucks flaming and exploding in the dark."

CCB's experience on March 29 and 30 was not dissimilar, in that it could hardly be described as a road march. Their zone of advance once again ran parallel to CCA's, but now it extended a few miles farther to the north. A blown bridge threatened to delay the advance, but an alternate route was used, and the column moved on with just a few minutes delay. Scattered groups of German soldiers were encountered along the way, and most of them surrendered without a fight.

A Fourth Armored Division column rolling through Germany (U.S. Army photograph, courtesy Darren Neely).

Abrams' main objective on the first day was Lauterbach, which fell at 1140 after 560 prisoners were bagged. The 51st Armored Infantry Battalion established its headquarters "in the home of a wealthy Kraut doctor." Though the day had been an easy one, the 51st suffered a heavy blow when S/Sgt. "Hoppy" Hobgood was killed by a German sniper. A member of the trains, Hoppy was one of the oldest men in the battalion, and his loss was taken especially hard by the battalion staff.

That wasn't the end of CCB's advance for the day. They pushed farther to the east, with C/704 moving into Angersbach and Landenhausen (the latter being four miles deeper into the German interior). Over the course of the 50 miles covered on March 29, the roads were strewn with wrecked vehicles and wagons. A countless number of Germans lay contorted along the roadside in the way that only dead men can.

On March 30, after incurring the imposed delay, CCB moved out at 1300 from their positions near Lauterbach. They advanced north on a route west of CCA. Their objective was the capture of Bad Hersfeld and the high ground immediately to the east.

While it may have seemed at times that the Germans had given up the fight, they had not. During the couple of days preceding the Fourth Armored's drive toward Bad Hersfeld, the German *7th Army* (now commanded by *General* von Obstfelder) tried to muster what forces they could to conduct a counterattack against the east flank of the Fourth Armored. The main element selected for the attack was a new unit, *Panzer Brigade Thüringen*. A training unit, it consisted of a tank battalion, assault gun battalion, and a *Panzer Grenadier* regiment (among its ranks were the slim remains of the *2nd Panzer Division*). Obstfelder hoped to complement this force with the reconnaissance battalion of the *11th Panzer Division*. Forty new tanks were due to arrive by rail.

The trains carrying the tanks and other elements of *Panzer Brigade Thüringen* reached their unloading point at Niederaula, where a major rail depot sits on the south edge of the town. Arriving at about the same moment were the tanks of B/35 and the armored infantry of B/51.

The timing completely favored the Americans. The Germans grabbed their small arms and offered stiff resistance, but it was not enough to hold off the firepower of the Shermans. Delk Oden's tanks tore up the two trains in the station. M18 tank destroyers attached to CCB added their firepower as well. Out of the estimated 40 tanks the Germans were trying to unload and deploy, less than a dozen escaped. The debacle forced *General* von Obstfelder to scrub the entire counterattack. CCB captured approximately 100 Germans during the melee.

While the B Team plastered the enemy, Lt. Colonel Abrams' main force bypassed the rail yard and attacked the town. Approximately 100 additional prisoners were taken there. Within Niederaula, 70 American and British POWs were rescued. A platoon each of tanks and infantry were left to mop up the town.

Though it was growing late in the day, there was still enough time for CCB to tackle Bad Hersfeld prior to nightfall. D/35 led the column toward the city. The light tanks advanced to the northeast on the main road running through a valley that leads from Niederaula to Bad Hersfeld. A little over three miles up the road, as they entered the village of Asbach, a *Panzerfaust* knocked out the leading tank.

A/35 and A/51 moved forward to attack Asbach in force. The armored infantry dismounted from the tanks for the attack. As the armor and infantry advanced into the town, they encountered "fanatical enemy resistance." Five *Panzers*, positioned north and west of the town, held up the advance until friendly artillery was brought into firing position. The subsequent barrage destroyed one of the *Panzers* and softened up the enemy infantry for the kill. The other four *Panzers* retreated toward the *Autobahn* a mile north of Asbach.

The artillery rounds set fire to most of the buildings in Asbach. The flames were still raging when the armored infantry made their way down the village streets. The threat of burning to death flushed many of the German soldiers from their positions. Asbach was cleared by 1900.

B/35 and B/51 took over the lead and resumed the advance toward Bad Hersfeld. About midway between Asbach and Bad Hersfeld, the road used for the advance crossed over an *Autobahn*. Here, two *Panzers* were destroyed.

Compared to many of the towns recently taken by CCB, Bad Hersfeld was of greater size and required a well-coordinated assault. B/35 and B/51 were called upon and placed under the command of Major Charles L. Kimsey. A deliberate plan of attack was formed: a platoon of tanks and infantry would drive cross-country over Hill 324 to the main road leading from the west into the city. They would then attack the west side of Bad Hersfeld with the objective of mopping up all the way to the city center. Meanwhile, the balance of the two companies would drive north up the main road and attack the southern portion of the city, clearing it up to the center, where they would connect with the platoon of tanks

15. Breakout from the Main River Bridgehead

attacking from the west. The stronger of the two forces would then clear out the section east of the main road. C/35 and C/51 would then be sent through to clear the north part of the city and assist in cutting all exits.

Given the size of Bad Hersfeld and the complexity of its streets, a high level of coordination was required to prevent confusion between the attacking forces as they struck from different directions. Complicating things somewhat for the 51st Armored Infantry was a recent shuffling of leadership. Only days before, they lost one of their veteran company commanders, Captain Daniel Beldon of B Company, who was seriously wounded in action. Beldon was replaced by Captain William Crane, the battalion S-2.

The attack kicked off at 1930 and met immediate, strong resistance at the entrances to the town. With darkness enveloping the battlefield, the advance through the narrow and winding streets was very difficult. The platoon attacking from the west became confused in the darkness and entered the city using the wrong street. An enemy tank, positioned at an intersection, knocked out the lead American tank. Enemy machine guns in position on the high ground north of the road delayed the infantry, leaving the tanks to advance on their own. The street was too narrow to bypass the now burning Sherman tank, so an attempt was made to find an alternate route. But at that point, with the attack breaking down, CCB issued orders to withdraw and assume positions alongside the *Autobahn*. Their work was done for the day.

As for CCR, their original mission on March 29 was to trail Abrams' CCB. However, Colonel Blanchard's orders were later modified. The Reserve Command would shift gears and drive on the right flank of CCA to help keep Colonel Sears' main supply route open.

The advance of the 10th Armored Infantry Battalion was not without incident. As the Service Company moved to a new location, they were attacked by an enemy force armed with machine guns and *Panzerfausts*. 2nd Lt Patrick R. Murren dismounted from his vehicle and led a successful counterattack.

Overall however, CCR did not encounter much opposition, and by 1700, had reached their objectives south of CCA. The 10th Armored Infantry Battalion ended the day at Herbstein, about nine miles west-southwest of the lead elements of CCA.

Before the end of March 29, the 10th Armored Infantry Battalion's commander, Lt. Colonel Cohen, received

Captain Harry Rockafeller (left) and Captain William Crane (right) of the 51st Armored Infantry Battalion (courtesy Michael Malone).

word that Task Force Baum had reached the prisoner of war camp and was returning with a large group of POWs. This was a better update than had been communicated from the Fourth Armored HQ much earlier, when at 0055, the message was, "No news of Baum." Unfortunately, the latest news received by Cohen was not entirely true.

On March 30, the division finally heard the news that the Presidential Distinguished Unit Citation had been awarded in recognition of their performance from December 22 through March 27. At the end of the war, the Fourth Armored was one of only two divisions to receive the honor (the other being the 101st Airborne Division). The 72 hours following the period of recognition would have been a worthy addition to the accolade. And it is fair to say that the advance made on March 29 and 30 had been much more than a simple road march.

The Advance Toward the Werra River

CCA had an easy morning on March 31, given that the orders for the day didn't arrive until 1315. Their objective once received: seize a bridgehead over the Werra River and then continue to the high ground near Eisenach. Given that sunset would come at 1855, covering the two dozen miles from their starting point at Ausbach before dark would be highly dependent upon the level of opposition they faced.

Colonel Sears' combat command moved out at 1400. The timetable was upset almost immediately. They ran into stiff resistance at Heimboldshausen, less than two miles northeast of the start line. While their opponents brought to bear the usual dose of late-war small arms and *Panzerfausts*, they were also dug-in and reinforced with supporting artillery. Among the defenders were SS troops who put up a spirited fight and knocked out one of the American tanks.

There were two Germans who never got the chance to turn their *Panzerfausts* against the advancing American tanks. As they were making their way uphill toward the town, Lt. Boas and Lt. Bill Lothian, commander of C Battery of the 94th, both walked to the side of the road to relieve themselves. As they approached the edge, they laid eyes on two unsuspecting enemy soldiers 30 feet below them, nestled within some bushes, *Panzerfausts* at hand. The two Americans officers drew their weapons before the Germans were aware of their presence. Their aim was true, and with four shots between them, they silenced the threat.

A single primary road led out of Heimboldshausen and crossed the winding Stankels River. After a portion of the column crossed the bridge, the Germans destroyed the span, splitting CCA in two. The balance of the column sought a detour through the Friede Forest. They followed a looping route to the north on the opposite bank of the river. The going was slow, as the road was only a logging trail and a recent rain had turned it into a muddy track. The column finally emerged from the forest a short distance west of Wölfershausen and proceeded to attack the town. A/8 led the assault, losing two Shermans to *Panzerfausts* before clearing out the enemy.

In the meantime, the portion of the column that made it safely across the river before the destruction of the bridge also advanced toward Wölfershausen but approached the town from the east side of the river. The column consolidated there and continued north, tracking along the west side of the Werra River.

The combat command was delayed when American artillery fire struck an enemy ammunition factory, setting it ablaze. The catastrophic secondary blasts prevented the column from drawing too close. The advance resumed once the explosions finally came to an end.

CCA moved on to capture the towns of Widdershausen and Dankmarshausen, four miles to the north. The B Team outposted the town of Heringen, two-and-a-half miles to the south on the east side of the river.

CCB had a much tougher time of it on the final day of March. The 51st Armored Infantry Battalion and 35th Tank Battalion moved out in darkness at 0400. The plan was to bypass Bad Hersfeld to the east and then attack it from the north, utilizing a task force led by Major Kimsey. The task force (comprised of the A and C Teams) would travel in a wide arc around the east side of the city, culminating at the town of Mecklar. There, they would cross the Fulda River and drive south to attack the city.

The C Team took the lead for the column. After advancing through Kerspenhausen, the task force was slowed by poor roads and trails near Hilperhausen. An alternate route was found, which bypassed Oberhaun and delivered the column to Unterhaun, where a roadblock barred entry into the town. While it was being cleared, an enemy self-propelled gun was destroyed.

The column moved another 2000 yards to the north. Upon reaching the *Autobahn*, they found another roadblock (this time undefended) that had to be cleared. Yet another roadblock forced the column to move cross country to the town of Sorga, two miles due east of Bad Hersfeld. At Sorga, they found an enemy supply installation and took 300 prisoners.

The column regained the original march route at Kathus, a mile northeast of Sorga. From there, the route took the form of a trail winding for three miles over wooded hills to Meckbach. The route was no more than a very poor logging trail, and multiple vehicles became mired in the mud. Scattered groups of Germans were found in the woods along the trail, but they surrendered without resistance. The total volume of prisoners was such that it imposed significant delays for the column as the Germans were processed.

At 1000, the lead elements of the column exited the woods and headed into the village of Meckbach. The Germans placed several 88mm anti-aircraft guns in defense of the town. In what the 51st Armored Infantry Battalion journal described as a "sharp, brisk fight," the task force destroyed eight 88s, twelve 20mm anti-aircraft guns, one *Panzer*, and numerous trucks and staff cars. One hundred and twenty five prisoners were taken.

Major Kimsey deposited a platoon of tanks and infantry in the town and spurred the rest of the task force due west toward Mecklar, nestled in a bend on the east bank of the Fulda River. After dealing with some dug-in *Panzerfaust*-armed infantry along the way, they arrived at the bridge site. Unfortunately, the Germans had destroyed it. The Fulda River was 60 yards wide at the crossing site, so the task force was stymied.

At that point, CCB received new orders. A decision was made to bypass Bad Hersfeld. The task force was directed to move back over the trail to an assembly area near Sorga, close to the *Autobahn*. The new instructions had them moving northeast at 1300, with the objective of seizing a bridge over the Werra River at the town of Creuzburg.

CCB sped down the *Autobahn* to the northeast. As the column raced on, some German armor was encountered, but Corporal John Eidenschink, gunner in Sergeant Ferraro's Hellcat, knocked out three *Mark IVs* and reduced the threat.

Farther down the route, just west of the town of Hönebach, an overpass crossed the *Autobahn*. After part of D/35 passed underneath, the Germans set off explosives that sent the roadway crashing down, blocking the *Autobahn*. The light tanks of D/35 that made it to the other side before the blast were immediately attacked by German infantry firing from dug-in positions. The armored infantry dismounted from the tanks and moved to engage alongside the light tanks. The tank crews relied on their machine guns to squelch the German defenders. Along with the armored infantry, the tankers wiped out the opposition. The engineers from A/24 came forward and used demolitions to break up the larger sections of debris, which the bulldozers then pushed out of the way.

In the meantime, the column bypassed the debris and continued their advance using an alternate route. With darkness approaching, the C Team moved due east on a road running parallel with the *Autobahn*. Hönebach lay less than a mile from the destroyed overpass, and it was the first of a series of towns to be cleared.

The Germans defended Hönebach with determination. The C Team responded with their own dose of increased resolve and left the town in flames. A/35 and A/51 moved along a secondary road leading northeast from Hönebach, clearing and outposting a trio of towns: Großensee, Raßdorf, and Bosserode.

The advance from Hönebach was two-and-a-half-miles. While transiting that route, A/35 came under fire from enemy artillery. The tankers tracked down the firing position and destroyed six artillery pieces. The C Team then cut through the *Autobahn* less than half a mile north of Raßdorf. Advancing two miles farther east of Bosserode, the B Team attacked the much larger town of Obersuhl and cut the *Autobahn* a half mile north of the town's center. All of this was done by 2200. The command post for the 51st Armored Infantry Battalion moved to Bosserode.

By 1900, the engineers had cleared the debris from the *Autobahn*, allowing the rest of the column to advance another mile or two to a point north of Bosserode, where they turned off the highway for the night. The Hellcats of C/704 outposted the town of Kleinensee, a half-mile south of Bosserode. Darkness having descended, the advance to capture a bridge over the Werra River waited until morning.

While CCA and CCB moved within striking distance of the Werra River, CCR followed the route of CCB, stopping near Bad Hersfeld at 1900. It was on this day that Patton started to make good on his promise to Brigadier General Hoge to replace the two companies lost on the Hammelburg raid. The wheels started turning on the requisition process for bringing the 10th Armored Infantry Battalion and 37th Tank Battalion closer to their normal complement of troops and equipment. By this point, the loss of Task Force Baum had been confirmed and conceded.

At their present position, the Fourth Armored Division had moved farther east than any other unit on the Western Front. General Bradley felt the need to halt the Third Army to allow the First Army to catch up on Patton's flank. However, that order was short lived after a German deserter of officer grade, taken into custody by the Fourth Armored, disclosed that a high-level German headquarters or communication center was to be found some 30 miles beyond the Werra River at the town of Ohrdruf. The information was credible enough that an airborne assault was considered but later ruled out because of the short notice. Instead, Eisenhower and Bradley agreed to turn Patton loose for another 24 hours to seize this tantalizing prize. The Fourth Armored, being the division closest to Ohrdruf, was given the task.

16

Ohrdruf

Another River—The Werra

Said the scribe of the unit diary of C Company, 704th Tank Destroyer Battalion, "Easter Sunday, but instead of a world at peace, war goes on just the same."

On April 1, CCB drove deeper into the heart of Germany. The C Team (C/35 and C/51) took the lead, with infantrymen taking their customary place atop the Sherman tanks. The command groups of both battalions followed behind them, followed by the A Team, the 66th Armored Field Artillery Battalion, the armored engineers of A/24, and the B Team. The rest of Abrams' combat command brought up the rear. The combat command sped along the *Autobahn* for four miles to the vicinity of Sallmannshausen, located on the east side of the Werra River. Abrams hoped to grab a bridge there, but as his tanks approached, the Germans succeeded in blowing the span.

While CCB approached the Werra, elements of CCA drove north along the west bank of the river. Sears' combat command drew up close on the right of CCB, and upon their arrival, took over engaging the Germans near Sallmannshausen. Released from the scene, Abrams followed the line of the Werra River to the northeast.

A mile up the road near Wommen, CCB encountered small pockets of German infantry that amounted to little more than a nuisance. Here, the twisting and turning Werra abruptly heads east, and CCB continued along the *Autobahn* which follows suit.

Near Herleshausen, two miles east of Wommen, a *Panther* tank was knocked out before it ever got off a shot. Its crew was taken prisoner. As the infantry-laden tanks of the 35th Tank Battalion rounded a blind curve closer to Herleshausen, they were ambushed, with serious casualties inflicted upon the vulnerable infantry. The advance stopped short of the town, and the column deployed in the open fields where they waited for further orders.

Several enemy vehicles, including two *Panzers*, were spotted moving south from Herleshausen on the road toward Lauchröden. CCA, which continued to track along CCB's right flank using secondary roads spliced between the *Autobahn* and the river, placed the *Panzers* under fire. Shermans from A/8 knocked out the two enemy tanks spotted by CCB, plus another two *Panzers* and several armored cars. Al Irzyk's tanks and infantry moved in and secured Herleshausen. On the outskirts of town, the Americans found what appeared to be an ordnance repair facility. Stripped-down tanks littered the field ... vestiges of the *Wehrmacht's* once mighty arsenal.

The two combat commands now came together on the *Autobahn*. CCA intended to cross the Werra using a railroad bridge at Hörschel, two miles farther to the east. As the column neared the bridge, the Germans once again displayed their prowess at demolitions and destroyed the span in the face of Colonel Sears' vanguard. Enemy machine gun and rifle fire erupted, hitting some of the infantrymen riding on the tanks. Rifle fire also erupted from the high ground to the left of the column, causing more casualties.

Not all the Germans challenged the lead units of the American column head-to-head. They either intentionally allowed the more heavily armed forward elements to pass, or inadvertently found themselves trapped behind the fast-moving American front. Some were inclined to surrender without a fight. Others continued to fight. On April 1, the 94th Field Artillery Battalion encountered the latter.

After the tanks and armored infantry had passed by, several German infantrymen crept back into slit trenches dug along the roadside and delayed the advance of the rest of the column. The Germans showed no willingness to put down their arms, so the men of the 94th were tasked with clearing the road. This was not typical work for the artillerymen, and they suffered several casualties in the process. When T/Sgt. Carl P. Bergman, T/5 James J. Coyle, and T/5 Nelson L. Sutherland were all wounded by machine gun fire, Captain Jacob Horowitz, T/3 Leo Pudwell, and T/5 Edward Rushin rushed to their aid, even though they were still under fire.

Elsewhere along the route, T/4 Michael DiGregorio of Battery B of the 94th was wounded by sniper fire coming from a cave. One of the M7s fired four HE rounds directly at the opening. Thirty-two Germans were flushed out, hands held high above their heads. They left three dead comrades behind. The 94th's tally for the entire day added up to 64 prisoners taken and six Germans killed.

CCA was ordered to hold in place while CCB was dispatched to the north. Abrams' column advanced along a road running parallel with a railroad track that ran parallel to the Werra River. At a turn in the road, a burning German truck blocked the way, delaying the column until it could be removed. While the road was being cleared, the infantry dismounted and moved forward along the railroad track. While out in the open, they were hit by rifle fire coming from the high ground to their left, right front, and rear. The only option for the infantrymen was to keep running with the tanks, using them for cover as best they could until some form of defilade could be found.

As they advanced over 500 yards of open terrain, seven G.I.s were killed and 14 wounded. When they finally found cover, two anti-tank guns opened fire, knocking out four Shermans before they were spotted to the north near the town of Spichra. The other Shermans followed up, knocking out both anti-tank guns as well as a self-propelled gun located near the bridge. The tanks also neutralized machine gun fire that had been plaguing the infantry. Lt. Colonel Alanis's men then deployed to take out the German infantry firing from the high ground to the left of the column.

CCB received orders to return to the *Autobahn* and head back to the vicinity of Herleshausen (the crossing site near Spichra was left to CCA). B/35 and B/51 moved four miles north to the town of Ifta. From there, they advanced east for three miles to Creuzburg, where they hoped to find a bridge over the Werra River. Creuzburg was nestled within a bend of the river that hugged the east and south edges of the town. It would be difficult to approach the lone bridge without clearing at least the southern portion.

While the B Team assembled for the attack on Creuzburg, the A Team backtracked to the town of Wommen before turning due north toward Markershausen and Lüderbach. The tanks and infantry then turned east for two miles before assembling on the high ground north of Ifta.

C/704 and the 25th Cavalry Recon Squadron, screening the left flank, advanced three-and-a-half miles to the northeast, where they outposted the village of Scherbda and the dense woods found between there and the Werra.

The tankers of C/704 found the woods infested with well-armed German infantry. The 3rd Platoon of C/704 took seven German prisoners and loaded them into the back of the ammo halftrack (the ammo being stored in a trailer hitched to the vehicle). When a *Panzerfaust* round whizzed by, the Germans bailed out of the halftrack and sought cover in a nearby ditch. The prisoners were kept under guard as the tank destroyers and other vehicles sent a hail of fire to cover the column as it turned around on the narrow road.

The German prisoners were as nimble as their captors and jumped back into the halftrack, which then made its way through the dense woods along with the other vehicles. The crewmembers fired every weapon they had into the trees and underbrush as they barreled through the woods toward Scherbda. As the column emerged out of the darkness, the maintenance vehicle at the rear of the column was almost fired upon by friendly tank destroyers. One of the men from C Company noted, "It was one of the most tense and dangerous situations we have yet been in. So ended our 'peaceful' Easter Sunday."

Before the day was out on April 1, CCA started the process of putting in a temporary bridge across the Werra River. The first step was for the 53rd Armored Infantry Battalion to establish a bridgehead near Spichra. Supporting the armored infantry was the 8th Tank Battalion's mortar platoon and the Sherman tanks of B Company. The 94th Armored Field Artillery Battalion went into position at Archfeld, four miles west of the crossing site, to fire in support of the forces at the bridgehead. The engineers from A/24 then came forward and worked through the night installing a 144-foot pontoon bridge.

The Germans were not willing to cede the crossing. Before sunrise, they launched an attack with assault guns and infantry in an attempt to eliminate the bridgehead. Lt. Frederick Moorby, the forward observer from the 94th Armored Field Artillery Battalion, called for artillery support to break up the German assault. He radioed in his adjustments from an exposed position, never flinching as he zeroed in the 105mm howitzers. The German attack wasn't without impact on the engineers' effort, as three of the 24th Armored Engineer Battalion trucks were destroyed, delaying the completion of the bridge.

By 0545 on April 2, all three infantry companies of the 53rd Armored Infantry Battalion had crossed the Werra and moved forward to occupy the high ground facing the river. At 0930, the first battalion of the 359th Infantry Regiment passed through the 53rd's positions to attack the town of Krauthausen. By 1600, the pontoon bridge was completed and vehicles began motoring across.

The Germans were determined to hold back the Americans at the line of the Werra River, but ultimately, they lacked the ground forces to stop the surge of the Fourth Armored. One resource they *did* have in strength was the *Luftwaffe*, which struck from the air in an attempt to destroy the temporary bridges erected by the American engineers. During a 24-hour period, 85 enemy aircraft attacked the Werra bridge sites. The 489th AAA Battalion knocked down 34 of them and damaged six (their largest tally of the war). The 94th Armored Field Artillery Battalion noted, "It was the biggest air show the battalion had ever witnessed. We only wish they were ours and that we were not the target. Sgt. Carl Rich of C Battery was killed during one of these air attacks."

The Attack on Creuzburg

CCB's work for April 1 wasn't done. The B team's attack on Creuzburg encountered stiff opposition. Enemy infantry held the town and were supported by two *Panzers* and three anti-aircraft tanks located on the high ground east of the river. From their vantage point on the elevated terrain, the Germans had a clear line of sight and could hit targets in the town with direct fire.

Shelling from the Sherman tanks started a considerable number of fires in the south part of the town. A strong wind coming out of the south spread the flames through the rest of Creuzburg, burning virtually all the houses except for a castle located at a high point near the center of town. Once the B Team cleared out that area, American artillery observers took up positions inside the castle, which provided an excellent vantage point for directing fire on the enemy positions in the area.

As the armored infantry mopped up the town, the Germans blew up the bridge located just to the south of Creuzburg. As darkness fell, the burning town illuminated the terrain. Patrols, moving slowly due to the light from the fires that made them easier to spot, searched for a suitable location to install a bridge. At 2300, they returned with a recommendation for a crossing site just south of the blown bridge.

Under the protection of a railroad grade, the engineers inflated a pontoon which was used as a ferry to take the infantrymen of B/51 across the river. C/51 followed and extended the crossing site to the left of B/51's positions. Thirty-seven prisoners were taken as they expanded the bridgehead.

The work of the armored infantry gave the engineers the elbow room they needed to work in relative safety. The task of getting the treadway portion of the bridge installed on top of the pontoon sections was aggravated when the engineers' crane failed to arrive. As a result, the bridge sections had to be moved by hand, which slowed the process. After working on the bridge all night and into the next morning, it was almost complete when at 0700 (April 2), three German planes attacked and ripped four of the pontoons with fragmentation bombs, further delaying the completion of the bridge.

Fifteen minutes later, about 50 enemy planes strafed the roads leading from the bridge site west toward Ifta. The 51st Armored Infantry Battalion journal noted, "The sky was full of more enemy air than we have seen in our push through Germany." The German planes were met with ferocious anti-aircraft fire, and six of them went to the ground in flames near the 51st's command post at Ifta. One aircraft crashed into a home less than a hundred yards from the battalion's maintenance section, leaving its tail section protruding through the roof. German civilians raced to the home and attempted to extinguish the flames, which threatened to spread through the town.

The rebuilding of the bridge commenced once a fresh set of pontoons were brought forward. No further enemy action interfered with the engineers' work, and the bridge was completed at 1500. The infantry-laden tanks of B/35 and C/35 were the first vehicles to cross. The lead elements struck out toward Ütteroda, Neukirchen, and Berteroda, and advanced a little over five miles before halting for the night.

Moving across a pontoon bridge was not an easy affair. The road track rested on inflated pontoons (i.e., a form of raft) floating on the water. Putting aside the unnerving fact that the men and equipment were moving across a bridge that could be zeroed in on by the enemy, the structure of the bridge itself didn't lend itself to speed. The weight of the vehicles, coupled with the fact that the bridge was not a fixed structure, resulted in an imposed speed limit of approximately 10 miles per hour (and in some situations, less than that).

As Harry Rockafeller later recalled, the Fourth Armored learned a valuable lesson during their training maneuvers in Tennessee when two tanks were too close together as they crossed a pontoon bridge. The bridge collapsed, and the tanks plunged into the river, taking their crews to their deaths by drowning.

To help ensure stability (and to avoid a clustered set of targets for the enemy), a large interval was maintained between vehicles (on a longer bridge, as much as 75 yards). The combination of a speed limit and the interval between vehicles resulted in a significant time requirement for moving a large armored formation across a bridged water obstacle.

Neither CCA nor CCB made the type of progress Patton and Bradley had anticipated. Even though the Fourth Armored stood 20 miles short of Ohrdruf, the prize was tantalizing enough that Bradley gave the okay for Patton to continue the effort on April 3.

Lt. Colonel Cohen Becomes a Prisoner

Lt. Colonel Hal Cohen's hemorrhoids kept him from leading the Hammelburg task force. Indeed, they were so grievous that he required medical attention. Cohen traveled to Dieburg (15 miles south of CCA's bridgehead on the Main River) for treatment at the 16th Field Hospital, where its 1st Platoon served the Fourth Armored Division.

As *Olympic* pushed farther north, the field hospital pulled up stakes and followed in the division's wake. Their destination was Lauterbach, more than a 50-mile road trip from Dieburg. A dozen trucks from the 136th Quartermaster Truck Company assisted the 1st Platoon with their relocation. When the hospital moved, 40 to 50 wounded or ill soldiers from the Fourth Armored were transported as well. As for Lt. Colonel Cohen, he apparently caught a peep ride with a major from the hospital staff. Accompanying the group was the commanding officer of the 106th Evacuation Hospital and his chief of surgery. Their purpose on the trip was to perform reconnaissance for the relocation of their own hospital.

While en route to Lauterbach, the 1st Platoon stopped outside of Assenheim (if he were aware of the town's name, Hal Cohen probably couldn't help but chuckle at the irony, given his condition). The medical unit set up a few of their hospital tents near the edge of some woods east of the town, where they tended to the patients being transported under their care. Among the medical staff were female nurses under the command of 1st Lt. Helen R. Cosma (other nurses were 1st Lt. Mildred E. Barnett, 1st Lt. Lillian G. Clark, 1st Lt. Lola Dickenson, Rosalou Freeland, Lula G. Harward, and 1st Lt. Marie C. Janes). Very close by was an encampment of the 620th Ordnance Company, which provided support to XII Corps.

Unbeknownst to Lt. Colonel Cohen and the hospital staff, not far to the west lurked the under-strength *6th SS Mountain Division Nord*, commanded by *SS-Gruppenführer* Karl Brenner. Cut off from their own lines by the rapid advance of Patton's Third Army, Brenner's division was desperately searching for an escape route to the east. (Lt. Colonel Irzyk traded blows with elements of the division two weeks prior at Rheinböllen.)

Brenner organized his division into two *Kampfgruppen* (task forces), one commanded by *SS-Oberführer* Johann-Georg Goebel and the other by *SS-Standartenführer* Helmuth Raithel. As they moved east, they picked up stragglers from a variety of other units. In total, Brenner's division probably numbered somewhere a little north of 4000 men. With surrender an option Brenner was unwilling to consider, their journey to avoid destruction was leading them dangerously close to XII Corps' main supply route (MSR).

Not long after sunrise on April 1, the advance guard of the formidable SS unit came upon the site occupied by the 620th Ordnance Company. The non-combat unit didn't put up much of a fight. However, when the Germans approached the hospital grounds, they encountered stiff resistance from the men of the 136th Quartermaster Truck Company.

Even though the G.I.s killed 10 of the *SS,* they were no match for the more numerous and highly-trained Germans. The Germans confiscated all the vehicles and supplies they could get their hands on. Given their depleted state, the pilfered material was invaluable.

The *SS* took the medical staff as prisoners, including the female nurses. The commanding officer of the 106th Evacuation Hospital joined the ranks of the captured Americans. Tragically, his chief of surgery (Major Fonde) was killed.

Lt. Colonel Cohen was apparently not at the camp at that moment, but he soon came through the nearby woods via the peep he shared with the hospital staff officer. Cohen explained it in a newspaper interview conducted soon after returning home in October 1945:

> At first we didn't notice them because their clothes blended in with the terrain and the vegetation. Then when we saw them we thought they were prisoners themselves. Well, I noticed that they had their caps on—something that captured Germans don't do is wear their caps or helmets.

Cohen turned to the major and said, "In case you don't know it, we're in one hell of a fix."

None of the men were armed, so when one of the *SS* troopers pointed a *Panzerfaust* directly at Cohen's peep, they had little choice but to surrender. The Germans searched them for concealed weapons and then took Cohen to their division headquarters.

Cohen wasn't the last American taken prisoner. As elements of the 16th Field Hospital and other support units traveled along the presumably clear road, they too were intercepted by the *SS*. But when a bus filled with more American women came to the German checkpoint, Brenner's men let them pass through, apparently not wanting the distraction of more females on their hands.

Cohen was "not so much scared as down-right embarrassed" by the fact he had fallen into enemy hands. He had in his possession an *Iron Cross*, taken as a battlefield souvenir (one of many in his collection). When the decoration was discovered by his captors, he was in the presence of an officer whom he believed to be the German division commander. The officer conducting his interrogation was, according to Cohen, a graduate of UCLA. Given that these were *SS*, it was perhaps surprising that his captors didn't punish Cohen for being in possession of the prestigious medal.

It appears that Cohen was a familiar name, particularly in terms of his relationship with Creighton Abrams. The officer even asked Cohen how Lt. Colonel Abrams was doing (no doubt with a tinge of sarcasm). Though a member of the *SS*, the officer earned a certain amount of respect from Cohen. The Lt. Colonel later reminisced, "This general was a soldier, every inch a soldier."

The *SS* were abundantly less sympathetic to the regular German troops who had previously surrendered and were being held by the Americans at a location near the hospital. Cohen witnessed the *SS* rounding up some of their brethren and machine gunning them as a penalty for not carrying out the standing order to fight to the last. The brutal action taken by the *SS* was in the spirit, if not the letter, of an order issued on March 5 by *General* Blaskowitz, commanding officer of *Army Group H*: "All soldiers … encountered away from their units … and who announce they are stragglers looking for their units will be summarily tried and shot."

SS-Gruppenführer Brenner kept his division moving to the east. Lt. Colonel Cohen was placed on a bus while other prisoners marched on foot. By noon, Brenner hoped to consolidate his two columns in the forest east of Assenheim. He then planned to reorganize before commencing movement during the early afternoon. He set up his division command post in the woods two miles east of Wickstadt.

Brenner's men fell well behind schedule. *SS-Oberführer* Goebel's column, comprised entirely of horse-drawn transport, was late in its departure. *SS-Standartenführer* Raithel's *Kampfgruppe*, which included the motor vehicles and constituted Brenner's primary fighting force, got an even later start. Lt. Colonel Cohen and the captured hospital staff travelled with the motorized column, though earlier in the day, the female nurses were left at a barn near the forest northeast of Erbstadt, unharmed and unguarded (they were discovered by a task force from the 5th Infantry Division before nightfall).

Movement along the forest's narrow trails was agonizingly slow for both *SS Kampfgruppen*. Matters were complicated further when an American spotter plan called in artillery fire. Despite the deadly crescendo, Raithel's damaged task force continued. During the night, the Germans abandoned most of the Fourth Armored Division's patients at the town of Staden, where they were recovered by American infantry closing in on Brenner's division.

Kampfgruppe Raithel reached the town of Wolf, located on the west edge of the Büdingen Forest. By midnight, the *Kampfgruppe* was tucked safely underneath the dense canopy of trees, and *SS-Standartenführer* Raithel went about the business of reorganizing. The columns were back on the march during the dark morning hours of April 2, hoping to get as far east as possible before sunrise.

During the pre-dawn hours, a series of battles ranging from skirmishes to vicious house-to-house fighting raged in several towns and villages east of the forest. Some of the most intense fighting occurred at Waldensberg, less than a half mile from the woods. Lt. Colonel Cohen was caught in the middle of incoming American artillery and mortar shells, neither of which discriminated between the Germans and their American prisoners. Cohen remembered, "This is when I really suffered. I knew I was going to die. But I was scared it wouldn't be by the Germans. I didn't want to be killed by the Americans. My shot had to come from the Germans."

During the shelling, Cohen gave aid to the German wounded. He pulled one soldier to safety. Then he went back for another. Eventually, he gathered 18 wounded enemy soldiers in a farmhouse on the north side of Waldensberg. When infantrymen of the 71st Infantry Division later approached the building, they heard a distinct American voice with a southern drawl yell out, "Don't throw your damned grenades in here. I'm an American colonel, and this place is full of dying and wounded men and two women." Along with Cohen was a lieutenant from the 620th Ordnance Company (Lt. Nemeth, taken prisoner the prior morning) and two German nuns who were caring for the wounded. Several of the SS men had already perished.

Cohen wasn't done. Angered by the atrocities he saw committed at the command of the SS officer, he grabbed a Garand rifle and went in pursuit, hoping to personally do him in. (Cohen later said the officer was killed by a direct artillery hit on his *Volkswagen*. However, Brenner, Goebel, and Raithel all survived the war. Whomever the "general" was remains a mystery.) Cohen didn't stay on the hunt for long, as he was shepherded to the 71st Infantry Division's command post in Langenselbold, where he provided the division G-2 (Lt. Colonel Foster) with an abundance of information about the composition of the enemy force.

In his memoir, Patton stated that perhaps 500 Germans were killed and about 800 taken prisoner after the unit was surrounded. He also noted rumors regarding atrocities committed by the *6th SS Mountain Division*, including the killing of medical personnel and the rape of nurses. Patton speculated that this might have influenced the actions of the American forces and accounted for the high number of Germans killed.

There was no truth to the ill-treatment of the nurses, nor evidence beyond the death of Major Fonde that the medical staff had been intentionally targeted (Patton went on to acknowledge as much). But given Cohen's account, it is possible that the rumor of atrocities grew from the SS treatment of their own countrymen. It is noteworthy that during their march, the SS also brutalized German civilians that had hung white sheets in surrender when the Americans originally captured the towns. The SS showed little tolerance for any German not willing to fight to the last.

Lt. Colonel Cohen soon began the trip to rejoin his battalion. The day prior to his rescue, his 10th Armored Infantry, still assigned to CCR, moved out at 1445 from the vicinity of Bad Hersfeld. They used the *Autobahn* the entire day to follow CCA and CCB. At 1800, the battalion command post was set up in Nesselröden, six miles west-southwest of Creuzburg. He had quite a long trip in front of him before catching up.

CCB's Attack on Gotha

On April 3, *Olympic* was reassigned to Major General Middleton's VIII Corps. Their next objective was the city of Gotha, 22 miles east-southeast of their bridgehead on the Werra River. Their plan was to bypass the city of Eisenach, staying north of the urban area. They would also avoid the *Autobahn* and main roads, opting instead for trails. As Hoge's division advanced east, the 65th Infantry Division would follow behind and scoop up the many prisoners the Fourth Armored sent marching on their own to the rear.

CCB began its drive at 0700. Little resistance was encountered, and pockets of enemy troops emerged from the woods and side roads eager to surrender. The American armor overran a *Panzer* school and two concealed airfields located within the forest. The 66th Armored Field Artillery Battalion fired at the airfield, destroying several parked aircraft.

A setback occurred during the morning when C/704's Lieutenant Callaway and First Sergeant Walter E. Mullen, Jr., both of C/704, failed to return after leading the 3rd Platoon to their positions. Concern was great that the two men had been killed or captured (indeed, they were captured, but escaped 10 days later and rejoined the company).

As Abrams' battalions drew closer to Gotha, the C Team was sent to secure Goldbach while the B Team occupied Metebach. The A Team captured Trügleben, two miles due west of Gotha.

Major Kimsey commanded the B Team, which was supplemented by Battery B of the 22nd Armored Field Artillery Battalion. His next action was to advance through a forest separating Metebach from Gotha. The woods narrowed as they approached the town, creating a finger-like appendage touching the northwest edge of the city. A trail connecting Metebach to Gotha ran down the spine of the forest. Kimsey would use this trail to reach the city.

As Task Force Kimsey started down the dirt tail, they discovered just how narrow it was. The trees hugged both sides, leaving no room for vehicles to maneuver, other than straight ahead. Once the column drover deeper into the forest, enemy infantry armed with *Panzerfausts* and 20mm guns opened fire. The battalion journal noted, "The majority of enemy riflemen had rifles equipped with telescopic sights." With the tanks limited to the trail, it was more difficult to clean out the enemy. When the task was done, three 20mm guns were destroyed, 15 German soldiers were killed, and 25 were taken prisoner.

TF Kimsey moved through the last sliver of woods into the outskirts of Gotha. Enemy snipers plagued the column, firing from buildings along the route. Supported by the tanks, the men of B/51 systematically cleared the houses on both sides of the street. As the head of the column drew near the square at the center of the city, an 88mm gun knocked out one of the Shermans. Rifles and *Panzerfausts* opened fire from all sides. Major Kimsey tried to move a platoon of infantry to the right to outflank the German positions, but they were stopped by fire on that approach as well. The outcome was the same when an attempt was made on the left.

It was clear that Major Kimsey had encountered resistance too strong for a task force of this size to overcome. He needed additional units for support on either his left or his right if the attack was going to succeed. After Kimsey placed a call for assistance, C/51 was dispatched to launch an attack from the north (Kimsey's left) using the main road leading into Gotha.

The attack by C/51 moved very slowly in the face of resistance much like what Kimsey's men had encountered. The addition of C/51 did little to relieve the pressure on TF Kimsey.

While C/51 attacked from the north, things got much worse for Kimsey when the company commanders of both B/51 (Captain Crane) and B/35 were killed by sniper fire. Kimsey ordered the withdrawal of the task force to the high ground on the edge of town from whence the attack commenced. A/51 came forward to relieve B/51 and then tied in their left flank with C/51. The two companies connected near the trail used by TF Kimsey to approach Gotha. B/51 then traveled back to Goldbach to reorganize and lick their wounds.

At 1930, the command post of the 51st Armored Infantry Battalion moved to Aspach, a mile-and-a half west of where CCB held the town of Trügleben. The armored infantry companies of the 51st outposted Delk Oden's tanks on the high ground during the night.

CCA's Drive to Gotha

CCA spent April 3 driving toward Gotha as well, advancing along a zone south of CCB. The 8th Tank Battalion, with A/8 leading, crossed the Werra River and passed through the positions held by the 53rd Armored Infantry Battalion. Lt. Colonel Jaques' infantry proceeded to join Lt. Colonel Irzyk's tanks in the column.

After taking the high ground north of Eisenach, the column picked up speed and headed east. D/8 lost its lone remaining officer when Lt. Spatz's tank was hit by a *Panzerfaust*. Irzyk placed Staff Sergeant Vollheim in temporary command of the company. But other than the loss of Lt. Spatz, the column proceeded with little interference until reaching Wenigenlupnitz, where small arms, *Panzerfausts,* and 20mm AA guns pelted the column. The 8th Tank Battalion gunners brushed them aside before they could do any damage, and the column sped on toward Sättalstädt, overrunning 10 German vehicles along the way.

As *Olympic* blitzed its way through town after town, it was not uncommon for the tanks to do the talking. Sergeant Nick Alexander of the 53rd Armored Infantry Battalion observed,

> Although we did have eyeball to eyeball fire fights in the villages, most of the big damage was done by the tanks, artillery and air corps. In my view, the American GI, young and old, came through with courage and dedication.

At Sättalstädt, the tankers found a lucrative target in the form of a series of railroad flatcars, some of which were loaded with vehicles. The tanks of the *Rolling Eight Ball* littered the rail line with the remains of the cars. After dispensing with the defenders of the town,

Irzyk decided to shift his column to the *Autobahn* running west to east through Sättalstädt. Irzyk's tanks enjoyed "the widest, smoothest, firmest road they had yet encountered."

Irzyk hoped to reach Gotha—10 miles east of Sättalstädt—in quick order. But at the six-mile mark, just north of Leinatal, the column slammed on the brakes when the pavement came to an abrupt end. The Germans had destroyed the overpass that carried the highway to the east.

Trailing behind the tanks and armored infantry came the 94th Armored Field Artillery Battalion. Their experience driving east was quite different than that of the 8th Tank Battalion. Not long after leaving the Werra River bridgehead, the road they were on deteriorated into a quagmire, resulting in several vehicles bogging down. The column diverted on a road taking them through the town of Stregda, where they were fired upon from the direction of the much larger town of Eisenach, not far to the south.

The artillerymen continued east for another two miles before reaching Hötzelsroda. As C Battery of the 94th moved through, they came under fire from a strand of woods southeast of the town. The crews of the M7s turned their ring-mounted .50 caliber machine guns on the wood line, while the M7 of S/Sgt. John J. Loebell leveled his 105mm howitzer and fired directly at the German position. Using the machine gun and HE fire as cover, 1st Sgt. Bernard Steinberg advanced with a detail of men; the M5A1 light tank from the headquarters unit joined them. The improvised combat team assaulted the woods, killing several of the defenders and taking 26 prisoners.

Back at the destroyed overpass, Lt. Colonel Irzyk decided to reverse the column. As the vehicles started to turn around, they were hit by heavy fire from two batteries of 88s. In rapid succession, the lethal enemy guns knocked out seven tanks and four half-tracks. Lt. Roger Boas (94th Armored Field Artillery Battalion) found himself in the middle of the barrage and took cover underneath his peep. By his estimation, there were four 88s zeroing in on them. The halftracks tried to maneuver cross-country but became mired in the muddy field. After much difficulty, most of the column managed to find cover or moved out of range.

Major Robert D. Franks, executive officer of the 94th AFAB, was positioned farther back in the column and saw the situation evolving in front of him. He ordered the battalion's M7s to pull off the roadway into hull-defilade positions. Some of the 105mm guns fired directly at the 88s while other sections fired at German infantry fleeing south toward the town of Waltershausen.

In the face of heavy enemy anti-aircraft fire, Lt. Edgar C. Smith flew his Cub observation plane over the battlefield to direct friendly artillery against the remaining enemy batteries. American aircraft also contributed to the response. The combined fire of the artillery, the mortar platoon from the 8th Tank Battalion, and the air support silenced the deadly 88s.

Lt. Colonel Irzyk consolidated his command and reorganized near the town of Hörselgau, where he was joined by the 94th Armored Field Artillery Battalion. Just before dark, German aircraft attacked again. And as they had done before, the gunners of the Fourth Armored brought some of the enemy pilots to the ground. One aircraft crashed within a hundred yards of A/94, scattering debris over the area.

Later that evening, Lt. Colonel Irzyk took stock of the condition of his battalion and observed that A Company had only three remaining Sherman tanks. B Company was in the best shape with a dozen, while C and D Companies each had 11. At full strength, the four companies were allocated 68 tanks. Now, they were down to 37. Of greater consequence was the shortage of manpower. The battalion was shy of their quota by 111 enlisted men and 15 officers.

To the rear of CCA, CCR's 10th Armored Infantry Battalion and 37th Tank Battalion moved out of Nesselröden at 1430 on April 3. They passed through Oesterbehingen at 1700 and settled in nearby for the night. In the 10th's journal, they noted that no word had been received from Task Force Baum. New equipment and vehicles were delivered as replacements for what was lost on the raid.

The Surrender of Gotha

At 0800 on April 4, the Americans received word that the Germans offered to turn Gotha over to the Fourth Armored (this coming after an ultimatum was issued demanding the surrender of the city by 1100). Given the heavy opposition CCB encountered the day prior, this was welcome news for all.

Gotha surrendered at 1030. Most of the enemy troops had withdrawn during the night, having chosen to fight another day. The initial occupation of the city was left to CCA. CCB withdrew to the high ground outside of the city and gathered themselves after the prior day's engagement.

At about noon, elements of CCA entered Gotha and began the process of ensuring the city was clear. While the tanks and armored infantry went to work, the supporting 94th Armored Field Artillery Battalion advanced to the town of Schwabhausen, three miles southeast of Gotha. The battalion commander (Lt. Colonel Parker) and Major Franks, traveling in separate peeps, advanced into the town along with the headquarters' light tank and the executive halftrack. They captured 33 prisoners, which added to the six prisoners picked up by C Battery outside of the town. The battalion went into firing positions at Schwabhausen, and during the next six days, executed counter-battery missions to the south.

CCR moved forward to assist CCA in securing and outposting Gotha. As CCR approached the city, the only problem they experienced occurred when German aircraft harassed the column. T/4 Charles R. Ross (10th AIB Service Company) manned a .50 caliber machine gun and drove off the enemy planes. The 10th Armored Infantry Battalion and 37th Tank Battalion arrived at Gotha at 1730, and by 1800, ensured that the roads leading into the city were secured and outposted.

Captain Lyons and his team returned with the 10th Armored Infantry Battalion S-2 halftrack on April 4. After Lyons provided the battalion headquarters with the latest update on Captain Baum's status, the decision was made to officially report all the battalion's task force personnel as MIA.

Even when a town or city surrendered, there remained ample work to do. Gotha was respectable in size, three-and-a-half miles across from west to east at its widest point, and a similar dimension from north to south. It would take time to search for weapons and any enemy forces, lone wolves or otherwise, that might be in hiding.

Captain Lyons was involved in that task. While in the city, his team discovered a large military hospital filled with "horribly wounded and crippled soldiers." Upon entering the office of the German medical corps colonel in command of the facility, Lyons ordered the officer to surrender all able-bodied combat personnel and weaponry.

As the firearms were loaded into a waiting trailer, the German colonel turned over a sabre he received upon graduation more than 30 years prior. With tears in his eyes, he handed Lyons the beautifully crafted wooden case housing the sabre. Lyons turned the officer's tears to expressions of gratitude when he told him he didn't consider the sabre a weapon. Lyons crafted a note explaining his position and gave it to the colonel, instructing him to show it to any American soldier who might challenge his possession of the artifact.

Back at his command post, Lyons was interrupted by a young English-speaking woman in search of the "*kommandant.*" She explained that her father owned a bakery a few streets from the command post. Slave laborers, freed during the American occupation of the city, were pillaging the shop. She felt that regardless of the wartime situation, law and order should be restored. From her perspective, it was the American's job to do it.

Lyons took some soldiers over to her father's store and broke up the crowd. He allowed the laborers to keep what they had already taken and sent them on their way. The woman then told Lyons of a rumor she had heard to the effect that the Allies would eventually turn over this part of Germany to the Russians. Lyons later wrote:

> *If I lived to be a thousand I'll never forget what I said to her: "Do you really think that we Americans are stupid enough to give over to the Russians vast areas of land we had conquered that had cost us thousands of dead and wounded?"*

At noon (well before CCR's arrival at Gotha) the 8th Tank Battalion entered the outskirts of the city. White sheets—the sign of surrender—hung from the windows. Reassured by the presence of the linen, Lt. Colonel Irzyk's tanks were able to move through the town at a good pace. Midway through the city, Irzyk was stopped by Colonel Sears, who was parked at the roadside waiting for the tank battalion commander to pass. Sears directed Irzyk to head south eight miles toward Ohrdruf, where the large communications complex was thought to be. At 1300, the 8th Tank Battalion and 53rd Armored Infantry Battalion headed across the gently rolling fields toward their objective.

North Stalag III

As *Olympic* drew close to Gotha, Meyer Levin (a war correspondent attached to the division) later recalled coming upon "cadaverous refugees." Never had the G.I.s seen anything of the sort. The poor souls were reduced to skeletal shapes with shaven heads and sunken eyes, zombie-like in their appearance. The malnourished, shriveled specimens of humanity identified themselves to Levin as Poles. The men pleaded with the Americans to go to the camp where they had been held prisoner. The encounter was likely the first hint of what would be discovered by the time the sun set on April 4. It would be a day unlike any other in the history of the Fourth Armored Division.

When Al Irzyk reached Ohrdruf, his plan was for the medium tanks to attack the town while the light tanks of D/8 screened the flanks. As they made their way closer to Ohrdruf, they ran into significant resistance from small arms, mortars, *Panzerfausts*, and occasional artillery. The enemy fire grew even stronger when they reached a road junction about three miles north of the town. But with their usual precision, they mopped up the resistance.

At 1430, elements of the 53rd Armored Infantry and 8th Tank Battalion entered Ohrdruf. The town was cleared by 1530 and the tank/infantry teams cut off the roads leading in and out of the town. An hour later, the 53rd set up its command post inside Ohrdruf.

During the process of screening Irzyk's left flank, the M5A1 tanks of D/8 moved over a minor road leading to some woods east of Ohrdruf. The lead tank, commanded by S/Sgt. Lester Guidry, entered the forest, and not far into it, came upon what seemed to be a prisoner of war camp (the other crewmembers in the tank were driver Orville Pirtle, BOG Jo-

The town of Ohrdruf viewed from the high ground to the east in 2019 (photograph by author).

seph Robbins, and gunner Raymond McMillan). Guidry radioed his battalion commander and reported his find, and Irzyk in turn dispatched elements from the 53rd AIB and the 8th Tank Battalion to reinforce D/8 at what was identified as *North Stalag III*.

The men of the Fourth Armored were not prepared for what they experienced there. It would forever change their view of the war and redefine why they fought. As "Doc" Buchanan of the 704th Tank Destroyer Battalion reflected years later, "…we had seen atrocities in the Ardennes, but never had we seen the full extent of the extermination policy of the Nazi regime against minorities." *North Stalag III* wasn't simply a prisoner of war camp. It was the first concentration camp discovered by Allied forces on the Western Front.

The first in a series of finds were several camp survivors hiding in the woods. Among them was Leo Laufer, a young Polish Jew who escaped four days earlier. He told his liberators how *SS* guards had murdered and burned 4000 inmates since December. The victims were Jews, Poles, and Russian prisoners of war.

The Americans came upon 31 bodies sprawled in the open. Too weak to march when the Germans attempted to evacuate the camp, each had been shot in the back of the skull at close range. It was starkly evident that they had suffered from severe starvation. The ground around them was soaked with blood. There were several nationalities among the victims, including an American pilot. His body was pointed out by two of the survivors.

Another discovery awaited in a nearby shed. Piled one atop another in a seemingly systematic and orderly fashion, akin to cordwood being stocked for winter—a sight that silently cried of inhumanity—were 30 more bodies, all naked and sprinkled with lime by the Germans in order to suppress the putrid odor of decaying flesh and organs.

Disposal pits were found in the woods adjacent to the camp. Bodies had been piled atop and within timbers, then set aflame. The charred skeletal remains were an abhorrent sight. Some described it as a barbeque pit for humans.

The camp contained several barracks for housing the prisoners and slave laborers. Nate Frankel of the 8th Tank Battalion described the structures as being like "a busted-out factory stinking amid high-growing weeds in one of America's uglier heartlands. We entered a stench of urine and vomit, and of decomposition—that ungodly mixture of feces and sulfur, hellfire in a sewer."

Corporal Edward McFarland (a clerk with the 8th Tank Battalion) noted:

> We also walked through some barrack like structures that appeared to be a place for the sick as signs indicated warnings of typhus. One former prisoner was sitting in a corner of this building just staring at the Americans.

McFarland also came across several structures he described as "sheds" (but which may have been the barracks Frankel referred to):

> Inside there were large timbers running the length of the shed on both sides of a center isle. These timbers had chains attached every few feet which had evidently been used to secure the legs of their prisoners. The same type of timbers and chains ran along the back walls of these buildings.

Lt. Colonel Irzyk left his command tank and took a peep to *North Stalag III*. Upon inspecting the bodies of those executed by gunshot, Irzyk noted that the wounds were made with

April 6, 1945. Victims of German atrocities at Ohrdruf (U.S. Army photograph).

a small caliber weapon. One can easily imagine the cold, calculated way the SS held their sidearm to the back of the neck of each prisoner, and one by one, unceremoniously ended each life with more concern for the cost of the bullet than the humanity they stole. Irzyk summarized his emotions:

> *I had been in combat since late July. I had seen the most horrible of wounds, soldiers on both sides killed, dismembered. I had watched helplessly as Germans and my own tankers had perished as flames engulfed their tanks after being hit. By this time, I believed I was somewhat hardened and understood deaths on the battlefield, but the deliberate and bestial suffering and death, which I had just examined, was far beyond my comprehension. As I stared at the Nazi slaughterhouse, I just could not accept that human beings could have such utter and total disregard for other human beings, and would callously, methodically, and unemotionally exterminate them. What depravity!*

While nearly all veterans of the Fourth Armored agreed on the level of revulsion they felt when seeing the German's barbaric and sadistic treatment of their captives, not all were affected to the same degree. Over the course of weeks and months of combat, many G.I.s had lived through countless encounters with death. The sight of a brutally mangled and disfigured corpse was nothing new. Sometimes their view of death came within seconds of life leaving the body. But more often, their experience with the dead was the ghastly sight of poor souls left to the elements for hours, days, or even weeks. For some of the most hardened, the horrors of Ohrdruf offered only a clinical difference. As Captain Lyons later described:

> *It may seem surprising to know that seeing this (Ohrdruf) was not a great shock to us. We had been seeing lots of dead people for quite some time so all these bodies really meant little to us. What did get our attention was the way the bodies were neatly stacked like cordwood and sprinkled with lime. It seemed that cremation was the logical way to get rid of them. I guess you could say that we weren't humanitarians, it was something that I had never heard discussed by anyone in the unit.*

Captain Lyons was certainly an exception. The lasting impact of what was witnessed at Ohrdruf was better captured by the words written in 1988 by Corporal McFarland:

> *Even though it has been 43 years since I witnessed this part of the war I still cannot think about it without a flow of tears. These atrocities did occur in our civilized world and I did witness a small portion of it.*

The inhabitants of the town of Ohrdruf claimed ignorance of the events that took place at *North Stalag III*. Among the first citizens to be brought to the camp was the mayor, Albert Schneider. While acknowledging that rumors had circulated about the events at the camp, he had always found them difficult to believe and dismissed them at face value. Now, he was shocked by what he saw first-hand.

Lt. Colonel James H. Van Wagenan (the Fourth Armored Division's military government officer) ordered the mayor to bring 25 to 30 of Ohrdruf's leading citizens to the camp the following day. When the mayor failed to appear at the agreed upon time, a soldier was dispatched to his home to retrieve him. Upon his arrival, he discovered the bodies of the mayor and his wife, their wrists slashed in an act of suicide.

The two dozen or so prominent citizens were subsequently paraded to the camp. They too claimed no prior knowledge of what happened in the deceivingly tranquil woods beyond their town. But in the wake of their visit, there was no denying the brutality and depravity that would be forever associated with Ohrdruf.

Throughout the time the Fourth Armored remained near Gotha, a point was made of touring American units through the camp to impress upon them the magnitude of the atrocities committed by the Nazis. On April 9, it was C/704's turn.

> We were taken to the German Concentration Camp near Gotha to view the atrocities committed by the Germans. It was the most horrible, gruesome sight we had ever seen. Prisoners, so emaciated, they were mere skeletons, had been shot and lay in the yard where they fell. In one building over a hundred naked bodies were piled in a heap and covered with lime. We went through the chamber where they were gassed. A Russian captive worker told us that at another camp close by, 1500 prisoners were burned each month and that here, 3500 a month were killed and burned. It was such a sickening and unbelievable sight that it made us sick to our stomachs.

On April 12, eight days after the liberation of the camp, Eisenhower, Bradley, and Patton travelled to Ohrdruf. Bradley was reportedly speechless. As for Patton, he retreated to the side of a building and vomited. Eisenhower made a point of inspecting every corner of the camp, anticipating the future need to provide testimony to the brutality of the Nazi regime.

Eisenhower was not alone in his sentiment for preserving the history of *Stalag III*. Numerous G.I.s, including First Sgt. John Harris from the 22nd Armored Field Artillery Battalion, took personal photographs of the gruesome scenes. There seemed to be an inherent feeling that the atrocities witnessed at Ohrdruf would be beyond belief unless one had been there to observe it. From Eisenhower down to Sgt. Harris, their actions proved to be wise. Who would believe that, more than 75 years later, with some of the witnesses still living to tell the tale, anyone would ever dispute the authenticity of accounts from Ohrdruf and all the other camps operated by the Nazis? Alas, as incredulous as it may be, those sentiments and people exist.

17

Beyond the Restraining Line

Recovery

With the surrender of Gotha on April 4, the Fourth Armored Division was spared what might have otherwise proven to be a costly battle to clear the city. Rather than continuing their drive to the east, the division received ample time to rest and gather itself. They remained near Gotha and Ohrdruf while the trailing infantry divisions came up and took over the front line.

CCB's 51st Armored Infantry Battalion spent April 5 cleaning their vehicles and weapons before moving to a new assembly area near Wechmar, four miles southeast of Gotha.

CCA's 53rd Armored Infantry Battalion remained near Ohrdruf, as did the 8th Tank Battalion. The 8th was still short tanks, enlisted men, and officers, but received a welcome addition when Captain Mac McGlamery returned from a month's leave in the United States. Lt. Colonel Irzyk reassigned McGlamery to the command of B Company. Ben Fischler, who commanded B Company in McGlamery's absence, was transferred to command of A Company. Lt. Ferguson, who had taken over A Company when Len Kieley was evacuated, was given command of D Company (which had not a single officer remaining in its ranks). Captain Paul Stephenson remained in command of C Company.

The 10th Armored Infantry Battalion and 37th Tank Battalion, still assigned to CCR, remained at Gotha, where they absorbed the replacements promised by Lt. General Patton. On April 5, the 10th AIB officially listed 208 members of TF Baum as missing in action while registering the addition of 216 replacements and a dozen returnees. The following day, the battalion received another 127 enlisted men and 15 new officers. Perhaps the most welcome returnee of all showed up on April 9 when Captain Baum arrived back at the battalion headquarters.

On April 5, the 37th Tank Battalion officially listed 73 enlisted men and four officers MIA. They received 22 replacements that evening and another 52 the following day, with which they could reconstitute C Company. On April 7, six new medium tanks arrived.

All remained relatively quiet at Gotha. The only disruption came from two separate attacks by small groups of enemy aircraft, neither of which caused damage. German stragglers continued to filter through the area. C/10 picked up eight prisoners from the *559th Flak Training Battalion;* the men had not been with their unit since January.

On April 6, the tank destroyers of C/704 left Cobstadt at 0700 to conduct a reconnaissance toward the city of Erfurt, nine miles to the northeast. After meeting strong infantry and artillery fire as they approached the city, they opted to return. That afternoon, the tank destroyers moved to a new location and their crews took on billets at Wechmer alongside the 51st Armored Infantry Battalion.

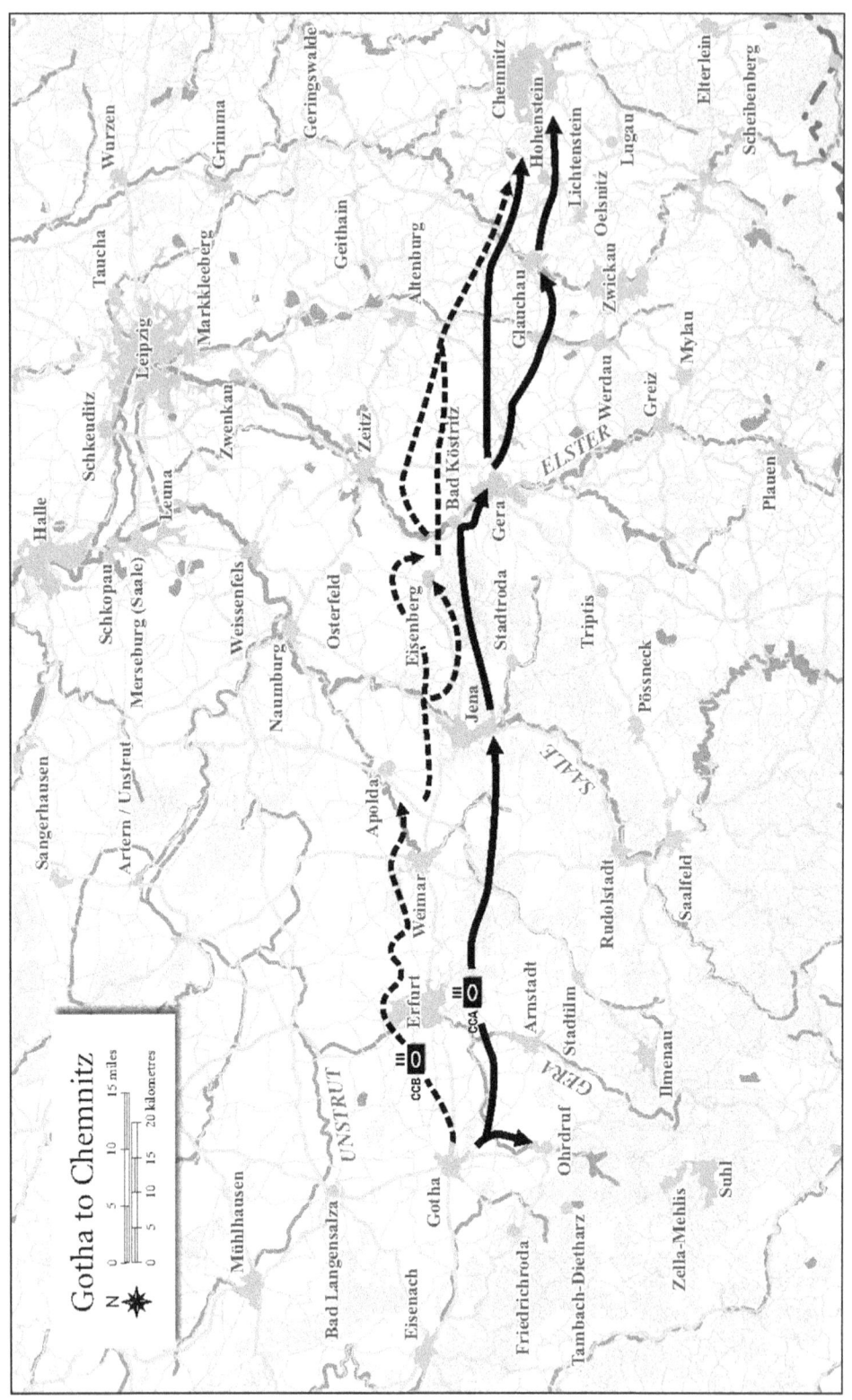

Gotha to Chemnitz (© Petho Cartography, 2020).

On April 7, the 53rd Armored Infantry Battalion was reassigned from CCA to CCR. They settled in for the accustomed dose of rest, maintenance, movies, and the always welcome Red Cross Clubmobile. That evening, the 80th Infantry Division began relieving the Fourth Armored at Gotha. The task was completed by 0945 the following day.

While the men of the Fourth hoped periods like this would be peaceful, danger continued to lurk. Sergeant Joseph Lopez, one of the original members of C/704 (but recently transferred to B Company) was ambushed and killed while taking his tank destroyer to ordnance.

Rescue Missions

As of the morning of April 7, the massive communications center originally believed to be at Ohrdruf had yet to be discovered. During the day, a signal corps officer from the Fourth Armored set out to the east in search of the facility. Accompanying his detachment was a high-ranking intelligence officer from Patton's G-2 staff, Colonel Robert S. Allen. Word filtered back that afternoon that the party was ambushed near Neudietendorf, nine miles east of Gotha.

A task force was formed and sent to the town with the hope of rescuing the group. The team consisted of C/35, C/51, C/704, and C Troop of the 25th Cavalry Reconnaissance Squadron.

When C/704 arrived at Neudietendorf, they found two dead Americans. The other members of the party had been captured and spirited away. The rescue force then encountered enemy infantry and entered a heated firefight. The 76mm guns on the tank destroyers and the .50 calibers mounted on the C Troop vehicles inflicted serious casualties. C/51 reported finding three dead Americans.

During the earlier firefight in which the other Americans lost their lives, Colonel Allen suffered a serious wound to his right arm. After his capture, he was taken to a German hospital in Erfurt where his forearm was amputated. On April 12, he was rescued by soldiers from the 80th Infantry Division. Though having lost his arm, he returned to duty on April 17, just 10 days after being wounded. (Allen was a well-known journalist prior to and after the war. He later wrote the book *Lucky Forward*, a history of Patton's Third Army.)

The communication center sought by Colonel Allen was located near Arnstadt, four-and-a-half miles to the south of Neudietendorf. As it turned out, it was not the lucrative target suggested by rumor. There was indeed a facility which had been constructed as a headquarters for the *Armed Forces High Command* (*OKW*) during the time of the Czechoslovakian crisis in 1938, but it was never used. More recently, *Reichsfuehrer SS* Heinrich Himmler ordered the expansion of the complex as a retreat for Hitler and his staff. Himmler intended to present it to Hitler for his birthday on April 20. When the Fourth Armored entered the area on April 4, they just barely missed a bigger prize. Within the 24 hours prior, *Generalfeldmarschall* Albert von Kesselring and the headquarters of *OB WEST* had been there and gone.

The mission to Neudietendorf was just one of two rescue missions conducted during the Fourth Armored's respite. As previously mentioned, Lt. General Patton sent the aide of France's General Giraud to ride along with the Fourth Armored with the expectation that Hoge's division would be the first unit to reach the area where Giraud's family was reportedly held captive. More precisely, Giraud's family was believed to be held prisoner at the town of Friedrichroda, nestled on the slope of a heavily forested mountain range. As it turned out, Friedrichroda … eight miles southwest of Gotha … was close to the Fourth Armored's axis of advance.

On April 6, in a move eerily reminiscent of the Hammelburg raid, a task force was assembled for the mission of rescuing the French general's family. The units were drawn from CCA and consisted of a company each of tanks and armored infantry, a platoon from the reconnaissance company of the 704th Tank Destroyer Battalion, a platoon of light tanks, an assault gun platoon, and a battery of M7s. The officer assigned to lead the task force was the S3 of the 8th Tank Battalion, Sam Diuguid.

The task force remained in its assembly area, waiting for the order to move. A decision was apparently made to dispatch only the reconnaissance unit toward the town. The entry from the 704th Tank Destroyer Battalion's diary is best left to speak for itself:

> From Gotha Captain Dowd of Rcn Company took a platoon into the town of Friedrichroda ahead of a task force of tanks and infantry to contact important P. W. s reported held there. An M8 was hit by a bazooka in the center of town, but the crew was able to pull out in a peep. In attempting to go in after the M8, Captain Dowd had his M20 hit by two bazookas which immediately transformed it into a mass of flame. The entire crew, unhurt, dodged to safety through buildings and back yards.

General Giraud's family was recovered, apparently after their captors surrendered under a white flag to other American troops. On April 7, the French family stayed overnight with Patton at his headquarters. The following morning, Patton sent them to Metz via a plane, which he felt was quicker and safer than travel by car.

The Respite Continues

On April 8, the Fourth Armored was reassigned to General Walker's XX Corps. That day, the Third Army received 90 brand-new Pershing heavy tanks, 50 of which were allocated to the 11th Armored Division. The remaining 40 were held in the Third Army combat vehicle pool. The Fourth Armored was offered the opportunity to take the new tanks, but declined, believing they were too heavy and presented a higher risk of bogging down. The M4A3E8 had become a tanker favorite and more than met their needs at this stage of the war.

The Fourth Armored entered its sixth day of recuperation. As the day progressed, there was no indication that the rest period would end anytime soon. Lt. Colonel Irzyk thought the time was right for a celebratory night with the officers of his battalion. Not wishing to get caught off guard by unexpected orders, he checked in with Division HQ as well as CCA's Colonel Sears, to whom he still reported. Both levels of command gave no indication that a change in status was imminent. Irzyk and his staff moved forward with the party that evening, hosting all the battalion's officers. He also allowed the enlisted men to uncork all the liquor they had at their disposal, both issued and captured. The alcohol flowed. The men celebrated their recent victories and remembered those lost during more than eight months of combat.

The revelry and reflection came to an abrupt halt at 2200. Over the radio, CCA called for the liaison officer (George Galvin) to report immediately to Colonel Sears' HQ. The battalion was instructed to be ready to move early the next morning. Party over.

The officers and men worked all night in their less than ideal state to ready for the move. As Irzyk stated, "Like a virgin in a whorehouse, a sober trooper would be difficult to find in the battalion area."

Galvin returned from CCA with orders for the following day. The battalion would set out at 0715. The plan of attack for April 11: both commands were to advance through the line held by the 80th Infantry Division. CCA would bypass Erfurt to the south while CCB advanced north of the city. Beyond that, the orders did not contain a specific objective. The combat commands were simply told, "Just push east."

The Advance Resumes to the East

The medium tanks of C/8, commanded by Captain Stephenson, took the lead for CCA. The column proceeded along the *Autobahn* running west to east below Erfurt. The route served them well until they reached a blown bridge. Unable to continue, the column took a detour on other east-bound roads.

The only opposition encountered by CCA came at Egstedt and Schellroda, two small villages flanking the *Autobahn* south of Erfurt. Elsewhere along the route, the task force knocked out two towed 88s and some anti-aircraft guns. German snipers wounded five Americans during the march. After a remarkable advance of almost 43 miles, the column reached the Saale River near the town of Maua, four miles south of Jena. As had happened so many times during their blitz across Germany, the bridge was blown in their faces.

On April 11, CCR was reconfigured to include the 35th Tank Battalion, 53rd Armored Infantry Battalion, and the 94th Armored Field Artillery Battalion (the 35th and 53rd were replaced in CCB by the 37th Tank Battalion and 10th Armored Infantry Battalion). CCR followed behind CCA and finished the night in positions west of Weimar, a dozen miles east of Erfurt. As CCR approached the city, they captured a German air corps headquarters, netting as prisoners 12 officers, 124 enlisted men, and 13 nurses.

Lt. Colonel Abrams must have been delighted to have his old tank battalion back under his command with CCB. He was probably just as pleased to be realigned with his good friend, Lt. Colonel Cohen. The 37th Tank Battalion had received 10 new medium tanks with which to reconstitute C Company in the wake of the losses suffered on the Hammelburg mission. Along with the replacement of manpower, both the 37th Tank Battalion and 10th Armored Infantry Battalion were ready to resume an active role. CCB's assigned units were the 37th Tank Battalion, 10th Armored Infantry Battalion, 22nd Armored Field Artillery Battalion, 177th Field Artillery Battalion (155mm howitzers), B/24, C/704, D/25, B/46, and C/489.

CCB moved out at 0645. The 25th Cavalry and the tank destroyers preceded the combat command and contacted the 80th Infantry Division to determine the point at which the main column would pass through their lines. The decision was made to advance through the 80th's positions at Alach, a small town three-and-a-half miles due west of Erfurt.

All did not go as planned. There was supposed to be a bridge in place over a small stream near Alach, and when the armored column arrived, it was discovered that the bridge had never been installed. CCB sent their own engineers to put a treadway in place. Once the bridge was completed, the column moved north to Tiefthal and then east to Gispersleben, a northern suburb of Erfurt. D/25 and C/704 led the column, followed by A/37 and C/10.

The column moved all the way to Gispersleben with no enemy contact. From there they advanced via a trail and circled around Erfurt to Kerspleben and Kleinmölsen. American aircraft reported five or six enemy tanks in the area, and the Hellcats were ordered to take care of them (the tanks were actually self-propelled guns). Destroying the enemy armor was easier than expected when it turned out that the vehicles were unmanned and apparently abandoned. Six more tanks were encountered near Kleinmölsen, which C/37 and B/10 destroyed. The 22nd Armored Field Artillery Battalion used direct fire against the tanks as well (C Battery claimed the destruction of a *Mark IV*). P-47s also supported the attack.

Once the column reached the vicinity of Ottstedt am Berge, Abrams split his command in two. A/37 and C/10 headed southeast toward Daasdorf while B/37 and A/10 peeled off to the north through the Ettersburg Forest. The southern task force ran into direct anti-tank fire coming from Daasdorf and Gaberndorf, which brought their advance to a halt.

The northern task force enjoyed better results. The team of B/37 and A/10 made good progress through the dense forest. At about 1400, while working their way east on a narrow road through the thick woods, the task force encountered and engaged elements of an *SS* unit. Stiff fighting took place near what the men of the 37th Tank Battalion later identified as a prisoner of war camp. The heaviest fighting reportedly took place just west of the camp. Some of the American tanks swept around the north side of the facility, while most of the force advanced to the south.

By 1430, the *SS* troops had been routed and the portion of the camp used by the German command staff was overrun by Abrams' tanks. In the battalion journal for that day, it was noted, "They liberated a PW Camp with 800–1000 Russian and French Prisoners." (In an after-action interview conducted on April 21, Captain Hays—the 37th Tank Battalion's Executive Officer—stated there were "several thousand" PWs. He also stated, "By the time CCB went through, the PWs themselves were in control and pretty well organized.")

What the men of CCB didn't know was that most of the *SS*, alerted to the presence of approaching American armor, had fled the camp at around 1000. The facility was largely left to the prisoners, who raided the armory and equipped themselves with over a thousand rifles, nearly a dozen machine guns, and over 100 *Panzerfausts*. The prisoners engaged in a brief firefight with some of the remaining guards and captured more than 100 of them. Some of the prisoners seized control of portions of the camp, while others fled to the surrounding countryside. Other prisoners made their way through the woods north of the camp, where they eventually encountered elements of the 6th Armored Division. Still others went south and entered the city of Weimer.

Traveling with the Fourth Armored were two observers from the Psychological Warfare Division: 1st Lt. Edward A. Tennenbaum and a civilian, Egon W. Fleck. Along the main highway near Weimer, they came upon thousands of armed prisoners marching in an organized column. While in poor physical condition, they managed to laugh and wave jubilantly, buoyed both by their freedom and the appearance of American forces. Among them were Poles, Jews, and Spaniards, as well as people from France and Holland. When the Americans ordered the column to return to the camp, the PWD observers decided to go with them. Upon their arrival at the main gate, they found more armed prisoners in control. Some of the prisoners were standing guard underneath the sign bearing the camp motto: "*Recht oder Unrecht, mein Vaterland*" (Right or wrong, my Fatherland).

Having dealt with the *SS*, B/37 and A/10 resumed their advance to the east with little interest in exploring the camp. The task force continued another two miles through the forest. At a point about a mile southwest of Kleinobringen, the column picked up a trail leading to the northeast. Near the east edge of the woods, they encountered *Panzerfausts*, resulting in some minor injuries and the loss of one tank. B/37 and A/10 were momentarily stopped after exiting the woods. The northern route turned out to be the better of the two, so A/37 and C/10 retraced their steps and switched to the route taken by B/37.

D/37 and the 37th's assault guns were brought forward and given the role of leading the attack toward Denstedt (D/37 was still operating short the platoon of tanks lost on the Hammelburg mission). When they approached the town, the light tanks ran into fire from small arms and *Panzerfausts*. No losses were incurred, but there was a slight delay in the attack. After clearing Denstedt, the light tanks and assault guns advanced to Schwabsdorf, which they secured and outposted for the night. A/37 and C/10 occupied Ulrichshalben. B/37 and A/10 seized Süßenborn. All roads leading north and east from Weimer had been cut and secured.

The 94th Armored Field Artillery Battalion proceeded to apply harassing fire on Weimar. The 80th Infantry Division, following behind the Fourth Armored, accepted the surrender of the city the following day (April 12).

Buchenwald

The prison camp deserves more attention than it received in the diary of the 37th Tank Battalion. Unknown to the men of B/37 and A/10, this "PW Camp" was the notorious concentration camp known as Buchenwald.

Given that Abrams' column spent no more time at the camp than it took to dispatch the *SS*, little if any attention was paid to the environs. The PWD observers (Tennenbaum and Fleck) may have well been the first Americans to enter the horrific areas of the compound. But not long after the departure of Abrams' tanks, elements of the 6th Armored Division, operating out of their positions at the town of Hottelstedt, entered the camp (apparently unaware that the Fourth Armored had already been there). The men of the "*Super Sixth*" soon experienced what the men of the Fourth Armored endured at Ohrdruf ... but on a much larger scale. Replete with a crematorium, the incinerator could reduce 18 bodies to ash in 20 minutes. The "strangling room" was a macabre killing ground where the living would plunge through a hole in the floor for 13 feet before striking concrete. If the fall didn't kill them, the *SS* waiting below would strangle them with a garrote. Then the body would be hung on a meat hook along the wall until it was time to send the victim to the incinerator.

As with Ohrdruf, the local citizens denied knowledge of the true purpose of the concentration camp. While it might be difficult to imagine worse atrocities than those committed at Ohrdruf, the limits of human imagination were exceeded when it was discovered that the original commandant's wife, Ilse Koch, collected the tattooed skin of prisoners to make lamp shades and ornaments. Her husband, Colonel Karl Otto Koch, commanded the camp from 1937 to 1941. Koch was among the most brutal of Hitler's concentration camp commanders. In December of 1941, Koch was replaced by Sr. Colonel Hermann Pister. While not as sadistic as his predecessor, his treatment of prisoners was no less barbaric. (Koch was later investigated by the *SS* for other criminal activity and subsequently imprisoned. He was executed by an *SS* firing squad on May 4 at Buchenwald, just one week before the Americans arrived.)

General Patton ordered citizens older than the age of seven to be brought into the camp and exposed to the horrors contained within. The famous reporter Edward R. Murrow visited Buchenwald shortly after the liberation of the camp. On April 15, broadcasting for 10 minutes on CBS Radio, he brought to the fore the depraved nature of Nazi Germany.

Among the prisoners liberated from Buchenwald was 16-year-old Elie Wiesel, who later made it his life's work to hunt down the Nazi savages responsible for such callous, inhumane treatment of their fellow man. He later wrote, "You were our liberators, but we, the diseased, emaciated, barely human survivors were your teachers. We taught you to understand the Kingdom of the Knight."

Liberating a concentration camp shocked the senses, leaving an indelible impression and haunting memories lasting a lifetime. But the truly toughest task was reserved for the rear element forces responsible for offering care to those who survived the horrors of the camp. The men of the Fourth Armored Division still had a war to fight, and they quickly moved on with their mission.

Across the Saale River

On April 12, CCB advanced along an axis extending north of Jena in pursuit of a bridgehead on the Saale River near the town of Kunitz. CCA remained south of Jena and would seek a crossing near Maua.

The 51st Armored Infantry Battalion drew the assignment of creating the bridgehead for CCA. At 45 minutes before midnight the day prior, Lt. Colonel Alanis led a small task force across the river and secured enough ground for the engineers to begin work on a bridge. The infantry drew small arms and 20mm fire until a strong response from American artillery silenced them.

The engineers came forward and completed the bridge at 1300, allowing the 51st (-C Company) and A/8 to move across the river. As they advanced toward the town of Schöngleina (six miles northeast of the crossing site) small arms fire struck the column from atop a ridge north of the road. The company commander of A/51 (Captain Plumley) was seriously wounded and required evacuation. D/8 lost another one of its light tanks. The resistance was quickly cleared, however, and the advance continued without meeting further resistance. Lt. Colonel Irzyk's task force tied in with Lt. Colonel Alanis's right flank and then continued advancing into the night.

Difficulties arose when the narrow road penetrated a densely wooded area. It was pitch black, which made the journey slow and methodical. Irzyk's lead elements advanced another three miles to the east and reached the town of Bobeck at 0200.

The 8th Tank Battalion suffered a loss that day that tore at their emotions. Sergeant Constance Klinga—famous within the division for his rallying cry "so they got us surrounded again, the poor bastards"—was shot in the forehead while manning the machine gun on the turret of his tank.

CCB began the day nearly a dozen miles west of CCA. They had a lot of catching up to do if they were to draw abreast of Colonel Sears' command.

Lt. Colonel Abrams' battalions moved out of the area near Kromsdorf at 0700. Once again, D/37 and the assault guns led the column. D/25 and C/704 screened the north flank and attempted to secure a bridge over the Saale River at the town of Dornburg. The bridge had been blown, however, before they arrived.

After the main column passed through Frankendorf unopposed, they ran into artillery fire west of Isserstedt. Abrams called for counterbattery fire, which silenced the enemy guns.

The column renewed their advance at 0950. When they arrived in the area south of Rödigen, eight rounds of enemy artillery fire struck near the column. D/37 and the assault guns sped toward Neuengönna with the hope of capturing the railway bridge intact. They found that the bridge had been destroyed, so they worked their way south down the line of the river toward another bridge indicated on their map. They found that bridge in ruins as well.

The closer CCB came to the river, the more deliberate the German defense became. Germans wielding *Panzerfausts* damaged two of A/37's Shermans before they reached the river. And the tenacious defense presented by the Germans soon led to the loss of one of the 37th Tank Battalion's most experienced leaders.

1st Lt. John Whitehill, the company commander for A/37, had arrived as a replacement officer in October of 1944. He was already a seasoned veteran, having led his unit in action through the tough autumn fighting and the arduous battles in the Ardennes. He now led his company of Sherman tanks toward the city of Jena's northern suburb of Zwätzen, which is built upon the slope of the valley carved out by the Saale River.

When Whitehill's company approached the north side of town, he spotted movement in a nearby cemetery. He grabbed his carbine and climbed down from his command tank to investigate. As he entered the hallowed grounds, three Germans, crouching behind headstones, opened fire on him. Whitehill sought cover behind another headstone and returned fire. One of the Germans raised a *Panzerfaust* and fired a projectile that smashed into the headstone. He was badly injured and evacuated (2nd Lt. Nolan assumed command of A/37).

At 1530, all four companies of the 37th Tank Battalion were brought up to the west bank of the Saale River to provide direct fire in support of a crossing to be conducted by the armored infantry of B/10 and C/10. Visibility was poor, and before the crossing commenced, American P-47s dropped three bombs on the west bank. Fortunately, friendly forces were unscathed.

With the tanks providing support, the engineers used pontoons to ferry the infantry to the east bank. Once across, they secured the town of Kunitz, the leading homes of which were not much more than 100 yards from the bank of the river. The armored infantrymen took between 150 and 250 prisoners in the process. With the crossing site secured, engineers from B/24 came forward at 1700 and began construction of a pontoon bridge. The structure was ready for traffic at 1930, and the vehicles of A/37, B/37, B/10, and C/10 made their way across.

Once on the far side of the river, the infantrymen of C/10 loaded onto the tanks of A/37 and moved out over the open fields east of Kunitz toward the tiny village of Laasen, a mile distant. Thirty-six Germans surrendered there without offering any resistance.

The other tank and infantry teams worked together to expand the bridgehead.

Captain John Whitehill, commanding officer of A/37 (courtesy Joe Whitehill).

C/37 and B/10 advanced south to secure and outpost the forested ground at the top of the valley, which offered a commanding view of Jena. The right flank of the bridgehead was secured by B/37 and A/10, and the two companies outposted a small town on the outskirts of Jena on the lower ground closer to the river. C/704 and D/25 took up positions on the north side of the bridgehead.

The National Redoubt

On April 12, a series of events involving the top American generals on the Western Front helped decide the future course of events for the Fourth Armored Division.

The day began with Eisenhower, Bradley, and Patton visiting the site of a hidden Nazi treasure, buried in the depths of an industrial salt mine near the town of Merkers. Currency, precious works of art, sack after sack of gold bars, gold coins, and looted treasures beyond itemized description were piled high, a half mile below the surface. The magnitude of the treasure was immense, leaving the generals in awe. From there, the trio travelled to Ohrdruf.

After leaving Ohrdruf, they returned to Patton's headquarters, where they conversed late into the evening. During their discussions, Ike revealed that Patton must stop his ad-

April 12, 1945. Shown at an airfield at Gotha, Germany, are (left to right) Major General Walton H. Walker, commanding general XX Corps, Major General Troy H. Middleton, commanding general VIII Corps, an unidentified major general, Lt. General George S. Patton Jr., General Dwight D. Eisenhower, and General Omar N. Bradley, commanding general 12th Army Group (U.S. Army photograph).

vance short of Chemnitz. The farthest TUSA was permitted to go was the line of the Mulde River, 10 miles west of the city. Eisenhower also expressed his concern about the possibility of the top German leadership fleeing south and consolidating their armed forces in the mountainous terrain of the Alps. The rumor surrounding Nazi intentions had grown to the point of being a near certainty. Dubbed the *National Redoubt*, the threat became a key factor in the dispersing of American forces during the days ahead.

Also discussed that night: the selection of officers that might be dispatched to the Pacific Theatre of Operations. The conversation carried on until near midnight.

The three generals eventually headed for their sleeping accommodations. Patton went to his trailer, while Ike and Bradley retired to separate rooms in a small house nearby. Patton turned his radio to BBC to set his watch to the official time, only to hear that President Roosevelt had passed away. He returned to the house to inform both Bradley and Eisenhower. Harry S. Truman was their new commander in chief.

CCA's Final Push toward Chemnitz

On April 13, CCA and CCB charged beyond the Saale River. Colonel Sears' CCA moved east beyond Waldeck and Bobeck, with one column moving rapidly through Bad Klosterlausnitz and Tautenhain while the other advanced along the *Autobahn* farther to the south.

To Al Irzyk's surprise, every time his southern column (consisting primarily of the 8th Tank Battalion) approached an area he thought ideal for the Germans to defend, he found it unmanned. Bridges that in past weeks would surely have been blown were left intact (he was especially fortunate to find undefended and undamaged a bridge over the Weisse Elster River). Roadblocks were non-existent.

Irzyk's good fortune continued late into the day. As he approached the Zwickau-Mulde River, he spurred his tanks on at full speed toward the bridge at Reinholdshain. Unlike the choke points he had passed through so easily the balance of the day, this one was defended by a modest contingent of German troops armed with *Panzerfausts*. The task force swept the enemy aside and secured the area east of the bridge.

It was only 1530 when the column was ordered to halt for the night. Irzyk pushed patrols to the east, well beyond the town. He established his command post a little more than a mile east of Reinholdshain. The balance of the day was uneventful … at least until 2100, when a disheveled G.I. was escorted to Irzyk's command post. The American had escaped from a prisoner of war camp located near Hohenstein, five miles farther east. As Irzyk later recalled:

> He reported that there were hundreds of stretcher cases, and that starvation was close at hand for many of those imprisoned. He also mentioned that there were now very few Germans left and that he had observed no movements of troops or equipment.

Irzyk resolved to ready a task force to go to their rescue the following morning.

The northern task force (consisting primarily of the 51st Armored Infantry Battalion) had a much different experience on April 13. As the column approached the town of Bad Köstritz, they discovered that the bridge over the Weisse-Elster River had been destroyed. Major Alanis was ordered to reverse course and fall in line behind the 8th Tank Battalion. They would use Irzyk's bridge to cross the river.

As the 51st Armored Infantry Battalion's column doubled back, it ran into the tail end of a horse-drawn enemy column. The Americans made quick work of it and took 72 prisoners. Alanis's column then moved on to the *Autobahn* and across the river.

After a brief stop to reorganize, the 51st AIB moved out at 1400. They advanced through Schmölin, then east to Gößnitz. After they reached Tettau, trouble emerged farther back in the column. Germans equipped with small arms and *Panzerfausts* sprung up to the rear at Gößnitz, now three miles behind the head of the column. The tanks and infantry halted at Tettau for the next hour while the disturbance at Gößnitz was cleared up. A platoon of infantry and the assault gun platoon remained behind to hold the bridge, just in case the enemy had other forces available to infiltrate the rear.

Once the tail of the column closed the gap with the tanks and infantry, the advance resumed through Oberwiera and picked up the main road leading into Waldenburg, only a dozen miles west of Chemnitz. The tanks and infantry moved through the town, seized the bridge, and occupied the high ground on Hill 318. Most of the lightly-armed Germans surrendered without a fight. One-hundred-and-forty prisoners were taken.

After the lead elements passed through Waldenburg, the 51st Armored Infantry established its command post there. Once the vehicles were positioned inside the town, some "fanatics" struck with a *Panzerfaust*. One of the halftracks from the machine gun platoon was hit, killing four and injuring five. A hunt ensued, and the culprits were found and dispensed with.

At 1630, the 66th Armored Field Artillery Battalion arrived in position north of Glauchau. From there, they supported CCA by firing on enemy gun positions, vehicles, a railroad bridge, and enemy infantry.

On April 14, the 51st Armored Infantry moved out at 0700 with the objective of seizing Limbach, eight miles east of their start line. The 66th moved out at 0905 and set up firing positions near Meinsdorf.

The task force moved rapidly until it reached Rußdorf, where enemy infantry and *Panzerfausts* delayed the column. The 66th hit the town with their howitzers, and the tanks and infantry moved in to clean out the resistance. During the fight, 25 enemy were killed and 280 prisoners were taken. Lt. Colonel Alanis had no way of knowing it at that moment, but for his men, this was their last action of the war.

Had Lt. Colonel Irzyk left matters up to the command post of CCA, his war might have been over as well. Eager to rescue the prisoners in dire straits at Hohenstein, he pushed his leading tanks on their way before sunrise on April 14. The task force rolled into Hohenstein unopposed. Before finding any trace of the prison camp, they came upon three trains in a depot, two of which were loaded with prime movers and staff cars. The third was a passenger train, with each car marked *Dresden*. The train was rolling down the track, so the reconnaissance platoon raced ahead of the locomotive and brought it to a halt. The passengers scattered from the cars like cockroaches caught in the glare of a kitchen light at midnight. The tanks proceeded to work over the equipment-laden trains.

Irzyk's task force discovered the hospital and adjacent prison camp, which the German guards had abandoned. There were hundreds if not thousands of American and British POWs, many of whom were in desperate physical shape. Irzyk's staff radioed higher command to report the location of the camp and the status of the prisoners. Hopefully, medical support would arrive soon. Irzyk could do little else for them and encouraged them to sit tight until help arrived.

Irzyk decided on his own initiative to push his task force farther east. The *Autobahn* was located a very short distance north of Hohenstein, and it wasn't long before his tanks were rolling toward Chemnitz. Three miles down the highway, just north of the town of Wüsterbrand, Irzyk pulled his command tank to the side of the road to talk to some of his advance elements. As he stood in the turret of his M4A3E8 Sherman, he suddenly heard loud banging on the side of the tank.

There stood his raging combat commander, Colonel Sears, who shouted, "Don't move another foot—you're already well beyond the restraining line." Irzyk, completely unaware of any such thing, immediately acknowledged the order and radioed his lead elements to stop in place. Sears climbed back into his peep and headed west. The men and vehicles at the tip of the spear headed the same direction. Irzyk consolidated his battalion at Wüsterbrand, where they set up outposts.

CCB's Final Push to the East

On April 13, Lt. Colonel Abrams' proceeded east using three separate columns. He had been criticized by Hoge for advancing on too narrow a front prior to this, and his decision to split the command in this way was a direct result of orders from Division HQ.

D/25 and C/704 met little opposition as they followed a 30-mile route extending east through the towns of Beutnitz, Mertendorf, Großhelmsdorf, Pötewitz, Rosenthal, Goßra, Droßdorf, Kayna, and Dölzig. The task force had originally planned on taking a bridge at Rossendorf, but when they discovered the bridge was out, they detoured south and captured a bridge at Rosenthal. In the open terrain between Nedissen and Kleinpörthen, gunners in the Hellcats commanded by Sergeant John Jesky and Sergeant John Ewantisko knocked out two anti-aircraft installations. The tank destroyers and cavalry then advanced another 15 miles to the east-southeast, coming to a halt at Heiersdorf. The tank destroyer crews and cavalrymen remained in their vehicles throughout the night.

A task force composed of A/37 and C/10, led by Captain Hays, also advanced without opposition. Starting from Laasan, his task force formed the middle of the three columns. After making a difficult crossing through the forested hills east of Laasan, he moved his force quickly toward the Weisse-Elster River and crossed using the bridge at Rosenthal. He then continued east before coming to a momentary stop near Nicklesdorf, where he provided protection for the bridgehead.

The main column consisted of the balance of CCB. Lieutenant Donahue's D/37 and the assault guns led the way through Laasan. As they pressed east through the forest, the narrow and twisting trails resulted in a slow pace. They finally emerged from the woods and cruised for the next three miles before encountering heavy small arms fire at Bürgeland, which they dealt with in the usual fashion.

At Hainspitz, a little under four miles east of Laasan, Major Hunter, commanding officer of the 37th, was wounded and evacuated (Captain Dwight assumed command of the battalion). Resistance at Hainspitz consisted of small arms and sniper fire, which Cohen and Dwight's men cleaned out before moving on.

The column diverted to Rosenthal to utilize the previously captured bridge for the crossing of the Weisse-Elster River. The HQ Company of the 10th Armored Infantry Battalion remained behind to guard the bridge while the balance of the task force continued east. The column was supposed to turn south toward Silbitz, but when one of the tanks on the route fell through a bridge spanning a canal, Abrams decided to place both the center and right columns on the same route through the Forest Zeitz.

The three columns converged at Mehna. Progress had been so fast and beyond expectations that Hoge ordered Abrams to press on, hoping a crossing over the Zwickau-Mulde River could be seized by day's end. Air reconnaissance reported that a bridge was intact at the town of Wolkenburg.

After passing through Burkersdorf, Mockzig, and Garbisdorf, D/37 moved forward to seize the bridge. Already low on gas, Lt. Donahue's tanks had barely enough in their fuel tanks to make it across the bridge. Once on the other side, they remained motionless as the other elements of CCB moved across the Zwickau-Mulde River. In anticipation of German aerial attacks against the bridge, Major Bautz positioned an anti-aircraft battery on the ridge overlooking the crossing site.

By 1830, the town of Kaufungen (one mile to the southeast) was cleared. The armored infantry companies advanced beyond the town to clear the high ground to the east, which overlooked a long, open slope leading down to the town of Niederfrohna. Fortunately, the medium tanks had just enough fuel to join infantry. The logistical situation wasn't made easier that night when a heavy rain turned the roads to muck, which kept the supply trucks from getting to the forward units.

The following morning (April 14), the three tank and infantry teams were dispatched on separate missions. At 1130, A/37 and C/10 moved out along the road southeast of Hartmannsdorf and advanced through Wittgensdorf to capture the high ground north of the town. Scattered small arms and *Panzerfaust* fire were quickly overcome. At 1200, C/37 and B/10 advanced through the towns of Niederfrohna, Mühlau, Chursdorf, and Burgstädt. They attacked to the southeast and captured the high ground south of the town of Taura. They also cleared a portion of Taura. Resistance was stiff, especially in the form of *Panzerfausts*.

B/37 and A/10 attacked Hill 300 near Burkersdorf. The enemy, mostly armed with *Panzerfausts*, was dug in along the road. A foot assault with running fire was employed to clear the positions. The tanks and infantry then carried the attack forward into the adjacent town of Burgstädt. Two to three hundred prisoners were taken. Unfortunately, Lt. Pielsk was killed during the battle; after being injured by a grenade, he was beaten to death by the Germans.

While CCB cleared the towns west of Chemnitz on April 14, C/704 and the 25th Cavalry Reconnaissance Squadron continued to screen the left flank of the combat command. The task force discovered a bridge intact at Penig (the 2nd platoon of C Company was left behind to guard the bridge). Once across the Zwickau-Mulde, the cavalry and tank destroyers advanced another five miles to the southeast through Mühlau and Hartmannsdorf. The task force then seized Hill 360, just outside of Hartmannsdorf, cutting the main road in the process.

The stealthy Hellcats and the armored cavalry made a lethal pairing. Colonel Roberts later commented,

> As German antitank guns generally can knock out any of our vehicles regardless of the thickness of their armor, we give the light tanks and tank destroyers almost any type of mission. Even medium tanks shed flat trajectory fire only occasionally. The M18 tank destroyer—light, fast and silent—has proved particularly good for escort missions because it can keep up with trucks. Tanks labor when performing such details.

The tank destroyers and cavalry came within five miles of the western edge of Chemnitz. Berlin was 115 miles to the north-northeast. The scribe of C/704's combat diary noted, "Berlin is only a very short drive from here and there doesn't seem to be any reason why we can't take it without any trouble."

CCR was also active. The 53rd Armored Infantry Battalion, 35th Tank Battalion, and

94th Armored Field Artillery Battalion left the vicinity of Langenburg at 0720 on April 14. Colonel Blanchard's command arrived at Weidensdorf at 1015, after which a task force was formed that worked with the 319th Infantry Regiment to clean out the town of Glauchau the following day. By 1700 on April 15, resistance was overcome and the 53rd's command post moved into Glauchau. CCR maintained defensive positions in the area through April 19.

While the main elements of CCR dealt with Glachau, the 94th Armored Field Artillery Battalion assembled a small task force from A Battery for an attack on the town of Gablenz. The party was led by Major Robert Franks and included Lt. Frank J. Vegh, S/Sgt. Charles J. LiVecchi, Sgt. Albert R. Conklin, and 1st Sgt. William Heesaker. The team took two half-tracks and two M7s to the high ground west of the town. The small force descended into Gablenz and engaged in a street fight that yielded the capture of three German officers and 51 enlisted men. Six enemy soldiers were killed.

The 94th Battalion HQ's light tank continued to be remarkably productive, taking 15 prisoners on another mission. The 94th also secured the town of Remse, capturing 17 prisoners in the process. The battalion remained in place at Remse for several days, mostly engaged in maintenance and sweeping in stray German soldiers.

Stopping at the Restraining Line

For the time being, it was the end of the road.

On April 15, most of the division was held in place. Lt Colonel Abrams visited the 10th Armored Infantry Battalion during the afternoon. Brigadier General Hoge visited the 37th Tank Battalion command post and personally congratulated Captain Dwight on the "fine manner in which he took over the battalion" after Major Hunter had been wounded and evacuated.

During the day, most of the activity along the division front amounted to tidying things up. That afternoon, the 3rd Platoon of C/704 had a little bit of action when they went to the aid of a light tank in trouble beyond their position. The Hellcats fired over 60 rounds of 76mm ammo and several hundred rounds of .50 caliber, killing an undetermined number of Germans and tearing apart the town where the enemy infantry resisted.

At CCA, Lt. Colonel Irzyk decided to send out patrols from his position at Wüstenbrand. He dispatched his reconnaissance platoon, reinforced with two light tanks, to check out the town of Siegmar, four miles to the east and less than three miles west of Chemnitz. Upon reaching the edge of town, the patrol was fired upon by dug-in civilians armed with *Panzerfausts*. The patrol reported the resistance to Irzyk, who called in an artillery volley on the town. Following the blasts, the town's *Bürgermeister*, accompanied by other town representatives, marched out under a white flag and surrendered.

Lt. Tremblay led a patrol back into Siegmar. When they arrived at the center of town, they found a huge pile of varied weapons. The Americans sorted the armaments and lined them up along a curb on the street. They took the pistols aside as souvenirs, and then they crushed all the rest underneath the treads of one of the light tanks. Upon his return, Lt. Tremblay proudly passed the pistols out as gifts. For his battalion commander, he reserved the finest: neatly packaged in a wooden box were two .22 caliber single shot dueling pistols (Irzyk treasured the gift his entire life).

By the end of the day on April 16, the 80th Infantry Division moved in and took over the positions held by the 8th Tank Battalion. Irzyk's command moved back a short distance to Hohenstein.

A shadow box containing the treasured dueling pistols and numerous decorations awarded to Brigadier General Albin F. Irzyk (courtesy Al Irzyk, Jr.).

The 10th Armored Infantry Battalion remained in position at Hartmannsdorf, except for one platoon from A/10 which moved into position on Hill 296 along with D/37. At 1315, three German planes strafed and killed a man from the 10th Armored Infantry. A platoon from C/10 and a platoon of tanks from A/37 met no resistance as they moved to positions at the bridge north of Draisdorf.

Around this time, Captain Lyons, commanding the 10th Armored Infantry Battalion's Headquarters Company, was on a hill overlooking the position held by one of the battalion's towed 57mm anti-tank guns. The gun was used to cover a road leading toward a forward enemy position. Lyons suddenly noticed a medical peep approaching from the rear. In the vehicle was Captain John R. Mabee, the battalion surgeon. It appeared to Lyons that Mabee's peep was not going to stop. If he did not, the doctor was at risk of continuing down the road directly toward the German position.

Lyons drew his .45 pistol and fired it in the air, hoping to draw Mabee's attention. When that didn't work, he took off his steel helmet and waved it wildly. Mabee noticed him, but he didn't appear to interpret it as a warning. He simply waved back at Lyons as his peep sped past the American anti-tank gun and drove unwittingly toward the enemy position. Lyons saw the surgeon captured by the Germans. (Captain Mabee was later repatriated by the 100th Infantry Division. While held captive, he worked with the professor of surgery at Heidelberg. A 1938 graduate of Harvard, Mabee went on to open a private practice after the war).

Captain Lyons had another chest-beating experience near Chemnitz. He and two of his men were riding along in their peep in search of an observation position. Atop a ridge, they noticed a large mound with a steel door entrance built into it (he said these were quite common and thought they had something to do with the local water systems). Lyons took one of his men with him to the top of the ridge to check out the perimeter of the mound, wanting to make sure no enemy troops were located around it.

As Lyons crawled forward, he saw two men laying on the ground about 50 yards away, both covered by a camouflaged poncho. He and his partner (his map sergeant) returned to the peep and told the driver, T/4 Oscar Bray, to man the .50 caliber machine gun. Lyons' orders were to shoot anyone not wearing an American uniform who might emerge from behind the mound.

A facility much like the one where Captain Lyons had a deadly encounter with a German sniper team (photograph by author).

Lyons drew his .45 pistol and returned alone to the left side of the mound. He approached the still bodies (he suspected they were sleeping). He kicked one of the boots, and suddenly one of the men whipped off the poncho, revealing himself as a German lieutenant. Alongside him was an enlisted man ... and two sniper rifles. Lyons motioned with his .45 for the officer to stand. As the officer rose, Lyons realized "he was a huge man and quite tall." The lieutenant made the mistake of reaching for his own holstered pistol, and Lyons immediately put a round in his chest.

The force of the .45 caliber slug at near point-blank range "knocked him backward about six feet and down he went turning almost immediately a sickly gray-green color—the death pallor."

Lyons searched the fallen officer for significant papers. As he did, the lieutenant regained consciousness and asked Lyons for a picture from his wallet ... a picture of a woman. Lyons fished out the photo and gave it to the mortally wounded man.

Lyons had the peep brought around. They loaded in the wounded lieutenant and forced the enlisted man to ride on the hood. After destroying the sniper rifles (which Lyons described as "beautiful pieces of work"), they drove back to their column with the prisoners. The German officer died within minutes despite attempts by the medical staff to save him.

18

Czechoslovakia

Pulled from the Line

Having reached the restraining line dictated by SHAEF, there was little need for the Fourth Armored to remain in a static position at the front. On April 16, the 80th and 76th Infantry Divisions relieved *Olympic*, giving them an opportunity to pull back for a rest. The following day, the Fourth was assigned to VIII Corps and took on billets at several towns west of Chemnitz.

The division's first days off the line were consumed with the customary activities associated with being outside the range of enemy guns. The veterans needed no reminders on how best to take advantage of a respite. They knew first-hand the benefits to be gained from disciplined preparation, and they wasted no time getting to work.

It wasn't long before the division was back on the road. Fearing the rumored assembly of German troops at the *National Redoubt*, Hoge's division was placed in Third Army reserve as a precaution. Their destination was the city of Bayreuth, 100 miles to the south.

The road march began on April 24. Though the *Autobahn* they used traversed an area of Germany previously cleared by Americans forces, there were a few points along the route where they encountered resistance from Germans operating behind American lines.

In one instance, a civilian brandishing a *Panzerfaust* knocked out a tank from the 35th Tank Battalion. In another, a tank recovery vehicle from the 94th Armored Field Artillery Battalion broke down on the *Autobahn* near the town of Schleiz. The three-man crew remained with the vehicle overnight and were ambushed the following morning by a band of Germans. T/4 John O. Pippin manned a machine gun and forced the German party to retreat, but not before T/4 William Eppele and T/5 Russell J. Dark were killed. A party from the 94th went in search of the Germans but found no trace of them.

In another incident involving the 94th, a group of German youth in ill-fitting uniforms approached the American column. Unarmed, they asked for cigarettes and chocolate. Not believing the young teenagers to be a threat, Lt. Boas and his men treated them to the luxuries. The boys scattered back to the field from whence they had emerged, and within moments, reappeared. Rifle and *Panzerfaust* fire erupted from the tall grass where the boys had apparently laid down their weapons. Before their lives came to an end, they knocked out two light tanks and killed two of the crew members. It was a total waste at this stage of the war.

At the end of the 100-mile trek, Brigadier General Hoge established his headquarters at Bayreuth and retained the 704th Tank Destroyer HQ and HQ Company for security. Colonel Abrams' units established billets in the surrounding towns (Abrams was promoted to full colonel on April 21). Effective the night prior, some changes had been made in the

18. Czechoslovakia

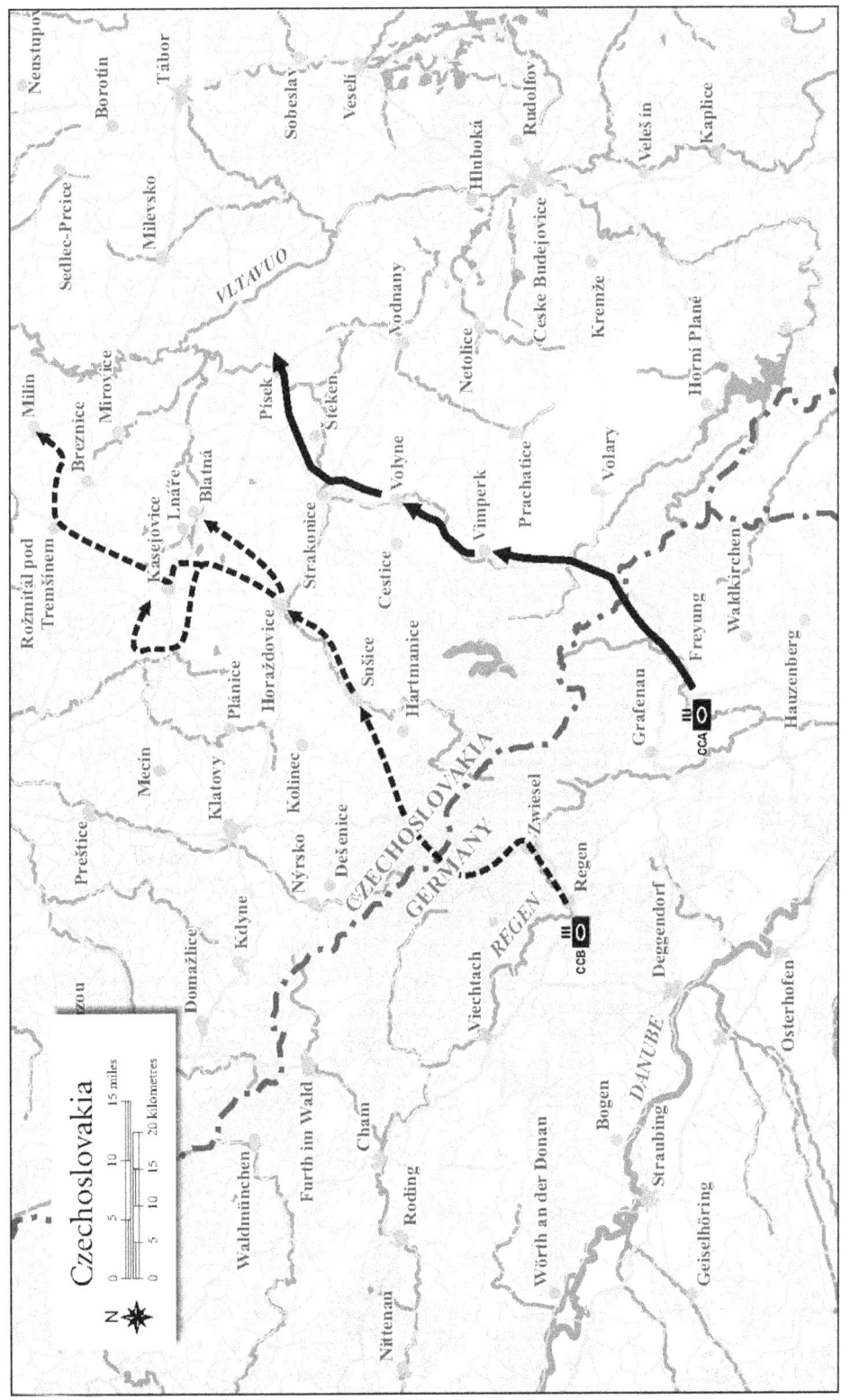

Czechoslovakia (© Petho Cartography, 2020).

command structure for the 37th. Major Ed Bautz took command of the battalion, while Captain Dwight resumed his prior position as executive officer. Captain Hays served as S-3 and Captain McMahon as S-2.

During the days that followed, maintenance, training, and recreational activities dominated the agenda. On the April 28, the division was placed in 12th Army Group Reserve. That same day, D/37 received four brand-new M-24 light tanks. Two of the 1st lieutenants from the 37th—Pancake and Whitehill—were promoted to captain.

Olympic's reserve status with 12th Army Group only lasted two days. On April 30, the Fourth was released to XII Corps.

News of events on the Western Front made its way to the front-line soldiers. The April 30 entry from C/704's unit journal serves as a roundup of what the men of the Fourth were thinking and feeling about world events:

> *War news all good yesterday. Stars and Stripes reported that Reds and Yanks meet. Hitler's Bertchestgarten retreat has been bombed further into the ground. Mussolini has been executed, Marshal Goering reported dead from heart failure and Herr Hitler reported dying of a heart attack. That would be too easy a death for the monster who ordered the atrocities we witnessed at Ohrdruf, but we should be happy if those rats are exterminated.*

Adolf Hitler had indeed met his end on April 30, though not by a heart attack. Having taken refuge in an underground bunker beneath the German Chancellery in Berlin, he opted to end his life with a self-inflicted bullet to the brain. At 0645 on May 2, Marshal Zhukov accepted the surrender of Berlin. A cease fire for the city went into effect at 1500.

A Dilemma in Prague

On April 25, American and Soviet ground forces made contact for the first time. The meeting came near Riesa, Germany (only 37 miles north-northeast of the easternmost positions held by the Fourth Armored 10 days earlier). However, on other parts of the front there remained significant distances between the Americans and the Soviets. Within the void between the two great powers, a significant number of *Wehrmacht* troops still occupied non–German soil. This was especially the case in Czechoslovakia.

Caught in the middle was the city of Prague. The British Chiefs of Staff, spurred by Churchill, discussed with their American counterparts the liberation of the Czech capital. The State Department agreed with the Brits that American forces should occupy the city before the Russians and urged President Truman to pursue it. Truman took the issue up with General Marshall, who in turn presented the British request to Eisenhower. There the matter died, for Eisenhower believed the Russians would arrive at Prague before General Patton possibly could (in truth, Patton was easily capable of getting to Prague first). Eisenhower kept in place the previously established stop line near the Czechoslovakian border. Much to Patton's consternation, the Czech capital was a prize reserved for Stalin.

The Czechoslovakian population grew restless. On May 4, the citizens of Prague launched protests in defiance of the German occupation. Demonstrators took to the streets, and the SS made a half-hearted attempt to clear the protesters. Eager to remove the yoke of oppression, the Revolutionary Czech National Council assembled and voted to begin a violent uprising against the Germans. Dr. Albert Prazak was chosen to lead the new government in revolt. The citizens of Prague were urged to erect barricades in the streets.

In light of the developments in Prague, Eisenhower announced that he would advance into Czechoslovakia as far as needed to clear the west bank of the Vlatva River (the river runs south to north from the southern Czech border through Prague itself). At 1930 on May 4, Bradley called Patton and give him the "green light" to enter Czechoslovakia. He asked how quickly he could move, and Patton told him it would be the following morning. The Third Army commander recalled that "[Bradley] was somewhat incredulous, but, as we were pretty well used to each other, he believed me."

The American drive into Czechoslovakia rubbed the Soviets the wrong way. They protested to Eisenhower that he was in violation of their prior agreements. Stalin asked that Eisenhower honor those agreements and not advance beyond Pilsen (50 miles southwest of Prague). Eisenhower agreed.

None of this assisted the Czechs in their struggle. During the night of May 4, an unauthorized delegation of Czech officers made their way from Prague to the small village of Shukomasty. They were in search of help from a very unlikely source: the Russian Liberation Army.

The Russian Liberation Army (ROA)

General Andrey Vlasov was a highly decorated Russian officer with a long and distinguished combat record. He played a pivotal role in reversing the Soviet's fortunes outside of Moscow when he led a counterattack that pushed the German army westward. His own fortunes changed on July 12, 1942, when he was captured by German forces during the battle for Leningrad.

During Vlasov's captivity, he renounced communism and expressed his belief that Stalin was a threat to the Russian people. He then went to work for the Nazis, becoming heavily involved in anti-communist propaganda campaigns within the occupied territories. Vlasov's long-term goal was an independent state for the White Russians (the most prominent faction combating Vladimir Lenin's Red Army during the Russian Revolution of 1917–1922). For that to be achieved, two things were required: the defeat of Stalin and Hitler's willingness to allow a self-governed state.

Vlasov advocated for the creation of an army comprised primarily of Russian prisoners who were aligned with him against communism. He was ready and willing to fight side by side with the *Wehrmacht* against the Soviet Army. Not trusting Vlasov, Hitler was opposed to the idea for quite some time, leaving Vlasov in despair. But in September of 1944, as Hitler faced a growing shortage of manpower for the *Wehrmacht*, he approved the creation of the Russian Liberation Army (ROA). Though nearly one million Russian prisoners were reportedly willing to serve, authorization was given to raise only two infantry divisions.

Armed and equipped with German weapons and uniforms, the ROA's First Division (commanded by General Sergei Bunyachenko) was ready for deployment by mid–February. On April 13, the First Division went into battle against their fellow Russians for the first time. While they fought bravely, the attack was unsuccessful. On his own initiative and against German orders, General Bunyachenko broke off the attack and withdrew his division.

No longer aligned with the Germans nor the Soviets, the First Division began a long march away from the front. Their only allegiance belonged to Mother Russia and one another. An army without a country, their destination was Czechoslovakia. It was the lone remaining refuge.

American military leadership was aware of the ROA's existence. On April 25, General Patton (he received his fourth star on April 14) was informed that 5000 of Vlasov's men tried to surrender to the 26th Infantry Division. Patton summed up the dilemma faced by the White Russians:

> *The question then arose as to whether they were prisoners of war or allies. We finally got a decision that they were prisoners of war, and they were and still are. In my opinion, they are in a very bad fix, because if the Russians ever get them they will unquestionably be eliminated.*

The men of Vlasov's First Division continued marching south. They crossed the Czech border and on May 4 arrived at the town of Beroun, 16 miles southwest of Prague. They held out hope that they could take refuge with the Americans.

The delegation of Czech officers came calling at midnight. They initially met with General Bunyachenko. Their ask: the Czechs needed help in their fight against the SS. Bunyachenko summoned General Vlasov and the conversation continued. The decision was made: the ROA would support the Czech uprising. As dawn broke on May 5, the lead elements of the ROA First Division were on their way to Prague.

The Battle for Prague

The battle between the Czechs and German SS troops intensified on May 5. The partisans gained access to the transmitter at the Radio Building in central Prague and sent a plea for help to the entire citizenry. With the assistance of an escaped Scottish prisoner of war (Private William Greig), a broadcast was also made in English (the Americans were close enough to Prague to capture the radio signal). With Greig as their spokesman, the Czechs urged the Allied forces to come to their aid.

Thirty thousand Czechs took to the streets to reclaim and defend their city. At 1400, the Czech National Committee announced that the Nazi occupying authorities had been overthrown. The new governing authority proclaimed control of the city. The Czech national flag flew above the capital.

Despite their matériel superiority (they even had air support available from a base east of Prague), the Germans failed to gain the upper hand. The SS sent out a call for reinforcements. As night fell on May 5, troops and armored vehicles from the *SS Division Das Reich* and the *SS Division Das Wallenstein* were on the way.

That same day, an OSS team led by Captain Eugene Fodor arrived in Prague. The American officer conducted talks with members of the German military and Czech civilian authorities. He then returned to American lines for a meeting with Patton.

After being briefed on the uprising, Patton was eager to go to the aid of the partisans. He asked General Bradley for permission. "For God's sake, Brad, those patriots in the city need our help. We have no time to lose." Bradley consulted with Eisenhower, who reinforced the order that the advance could not go as far as Prague. In turn, Bradley relayed to Patton that his request was denied. (Eisenhower did broach the topic with the Soviet General Staff. Rebuffed, he kept the restraining line in place.) At the very least, Patton hoped that he could push his reconnaissance units as far as the Czech capital. But even this was no longer a possibility.

Unhampered by politics and driven by an appetite to consume as much territory as possible, the Soviets ramped up their effort to reach the city. The Soviet leaders were aware of the political importance of the Czech capital, especially when considering their desires for the post-war occupation of Eastern Europe. But as of May 5, the tanks and infantry of the 1st Ukrainian Front were still more than 120 miles from the capital. In the face of continued German resistance, the Soviets would likely not reach the capital for another four days.

Liberators Once More

Perhaps sensing an opportunity, Patton began moving his pieces on the chess board even before the situation in Prague came to a boil. On May 2, *Olympic* was already rolling toward Czechoslovakia. The 37th Tank Battalion departed at 0700 that morning for a 155-mile road march. By the time the uprising began in earnest, Hoge's division was assembled in the Dreggendorf-Regen area. Elements of the Fourth were within striking distance, only 10 miles from the Czech border.

On May 4, *Olympic* received their orders. The following day, they would advance across the Czech border and onward to Prague (despite all we know about the conversations among those in positions of higher command). For CCB, the plan was for Captain Donahue's D/37 to lead the charge to the north, followed by C Company of the 704th Tank Destroyer Battalion. Their route would take them through the difficult Böhmerwald Mountains.

The units moved into their assembly area and waited for the green light. But word never came, and the men were ordered to return to their billets. The frustration was palpable and reflected in the 37th Tank Battalion's diary:

> *This move proved to be the greatest abortion of false prenancy (sic) that this unit has experienced either in maneuvers or in the present war.*

The go-ahead finally came on May 6. The division advanced through the lines of the 5th and 90th Infantry Divisions and headed toward Prague. The 177th Field Artillery Group, consisting of the 179th Field Artillery Battalion with their 155mm howitzers, and the 276th Armored Field Artillery Battalions with their M7 105mm howitzers, were attached for additional support.

CCA formed the eastern column and advanced through the Freyung Pass while CCB entered Czechoslovakia via the Regen Pass. Both columns moved 25 miles across the border without meeting resistance. CCA established its command post at Strakonice while CCB established theirs at Horazdovice, 10 miles to the northwest of CCA. CCR, which trailed behind CCA, set up their command post at Volyně, six miles south of CCA. Hoge established his division HQ at Sušice.

When *Olympic* crossed the German border in February, Hoge's men were not viewed as liberators. They were invaders. Conquerors. The enemy. Upon entering Czechoslovakia, the tankers were taken aback when the civilians seemed to look at the rolling column of vehicles with the same disdain, sunken hearts, and suspicion as had so many thousands of Germans the past three months. But this was the *Sudetenland*, home to people predominately of German heritage. The German-speaking civilians were no more thrilled to see the Americans than their nearby German cousins.

After a dozen or so miles across the border, civilian temperament changed in dramatic fashion. As the Sherman and Stuart tanks, halftracks and peeps, Hellcats and M7 self-propelled artillery, and every other form of vehicle in the armored division's arsenal rolled deeper into Czech territory, the Americans were greeted by a populace every bit as delirious about their arrival as had been the people of France during the drive across the breadth of that country. As one anonymous G.I. said to Pfc Charles Wilson, "How do you like this liberating? It beats the hell out of conquering!"

C/704 crossed the Czechoslovakia border shortly after noon on May 6. They followed behind D/37 as previously planned. Their journal entry sums up the spirit of the day:

> *(We) were given a royal welcome by the crowds along the way. We never saw so much pastry in our lives and had to duck to keep from getting hit with bread, cakes and pies. We rode 95 miles to the small town of Lnare where we got billets and took up positions of outpost. The excitable Czechoslovakia got us out of bed at midnight with the rumor of Heinie tanks and 3000 Krauts supposedly on the edge of town. We spent the rest of the night waiting but nothing happened. A dance being held in town broke up in a hurry.*

Lnáře was another 10 miles north of CCB's command post. Two miles shy of there, the 10th Armored Infantry Battalion and 37th Tank Battalion outposted the town of Pole. They took in 800 German prisoners during the night that followed. The 37th Tank Battalion received instructions that they were not to move beyond the restraining line at Lnáře unless released by SHAEF.

During the night of May 6, Czech partisans in contact with Captain Donahue reported large concentrations of Germans and vehicular movement to the north and on the flanks of the American positions. The 37th Tank Battalion asked permission to fire artillery at the reported area, but higher headquarters denied the request. Patrols conducted the following morning didn't find evidence of the enemy. The reports from the partisans were subsequently characterized as being "greatly exaggerated."

Members of C/25 pose with welcoming civilians (courtesy Jim White).

The lead elements of CCA advanced as far as the city of Pisek, 35 miles beyond the border and 52 miles south of Prague. Captain Kermit A. Bernard commanded the first unit to enter the city (A Troop, 25th Cavalry Reconnaissance Squadron). Seven hundred Germans surrendered to the armored cavalrymen. The reborn Czech army honored Bernard by naming a regiment after him.

By the close of the day, the Fourth Armored reached the restraining line established by Eisenhower. Patton was reminded that no advance was to be made beyond the line running through Pilsen. The only exception allowed was for the conduct of security reconnaissance (up to about five miles beyond the line). Patton was none too pleased and expressed as much in his memoir:

> *I was very much chagrined, because I felt, and I still feel, that we should have gone on to the Moldau River and, if the Russians didn't like it, let them go to hell. I did not find out until weeks afterward the reasons, which were sound, which implemented General Eisenhower's decision to order us to stop where he did.*

Patton also heard a report that 100,000 White Russians (elements of Vlasov's Russian Liberation Army) were attempting to surrender, along with women and children in their company. In his diary, he wrote:

> *These people have fought for the Germans against the Russians and are in a pitiable state. However, they will have to be treated as displaced persons. I am having them moved west of the Czechoslovakian border (to save them).*

The Battle for Prague Continues

The German reinforcements arrived at Prague during the early hours of May 6. The commander of the relief force, *SS Gruppenführer* Friedrich von Pückler-Burghauss, drew up orders for an attack to commence at dawn. The Czechs, aware of the arrival of German armor, barricaded the streets with hopes of keeping the enemy tanks at bay. But with all too few anti-tank weapons, their chances of mounting a successful defense did not equal their will. As the day wore on, the situation became increasingly desperate for the Czechs.

Though the Germans achieved tactical success within Prague, they knew their long-term fate was dependent upon which army—the American or the Soviet—they eventually faced. To help improve their chances of survival (or perhaps to sow division between the Americans and Soviets), the Germans offered to allow Patton's forces into Prague. They were willing to embrace a cease-fire if they could surrender to the Americans. However, Eisenhower remained unwilling to release Patton for the mission. The opportunity was denied.

The citizens of Prague were desperate for help as they battled the SS. Patton chomped at the bit to go to their aid, and the men of the Fourth Armored were ready, willing, and able to come to their rescue. Shackled by Eisenhower, the savior of Prague would come from a different direction, flying a very different flag.

On May 7, one regiment of General Vlasov's Russian Liberation Army (ROA) arrived in Prague and became engaged in the fight. General Bunyachenko sent another of his regiments to seize the airfield at Ruzne. Other elements of the ROA First Division cut off access to Prague from north and south. As the day progressed, the tide turned in favor of the Czechs. The ROA's intervention saved countless civilian lives.

The Soviets were aware of Vlasov's whereabouts, and they were determined to bring him to justice. To improve the odds of capturing him, a special operations unit was formed from the Soviet 25th Tank Corps. If it turned out that Vlasov and Bunyachenko sought refuge with the Americans, this unit would go after them (even if it meant going behind American lines).

By the morning of May 8, the situation in Prague was stable. But Vlasov faced a dilemma: the American advance had come to a halt. The Soviets, on the other hand, continued to press forward and would soon be on the doorstep of the capital. Vlasov and his men knew they would be treated as traitors by Stalin (even though they had turned against the Germans in this last large-scale battle). Complicating matters further, Czechs loyal to the Soviets suddenly turned on Vlasov's division. They disavowed the request for help made by the rogue Czech officers and urged Vlasov to surrender to the Soviets upon their arrival.

The ROA First Division broke off their fight with the SS. Their only hope for survival was to surrender to the Americans. Vlasov left Prague in the hands of the Czech partisans and ordered his division to move toward the American lines. Without the benefit of the ROA's heavy weapons, it didn't take long for the SS to regain the initiative. Within a matter of hours, the Germans were back within the city's center in force.

The SS ramped up their terror tactics, slaughtering civilians regardless of whether they had taken up arms to defend their city. Just when things looked the bleakest for the Czechs, *General* Rudolf Toussaint (overall commander for the German forces in Prague) reached a negotiated peace with the Czech rebels. Fearing the approaching Russian forces, he agreed to a cease fire. In exchange, the Germans would be granted free passage through Prague and would turn over their weapons to the Czech Army before reaching American lines. The agreement was made at 1800. Within 15 minutes, the leading German column, spearheaded by 27 tanks and 3000 infantrymen, headed toward the American front. Some die-hard SS troops remained behind, unwilling to surrender to anyone.

On the morning of May 9, Soviet tanks occupied the city center. The few remaining Germans within the city surrendered. While the Soviets were well received at that moment, perspectives would change soon enough. For decades to come, the citizens of Czechoslovakia paid the price for the political decisions made by the leadership of the United States of America.

At a press conference, Patton was asked by a reporter why he did not advance to Prague. He answered,

> *I can tell you exactly—we were told not to. I don't know the exact reasons but those were the orders. Of course there are probably many reasons which we don't know which would explain this, as there may be cause of international incidents up there we don't know anything about.*

Chomping at the Bit

As the sun rose on May 7, the men of the Fourth Armored were aware that the uprising in Prague continued. Despite the desire to play a role in helping the Czech citizens, they were forced to sit on their hands. They pushed the envelope via their patrols, but that was the extent of their ability to influence events.

A task force led by Lt. Colonel Cohen, comprised of C/37 and B/10, swept through the towns of Kotouň, Kladrubce, Budislavice, Dožice, Radošice, and Mlady Smolivec, taking 700 prisoners along the way. A/37 and C/10 went into position north of Zahorčichy. D/37 pushed out the most aggressively, venturing as far as 10 miles north of their outpost at

Lnáře. The Stuarts and brand-new Chaffee tanks went through the towns of Blatna, Kasejovice, Hvozdany, and Rožmitál without encountering German resistance.

At 1800, the 37th Tank Battalion received a message that Czech forces had reported 1200 *SS* troops and 20 *Panzers* headed for Rožmitál (where D/37 had pushed its farthest patrol earlier that day). A/37 and C/37 were dispatched to take up defensive positions north of Lnáře. But as had occurred with other reports from the partisans, it turned out to be a false alarm.

Another message was also received at 1800. This one came from higher command via radio, ordering all offensive action to cease and for units to take up defensive positions. Another order came with it, and it was viewed as an odd directive: the Americans were to protect German troops from the hands of the Czech partisans. The 37th Tank Battalion carried out the order "without the usual enthusiasm." They were hard pressed to accept a role as saviors of the *SS*.

The German Surrender

At 0141 Central European Time on May 7, the unconditional surrender of Germany was agreed to and signed at the city of Rheims, France. There was considerable disagreement between the Russians and Americans regarding the language in the document. There was also a demand that another signing would take place near Berlin. Despite those wrinkles, the net effect was nearly the same as far as the American solider was concerned.

May 7, 1945. Lt. General Walton H. Walker, left, and Lt. General George S. Patton, Jr., on their way into a horse show at St Martin, Austria, at which Robert P. Patterson, Under Secretary of War, also was in attendance (U.S. Army photograph).

Word of the surrender began making its way to the front-line troops. The 53rd Armored Infantry Battalion (then in CCR) received an order to halt all offensive operations at 1555 and to remain in their present positions. CCB's 10th Armored Infantry Battalion received the news at 1800, as did the 37th Tank Battalion. Offensive actions were to cease immediately, and all units were to assume defensive positions.

The unconditional surrender of German forces would be in effect at 0001 on May 9. There was no telling how long it might take for all German units to receive word that an end to hostilities had been agreed to, so a warning was issued for all units to remain prepared for action.

From General Patton's perspective, there was little to celebrate on May 7. He spent much of the day in the company of Under Secretary of War Robert P. Patterson. Part of their time together was consumed by a visit to the Imperial Spanish Riding Academy. The recently repatriated Major Stiller was back at Patton's side.

After having lunch and attending a riding exhibition, Patton and Patterson had ample opportunity to talk. According to Stiller, Patton spoke at length about his desire to keep the U.S. Army intact and in a state of readiness during the post-war period. Patton was of the belief that if a show of force was not maintained in front of the Soviets, America would have defeated Germany but lost the war.

Patterson asked Patton what *he* would do. Patton suggested the proper course was to order the Soviets to withdraw their forces back to their own borders. If they did not do it within a reasonable time, the Western Allies would push them back by force. The secretary suggested to Patton that he was underestimating the strength of the Soviets. Patton countered by criticizing the state of Russian logistics.

May 7, 1945. Nearest the camera: Under Secretary of War Robert P. Patterson and General Patton leaving the building where they had attended a horse show at St. Martin, Austria (U.S. Army photograph).

They could probably maintain themselves in the type of fighting I could give them for five days. After that it would make no difference how many million men they have, and if you wanted Moscow, I could give it to you.

On the one hand, Patton was brilliantly forecasting the coming Cold War. But one cannot avoid speculating that the primary catalyst for his appeal was his relentless and insatiable urge for combat. In the absence of receiving a nod for a role in the Pacific, turning on the Soviets was the only option for satisfying his warrior spirit.

The Hunt for Vlasov—and One Final Battle

On May 10, Captain Donahue's D Company of the 37th Tank Battalion moved north to the town of Hvoždany with the intent of handling the anticipated flow of tens of thousands of German troops fleeing from the Soviets. When Donahue's force arrived, he found the town occupied by Vlasov's men. The veteran company commander, on the order of higher command, continued up the road to contact the German *SS* forces.

Captain Donahue suddenly found himself in the middle of a battle taking place between the White Russians and the *SS* near the village of Milín (*SS Gruppenführer* Friedrich von Pückler-Burghauss, having fled Prague, was in command). The spark for the battle occurred when the local partisans fired upon the German column. The *SS* returned fire against the partisans, and then the White Russians came to the partisans' aid. A pitched battle ensued, and by the time Captain Donahue arrived, a dozen Germans had been killed. Donahue, flying an American flag on his peep, drove between the lines of the two forces and brought the situation under control.

Though the Germans wished to be taken prisoner by the Americans, the standing order from high command prohibited it. As noted in the 37th Tank Battalion journal, "A German Corps Commander with his staff was put in charge of all the enemy bivouac areas." That "Corps Commander" was likely Pückler-Burghauss.

Denied the option of surrendering to the Americans, *SS Gruppenführer* Pückler-Burghauss' men retained their arms. They were unwilling to surrender to the Soviets and would fight to the last if necessary. In the meantime, Marshal Maklinovsky's 2nd Ukrainian Front was tasked by higher Russian command to deal with the intransigent *SS*. The Soviets asked the Americans to assist by blocking the Germans' route of retreat. Eisenhower agreed. The Fourth Armored Division was ordered to bar the door. *SS Gruppenführer* Pückler-Burghauss dug in his troops in a forested area near Milín and Slivice. This was the ground chosen for the final battle of the vaunted *SS*.

Marshal Maklinovsky's units ... much greater in number than the estimated 6000 troops remaining under the command of Pückler-Burghauss ... closed in on the German positions on May 11. That evening, the desperate *SS* soldiers fended off the Soviet's initial attacks, which included a deadly barrage of Katyusha rockets.

The Soviets again asked for assistance from the Americans. The commander of the 104th Guards Rifle Division (Major General Sergei Seryogin) met with an American officer at the Old Mill House in Čimelice, 11 miles south of Milín. Here, they coordinated an artillery barrage that would strike the German positions from both west and east.

The artillery added considerably to the crushing blow received by Pückler-Burghauss. Still, the *SS* refused to surrender, and it took a final assault by the Soviet infantry to deliver the fatal blow. *SS Gruppenführer* Pückler-Burghauss finally decided that enough was enough, and at 0900, he met at the Old Mill House with Major General Seryogin and an American representative. He signed the unconditional terms of surrender, turning his men over to the Soviets. The following day, rather than turn himself over to the Russians, SS *Gruppenführer* Pückler-Burghauss committed suicide. (To this day, the Battle of Milín—Slivice is commemorated with an elaborate reenactment by the Czechs. A monument erected in 1970 marks the site of the battle.)

The Russians had an additional goal when they arrived on May 11. The special task force formed on May 7 was ready to be let loose in dogged pursuit of Vlasov. The task force consisted of a motorized battalion of the Soviet 162nd Tank Brigade and was led by Major Ivan Yakushev, whose orders were to capture Vlasov and the members of his army.

Generals Vlasov and Bunyachenko were engaged in discussion with Captain Donahue at Lnáře's 17th Century castle. Meanwhile, a patrol from the Soviet motorized brigade reached the American front lines. The patrol leader asked an American officer if he knew the whereabouts of Vlasov and his division. The officer revealed to the Soviet patrol the positions of the American, German, and ROA forces in the area. It was a treasure trove of information for Lt. Grigory Sukhorukov.

On the morning of May 12, as the SS were in their final throes near Milín-Slivic, Donahue met once again with Vlasov and Bunyachenko. The captain informed them that the Soviet 25th Tank Corps would soon arrive, and when they did, the town of Lnáře would be turned over to them. Donahue was sympathetic toward the plight of the ROA, but nevertheless informed Vlasov that his men would not be allowed to flee behind American lines.

General Bunyachenko drove to his headquarters one mile north of Lnáře. He delivered the sobering news that surrendering to the Americans was not an option. His last order to the division was to disband and head out in small groups for southern Germany.

The men of the ROA abandoned their weapons and attempted to melt into the nearby forests. Some of the men changed into civilian clothes in a desperate effort to blend in with the populace. Others attempted to pass through the lines of the 10th Armored Infantry Battalion. In accordance with the orders previously received, the Americans turned them back.

The motorized battalion led by Major Yakushev was hot on Vlasov's trail. The day prior, they learned from a captured ROA officer (Colonel Artiemiev of the 2nd Regiment) that Vlasov and Bunyachenko were at Lnáře. Colonel Artiemiev was aware that the generals would soon be leaving Lnáře for Horazdovice (site of CCB's headquarters). Now, on the morning of May 12, Yakushev and his lieutenant took off in an armored car with the hope of intercepting the generals. With them came ROA officer Captain Kuchinsky, who agreed to identify Vlasov once in Yakushev's grasp.

Their options exhausted, Vlasov and Bunyachenko turned their focus toward self-preservation. They and their party formed a small caravan and departed Lnáře at 1400. Bunyachenko rode in the lead vehicle while Vlasov occupied a seat in the last (some accounts claim a small contingent of American troops accompanied them on their route to Horazdovice).

After traveling only two miles to the east, a Soviet Army vehicle overtook the lead car and swerved in front of the column, bringing it to a stop. Soviet soldiers surrounded the automobiles, machine guns at the ready. They knew from their informant which of the cars belonged to Vlasov, and they turned their attention there first. There are varied accounts of what exactly transpired as Vlasov was taken into custody, but all agree that he was an easy catch for Major Yakushev.

Back at Lnáře, eight members of the ROA remained in the company of Captain Donahue, including Lt. Colonel Nikolai Tenzorov (Vlasov's intelligence chief) and Rostislov

Antonov (Vlasov's adjutant). While it was too late for Vlasov, Donahue spirited the party to safety 35 miles behind American lines. After supplying them with food and water, he left the group to their own devices. His actions changed their lives forever.

Vlasov, Bunyachenko, and General Mikhail Meandrov were not as fortunate. It was simply a matter of time before they met their fate. After a trial, all three were hanged for treason. Nearly 30,000 of their men suffered a variety of fates. Almost all were tried and either executed or sentenced to years of captivity and hard labor.

Prison Duty

May 8, 1945. The day that marked the end of the war in Europe. There was still much work to be done, but on that day, celebrations among the civilians were spectacular. Within the American lines, Czech citizens turned out in droves to take part in parties and street dances. Beer flowed. Fraternization was difficult to restrain.

For many American soldiers, the announcement was met with a sober perspective. At the village of Lnáře, the men of C/704 had yet to receive formal word of the surrender (though they heard rumors of it). The diary entry for May 8 read:

> War is rumored to be over and perhaps it is but there is no celebrating, no jubilation, because even if it is over, so what, there is still war in the Pacific, or Army of Occupation, so it means very little to us here. We all hope for the sake of all the persecuted people of Europe that the rumors are true.

In the territory between the Fourth Armored Division and the Russian lines, a sizeable area remained within Czechoslovakia that was yet to be controlled by either the Americans or the Russians. The German forces being squeezed between the two advancing armies had a dilemma on their hands. If they surrendered to the Soviets, they had much to fear, including the loss of their lives. If they made their way to the American lines, the prospects for fair treatment were incredibly higher. Of course, the latter was the preferred option. However, they were unaware of the agreement struck between the Western Allies and the Soviets. Any Germans fleeing the prescribed Russian zone in favor of reaching American lines would be restrained, detained, and turned over to the Russians. What was about to unfold was a nightmare for the German soldier.

On May 9, General Patton issued orders for the Third Army to take control of Czechoslovakia up to the stop line. Patton's men were to prevent German units from crossing the American lines (though civilians would be allowed). Re-

An elderly German civilian reads the news of his nation's surrender to the Allies (U.S. Army photograph).

ports that day indicated that up to 120,000 German troops might flee toward the Fourth Armored in their attempt to avoid becoming Stalin's prisoners.

The American troops were reminded of the surrender terms:

> All weapons to be collected and stored except officers' pistols and 1 rifle with 10 rounds of ammo per 100 men.
> All Germans including civilians to halt in place and bivouac.
> Germans to report location and strength to nearest Allied unit, and await further orders.

After May 8, 80,000 Germans tried to return to their homeland through the lines of the Fourth Armored Division. Some attempted to surrender, while others tried to pass through undetected and were caught in the web of frontline outposts. Perhaps the most unusual effort was made by three members of the *Luftwaffe* when they glided a small observation plane onto an open field adjacent to one of the encampments. Sergeant Bod Oakley of the 35th Tank Battalion accepted their surrender.

The Germans were detained in makeshift camps near the restraining line. It was a daunting task to provide for the well-being of such a large quantity of prisoners in such a short time. To help make the effort a success, the staff of the *17th Army* (which surrendered to CCA) was called upon to organize their fellow prisoners. To help set them apart, German officers were adorned with white armbands which read *Liaison Officer With U.S. Army*. All of this was temporary in nature, as it was just a matter of time before the captives were turned over to the Soviets.

Some of the prisoners tried to avoid their fate. The night before they were to be turned over to the Russians, 20 Germans attempted to escape and were shot by Fourth Armored tankers. A *Wehrmacht* colonel, presumably not wanting to fall into Soviet hands, killed his aide and his mistress, then shot himself.

The Germans had more to fear than falling into the hands of the Russians. On the evening of May 8, Czech citizens lined up five "arrogant" *SS* soldiers in Lnáře and executed them. The following day, two more *SS* dressed in civilian clothing were caught by locals. In preparation for their execution, the men were forced to dig their own graves. American soldiers stepped in to prevent the atrocity. That evening, a long column of Germans appeared at the town and turned in their weapons. Within the column were members of the *SS*. Even in defeat, they displayed "…arrogant attitudes and smirking faces…" But there was little doubt that, as cocky as they may have been, they were in no hurry to face the Russians. They were desperate in their attempt to surrender to the Americans.

On May 9, D/37 and B/704 received orders to set up outposts at Hvozdany and Blatna (the units moved to those positions the following day). The 66th Armored Field Artillery Battalion also set up a camp, as detailed in their battalion diary:

> Roads from the east were suddenly jammed with fleeing German columns, who were trying desperately to surrender to the Americans, than to the Russians although, they had been ordered to stay in place. The columns included motor transport, armored vehicles, commercial cars, farm tractors hauling wagons, teams of horses and oxen hauling wagons and carts and hundreds trudging on foot. The battalion quickly assigned each battery an area and the disorganized German columns were herded off the highways into camps. The sorting and bivouacking of Germans lasted about two and one half days. The battalion guarded approximately 12,000 pw's.

The 10th Armored Infantry Battalion's HQ Company (commanded by Captain Lyons) was assigned the task of establishing a prisoner of war cage for CCB. Lyons chose an eight-acre site on the outskirts of Horazdovice. It was a relatively open field that sloped gently toward a lake 300 yards west of the road connecting Horazdovice with Velky Bor. Having never been trained for the task and lacking the resources to construct barb wire fencing, guard towers, or any of the things normally associated with a prison camp, Lyons improvised. He placed his company vehicles in a circle and turned them inward toward the center. The vehicles and their manned weapons served as containment for the thousands of prisoners soon to arrive. Two men were on alert on each of the .50 caliber machine guns. They remounted all the headlights they could find to keep the compound lit at night. Once established, he notified Lt. Colonel Cohen they were ready to receive prisoners.

It was nightfall before the first prisoners arrived. They came by the truckload in long columns from both directions, lights blazing. Women and children accompanied some of the German soldiers. Some even brought horses with them (200 of which were allowed inside the encampment). On the second day, Lyon's force was reinforced with a platoon from A/10. Over the next few days, the population inside the compound grew to an estimated 8000 prisoners (no official processing was conducted). Organizing the prisoners was a challenge, and it was difficult to satisfy the most basic sanitation and dietary needs.

From Lyons' perspective, the prisoners lacked discipline and seemed little inclined to

May 8, 1945. German soldiers in this P.O.W. camp appear relieved that the war is over. In this camp at Lambach, Austria, they are waiting to be taken away to prisoner of war cages. German women and girls from nearby towns comfort the soldiers before leaving the camp (U.S. Army photograph).

improve their own situation. After three days of this, he had a terse conversation with the senior German officer. From that point forward, the prisoners began to pull themselves up by their bootstraps and restored order. By the fourth or fifth day, relief supplies finally arrived and the prisoners were better fed. The HQ Company, with supporting infantry, remained on guard duty until at least May 15.

The corralling and care of thousands of Germans was a chore. A sergeant from the 35th Tank Battalion summed it up well: "Those prisoners were more damn work than six months of combat."

As the Americans went about the business of creating makeshift POW pens and wiping out the remaining German fanatics within their lines, the Russians gobbled up Czech territory. On May 11, the Soviets showed up in force and contacted the Fourth Armored at the towns on the American side of the restraining line.

The routines of a peacetime army started creeping back in not much more than a week after the official end of hostilities. The men of the 704th Tank Destroyer Battalion went through rugged physical examinations to determine their fitness. But there was still ample time for recreation, including swimming and organized sporting events. Men from the 704th confiscated some of the saddle horses kept at the camp guarded by the 10th Armored Infantry Battalion. They added horseback riding (and blisters) to their recreational pursuits.

Things started to settle down a bit as the flow of fleeing Germans abated. Preparations began for pulling the division out of Czechoslovakia. Billeting teams travelled to Germany to scope out the area near Landshut, Germany. This would soon be the new home for the Fourth Armored Division.

For some, thoughts started to turn toward their *real* home: The United States of America. The men of C/704 took stock of their situation:

> Most of us went swimming and everybody busy trying to figure out their points and trying to make them stretch into enough points to enable them to go home. Many of the newer men who have wives and children, bronze stars, and purple hearts, now have enough points to be able to be among the first to go home. Eighty-five points are needed according to the point system announced. Not too many except the old timers or the young married men with children have the needed points.

The German prisoners could only dream of going home. Many of those held by the Fourth Armored Division would never see their dreams realized. Before the division moved to Landshut, the Americans completed the task of turning over to the Soviets the German prisoners held in their custody since VE Day. On May 14, the 66th Armored Field Artillery Battalion marched their captives to the east of Risek where in accordance with the international agreement, they turned them over to the Russians. Captain Donahue, commander of D/37, handed over 3500 prisoners that day. On May 17, the 53rd Armored Infantry Battalion turned over another 12,000 to the Soviets.

The stroke of a pen in Reims had not been enough to shift from war to peace on every sector of the front. Those killed after the official surrender of Germany are perhaps the most tragic deaths of the war.

On May 9, Lt Boas of the 94th headed off with Sgt. Peter Stackonis and four enlisted men for an afternoon of R&R. They packed a load of sandwiches and hard-boiled eggs into two peeps and departed for the countryside. A "large, beautiful rock" at the center of a gorgeous lake lured them into the water. They swam to the rock and basked in the sunlight like a half-dozen turtles. When all others returned to the water, Sgt. Stackonis remained on the rock in solitude. Suddenly, a shot rang out, striking him in the collar bone. According to the battalion journal, "Two avenging patrols were sent out, one patrol took one prisoner and killed one while the other captured eight Germans."

On May 14, Pfc Oscar Oakman and T/5 Garland J. Bunch were ambushed in the woods by German soldiers. Private Oakman was killed. A patrol from A/94 went out in search of the bastards that killed him. By the time their mission ended, they killed 15 Germans and brought back eight prisoners.

19

The Occupation

The Occupation Zone

Nearly three weeks had elapsed since the end of the war in Europe. Within the borders of Germany, the challenges faced by the victors were monumental. There were few spoils to be had. Their reward was peace and the opportunity to return home.

To the victors went toil. Germany was a wreck. Cities had been leveled. Hundreds of thousands of civilians were displaced, roaming the country in search of family members or familiar faces. Displaced persons from other countries, victims of the Nazi regime, were even more desperate, their plight sometimes manifesting itself in crime and the victimization of German citizens. Hundreds of thousands of others remained prisoners of the Allied armies.

What governance remained was ineffective. As part of the "denazification" process, members of the Nazi party were culled from positions of power. Given that approximately 70 percent of adults were members of the party, it made it difficult to find competent individuals to fill important roles.

The economy was in shambles. Mass starvation was a very real possibility, and the challenge of a population ill-prepared for the hardship of the coming winter was already on many minds.

The war in Europe had drawn to a close, but the same was not true half a world away in the Pacific Theater. The battle for Okinawa raged on while planning for the invasion of Japan was underway. The highest priority for the U.S. forces in Europe was the sharing of resources needed for the defeat of Imperial Japan. All else was secondary.

As Eisenhower noted in his memoirs, the greatest need in the Pacific was for support services. However, in direct conflict with that demand, logistics personnel and assets were the top priority for a successful occupation of Germany. One theater or the other had to receive priority, and it was the Pacific that earned the nod. In anticipation of Germany's defeat, the headquarters responsible for managing the transfer of assets from Europe to the Pacific had been established back on April 9.

In addition to the shift of resources from Europe to the Pacific, there was a demand for experienced talent for the execution of the final stage of the war against Japan. The end of hostilities in Europe freed up many senior leaders. General Spaatz was soon transferred to the Pacific. General Courtney Hodges (U.S. First Army) was transferred before the conflict in Europe had even drawn to a close.

There were needs in other arenas as well. Over a stiff drink of bourbon, Eisenhower broke the news to General Omar Bradley that President Truman had requested he serve as the new leader of the Veterans Administration (Chief of Staff General George Marshall had endorsed his selection). This was devastating news for Bradley. Like Patton, he preferred to

The devastated city of Frankfurt, cut off from the east by the Fourth Armored Division (U.S. Army photograph).

continue in command of combat troops, even if it meant a reduction in responsibility from army group command to that of a single army. However, in the spirit of serving wherever the Commander in Chief felt he added the most value, he accepted the assignment in Washington, D.C.

In Germany, the occupation zones had previously been agreed upon by the leadership of the four key members of the Western Alliance: America, Great Britain, France, and Russia. The Americans were responsible for the region of Bavaria, and Eisenhower (appointed by the U.S. Joint Chiefs of Staff to the role of commander in chief, U.S. forces European Theater) was named head of the military government in the American Zone. Ike subsequently divided responsibility for the American Zone between the U.S. Seventh and Third Armies. The Seventh Army would control the Western Military District, and Third Army the Eastern. Patton's district encompassed 25,000 square miles of German soil, populated by more than seven million Germans and approximately two million displaced persons.

Patton's role changed virtually overnight on May 8. His time as a wartime general in command of a powerful army more than half-a-million men strong was over. He was now an administrator, charged with maintaining order, promoting the physical welfare of the population, and finding a way to help the defeated Germans get back on their feet. He had to achieve this while under strict orders prohibiting fraternization (though those chains would be loosened and later abandoned). Wiping away the vestiges of Nazism (denazification) was also engrained into the mission (a responsibility that would haunt Patton during the months ahead).

General Patton was ill-equipped for the task assigned to him by Eisenhower. He had not the skill set nor the temperament for governing. The same could be said for many (if not most) of the men under his command. His Chief of Staff (Hap Gay) showed no more interest for the task than Patton himself. Rather than embrace his new role with a determination to succeed in his mission, Patton remained hopeful for a role in the Pacific Theater.

In victory, Patton's reputation soared among the citizens of the United States. He basked in the adoration. But not everyone was a fan, and he found critics in the press of the day. The media did him no favors and could be rightfully criticized as being unjust towards him. (The history of the Cold War would prove Patton right on many of the points that reporters and editors vilified him for.)

The Fourth Armored Finds a New Home

Their work done in Czechoslovakia, it was finally time for the Fourth Armored Division to depart for Germany.

On May 27 and 28, the division assembled in columns for the 100-plus mile trip to Landshut, a city bisected by the Isar River. Upon its arrival, the division established its headquarters in the *Schoch Kaserne,* previously a German army barracks. The men of the 704th Tank Destroyer Battalion shared the barracks. Sheltered five or six men to a room, it was the first time in over four months that the entire battalion assembled in one place. "We will doubtless remain as a part of the Army of Occupation. Some of us hope to go home soon."

The 10th Armored Infantry Battalion departed Czechoslovakia on the morning of May 28. They bivouacked the following day near Hohenpfahl. The 37th Tank Battalion occupied towns 60 miles to the northwest of Landshut. Billets were established at Neumarkt, Mühlhausen, Pfoffenhofen, and Berngau.

The 53rd Armored Infantry Battalion moved into the towns of Essenbach, Wörth, Ergolding, Altdorf, and Altheim. Sgt. Nick Alexander of A/53 had a fair number of points (85), but not enough to return home with the earliest group of men (he returned to the United States in October). His company was stationed in Wörth.

My platoon lived in a vacant two-story train station. I had a private room and the squad leaders shared rooms that housed the rest of the troops. The other platoons lived in scattered buildings elsewhere in the village. The officers lived in private homes. Our company commander had a big home with a private cook and once hosted a dinner for the non-coms. We ate all of our meals at a mess hall which I think was an abandoned school house. Worth was a sleepy village and did not require much policing.

Despite higher command's prohibition against fraternization, it was difficult to avoid. Alexander continued,

We were not allowed to fraternize with the population although we did use the local barber and had our clothes washed by one of the housefraus. A couple of the Wehrmacht veterans living in the village worked in the mess hall and kitchen for our cooking staff. In spite of the ban on fraternization, some of our guys contacted VD from itinerant German WACS who made a stopover on their journey home.

While there was much work to do, there was also ample time for rest and relaxation. The Fourth Armored certainly deserved it.

(It) was an easy duty of occupation for me as a platoon sergeant. I had a three day pass to Paris in June. We made trips to Regensburg for viewing movies and spending some leisure time there. I attended a course on photography. We had a company softball team that won the battalion championship with me as the pitcher. My pitching was greatly helped by some excellent backup in the field.

The 8th Tank Battalion established its headquarters near Vilsbiburg, 10 miles southeast of Landshut. Lt. Colonel Irzyk faced the same challenge as his peers in the other battalions. In his case, he was given the responsibility of being the Commandant of *Kreis* (county) Vilsbiburg. Among his first acts was the conduct of reconnaissance by his company commanders. The territory was unknown to them, and the need was great to quickly size up the state of civilian affairs. Irzyk's company commanders returned with bad news: there was no functioning government. Hand in hand with that, no police force existed nor any form of services. Roads were in disrepair and communications were non-existent.

While Irzyk was confident in his men and officers, he recognized they had no experience dealing with what was now asked of them. What he quickly discovered, however, was that within the ranks of almost a thousand citizen soldiers there resided plumbers, electricians, carpenters… many of the skills needed to help get the German communities back on their feet.

With the help of the Americans, the Germans started to demonstrate the industriousness their culture was famous for. Having sacrificed their most virile citizens to the war effort, few young men remained in the town, but the elders soon picked themselves up and brought forward their own talents. It wasn't long before the Americans were viewed less as the enemy and more as an ally in helping to reconstruct their battered communities.

Finding a Purpose

On June 1, not long after the Fourth Armored assumed their new responsibilities, General Patton issued a directive to his command regarding items of personal concern to him. A highlight of his order included the need to maintain military discipline and to respect the assets of the U.S. government. He also emphasized the maintenance of superior military appearance. He bemoaned his soldiers who "wander about like furtive pickpockets with your shoulders slipping, your stomachs sticking out, and your heads hanging down…. Show the world how great you are. Look like soldiers!" He also wanted military maneuvers and training to continue, up to and including the battalion level. And lastly, he wanted all units to embrace the conduct of ceremonies, believing they created a favorable impression upon the defeated Germans as well as America's allies.

While he closed the letter of instruction with a warning that he would personally inspect all the above points, Patton left almost immediately for the United States on a tour to help sell war bonds. Before his departure, he showed no interest in the task of raising funds. His main goal remained the attainment of a combat assignment in the Pacific.

The welcome that General Patton received upon his return to the United States was of a magnitude that he didn't anticipate. An estimated one million people greeted him as he motored through the streets of Boston. When the bond tour reached the Pacific coast, 100,000 people came to hear him speak at the Los Angeles Coliseum.

Unfortunately, Patton's month-long visit to the U.S. was marred by an unfortunate comment he made while addressing a crowd of 20,000 in Boston. During his remarks, Patton suggested that some of the veterans who died in the war were fools because of the manner in which they met their end … and that the real heroes were just like the 400 wounded veterans of the Third Army sitting in a reserved section at the front of the audience, slightly to Patton's left of center and in the shadow of the microphone-adorned podium. His comments were ill-worded, but any fair-minded observer would readily understand what he meant to say, even if uttered so clumsily. Most people did not assign a negative or hurtful intent to his comment. Some who found it offensive forgave him his transgression once he clarified his statement. Only those predisposed to stand against him would fail to embrace his interpretation and explanation after the fact. But those people … especially in the media … were out there. And unfortunately for Patton, the strength of their voice was out of proportion to their number. The segment of the media that had a history of granting Patton little respect seized upon the opportunity to exploit his comments.

Two weeks after General Patton's instructions for how his troops should conduct themselves, the Fourth Armored held a ceremony that only one other division in the United States Army would have been able to duplicate. On June 14, under the bright sunlight of a waning spring, General Jacob Devers (commander of the 6th Army Group) delivered the Presidential Distinguished Unit Citation. All units of the division were assembled for the occasion on a large, open field. A platoon of M4A3E8 tanks, perfectly aligned and presented, were parked before the reviewing stand. After the citation was read aloud to the troops, they watched proudly as General Devers tied the blue streamer of the citation to the lowered staff flying the division colors. He saluted the flag and then stepped to the microphone to address the division. Devers acknowledged that he had no words that would adequately build upon the citation itself. "Each of you knows what he did."

Three days later, having drawn an assignment in the Pacific, Major General Hoge left the division. For a brief period (June 20 through July 15) Brigadier General Bruce Clarke returned to command the division before he too was called for duty in the Pacific. Brigadier General Roberts then took command of the Fourth for the next two months.

While Patton was preoccupied on other fronts, much of the heavy lifting was being done on the initiative of the lower levels of command. Men such as Lt. Colonel Irzyk succeeded despite the lack of focus from the commander of the Eastern Division.

Patton's interest remained in the Pacific, and his frustration over bring trapped in Europe was expressed in a letter to his wife on July 7:

> I am still confused as to just what one has to do. I have five corps and some 30 divisions. I will know more in a day or two. I love and miss you.

On July 14, believing that adequate progress had been made in denazification, Eisenhower relaxed the ban on fraternization, thus aiding the effort of those seeking collaboration with the population. Better communication led to better relationships and better results. Also this day (and perhaps this facilitated his decision regarding fraternization), SHAEF ceased to exist and Eisenhower's command was limited to that of American forces.

An area of emphasis became the condition of German youth. Organizations were formed under the supervision of the military government at the *Kreis* level. Youth in the range of 10 to 18 years of age were permitted to form international branches of organizations such as the Boy Scouts, Young Men's Christian Association (YMCA), and their equivalents for girls (though any activity approaching paramilitary training was prohibited). Within one year of implementation, approximately 481,000 youth out of an estimated 2.1 million participated in the various programs.

From Teacher to Student

On August 9, Lt. Colonel Irzyk was granted a unique opportunity. Along with a tank platoon leader and tank company commander, he was invited to meet with General Patton to discuss the conduct of armored operations. The trio departed the following morning by peep for Third Army HQ at Bad Tölz. After being greeted by Patton's Chief of Staff (Hap Gay), they were ushered into a briefing room where sat several staff officers, apparently there to observe the session. Al and his two companions were seated in folding chairs in front of a long wooden table that took up much of the width of the room.

The three warriors were seated for only a minute or two before General Patton strode through a door directly behind the table. In one hand was a leash attached to Willie, his frequent canine companion. In the other hand, he clutched a tablet of paper and two pencils. All rose upon his entrance, and Patton quickly told them to be seated. Al was struck by how Patton appeared to have aged since he last saw him at the village of Domnom-lès-Dieuze, shortly before the Battle of the Bulge. Al took note of Patton's "crooked smile" and the heaving of his chest as he drew his breaths.

Patton wasted no time after taking his place at the table. His questions focused on the strategy and tactics utilized at the levels of command represented at the table. How was a platoon of five tanks best employed? How did a company commander fight his three platoons? How did Lt. Colonel Irzyk lead his battalion? The discussion ranged from the smallest tactical considerations to the broader elements of strategy and logistics. Patton took steady notes as the tankers shared their experiences and opinions for the next two-and-a-half hours. Irzyk noted that throughout the session, Patton was studious, almost academic. The braggadocios elements of his personality were nowhere to be seen. Being a student of military history was one of Patton's higher qualities, and he was firmly planted in that persona as he capitalized on the experience of the seasoned veterans assembled before him.

The Dwindling Ranks—and Patton's Final Days

As the occupation period progressed, the composition of the division changed dramatically. Given the veteran status of the Fourth Armored, many within the division's ranks

Some of the first returnees to the United States from the 37th Tank Battalion. Captain William Dwight is at lower right (author's collection).

were among the first to earn a ticket home to the United States. One third of the members of the division were immediately eligible and soon departed.

1st Sgt. John Harris (22nd Armored Field Artillery Battalion) had 106 points. He was the first to leave his unit, departing on May 21. He boarded a C-47 transport plane destined for France. He was trucked to Le Havre, where he waited at Camp Twenty Grand for a Liberty Ship that would take him and his fellow high-pointers home.

> Finally we were at sea and for those with money were gambling (mostly Craps). I remember one Sergeant who had a bundle of money and had about $5000 bet it all. Finally it was covered by several soldiers. The dice were rolled and he made his number. He collected his winnings and never played again.

Upon his arrival in Boston, Harris was shipped to Camp Myles Standish for processing. He had departed for the European Theater through the same camp on December 29, 1943. Now he was back and enjoyed the overwhelming adoration of the American public. On June 16, he arrived at his final destination. Home!

In mid–July, Lt. Colonel Irzyk learned that 229 of his men had earned enough points to return to the United States. On July 16, he gave them a send-off at a battalion review near Vilsbiburg. According to the division's own history, "By October, more than 14,000 men, a total higher than the division's strength, had been redeployed." The thousands of G.I.s crammed into troop ships heading west across the Atlantic were of much different mind and character than when they sailed east. They were forever changed. The departure of so

Final assembly of the 8th Tank Battalion (author's collection).

many created mixed emotions among those who remained behind as well as those who left for home.

Like his peers in the other battalions, Irzyk was faced with the challenge of rebuilding his unit in the face of the departures. But in early August, Irzyk's own fate and focus changed when he was reassigned to the position of division G-1. After several weeks in that role, he moved yet again, this time to the G-3 slot.

On September 7, Major General Fay Brink Prickett was assigned as the division commander. During the months to come, he would lead the Fourth in their assigned Occupation Zone, which soon expanded from eight to 32 counties. (Lt. Colonel Irzyk became Prickett's Chief of Staff.) On November 11, the division command post moved to the city of Regensburg, nestled along the famous Danube River. The division controlled 7,500 square miles of Germany.

Many enlisted men and officers had departed. But General Patton was among those who remained. Unlike Lt. Colonel Irzyk, increased responsibility was not on the horizon for the commander of the Third Army. And with the war in the Pacific drawing to a close, opportunities were evaporating quickly. Patton had already suffered through the departure of several of his peers for the Pacific Theater. And now, even the remaining opportunities in the United States were being taken by others.

In mid–August, General Gerow was appointed Commandant of the Army War College. It was a position that Patton would have declined if choosing between that and service in the Pacific. But Japan had surrendered on August 15, and that possibility was now forever gone. Given the choice between the War College and his current duties, he would have surely embraced the former. In his diary, he sulked about Gerow's mediocrity, and how this development left nothing else available to him.

His options exhausted, Patton focused more attention on matters of governance. He had a genuine concern about the coming winter and the impact the harsh conditions would have on the general population and displaced persons. Unfortunately, his renewed focus also lent itself to increased chatter relating to denazification. He increased his advocacy for tapping into the human potential of those previously aligned with the Nazi party. He recognized their favorable virtues at the expense of being either politically incorrect or in outright conflict with the directives under which he was to operate.

Combined with his knack for ill-worded commentary, Patton found himself in deeper water as a subordinate. An episode that haunted him centered on an analogy he employed when comparing the Nazi party to any other political party or apparatus. The gaffe occurred when he used the American Democrat and Republican parties to make his point. Certain elements of the press circled and attacked like sharks to chum.

On September 22, following the normal Sunday morning briefing conducted by the Third Army press officer, Patton entertained questions from 11 correspondents in attendance. The hour-long affair did not go well. Several of the reporters baited Patton on the topic of denazification. Their line of questions brought out his temper.

The slanted reporting that followed signaled the final curtain for Patton's current role in Europe. Exactly one week later, he was relieved of command of the United States Third Army and appointed commander of the U.S. Fifteenth Army, a largely paper organization responsible for studying the European campaigns and recording the lessons learned. On October 7, he gave his farewell address to the assembled officers and men of TUSA.

Toward the end of November, it was Eisenhower's turn to depart. He was pegged to replace Marshall as Chief of Staff (a position he assumed officially on December 3). When General Eisenhower relinquished his command, he issued a message to all members of the Allied Expeditionary Force. His closing statement summed up the spirit of what every soldier wished for their brothers in arms:

> Now that you are about to pass to other spheres of activity, I say good-bye to you and wish you good luck and God-speed.

General Patton pressed on with the mission of the Fifteenth Army. There was an element of the job that appealed to him, even though it was far from his first choice of assignments.

On December 9, the day before he was scheduled to depart for the United States, General Patton set out with Hap Gay on a pheasant hunting excursion. As is well known, an accident occurred when a military truck turned in front of his limousine. Though both vehicles were traveling at low speeds, Patton suffered a devastating injury, rendering him paralyzed below the neck.

During the days that followed, there were some encouraging signs as he regained some feeling and function in various parts of his body. From the time of his accident, he had not lost his ability to speak and was, indeed, very communicative. But after a week of promise, his condition deteriorated. He passed away on December 21, 1945.

One could not have imagined on that same date in 1944, during the height of the Battle of the Bulge, how much would have changed just one year later. On December 23, the Fourth Armored Division provided several members of the honor guard at General Patton's burial at the Hamm Cemetery in Luxembourg.

The United States Constabulary

In response to the changing realities within the American Zone, another organizational design was considered for policing the occupied territory. The *United States Constabulary* was formed. The anticipated force of 38,000 would be an elite organization, created from superior units that could bring a high level of leadership, competence, and morale to the assignment. On January 10, 1946, Major General Ernest Harmon was appointed the commander of the new organization.

Given the desired qualities, it is no surprise that the Fourth Armored Division was called upon. The consequence, however, would be the deactivation of the division. Its component units were reorganized and assigned new titles. Division HQ became the 1st Constabulary Brigade Headquarters. CCA and CCB became the 2nd and 3rd Constabulary Brigade Headquarters, respectively.

The various battalions were reformed into constabulary squadrons and assigned to new areas within the American Zone of Occupation. The TO&E for the cavalry reconnaissance squadron would be employed as the design for the constabulary squadron. Thus, the division turned in its heavy equipment. Tanks, halftracks, self-propelled howitzers … almost everything was exchanged for lighter vehicles with which to conduct the work of the constabulary. New uniforms were issued, characterized by a golden-yellow scarf and a shoulder patch unit insignia that incorporated the colors of the cavalry, infantry, and artillery.

The transition took time. In February, the constabulary headquarters was established in Bamberg. For the constabulary to perform at a high level, specialized training was required, and so a constabulary school was established at Sonthofen. Officers were immersed in a curriculum that included the theory and practice of criminal investigation, the apprehension of wanted persons, self-defense, and the maintenance of police records. After March, 650 students per month attended the school. The newly trained officers then returned to their units and began training their Troopers (as they were known).

By May 15, 1946, the reorganization was complete. The units of the Fourth Armored Division were re-designated. On July 1, the constabulary became operational. The history of the Fourth Armored Division … vanguard of Patton's Third Army and the most accomplished armored division in the history of the United States of America … had drawn to a close.

Legacy

In the hearts and minds of those who served, the division lived on. Not long after the war, the Fourth Armored Division Association was formed. Chapters were established across the country, their ranks filled with men who shared the unique bond known only to those who experienced the danger and exhilaration of combat. Many veterans joined the association immediately. Others waited for years or even decades before reconnecting with their brothers in arms.

Many members of the division—especially those in the officer ranks—were professional soldiers long before the division saw combat. Tempered and hardened by the action they saw in Europe, they continued their careers through Korea, Vietnam, and the protection of Western Europe from the Soviet threat. They rose in rank, taking on positions of responsibility even greater than they possessed during World War II. The most famous and highest ascension was made by Creighton Abrams, who became chief of staff of the United States Army in 1972 (Abrams served until his untimely passing on September 4, 1974). Among those who joined Abrams in Vietnam were Al Irzyk, who rose to the rank of brigadier general and commanded the Army's Headquarters Area Command in Saigon (during which time he led the military police force that made the initial response to the TET Offensive) and Jimmie Leach, who became a colonel in command of the 11th Armored Cavalry. There were many other ascensions with service given around the globe.

In pure military terms, the legacy of the Fourth Armored Division lives on in the form of military doctrine. For all the decades that followed, up to and including the present day, the lessons gleaned from the history of the Fourth Armored have been applied extensively by military professionals. Major General John S. Wood's impact on the United States Army far exceeds the degree to which the public is familiar with his name. Many of his disciples carried forward his teachings (most notably, General Abrams, who certainly added his own dose of drive and leadership to the formula). Major General Wood and the men he commanded can be credited with impacting the American use of armor and mechanization in a way that no other combat unit ever achieved.

For most members of the division, their service with the Fourth Armored marked the beginning and the end of their military career. Enough was enough. They had done their duty in magnificent fashion and were eager to move on to the next phase of their lives. They excelled at that as well. Over the next 50 years, along with 16,000,000 fellow Americans who served during World War II, they built the America that we know and cherish today. The veterans of the Fourth Armored contributed at every level of society, from blue collar workers to businessmen. Physicians and educators to government officials and public servants. Entrepreneurs and men of the cloth. They became better educated than any generation before them, and they were arguably more productive, industrious, and ingenious as well. Some struggled, unable to fully cope with the indelible memories of war.

We owe every one of them a debt of gratitude, no matter the path they travelled.

I hope this work helps keep alive the memory of the division and the individuals who selflessly served in support of not only their country, but also the oppressed peoples of Europe. Let us remember their actions and accomplishments. Their sacrifices and valor. Let us always know them…

By their deeds alone.

Bibliography

Books

Allen, Robert S. *Forward with Patton: The World War II Diary of Colonel Robert S. Allen*. Edited by John Nelson Rickard. Lexington: University Press of Kentucky, 2017.

Atkinson, Rick. *The Guns at Last Light: The War in Western Europe. 1944–1945*. New York: Henry Holt & Co., 2013.

Baldwin, Hanson W. *Tiger Jack*. Ft. Collins, CO: The Old Army Press, 1979.

Baron, Richard; Baum, Abraham; Goldhurst, Richard. *Raid! The Untold Story of Patton's Secret Mission*. New York: Dell Publishing Co., 1981.

Belpulsi, Peter A. *A GI's View of World War II*. Salem, MO: Globe Publishers, 1997.

Blumenson, Martin. *Patton: The Man Behind the Legend, 1885–1945*. New York: Quill-William Morrow, 1985.

Blumenson, Martin. *The Patton Papers 1940–1945*. New York: Houghton Mifflin, 1974.

Boas, Roger. *Battle Rattle: A Last Memoir of WWII*. Kindle edition: Stinson Publishing, 2015.

Bradley, Omar N. *A Soldier's Story*. New York: Henry Holt & Co., 1951.

Bradley, Omar N., and Clay Blair. *A General's Life*. New York: Simon & Schuster, 1983.

Buchanan, Richard R. *Men Of The 704th: A Pictorial and Spoken History of the 704th Tank Destroyer Battalion in World War II*. Latrobe, PA: Publications of the Saint Vincent College Center for Northern Appalachian Studies, 1998.

Clinger, Fred, et al. *The History of the 71st Infantry Division*. United States Army, 1946.

Cole, Hugh M. *The Ardennes: Battle of the Bulge: United States Army in World War II: The European Theater of Operations*. Washington, D.C.: Office of the Chief of Military History, 1965.

Cosmas, Graham A., and Albert E. Cowdrey. *Medical Service in the European Theater of Operations*. Washington, D.C.: Center for Military History, United States Army, 1992.

Dando-Collins, Stephen. *The Big Break*. New York: St. Martin's Press, 2017.

D'Este, Carlo. *Patton: A Genius for War*. New York: HarperCollins, 1995.

D'Este, Carlo. *Eisenhower: A Soldier's Life*. New York: Henry Holt & Co., 2002.

Diczbalis, Sigismund. *The Russian Patriot*. Great Britain: The History Press, 2008.

Dyer, George, Lt. Col. *XII Corps, Spearhead of Patton's Third Army*. London: Arcole Publishing, 2017 (originally published 1947).

Eisenhower, Dwight D. *Crusade in Europe*. Garden City, NY: Doubleday, 1948. 2000.

Fifth Division Historical Section. *The Fifth Infantry Division in the ETO*. Nashville, TN. Reprint by Battery Press, 1997 (originally published in 1945).

Forty, George. *Patton's Third Army at War*. Havertown, PA: Casemate Publishers, 2015.

Forty, George. *The Armies of George S. Patton*. London: Arms & Armour Press, 1996.

Fox, Don M. *Patton's Vanguard: The United States Army Fourth Armored Division*. Jefferson, NC: McFarland, 2003.

Ganz, A. Harding. *Ghost Division: The 11th "Gespenster" Panzer Division and the German Armored Force in World War II*. Mechanicsburg, PA: Stackpole Books, 2016.

German Army Publishers. *2nd Panzer Division, 1935–1945*. 1998.

Gilbert, Martin. *The Second World War*. New York: Henry Holt & Co., 1989.

Hirshson, Stanley P. *General Patton: A Soldier's Life*. New York: HarperCollins, 2002.

Hynes, Samuel, et al. *Reporting World War II: American Journalism 1938–1946*. New York: The Library of America, 1995.

Irzyk, Albin F. *He Rode Up Front for Patton*. Raleigh, NC: Pentland Press, 1996.

Irzyk, Albin F. *Patton's Juggernaut: The Rolling 8-Ball*. Oakland, OR: Elderberry Press, 2017.

Irzyk, Albin F. *A Warrior's Quilt of Personal Military History*. Raleigh, NC: Ivy House Publishing Group, 2010.

Irzyk, Albin F., et al. *The Legacy of the 4th Armored Division* Paducah, KY: Turner Publishing Co., 1990.

Jones, Michael. *After Hitler: The Last Ten Days of World War II in Europe*. New York: Penguin Random House, 2015.

Kershaw, Alex. *The Longest Winter*. Cambridge, MA: Da Capo Press, 2004.

Koyen, Kenneth. *The Fourth Armored Division: From the Beach to Bavaria*. Munich, Germany, 1946.

Lande, D.A. *I Was with Patton: First-Person Accounts*

of WWII in George S. Patton's Command. St. Paul, MN: MBI Publishing Co., 2002.
Le Tissier, Tony. *Patton's Pawns: The 94th US Infantry Division at the Siegfried Line*. Tuscaloosa: University of Alabama Press, 2007.
Lee, Ulysses. *United States Army in World War II: Special Studies: The Employment of Negro Troops*. Washington, D.C.: Center of Military History, United States Army, 1963.
Liddell Hart, Basil Henry, Sir. *History of the Second World War*. New York: Putnam, 1971.
Lyons, Stanley. *Pass in Review*, (n.p.) 1996.
MacDonogh, Giles. *After the Reich: The Brutal History of the Allied Occupation*. New York: Basic Book, 2007.
McDonald, Charles B. *The Last Offensive*. Washington, D.C.: Center of Military History, 1973.
McManus, John C. *Hell Before Their Very Eyes*. Baltimore, MD: John Hopkins University Press, 2015.
Neely, Darren. *Forgotten Archives 1: The Lost Signal Corps Photos*. United Kingdom: Panzerwrecks, 2015.
Neely, Darren. *Forgotten Archives 2: The Lost Signal Corps Photos*. United Kingdom: Panzerwrecks, 2017.
Patton, George S. *War As I Knew It*. New York: Houghton Mifflin, 1947.
Phillips, Henry Gerard. *The Making of a Professional: Manton S. Eddy, USA*. Westport, CT: Greenwood Press, 2000.
Prefer, Nathan N. *Patton's Ghost Corps*. New York: Presidio Press, 1998.
Province, Charles M. *Patton's Third Army: A Chronology of the Third Army Advance, August 1944 to May 1945*. New York: Hippocrene Books, 1992.
Reagan, Bruce W., and Jack N. Duffy. *An Odyssey with Patton: A Revised History of the 150th Engineer (Combat) Battalion, XII Corps, Third Army, Europe, 1944-1945*. Bennington, VT: Merriam Press, 4th ed., 2007.
Rusiecki, Stephen M. *In Final Defense of the Reich: The Destruction of the 6th SS Mountain Division "Nord."* Annapolis, MD: Naval Institute Press, 2011.
Schillare, Quentin W., Major. *Battle of Aschaffenburg: An Example of Late World War II Urban Combat in Europe*. Pickle Partners Publishing, 2014 (Kindle edition).
Shapiro, Milton J. *Tank Command: General George S. Patton's 4th Armored Division*. New York: David McKay Co., 1979.
Shirer, William L. *The Rise and Fall of the Third Reich*. New York: Simon & Schuster, 1959.
Sorley, Lewis. *Thunderbolt: From the Battle of the Bulge to Vietnam and Beyond: General Creighton Abrams and the Army of His Times*. New York: Simon & Schuster, 1992.
Steenberg, Sven. *Vlasov*. New York: Alfred A. Knopf, 1970.
Toland, John. *The Last 100 Days: The Story of the Bulge*. New York: Random House, 1965, 1966.
Weigley, Russell F. *Eisenhower's Lieutenants: The Campaign of France and Germany 1944-1945*. Bloomington: Indiana University Press, 1981.
Whiting, Charles. *48 Hours to Hammelburg*. New York: Berkley Publishing Group, 1970.
Yeide, Harry. *Fighting Patton: George S. Patton Through the Eyes of His Enemies* Minneapolis, MN: Zenith Press, 2011.
Ziemke, Earl F. *The U.S. Army in the Occupation of Germany 1944-1946*. Washington, D.C.: Center of Military History, United States Army, 1975.

Papers, Reports and Articles

"Col. Cohen Gave Nazis Unwanted Lessons." *Spartanburg Herald-Journal*, Oct. 28, 1945.
Irzyk, Albin F., Brig. Gen. U.S. Army (ret.). *Genesis to Greatness 1940-1945*. Fourth Armored Division Association, 1982.
Irzyk, Albin F., Brig. Gen. U.S. Army (ret.). "Lt. Gen. George S. Patton—Maj. Gen. John S. Wood." (n.p.) 2001.
Irzyk, Albin F., Brig. Gen. U.S. Army (ret.). "Tank vs. Tank." *Military Review*, January 1946.
Irzyk, Albin F., Brig. Gen. U.S. Army (ret.). "The 'Name Enough' Division." *Armor Magazine*, July-August 1987.
"Memoir of a Tank Killer." *Purple Heart Magazine*, May/June 1997. Assorted recollections from members of the 704th TD Battalion.
Ozark Replay: POW experiences of Jay Drake, 2nd Lieut, 379 FA Btn. Jay Drake (n.p.) undated.
Whitaker, Richard. "Task Force Baum and the Hammelburg Raid." *Armor Magazine*, Sept.-Oct. 1996.

Combat Histories, After Action Reports and Interviews

After Action Report by Colonel Hoppe—German report on action at Hammelburg.
After Action Report 51st Armored Infantry Battalion—July 1944 Through May 1945 (n.p., n.a.).
After Action Report 53rd Armored Infantry Battalion—July 1944 Through May 1945 (n.p., n.a.).
After Action Report for Unit Citation—Bastogne. 51st Armored Infantry Battalion, Dec. 19, 1944-Jan. 10, 1945 (n.a.).
After Action Report 704th TK DES Battalion—July Through Nov 44, Jan Through Mar 45, May 45.
After Action Report 66th Armored F.A. Battalion—July 1944 Through April 1945.
After Action Report 22nd Armored Field Artillery Battalion—July 1944-May 1945 (n.p., n.a.).
Armored Special Equipment—The General Board, United States Forces, European Theater. Study Number 52 (n.d.)
Battalion Diary: 37th Tank Battalion, 4th Armored Division. By "Unknown Soldier," U.S. Army Command and General Staff College, Fort Leavenworth, KS.
Battalion S-3 Journal—35th Tank Battalion: January-May 1945.
Bautz, Edward. Rutgers College Class of 1941, Oral History, October 15, 1999.
Citation for DSC: Captain Abraham J. Baum, 10th AIB.
Citation for DSC: Lt. Col. Harold Cohen, 10th AIB.

Combat Diary of the 704th TD Company C—Walter E. Mullen and Norman E. Macomber. Saint Vincent College Center for North Appalachian Studies/ Oral History Program.

Combat Diary of the 10th Armored Infantry Battalion. 1944–1945 (n.p., n.a.).

Combat History 51st Armored Infantry Battalion. 1944–1945 (n.p., n.a.).

Combat History of the 4th Armored Division. 1944–45. U.S. Army Command and General Staff College. Fort Leavenworth, KS.

Drive Toward Bastogne: 51st Armored Infantry Battalion. Period Dec. 24–31, 1944. Based on interview with Lt. Col. Dan Alanis, CO 51st AIB, and Maj Harry Rockafeller, Ex O, 51st AIB. Interview conducted Feb. 16, 1945.

Events Preceding Entry into Bastogne. Report by Capt. Dwight regarding CCR action on 25 Dec and 26 Dec 45.

Experiencing War: Veterans History Project (Library of Congress). Bruce Donald Fenchel, Personal Narrative. Account by tank driver in 8th Tank Battalion.

The First Year of the Occupation—Occupation Forces in Europe, Series 1945–1946. Office of the Chief Historian, European Command Frankfurt-AM-Main, Germany.

Fourth Armored Division Monthly After-Action Reports—January–May 1945.

Fourth Armored Division Notes on Staff Meeting— May 4, 1945.

Fourth Armored Division Reports on Staff Conferences—May 1945.

FM2-20 Cavalry Reconnaissance Troop Mechanized—War Department, 24 February 1944.

History of the 94th Armored Field Artillery Battalion in The European Theatre of Operations 29 December 1943 to 9 May 1945 (n.a.).

History of the 704th Tank Destroyer Battalion from D Plus 36 to V-E Day.

History of the 318th Infantry Regiment. Compiled by Robert T. Murrell, PNC Company M, 318th Infantry, 80th Infantry Division.

Headquarters Twelfth Army Group APO 655 Immediate Report No. 85. (Combat Observations). Interview with Colonel Toben, XII Corps Ordnance Officer. Oct. 24, 1944 (topic: M4A3E2 Sherman tank)

Headquarters Twelfth Army Group APO 655 Immediate Report No. 85. (Combat Observations). Interview with Colonel Yuill, CO, 11th Infantry Regiment and staff. Oct. 24 1944 (topic: quality of infantry replacements).

Headquarters European Theater of Operations United States Army –APO 887 Immediate Report No. 92 (Combat Observations). Lt. Col. Jarrell, Combat Observer with VII Corps. March 20, 1945. G-2 Report, Apprehension of German Soldiers in Civilian Clothes.

Headquarters European Theater of Operations United States Army—APO 887 Immediate Report No. 119 (Combat Observations). Interview with Colonel W.L. Roberts, Asst. Div Comdr, 4th Armored Div. April 27, 1945. Mission for light tanks and tank destroyers; tank destroyers.

Headquarters European Theater of Operations United States Army—Immediate Report No. 98 (Combat Observations) Colonel B.C. Andrus, Combat Observer with III Corps. Captured document detailing German Sabotage Instruction.

Holdings and Opinion, Board of Review—Volumes 11, 17, 18, 22, 26, 28. Branch Office of the Judge Advocate General, European Theater of Operations, 1946.

Interview with Abraham Baum. Conducted by Gene Santoro, published *WWII Magazine*, April 2013

Interview with Capt. Abraham Baum and Sergeant Graham—HQ 4th Armored Division, April 10, 1945

Interview with Capt. Harold V McCoy, asst S3, 4th Armored Div Arty. Describing artillery support provided by 4th Armored Div Arty, during relief of Bastogne. Interview conducted on Feb. 12, 1945.

Interview with Lt. Colonel (ret.) Len Kieley. Conducted by Don Fox on December 7 and 8, 2019, in Salem, MA.

Interview with Hauptmann Franz Gehig. Conducted by Hanns-Helmut Schnebel

A Memoir: B Company, 37th Tank Battalion, 4th Armored Division. By Francis N. Magliozzi. U.S. Army Command and General Staff College.

Notes on Service Troops—Organization Branch, G-4 Headquarters, 12th Army Group. 18 July 1945.

Operations of Task Force Baum, 4th Armored Division, Between Aschaffenburg and Hammelburg, Germany, 27–28 March 1945.

Reluctant Valor—Oral History of Captain Thomas J. Evans

Thompson, Shelden L., Capt., Advanced Infantry Officers Course, Fort Benning 1948–49.

Correspondence

Letter from Dwight D. Eisenhower to General George Marshall, Aprl 15, 1945. Update on Western Front and Patton's commission of TF Baum.

Letter from Mrs. Helen Gniot to 1st Lt. Earl J. Kelly. Regarding the death of her husband.

Letter from James G. Kelly to Don Fox, July 3, 2001. Regarding Lt. Earl J. Kelly

Letter from Brig. Gen. Hal C. Pattison to Michael R. Peed, October 23, 1977. Regarding the relief of Major General Wood from his command of the Fourth Armored Division.

Letter from Joe Morris to Don Fox, July 9, 2004. Regarding his experiences with the 22nd Armored Field Artillery Battalion (member of C Battery)

Letters from Robert Calvert, Jr., to Don Fox. March 18, 2004 and April 22, 2004. Detailed account of his experiences with C Company, 51st Armored Infantry Battalion.

Letter from Kevin Cook to Bill Rowe—June 3, 2001— Relaying his father's account of his role in TF Baum.

Letter from Bill Mackin to Bill Warthren May 31, 2001 Mackin relaying his experience during TF Baum as 1st Sgt. A/10

Letter from Bob Zawada to Mr. S (unknown) September 27, 1981. Experience on TF Baum.

Email Correspondence

Chaplain Jack Ammon to Don Fox, Dec. 23, 2006. Acknowledging his photograph appearing in *Patton's Vanguard*

Nick Alexander to Don Fox, Dec. 7, 13, 14, and 16, 2004. Recollections from A/53.

Nick Alexander to Don Fox, Sep.14, 2018. Renewal of contact from 2004.

Nick Alexander to Don Fox, Sept. 17, 2018. Recollections from January 45 rest period.

Nick Alexander to Don Fox, Dec. 4, 2018. Views on replacement troops.

Nick Alexander to Don Fox, Dec. 10, 2018. Recollections on occupation period.

Nick Alexander to Don Fox, April 18, 2019. Details regarding the Main River crossing at Großauheim.

Al Irzyk, Jr., to Don Fox, Nov. 23, 2018, Confirming outcome of Lt. Art Irzyk's wounds suffered in combat.

Edward Bautz to Don Fox, Sept. 16, 2002. Comments on the table of organization in respect to assault guns.

Harry Feinberg to Don Fox, multiple emails from June 30, 2001 Through Feb. 2, 2003. Recounting experiences as a tank commander in the assault gun platoon of HQ Company, 37th Tank Battalion.

John Harris to Don Fox, Dec. 11, 2018. Account of his return home at the end of the war.

James Kelly to Don Fox, June 25, 2001. Forwarding information regarding his father, Lt. Earl J. Kelly (10th AIB, A Company).

James Kelly to Don Fox, Dec. 21, 2018. Forwarding information regarding his father, Lt. Earl J. Kelly (10th AIB, C Company).

Milton B. Koshiol to Don Fox, Jan. 9, 2005. Member of A Company, 10th Armored Infantry Battalion.

King Pound to Don Fox, Dec. 17, 2004. Regarding New Year's Eve events.

Captain John Power to Don Fox, April 4, 2002. Regarding taking command of A/35 in early Jan. 45.

Paul H. Stephenson to Don Fox, Jan. 16, 2005. General information on war experience with the 8th Tank Battalion.

Harry Traynor to Erwin Verholen, multiple emails between February 6, 1989 and May 24, 1995. Predominately relating to the battle at the Bannholz Woods.

John Whitehill to Don Fox, April 21, 2001. Regarding addition of extra armor to Shermans after the Bulge, and the receipt of new M4A3E8 tanks.

Instant Messenger Correspondence

John Harris to Don Fox, Aug. 16–18, 2018. Description of and preference for ration types.

John Harris to Don Fox, Dec. 9, 2018. Regarding the point system and return trip from Europe

Internet Sources

Advocates for Harvard ROTC—https://www.advocatesforrotc.org/harvard/SilverStar.pdf Background information on Captain John R. Mabee.

Anthony v. Hunter, 71 F. Supp. 823 (D. Kan. 1947) https://law.justia.com/cases/federal/district-courts/FSupp/71/823/1674744/.

Baum Raid by Eric Nideros https://warfarehistorynetwork.com/daily/wwii/witnessing-pattons-failure-a-prisoners-view-of-the-task-force-baum-raid/.

Buchenwald and Mittlebay-Dora Memorials Foundation—Chronology of the Liberation of Buchenwald—www.buchenwald.de/en/473/.

Combat: A World War II Story of Cav Recon with Patton by Steve Chicoine. https://freedomhistory.com/combat-a-world-war-ii-story-of-cav-recon-with-patton/.

The Hammelburg Affair—Oflag 64 Association http://oflag64.us/the-hammelburg-affair.html.

History of the 94th Infantry Division In World War II—https://archive.org/stream/HistoryOfThe94thInfantryWWII/HistoryOfThe94thInfantryWWII_djvu.txt.

Library of Congress World War II Military Situation Maps. https://www.loc.gov/collections/world-war-ii-maps-military-situation-maps-from-1944-to-1945/?sp=2.

The Mad Russian: The Life and U.S. Army Service of Alexis Ureyvitch Sommaripa by Paul Roberts. Army Historical Foundation. https://armyhistory.org/3978-2/.

94th Infantry Division Historical Society—www.94thinfdiv.com

Peter Domes and Martin Heinlein—Task Force Baum Website—www.taskforcebaum.de.

Warfare History Network—Witnessing Patton's Failure: A Prisoner's View of the Task Force.

Warfare History Network—WWII Concentration Camps: The Horrific Discovery of Buchenwald by Flint Whitlock—https://warfarehistorynetwork.com/daily/wwii/wwii-concentration-camps-the-horrific-discovery-at-buchenwald/.

WWII Courts Martial Cases: ETO Review Board Documents. http://www.paperlessarchives.com/wwii-courts-martial-documents.html.

WWII Military Hospitals—European Theatre of Operations. https://www.med-dept.com/articles/ww2-military-hospitals-european-theater-of-operations/.

Military Unit Index

American

I Armored Corps 11
First Army 3, 7, 14, 19, 22-3, 28-9, 49, 50, 56-7, 61, 64-5, 93, 115, 149, 225, 232, 284
1st Constabulary Brigade Headquarters 293
2nd Armored Division 11, 19
2nd Cavalry Group 20, 51, 53
2nd Constabulary Brigade Headquarters 293
2nd Infantry Regiment 90, 129
2nd Mobile Radio Broadcasting Company 103
Third Army 1-3, 7-9, 11, 14-5, 20, 22-3, 25, 28-9, 39, 49, 50, 56, 64-5, 69, 74, 78, 96, 107, 115, 119, 127, 133, 136, 138, 149, 155-7, 161, 180, 183, 203, 211, 214, 218, 221, 223, 225, 232, 237, 251-2, 266, 269, 279, 286, 288-9, 291-3, 295-6
3rd Cavalry Group 53
3rd Constabulary Brigade Headquarters 293
III Corps 11, 53, 58, 60-1
4th Infantry Division 3, 27, 49
5th Infantry Division 25, 30, 49, 50, 56-61, 63, 79, 90-1, 93-7, 99, 129, 131, 133, 141, 156-9, 161-3, 239
5th Ranger Battalion 36, 47
6th Armored Division 14-6, 18, 53, 254-5
6th Army Group 5, 28, 138, 218, 288,
6th Cavalry Group 53, 58
Seventh Army 2, 127, 138, 173, 177, 203, 211, 286
VII Corps 78, 200, 297
7th Engineer Battalion 95
8th Armored Division 38-40
VIII Corps 11, 12, 14, 18-9, 53, 63, 240, 258, 266
8th Tank Battalion 3, 11-2, 15, 19, 25-8, 31, 51, 66-70, 75-9, 81, 88, 90-1, 98-9, 107, 113, 117-9, 127, 130, 136-7, 139-40, 144-6, 154-6, 162-3, 166-8, 175, 201, 218, 225-6, 230, 233, 235, 241-2, 244-6, 249, 252-3, 256, 259, 263, 287, 291, 297-8
9th Armored Division 109-10, 161
Ninth Army 53, 64, 218
10th Armored Division 64, 78, 133, 138
10th Armored Infantry Battalion 11-2, 14-9, 25, 27, 31, 51-6, 61, 64, 66-77, 79-81, 87-8, 92, 96-7, 99, 101, 105-6, 110, 112, 116, 124-6, 130, 132-6, 139, 142-4, 149-52, 154, 162-3, 165, 170-2, 176-7, 180, 182-6, 195, 198-9, 210, 213, 217, 221, 225, 229, 232, 240, 243, 249, 253-5, 257-8, 261-5, 272, 274, 276, 278, 280-2, 286, 296-9
10th Infantry Regiment 49, 56
11th Armored Cavalry 294
11th Armored Division 19, 53, 110, 133, 157, 252,
11th Infantry Regiment 59, 90, 93, 95, 116, 124, 140-1, 159, 297
12th Army Group 1, 5, 7, 18-9, 23, 49, 53, 56, 96, 115, 127, 138, 149, 172, 218, 258, 268, 297
XII Corps 2, 20, 25, 29, 31, 49-51, 53, 57, 60, 63, 65, 78, 90, 93, 127, 130, 156, 173, 178, 181, 226, 237, 268, 295-7
14th Armored Division 211
Fifteenth Army 292
16th Field Hospital 237-8
17th Airborne Division 14, 53
XIX Tactical Air Command 10, 28, 64, 78, 90, 133, 135-6, 142-3, 161, 172
XX Corps 20, 23, 26, 34-5, 53, 64, 252, 258
22nd Armored Field Artillery Battalion 11-2, 18, 20, 22, 26-7, 51, 57-8, 60, 63, 81, 83-7, 96, 100-1, 118, 130, 134, 142-3, 163, 167, 184, 217, 219, 240, 248, 253-4, 290, 296-7
XXIII Corps 161
24th Armored Engineer Battalion 12, 15-6, 18, 27, 59, 66, 96, 98, 130, 149, 232-3, 235, 253, 257
25th Cavalry Reconnaissance Squadron 16, 19-20, 27, 74, 80-1, 87, 91, 96-8, 100, 112, 118, 120, 131-2, 142-3, 153-4, 161, 163-4, 176, 221, 235, 251, 253, 262, 272-3,
26th Infantry Division 175, 177, 186, 215, 217-8, 270,
34th Evacuation Hospital 211-2
35th Armored Regiment 27
35th Infantry Division 11-2, 15, 207
35th Tank Battalion 3, 9, 11-2, 16, 27, 31, 56, 60, 63, 107, 113, 116, 120-1, 123-4, 127, 130, 141, 150-1, 153, 154, 157, 172, 175, 186, 217, 219-20, 228-9, 231, 233-4, 236, 241, 251, 253, 262, 266, 280, 282, 296, 298
37th Tank Battalion 11-2, 14-5, 18-9, 27, 31, 61, 78-9, 81-7, 90-2, 95-7, 99-100, 103-5, 110, 112-3, 116, 124-6, 130, 132-3, 135-6, 139, 142-4, 149-52, 163, 165, 170-72, 177, 180, 182-4, 186, 188, 207, 217, 220, 225, 232, 243, 249, 253-8, 261-4, 268, 271-2, 274-7, 280, 282, 286, 290, 296-8
45th Infantry Division 208
46th Armored Medical Battalion 27, 96, 224, 253,
51st Armored Infantry Battalion 9-10, 12, 15, 19, 23, 27, 51, 53-4, 56, 58-60, 62-4, 66, 68, 70-1, 73, 75, 77-8, 81-7, 107, 116, 120-4, 127, 130, 137, 141, 150-1, 153, 157, 172, 175, 186, 217, 219-20, 227-9, 231-4, 236, 241, 249, 251, 256, 259-60, 296-7
53rd Armored Infantry Battalion 12, 15, 17-20, 24-5, 27, 51, 54, 56, 58-61, 63-4, 66-70, 72, 78-9, 81, 85, 88-91, 98, 101, 107, 113, 115, 118-9, 124, 127, 130, 136-

7, 139, 144, 154-6, 163, 167-9, 175, 215, 222, 235, 241, 244-5, 249, 251, 253, 262, 276, 282, 286-7, 296, 298
65th Infantry Division 240
66th Armored Field Artillery Battalion 12, 16, 20, 27, 56-61, 63-4, 83, 87, 96, 97, 100, 105, 112, 120, 123, 127, 130, 139, 143, 150-1, 157-8, 184, 217, 233, 240, 260, 280, 282, 296
66th Infantry Division 32
71st Infantry Division 239, 295
76th Infantry Division 53, 57, 90, 93, 266
80th Cavalry Reconnaissance Troop 60
80th Infantry Division 27, 51, 54, 56-64, 66, 68, 78, 88, 90, 93, 165, 251, 253, 255, 263, 297
82nd Airborne Division 103
87th Infantry Division 14, 25, 53, 127
90th Infantry Division 27, 34, 53, 78, 129-30, 132-3, 151, 157, 271
94th Armored Field Artillery Battalion 12, 20, 27, 66, 68, 71-2, 79, 89-90, 98, 101, 106-7, 130, 136, 144, 146, 162, 166-7, 226, 230, 234-5, 242-3, 253, 255, 263, 266, 282-3, 296-8
94th Infantry Division 32-47, 53, 91, 223-4, 298
94th Intelligence and Reconnaissance Platoon 43
99th Infantry Division I & R Platoon 174
100th Infantry Division 264
101st Airborne Division 3, 9, 12, 15-6, 188, 230
106th Evacuation Hospital 237-8
106th Infantry Division 174
126th Armored Ordnance Battalion 12-3, 24, 27, 31, 92, 96
136th Quartermaster Truck Company 237-8
150th Engineer Battalion 80, 161, 296
177th Field Artillery Battalion 253
177th Field Artillery Group 271
179th Field Artillery Battalion 84, 146, 271
191st Field Artillery Battalion 184, 217
204th Engineer Battalion 159
255th Field Artillery Battalion 20, 27, 51
276th Armored Field Artillery Battalion 79, 120, 146, 271
301st Infantry Regiment 36, 42
305th Engineer Battalion 59
318th Infantry Regiment 54, 58-60, 165, 297
319th Infantry Regiment 51, 56, 58, 60, 63, 66, 68, 70, 77, 263
328th Infantry Regiment 215
376th Infantry Regiment 39, 45
417th Infantry Regiment 57
452nd Anti-Aircraft Battalion 136, 156
489th Anti-Aircraft Artillery Battalion 12, 136, 156, 235,
620th Ordnance Company 237, 239
704th Tank Destroyer Battalion 12, 15-6, 18, 27, 32-3, 35-38, 40-48, 64, 66, 71, 83, 85, 91, 96, 101, 112, 118, 124, 130-1, 142-3, 150-1, 153-4, 157, 163, 221-2, 176, 225, 227, 232-5, 240, 245, 247-8, 249, 251-3, 256, 258, 261-3, 266, 268, 271-2, 279-80, 282, 286, 295-7
974th Field Artillery 79
995th Engineer Treadway Bridge Company 66
CCA/4 9-12, 14-16, 18-20, 27, 32, 56, 64, 73, 79-81, 85, 88-90, 93, 98-9, 101-2, 106-9, 113-8, 127, 130-1, 133, 136-40, 144-5, 154-7, 161-6, 169-70, 172, 175-7, 186, 215, 217-21, 224-7, 229-35, 237, 240-1, 243, 249, 251-3, 256, 259-60, 263, 271, 273, 280, 293
CCA/6 14
CCA/8 38-9
CCB/2 11
CCB/4 11-2, 15-8, 20, 27, 32, 51, 56, 60-3, 64, 66-8, 75, 78-9, 81-93, 96-101, 103-10, 112-3, 115-6, 118, 120-4, 127, 130-44, 149-57, 161, 163, 165-6, 169-72, 175-7, 180, 182-3, 186, 201, 215, 217, 219-20, 224, 226-9, 231-7, 240-1, 243, 249, 253-4, 256-7, 259, 261-2, 271-2, 276, 278, 280, 293
CCB/9 161
CCB/14 211
CCR/4 11, 15, 20, 27, 32, 81, 107-8, 115-6, 118, 124-5, 130, 133, 137, 140-1, 150, 157, 161, 166, 172, 175, 186, 217, 220, 224, 229, 232, 240, 243-4, 249, 251, 253, 262-3, 271, 276, 297
SHAEF 5-8, 18, 20, 28, 56, 64, 78, 127, 218, 266, 272, 289
Task Force Alanis 12
Task Force Baum 178-211, 217, 225, 230, 232, 243, 296-8,
Task Force Ezell 3, 138
Task Force Irzyk 156
Task Force Jaques 156
Task Force Kimsey 240-1
Task Force Oboe 51-3
Task Force Oden 12, 16
Task Force Young 16
Task Force Withers 12

British

21st Army Group 5, 64, 218

German

1st SS Panzer Division 3, 9
2nd Mountain Division 48
2nd Panzer Division 69, 73, 78, 81, 83, 93, 98, 136, 140, 143, 155, 159, 212, 228, 295
2nd Panzer Grenadier Regiment 69
5th Fallschirmjäger Division 3
6th SS Mountain Division Nord 129, 136, 237-40, 296
6th SS Panzer Army 28
7th Army 93, 107, 118, 127, 133, 138, 155, 159, 162, 169, 227
9th Flak Division 133
9th Volksgrenadier Division 78, 81
10th Signal Training and Replacement Battalion 196
11th Panzer Division 36-9, 43-5, 218, 228
XIII Corps 93, 159
15th Army 93
17th Army 280
34th Regiment 112
40th Wood-Chopping Command 101
47th Volksgrenadier Division 153
53rd Artillery 97
LIII Corps 93, 99
54th Nebelwerfer Regiment 153
LXVI Corps 109
LXVII Corps 109
79th Volksgrenadier Division 98
80th Battalion 112
LXXX Corps 93

LXXXV Corps 169
159th Volksgrenadier Division 129, 159
172nd Volksgrenadier Division 112
198th Infantry Division 133, 143, 150
226th Snow-Shovel Company 101
246th Volksgrenadier Division 93, 98
251st Heavy Tank Destroyer Battalion 196, 208
256th Volksgrenadier Division 45
276th Volksgrenadier Division 78
305th Regiment 133-4
326th Regiment 133
340th Volksgrenadier Division 17, 98-9
352nd Volksgrenadier Division 53, 73, 78
413th Infantry Division 206
416th Infantry Division 34
559th Flak Training Battalion 17
559th Volksgrenadier Division 159
560th Volksgrenadier Division 135
669th Assault Gun Brigade 143-4
696th Regiment 17
714th Regiment 34
915th Regiment 53
Kampfgruppe Goebel 237, 239
Kampfgruppe Raithel 237-239
OB West 251
OKW 251
Panzer Lehr Division 2
SS Division Das Reich 270
SS Division Das Wallenstein 270

Russian

1st Ukrainian Front 271
2nd Ukrainian Front 277
25th Tank Corps 274, 278
104th Guards Rifle Division 277
162nd Tank Brigade 278
ROA First Division 270, 273-4
Russian Liberation Army (ROA) 269-70, 273-4, 278-9

General Index

Abenheim 155
Abrams, Creighton 3, 14, 79, 82-3, 86-7, 90, 103, 110, 115-6, 124, 130, 133, 135-6, 139, 141, 144, 150-1, 155-7, 163, 165-6, 169-71, 176-7, 180-3, 186, 203, 271, 219-20, 227-9, 233-4, 238, 240, 253-6, 261-3, 266, 294, 296
Aita, Cpl. 176
Alach 253
Alanis, Dan 9, 12, 51, 60, 217, 234, 256, 259-60, 297
Albert, Alfred 88, 92
Albig 155
Alexander, Nicholas 24, 30, 169, 222, 241, 286-7, 298
Alflen 127
Allen, Leven 78
Allen, Robert 251, 295
Alphonese, Sgt. 121
Alphonse, Clovis 23
Altdorf 286
Altenbamberg 136, 139
Altenstadt 218
Altheim 166, 286
Altscheid 81
Alzey 151-3, 155
Ammon, Jack 298
Andernach 93, 104, 112, 124
Anderson, Woodrow 59
Angersbach 227
Antonov, Rostislov 278
Archfeld 235
Ardennes 2, 5-6, 8-9, 12, 22, 28, 34, 161, 245, 257, 295
Argenschwang 137
Armsheim 155
Arnstadt 251
Artiemiev, Col. 278
Asbach 228
Aschaffenburg 166, 170-2, 176-7, 184, 215, 217, 225, 296-7
Assenheim 237-8
Assenois 3, 11, 18
Auschwitz 29
Autobahnen 104, 165, 228-9, 231-4, 240, 242, 253, 259-60, 266
Axmann, Artur 215

Babenhausen 166, 217, 225
Bad Hersfeld 226-9, 231-2, 240
Bad Homberg 134

Bad Klosterlausnitz 259
Bad Köstritz 259
Bad Kreuznach 131, 133, 135, 137, 139, 140-4, 157
Bad Münster 135, 137, 139
Bad Tölz 289
Badem 83, 95-6, 98
Baloga, T/Sgt. 32
Bamberg 155, 293
Bannholz Woods 38, 42-46, 298
Barbieri, Mickey 121
Barnett, Mildred 237
Basham, Truman 107
Bassenheim 107, 113
Bastogne 3, 8-12, 15-6, 18-9, 28, 32, 56, 61, 138, 188-9, 297-7
Battle of the Bulge 3, 7-8, 12, 14, 18, 20, 25, 28-9, 34, 49, 73, 78, 118, 144, 161, 174, 183, 201, 289, 292, 295-6, 298
Baudo, Richard 154
Baum, Abraham 15, 51, 138, 180-8, 190-3, 195-6, 198-213, 230, 243, 249, 295, 296-7
Baustert 79
Bautz, Edward 262, 268, 296, 298
Bayreuth 266
Beaghler, Edwin 176
Beaufort 54
Beaulieu, Willard 60
Bechtheim 155, 157
Behney, Theodore 177
Behrens, Pvt. 226
Beldon, Daniel 229
Belgium 6, 50
Beltershain 220
Beltheim 133
Bennick, Cpl. 157
Berdorf 60, 63
Bergman, Carl 234
Berlin 29, 159, 200, 218, 262, 268, 275
Bermersheim 155
Bernard, Kermit 273
Berngau 286
Beroun 270
Berstadt 218
Berteroda 236
Besch 35-6, 40
Bettel 54, 58-60
Bettembourg 41
Bettendorf 51, 54

Betts, T.J. 8
Beulich 130
Beutnitz 261
Biebelsheim 140
Bigonville 3
Bingen 136, 155, 161
Bingenheim 218
Binningen 120, 123, 127
Birkenau 29
Bitburg 53, 57, 59-60, 63, 79, 83-4, 90-1, 93, 108
Black, Russell 17
Blanchard, Wendell 15, 108, 133, 137, 140-1, 150, 224, 229
Blaskowitz, General 238
Blatna 275, 280
Blumenson, Martin 39, 178, 181-2, 295
Boas, Roger 68, 107, 230, 242, 266, 282, 295
Bobeck 256, 259
Bockenau 135
Bodinsky, Michael 83
Böhmerwald Mountains 271
Bollendorf 57-9, 61
Bonnland 205
Borg 44-5
Bornheim 155
Bosserode 232
Boston 288, 290
Bothwell, Herbert 107, 131, 146
Bouck, Lyle 174, 202, 206-7, 210
Bourcy 16
Brachtendorf 124
Bradley, Omar 1, 5, 7, 19, 23, 28, 49, 53, 60, 64, 78, 110, 115, 127, 138, 149, 156, 161, 181, 210-1, 213, 218, 225, 232, 237, 248, 258-9, 269-70, 284, 295
Brasseur Hotel 100
Bray, Oscar 264
Brecht 79-81
Brenner, Karl 237-9
Bretzenheim 139
Brimingen 75-7, 79
Brittany 1, 32
Brodenbach 129
Brooke, Sir Alan 8
Brown, Robert 97
Bryan, Lt. 120-1
Buchanan, "Doc" 41, 245, 295
Büchel 104

303

Buchenwald 255, 298
Budislavice 274
Bull, Harold 8, 64
Bunch, Garland 283
Bunyachenko, Sergei 269-70, 273-4, 278-9
Bürgeland 261
Burgen 132
Burgsinn 192
Burgstädt 262
Burkersdorf 262
Burkett, Harry 46
Burnon 144
Bush, Eugene 66
Butzdorf 35-6

Callaway, Charles 154, 240
Calvert, Robert 23, 58, 62-3, 70, 120-3, 297
Camp Myles Standish 290
Camp Twenty Grand 290
Campholz Woods 45
Canine, Ralph 178
Capri, Sam 17
Cardenas, Albert 112
Casanova, Alfonso 126, 198, 208
Casteel, George 183, 199
Cavender, Charles 174
Chaumont 3, 11, 15, 17, 145
Chemnitz 259-64, 266
Churchill, Winston 218, 268
Chursdorf 262
Čimelice 277
Clark, Lillian 237
Clarke, Bruce 1, 288
Cobra King 3, 188, 189, 192, 204
Cobstadt 249
Codman, Charles 213
Cohen, Harold 11, 15, 51, 55-6, 61, 64, 79, 80, 87-8, 130, 162, 170, 177, 180-1, 183, 229-30, 237-40, 253, 261, 274, 281, 296
Cologne 23, 64-5
Compton, Pfc 157-8
Conklin, Albert 263
Contern 19-20
Cook, Capt. 68
Cook, James 207-8
Cook, Kevin 297
Cooperman, Barnet 55-6, 70, 76
Cosma, Helen 237
Costanzo, Canio 36
Coutcher, Ralph 76
Coyle, James 234
Crane, William 229, 241
Creuzburg 231, 234-6, 240
Crevier, Francis 96
Crider, John 29
Crise, Donald 112
Crumstadt 163
Curtis, Lawrence 16
Czechoslovakia 266-74, 279-82

Daasdorf 254
Dager, Holmes 3, 15, 27, 61, 66, 79, 86, 90, 96, 98, 101, 110, 162
Dalberg 137
Danic, Radovan 201

Dankmarshausen 231
Danube River 291
Dark, Russell 266
Darmstadt 162, 172
Darmstadt-Eberstadt 163
Darscheid 101, 108
Dasburg 28
Daubach 141
Daun 101
Dautenheim 155
Davenport, Charles 16
Davis, Lt. 226
Dawda, Michael 176
Deane, John 175
Demchak 201
Denstedt 255
Devers, Jacob 5, 138, 218, 288
Dexheim 156
Diamantes, Captain 11
Dickenson, Lola 237
Diebach 196
Dieburg 166, 237
Diekirch 25, 28
Dienheim 156-7
DiGregorio, Michael 234
Dillingen 54, 58-9
Dintesheim 151
Dittelsheim 155
Diuguid, Sam 146, 149, 252
Dlugosz, Bronislaw 176
Dölzig 261
Domes, Peter 183, 298
Dommershausen 132-3
Domnom-lès-Dieuze 289
Donahue, Richard 97, 105, 171, 261-2, 271-2, 277-9, 282
Donnelly, Thomas 144
Doran, Lt. 58, 96, 120
Dornburg 256
Dorweiler 133
Doughty, Harry 154
Dowd, Capt. 252
Dožice 274
Draisdorf 264
Dreiweiherhof 136
Droßdorf 261
Duan 126
Dufoe, Lt. 86
Düngenheim 133
Dunn, Irene 25
Duston, Leonard 93, 95
Duty, Lt. 96
Dwight, William 3, 110, 180, 261, 263, 268, 290, 297

Earnest, Herbert 9, 12, 15-6, 20, 27
Echternach 53, 57, 61
Eckelsheim 150
Eckweiler 141
Eddy, Manton 2, 25, 29, 49, 53, 61, 65, 78, 90, 127, 130, 133-4, 156, 173, 178, 181, 203, 213-4, 296
Edwards, Capt. 100
Egstedt 253
Eich 157
Eichen 218
Eidenschink, John 231
Einig 120

Eisenach 230, 240-2
Eisenhower, Dwight D. 1, 3, 5-8, 23, 53, 56, 110, 115, 122, 127, 138, 149, 161, 212-3, 218, 232, 248, 258-9, 268-70, 273, 277, 284, 286, 289, 292, 295-7
Ellern 137
Emmelshausen 131
Emmett, Paul 107
English, Lt. 68
English, Samuel 77
Enz River 68, 70-1
Eppele, William 266
Eppelsheim 151
Erbes-Büdesheim 151
Erbstadt 239
Erdmann, Roy 136
Erdorf 84, 95-6
Erfelden 165
Erfurt 249, 251, 253
Ergolding 286
Eschollbrücken 163
Essenbach 286
Étain 13
Ettersburg Forest 254
Evacuation Hospitals 74, 211-2, 223, 237, 238
Evans, Thomas 41, 297
Eveshausen 132
Ewantisko, John 261
Ezell, Bert 3, 138, 146, 149

Feilbingert 136
Feilsdorf 79-80
Feinberg, Harry 298
Felber, Hans-Gustav 64, 93, 136, 140, 162, 169, 176
Fenchel, Bruce 117, 297
Ferguson, Irvin 70
Ferguson, Lt. 107, 163
Ferraro, Sgt 231
Ferschweiler 63
Field Hospitals 223-4, 237-8
Fields, James 68-9
Fieux, Lt. 176
Fife, Lt. 96
Fischler, Ben 154, 249
Fisher, Dave 76
Fleck, Egon 253-4
Fleißem 85
Flonheim 155
Fodor, Eugene 270
Fonde, Major 238, 240
Forest Zeitz 261
Försch, Anton 195
Ft. Belvoir 188
Foster, Lt. Col. 239
Fouhren 51
Fox, Willard 36, 153
Frankel, Nate 246
Frankendorf 256
Frankfurt 65, 173, 203, 211, 285
Franks, Robert 242-3, 263
Freeland, Rosalou 237
Frei-Laubersheim 139, 143
French, Robert 71, 77, 82, 86
Freyung Pass 271
Friede Forest 230

Friedrichroda 252
Friemersheim 153
Frisange 25, 51, 56, 61
Fuchs, Hauptmann 200-1
Fuchsstadt 199, 208
Fulda River 231
Fürfeld 139, 141-4, 150-1

Gaberndorf 254
Gablenz 263
Gaffey, Hugh 2, 9, 11-2, 18-20, 59-61, 65, 69, 78, 88, 90, 134, 141, 155, 161
Galvin, George 252-3
Gamlen 124
Garbisdorf 262
Gau-Bickelheim 144-5
Gau-Heppenheim 155
Gay, "Hap" 211, 286, 289, 292
Gehig, Franz 206, 297
Geichlingen 66
Geisbüsch Woods 45
Gemünden 190-2
Gensingen 137
Gentingen 64
Georgenhausen 166
Gerow, Leonard 291
Gersdorff, General von 136
Gethsemane 226
Giessen 219, 221
Gill, Lt. 137
Gillenbeuren 124, 130
Gilsdorf 51
Gindorf 98-9, 101
Giraud, Henri 225, 251-2
Gispersleben 253
Glauchau 260, 263
Glaz, Paul 152
Glenn, Lumpkin 112
Göbelnrod 220, 225
Gödenroth 133
Goebel, Johann-Georg 237, 239
Goeckel, General von 200
Goldbach 240-1
Gondershausen 130-1
Goode, Paul 174, 200, 202, 207, 213
Gordon, Albert 176
Gößnitz 260
Goßra 261
Gotha 240-4, 247-9, 251-2, 258
Gräfenbacherhütte 137
Gräfendorf 193-5, 206
Graham, Charles 73, 183, 198, 200, 208, 211, 297
Grandru 11
Greig, William 270
Greimersburg 123
Griffith, Lt. 89
Groß-Zimmern 166
Großauheim 166, 168-9, 175-6, 215, 298
Großenlüder 225-6
Großensee 232
Großhelmsdorf 261
Großostheim 176
Grünberg 215, 219, 221, 225
Grünmorsbach 187
Guidry, Lester 244-5

Guild, Donald 107
Güls 118
Gumbsheim 150
Gutenberg 137

Hackenheim 142-3
Hahn 165
Hähnlein 165
Haibach 187
Hain 190
Hainspitz 261
Hainstadt 175
Hallgarten 136
Hamburg 133
Hamm Cemetery 202
Hammelburg 173-4, 180-1, 185, 187-9, 191, 193, 195-6, 198-9, 204, 206, 210-3, 232, 237, 252-3, 255, 296-8
Hanau 161, 186, 215, 218-9
Harkins, Paul 211
Harmon, Ernest 293
Harris, John 22, 84, 167, 248, 290, 298
Hartmannsdorf 262, 264
Harward, Lula 237
Hassel 19-20
Hassell, Dennis 55
Hatzenport 129-31
Hauser, Ernest 28
Hays, Capt. 254, 261, 268
Heesaker, William 263
Heger, Frank 36
Heierstein 261
Heimboldshausen 230
Heimersheim 151
Heinlein, Martin 183, 298
Heinold, Lester 71
Hensen, Joe 210-1
Herbstein 225-6, 229
Heringen 231
Herleshausen 233-4
Hermesdorf 81
Herrnsheim 155
Heßdorf 205
Highway 26 187, 190-1
Highway 27 187, 191, 195-6, 202-3, 205-6
Hill 236 76
Hill 271 146, 148
Hill 296 264
Hill 300 262
Hill 318 260
Hill 340 205
Hill 360 262
Hill 366 82
Hill 405 70-1
Hill 408 63
Hill 418 84
Hill 426 76
Hill 427 195-6, 205, 207-9
Hill 431 85
Hillartshausen 226
Hilmes 226
Hilperhausen 231
Himebauch, Gordon
Himelick, John 68-9
Himmler, Heinrich 251

Hitler, Adolf 1-3, 6-8, 22, 28-9, 34, 63, 104, 109-10, 119, 159, 174, 215, 220, 251, 255, 268-9, 295
Hitler Youth 215, 217
Hobgood, "Hoppy" 227
Hochborn 155
Hochstätten 135-6, 139, 142
Hodges, Courtney 3, 14, 23, 28-9, 49, 56, 61, 64, 93, 110, 115, 149, 284
Hoesdorf 51, 53-6, 88
Hoffman, Kenneth 170
Hoffner, Norman 162, 183, 192-3, 205-6, 211
Hoge, William 110, 161, 173, 178, 180-2, 203, 213, 218, 225-6, 232, 240, 251, 261-3, 266, 271, 288
Hohenpfahl 286
Hohenstein 259-60, 263
Höllrich 205-7
Homa, Joseph
Hönebach 231-2
Hood, Carvel 135
Hope, Capt. 58
Horazdovice 271, 278, 280-1
Horchheim 152
Horn, William 41
Horowitz, Jacob 234
Hörschel 233
Hosey, Phil 221-2
Hottelstedt 255
Hötzelsroda 242
Houffalize 19, 49-50
Hoy, James 69
Hüffelsheim 135
Humpick, Freddie 192
Hungary 28
Hungen 218, 225
Hunsruck Mountains 137
Hunter, William 79, 110, 177, 180, 261, 263, 298
Huttingen 96
Hvoždany 275, 277, 280

Idar-Oberstein 218
Ifta 234, 236
Ike, Joe 148
Illerich 123
Ippenscheid 141
Ippesheim 140, 144
Irwin, Stafford Leroy 129-30, 156, 158-9
Irzyk, Albin F. 3, 11, 24-5, 27-8, 79, 90, 98-9, 113-8, 131, 136-7, 140, 142-9, 154, 156-7, 163, 175, 218, 225-6, 233, 237, 241-2, 244-7, 249, 252, 256, 259-61, 263-4, 287-91, 294-8
Irzyk, Art 142-3, 298
Isar River 286
Isserstedt 256
Iuppa, Dr. 143

Jackson, Curtis 16
Janes, Marie 237
Janetos, Theodore 97
Japan 284, 291
Jaques, George 51, 54, 60, 64, 69, 89, 156, 241

Jena 253, 256-8
Jenkins, Lt. 154
Jennings, John 142
Jesky, John 36, 150, 153, 176, 261
Judge Advocate General 119, 297

K Rations 21-2, 60
Kachline, George 176
Kaifenheim 124
Kaisersesch 104-5, 125
Kaiserslautern 133, 161
Kaltenengers 118
Kaminsky, Lt. 162, 175
Karden 116, 120-3
Kasejovice 275
Kassel 149
Kasserine Pass 174
Kathus 231
Katzengraben River 98
Kaufungen 262
Kayna 261
Keenan, Jack 143
Kehrig 105, 120
Keil, Raymond 183, 192
Kelly, Earl 11, 75-6, 297-8
Kerben 107
Kerspenhausen 231
Kerspleben 253
Kesselheim 118
Kesselring, Albert 169, 251
Kettig 110, 112, 118, 124
Kieley, Len 22, 66, 69, 72, 139-40, 144-6, 155, 163, 249, 297
Kimsey, Charles 41, 141, 228, 231, 240-1
King, William 41
Kingery, James 176
Kladrubce 274
Klein-Auheim 166
Kleinensee 232
Kleinmölsen 253-4
Kleinobringen 254
Kleinpörthen 261
Kleinreisdorf 55
Klinga, Constance 256
Kneiss, General 169
Koblenz 65, 104-5, 109, 112, 118, 124-5, 149
Koch, Ilse 255
Koch, Karl 255
Köhl, Richard 196, 198
Koosbüsch 81
Koshiol, Milton 210, 298
Kotouň 274
Koyen, Ken 70, 295
Krauthausen 235
Krewsky, Sgt. 157
Kromsdorf 256
Kronprinz-Wilhelm Bridge 109, 113-5, 116-7
Kruft 112, 124
Kuchinsky, Capt. 278
Kunitz 256-7
Kyll River 66, 79, 83-5, 90-9, 107, 123
Kyllburg 92, 165
Kyllburgweiler 96

Laasan 261
Laasen 257
Lager Hammelburg 174, 198-9, 204, 206
Lamay, Danny 153, 157
Lamb, David 41
Lamberth, Emil 184
Landenhausen 227
Landkern 123
Landshut 282, 286-7
Lane, Richard 169
Lang, Will 28
Lange, Robert 135, 183, 199
Langenlonsheim 137, 139
Langenprozelten 191
Langenselbold 239
Lanzendorfer, Erwin 176
Larrocco, Dominic 126
Laubach 104, 132-3
Lauchert, Meinrad von 155
Lauchröden 233
Laufach 187-88, 190
Laufer, Leo 245
Laughlin, Lt. 23, 122
Lauterbach 227, 237
Leach, Jimmie 3, 61, 294
Leanord, Lt.
Lee, William 97
Leech, Lt. 55
Leeheim 163, 225
Lehmen 118
Leichtman, Pfc 158
Leinatal 242
Leiper, Edwin 41, 46
Leiselheim 151
Lenin, Vladimir 269
Leningrad 269
Leudelange 60-1
Levin, Meyer 244
Lich 220
Liese, Bernard 61, 82, 100, 105, 142
Liesenfeld 131, 136
Ließem 82
Limbach 260
Lipsitz, Charles 76
LiVecchi, Charles 263
Livingston, Lt. 120
Lnáře 272, 275, 278-80
Loebell, John 242
Lohr 190-1
Longchamps 12
Longsdorf 51
Lopez, Joseph 251
Lorient 32
Los Angeles Coliseum 288
Lothian, Bill 230
Lucas, Richard 73
Ludendorff Bridge 110, 115
Lüderbach 234
Luneville 138
Lutrebois 9
Lutz 129
Lützel 118
Luxembourg 6, 15, 18-20, 24-6, 35-6, 41, 49, 56-7, 64, 66, 100, 127, 138, 218, 292
Luxembourg City 18-9, 24-5, 55, 61
Lyons, Stanley 73-4, 106, 163, 170-1, 177, 183, 186, 195, 215, 225, 243-4, 247, 264-5, 280-1, 296
Lytle, Nathaniel 144

Mabee, John 73-4, 264, 298
Mabrey, James 186
Macik, John 76
Macken 132
Mackin, William 73, 201, 297
Main River 134, 161, 166, 168-70, 173, 175-6, 186, 190-1, 213, 215-6, 218-9, 225-6, 237, 298
Mainz 133, 138, 149, 151, 161
Maklinovsky, Marshal 277
Makowski, Edward 72
Malberg 88, 92
Malbergweich 85, 87-8
Malinski, Frank 186, 188
Malony, Harry 32, 34-5, 39-40, 44-6
Mandel 135
Mankin, Buell 44, 47
Markershausen 234
Markowski, Lt. 96
Marshall, George 161, 212, 268, 284, 292, 297
Marshall, Horace 176
Marshall, William 98, 201
Martasin, William 72
Mascara, Pat 176
Matheson, Robert 41
Matzen 83, 88-91
Maua 253, 256
Mauel 63
Mazza, Anthony 89
McDonald, Charles 18, 57, 169, 225, 296
McDonald, Curtis 17
McElwrath, Brooks 125
McFarland, Edward 246-7
McGee, Carl 126
McGinnis, William 97
McGlamery, Mac 249
McGrew, Sherman 169
McInerney, William 167
McKeown, Douglas 41
McMahon, John 110, 126, 268
McMillan, Raymond 245
ME-109 105, 124, 139, 157
ME-262 135-6, 155, 177
Meandrov, Mikhail 279
Meckbach 231
Mecklar 231
Meerane 119
Mehna 262
Meinsdorf 260
Meisberg 100
Merkers 258
Merriam, John 107
Mertendorf 261
Metebach 240
Mettendorf 57, 63
Metterich 96, 98-9
Metternich 113
Metz 124, 252
Metz, Joseph 87
Metzler, Charlie 169
Michelau 195

Middleton, Troy 11-2, 14-5, 53, 63, 78, 240, 258
Milín 277-8
Miller, Crosby 41
Miller, Robert 143
Millikin, John 11, 53, 60
Miner, Gordon 121
Minkelfeld 107
Mitchell, Lt. 120
Mittelbuchen 219-20
Mlady Smolivec 274
Mockzig 262
Modlin, Pfc 154
Moestroff 51
Moldau River 273
Mondercange 26, 66
Montgomery, Bernard 5, 7, 19, 22, 49, 53, 110, 115, 149, 156, 218
Monzernheim 155
Moomaw, Stevenson 168
Moorby, Frederick 235
Moosburg (POW Camp) 210, 213
Morris, Joe 297
Morshausen 130
Moscow 8, 175, 269, 277
Moselle River 1, 56, 96, 98, 111, 115-20, 122-4, 126-33, 138
Moselsuersch 118
Moses, Alan 97, 183
Motzfeld 226
Müden 129-30
Mühlau 262
Mühlhausen 286
Mulde River 259, 262
Mülheim-Kärlich 113, 115
Mullen, Walter 240, 297
Mulregan, Lt. 121
Münstermaifeld 118
Munzel, Oskar 155
Münzingen 46
Murrow, Edward R. 255
Murschell, William 76

Nack 153
Naddy, Lt. 226
Nahe River 130-1, 133, 135-7, 139, 151, 156
Nancy 1, 119
National Redoubt 258-9, 266
Nattenheim 85, 87
Nebelwerfer 27, 59, 97, 101, 107, 225
Nedissen 261
Neffe 15-6
Neiderhausen 151
Nemeth, Lt. 239
Nennig 35-8, 40-1, 48
Nesselröden 240, 243
Neudietendorf 251
Neuendorf 118
Neuengönna 256
Neuhuette 137
Neukirchen 236
Neumarkt 286
New York Times 29
Newhaus 75-6
Newton, Capt. 55-6, 177
Nicklesdorf 261
Nieder-Flörsheim 153

Nieder-Ramstadt 163
Niederaula 228
Niederberg Ridge 51
Niederfrohna 262
Niedergeckler 69-71, 75
Niedernberg 170, 186, 195
Niederstadtfeld 101, 106
Nierstein 156, 159, 162
Nilkheim 170-1, 176
Nims River 59, 79, 82-3, 88, 90
Nita Patton 173
Noel, Joseph 17
Nolan, Lt. 257
Norheim 135
Normandy 1, 6, 51, 73, 103, 113, 157
North Stalag III 244-7
Nutto, William 183, 188, 192, 199-200, 202-07

Oakley, Bod 280
Oakman, Oscar 283
Ober-Beerbach 170
Ober-Ramstadt 16, 166
Obereschenbach 196
Obergeckler 78
Oberhaun 231
Oberhausen 135
Oberkail 99, 101
Obernau 172
Obernaumen 36
Oberperl 36, 41
Obersgegen 64, 66, 78
Oberstadtfeldt 99-100
Obersuhl 232
Oberweis 80
Oberwiera 260
Obstfelder, General von 227-8
Ochtendung 104-7, 110
O'Conner, Francis 107
Oden, Delk 12, 16, 56, 217, 219, 228, 241
Oder River 29
Odom, Col. 211
Oesterbehingen 243
Offenheim 153
Oflag XIII-B 173-5, 182, 184, 187, 195, 197, 199-200, 207, 210-1
Oflag LXIV 174
Ohrdruf 232-3, 237, 244-49
Oliver, Lt. 143
Olson, John 168-9
Oppenheim 156-7, 159, 162
Oriola, General von 159
Orleno, Frank 83
Orsfeld 96
Osborne, Lt. 96
Ostheim 218
Osthofen 155
Ottstedt am Berge 254
Our River 28, 49-51, 53-5, 56, 63-4

P-47 Thunderbolts 38, 64, 82, 133, 135, 142-3, 150, 155, 254, 257
Pacific Theater 259, 277, 279, 284, 286, 288, 291
Pancake, Richard 184-6, 268
Paris 25, 55, 61, 65, 78, 119, 163, 212, 287

Parker, Bob 146, 162, 243
Patch, Alexander 138, 211
Patterson, Robert 275-6
Pattison, Hal 9, 12, 26, 161, 297
Patton, Beatrice 56, 161, 172-4, 203, 211-3, 288
Patton, George S. 1-3, 7-9, 11, 14-5, 18-21, 23, 26, 28-9, 34, 39, 49, 53-4, 56-7, 60-1, 64-5, 68-9, 78, 90, 93, 99-100, 109, 115, 127, 133, 138, 149, 156-7, 159, 161-2, 172-5, 177-8, 180-3, 201, 203, 210-14, 218, 225, 232, 237, 239-40, 248-9, 251-2, 255, 258-9, 268-71, 273-7, 279, 284, 286-89, 291-3, 295-8
Pendergast, Lt. 18
Penig 262
Perkins, George 87
Perrine, Cpl. 157
Peterson, Arthur 11
Pfeddersheim 151, 154
Pfifflingheim 151-2
Pfoffenhofen 286
Pfrimm River 151-2
Pfungstadt 163
Philippshospital 163
Phillips, Henry Gerard 214, 296
Pielsk, Lt. 262
Pilsen 269, 273
Pippin, John 266
Pirtle, Orville 244
Pisek 273
Pister, Hermann 255
Plaidt 110, 124
Plecinski, Hubert 61
Pluff, Andrew 112, 170, 177, 183
Pluff, Charles 177
Pluff, Lavern 177
Plumley, Capt. 256
Podesta, Silvio 118-9
Polch 105, 107, 127
Pole 272
Pontpierre 62-3
Pötewitz 261
Pound, King 9, 298
Powell, Lester 184-5
Powers, James 107
Prague 268-71, 273-4, 277
Prazak, Albert 268
Presidential Distinguished Unit Citation 230, 288
Prickett, Fay Brink 291
Province, Charles 155
Pruett, John 121
Prüm 28, 53, 65, 73
Prüm River 59, 63, 79-82
Prusaczyk, Johnny 43-4
Pückler-Burghauss, Friedrich von 273, 277-8
Pudwell, Leo 234
Puttkamer, Karl-Richard von 69-70, 72
Pützborn 100-1

Quigley, Lt. 14
Quinn, Sgt. 157

General Index

Radošice 274
Raithel, Helmuth 237, 239
Ranson, Ellsworth 136
Raßdorf 232
Rechtenbach 189-90
Red Cross Clubmobile 23, 25, 61, 251
Regensburg 287, 291
Reid, Matthew 202, 206-7, 210
Reinheim 170
Reinholdshain 259
Reisdorf 51, 53, 55
Remagen 110, 115, 117, 149, 159, 161
Remse 263
Reussenberg Mountains 174, 205
Revolutionary Czech National Council 268, 270
Reynolds, Herbert 198
Rhaunen 134
Rheims 275
Rheinboellerhuette 137
Rheinböllen 136-7, 237
Rhine Plain 170
Rhine River 1, 6-8, 28-9, 62, 64-5, 93-4, 96, 99, 103, 106-18, 120, 124-8, 133, 136-8, 141, 149, 151-2, 154-62, 166, 213, 215
Rhodler, Pfc 158
Rich, Carl 235
Rieneck 193
Riesa 268
Righton, Wally 163
Rittersdorf 81-3, 87, 89
Robbins, Joseph 245
Roberts, Williams 138, 180, 262, 288, 297
Rockafeller, Harry 12, 141, 150, 229, 236, 297
Rodgers, Fred 45-6
Rödigen 256
Rodriquez, Salvatore 17
Roer River 56
Roes 124
Rollingen 51, 60
Rommersheim 154
Roosevelt, Franklin D. 212, 259
Rorem, Elden 107
Rosenthal 261
Ross, Charles 243
Roßdorf 166, 218, 225
Rossendorf 261
Roth 54, 64
Rothenbuch 190
Rothenbucher Forest 190
Rothkirch, Kau von 99-100
Rowe, William 55
Rožmitál 275
Rübenach 113, 115, 118
Rubin, Mandel 147
Rüdesheim 135
Ruhr 5, 7, 218
Rundstedt, Gerd von 7, 110
Rupprecht, Cpl. 112
Rushin, Edward 234
Rußdorf 260
Ruzne 273

Saale River 191, 193, 195, 198, 253, 256-7, 259
Saar Basin 5
Saar-Palatinate 115
Saar River 46, 95
Saffig 110
St. Nazaire 32
St. Vith 161
Sallmannshausen 233
Salm 97, 100
Sanders, Lt. 62, 120
Sankt Johann 144-9
Sankt Sebastian 118
Sättalstädt 241-2
Saturday Evening Post 28
Schellroda 253
Scherbda 234-5
Schleiz 266
Schlitz 226
Schmitt 127
Schmölln 260
Schnee Eifel 174
Schoch Kaserne 286
Schöngleina 256
Schu Mine 36, 55
Schwabhausen 243
Schwabsdorf 255
Schweinfurt 196
Schweinheim 172, 184-7
Schweppenhausen 137
Sears, Hayden 27, 79, 81, 98-9, 101, 115, 117-8, 131, 137, 139-40, 144-5, 154-5, 157, 162-3, 175, 177, 218-9, 221, 225, 229-30, 233, 244, 252, 256, 259, 261
Seaver, Capt. 56
Seffern 88, 92
Sefferweich 85-88, 90
Seinsfeld 97, 107
Seligenstadt 166
Serrig 46-48
Seryogin, Sergei 277-8
Shankweiler 64
Shönbach 101
Shukomasty 269
Sidles, John 201, 209-10
Siefersheim 149
Siegmar 263
Silbitz 261
Simmern 133, 137, 140, 156
Simmern River 133
Simmertal 134
Sinn River 193
Sinspelt 68, 70-3, 75, 77-9
Sinz 38-40, 42-5
Slaninka,Charles 122
Smail, Gomer 69
Smith, Bow 226
Smith, Edgar 86, 105-6, 242
Smith, Kenneth 204
Smith, William 184
Snyder, Donald 71
Sommaripa, Alexis 101-3, 105, 220, 298
Sonthofen 293
Soon Forest 134, 136
Sorga 231
Sorrentino, Dominik 83, 150

Spaatz, General 284
Spabrücken 137
Spatz, Lt. 241
Spessart 190
Spichra 234-5
Spiesheim 154
Sponheim 135
Sprendlingen 144, 157
Stackonis, Peter 282
Staden 218, 239
Stalag XIII-C 174, 200
Stalin, Joseph 5, 8, 218, 268-9, 274, 280
Stankels River 230
Stanley, Jack 198, 208
Stars and Stripes 130, 218, 268, 282
Stasi, Sgt. 83, 150
Steele, William 71
Stein-Bockenheim 150-1, 157
Steinberg, Bernard 242
Steinborn 97
Stephenson, Lyndon 36, 176
Stephenson, Paul 249, 253, 298
Stewart, Bryon 71
Stiller, Alexander 173, 178, 180-1, 183, 198-9, 201-3, 207, 209-11, 213, 276
Stockstadt am Rhein 165
Stregda 242
Stromberg 137
Stübinger, Karl 193, 195
Stürzenberger, Karl 195-6
Sudetenland 271
Sukhorukov, Grigory 278
Sulzheim 154
Sûre River 25, 49-51, 54-61, 63-4, 66, 68, 78
Sušice 271
Süßenborn 255
Sutherland, Nelson 234
Sutton, Elmer 183, 192
Szubin 174

Taake, Marion 43-4
Taben-Rodt 46
Taura 262
Tautenhain 259
Taylor, Robert 157
Tedder, Sir Arthur 8
Teller-Mine 36, 46, 59
Temple, Capt. 68, 167
Tennenbaum, Edward 254-5
Tennessee Maneuvers 236
Tenzorov, Nikolai 278
Tessier, Adrien 55, 184-6
Tettingen 34-6, 44
Thompson, Sheldon 202, 297
Tiefenbach 133-4, 140
Tiefenthal 151
Tiefthal 253
Time-Life Magazine 28
Tittendorf 88
Toben, Colonel 31, 297
Tomillo, Lou 169
Tone, Solomon 176
TOTE 190
Toussaint, Rudolf 274
Tracy, Spencer 25

General Index

Traynor, Harry 43-4, 298
Treis 116, 120, 123, 129
Treis-Karden 116, 120, 123, 129
Tremblay, Lt. 263
Trier 78, 138, 161, 223
Tripodi, Salvatore 36
Trover, Charles 3
Trügleben 240
Truman, Harry S. 259, 268, 284
Turner, Clifford 55, 101
Tytus, John 46

Üdersdorf 101, 106-7
Ulmen 101, 104, 107-8
Ulrichshalben 255
U.S. Army National Museum 188-9
Unterbessenbach 187
Unterhaun 231
Urmitz 109, 113-4, 116, 118, 124
Utscheid 75, 77-8
Ütteroda 236

Vacha 226
Van Auken, Clifford 71
Vannett, Robert 186, 188
Vegh, Frank 263
Velky Bor 281
Vendersheim 154
Vianden Bulge 63
Vilsbiburg 287, 290
Vlasov, Andrey 269-70, 273-4, 277-9, 296
Vlatva River 269
Vollheim, Sgt. 241
Volmerange 32
Volxheim 141, 143-4, 149
Volyně 271

Wachal, Elmer 72
Wahlheim 153
Waldeck 259
Walden, Thurnon 226
Waldenburg 260
Waldensberg 239
Waldlaubersheim 137
Waldorferhof 107
Walker, Walton 26, 34, 53, 64, 78, 252, 258, 275

Wallace, Neil 61, 157
Wallenborn 97, 100
Wallendorf 49, 57, 59, 63
Wallertheim 154
Wallhausen 137
Waltershausen 242
Warnach 3
Washington D.C. 188, 285
Waterhouse Curve 190
Waters, John 174-5, 177-8, 183, 200-1, 203, 211-13
Weaver, William 170-1, 183, 186-8, 190, 193, 201, 204, 208
Wechmar 249
Weiberhof 187
Weickersgrüben 195-6, 208
Weidenbach 97, 100
Weidensdorf 263
Weidingen 81
Weimar 225, 253, 255
Weinsheim 135, 141, 151
Weisse Elster River 259, 261
Weißenthurm 124-5
Wendell, Capt. 120
Wendelsheim 150-1
Wenigenlupnitz 241
Werra River 230-5, 240-2
Westberry, Morrison 17, 198
Westhofen 155
Westmann, Hans 200
Westwall 2, 6, 34, 36-7, 40, 45, 49-50, 53, 59, 63, 138
Weyland, Otto 78
White, Lawrence 198, 208
Whitehill, John 3, 18, 86, 92, 142, 171, 257, 268, 298
Whiteley, John 28
Wickstadt 238
Widdershausen 231
Wierschem 118
Wiesel, Elie 255
Wilhelm, Capt. 100
Wilson, Capt. 41
Wilson, Charles 164, 272
Wilson, T/5 157
Windesheim 137
Winkhaus, Capt. 154
Winningen 118
Winterbach 134, 141

Winterborn 151
Winterburg 135, 141
Wirfus 123
Withers, William 9, 12, 27
Wittgensdorf 262
Wolf 239
Wölfershausen 230
Wolfsheim 145-8, 154
Wolfskehlen 163, 165
Wolken 113
Wolkenburg 262
Wollmerath 127
Wöllstein 143-4, 149
Wommen 233-4
Wonsheim 150
Wood, Billy 90, 131, 166
Wood, George 107
Wood, John S. 1-2, 9, 11-2, 26, 161, 294, 296-7
Worms 133, 149, 151-3, 155-7, 161
Wörrstadt 154
Wörth 286-7
Wright, Fred 176
Wrolson, Walter 183
Wüstenbrand 263
Wyatt, George 188, 198
Wyland, James 71

Yakushev, Ivan 278
Yocca, Nicholas 71
Yoerk, Donald 188, 193, 198, 201, 208
Yosefovitch, Dragon 200-1
Young, Hugh 15-6
Yuill, Charles 30, 297

Zahorčichy 274
Zamora, Sgt. 153
Zawada, Robert 209, 297
Zelinski, Walter 107
Zeljak, George 176
Zellhausen 175
Zeno 201
Zhukov, Georgy 29, 268
Zotzenheim 140, 144
Zwätzen 257
Zwickau-Mulde River 259, 262

www.ingramcontent.com/pod-product-compliance
Lightning Source LLC
Chambersburg PA
CBHW080759300426
44114CB00020B/2762